TRIAL OF
SAMUEL CHASE

VOLUME I

TRIAL OF SAMUEL CHASE

*An Associate Justice of the Supreme Court
of the United States*

*Impeached by the House of Representatives
for High Crimes and Misdemeanors Before
the Senate of the United States*

VOLUME I

DA CAPO PRESS · NEW YORK · 1970

A Da Capo Press Reprint Edition

This Da Capo Press edition of the *Trial of Samuel Chase* is an unabridged republication of the first edition published in Washington, D. C., in 1805. It is reprinted with permission from a set in the George Peabody Branch, Enoch Pratt Free Library, Baltimore, Maryland.

Library of Congress Catalog Card Number 69-11324
SBN 306-71181-8

Published by Da Capo Press
A Division of Plenum Publishing Corporation
227 West 17th Street, New York, N. Y. 10011
All Rights Reserved

Manufactured in the United States of America

TRIAL

OF

SAMUEL CHASE,

AN ASSOCIATE JUSTICE

OF THE

SUPREME COURT OF THE UNITED STATES,

IMPEACHED

BY THE

HOUSE OF REPRESENTATIVES.

FOR

HIGH CRIMES AND MISDEMEANORS,

BEFORE THE

SENATE OF THE UNITED STATES.

TAKEN IN SHORT-HAND,

BY SAMUEL H. SMITH AND THOMAS LLOYD.

VOLUME I.

WASHINGTON CITY:

PRINTED FOR SAMUEL H. SMITH.

....

1805.

DISTRICT OF COLUMBIA, *to wit:*

BE IT REMEMBERED, *that on this twenty third day of April, in the year of our Lord eighteen hundred and five, Samuel H. Smith, of the said district, hath deposited in the clerk's office of the district court of the United States for the district of Columbia, the title of a book the right whereof he claims as author, in the words following, to wit:* " *The trial of Samuel Chase, an associate* " *justice of the supreme court of the United States, impeached by the House* " *of Representatives for high crimes and misdemeanors, before the Senate* " *of the United States, taken in short hand by Samuel H. Smith and Thomas* " *Lloyd,*" *in conformity to the act of Congress of the United States entitled an act for the encouragement of learning by securing the copies of maps, charts and books to the authors and proprietors of such copies during the time therein mentioned.*

G. DENEALE, CLK. DIST. COLUM.

THE following report of the trial of Samuel Chase has been drawn up with the greatest care. To guard against misconception or omission, two individuals, one of whom is a professional stenographer, were constantly engaged during the whole course of the trial; and the arguments of the managers and counsel have in most instances, and wherever it was attainable, been revised by them. It is with some satisfaction that the editor of this impression is enabled, under these circumstances, to submit to the public a tract, whose fidelity and comprehensiveness, he hopes, will amply reward the interest so deeply excited by the progress and issue of this important trial.

The second volume is in the press, and will be published in a short time.

IMPEACHMENT OF SAMUEL CHASE.

MEASURES PRELIMINARY TO THE TRIAL.

ON the fifth day of January 1804, Mr. *J. Randolph*, a member of the House of Representatives of the United States, rose and addressed that body to the following effect :

He observed " That no people were more fully impressed with the importance of preserving unpolluted the fountain of justice than the citizens of these states. With this view the constitution of the United States, and of many of the states also, had rendered the magistrates who decided judicially between the state and its offending citizens, and between man and man, more independent than those of any other country in the world, in the hope that every inducement, whether of intimidation or seduction, which could cause them to swerve from the duty assigned to them, might be removed. But such was the frailty of human nature, that there was no precaution by which our integrity and honor could be preserved, in case we were deficient in that duty which we owed to ourselves. In consequence, sir," said Mr. Randolph, " of this unfortunate condition of man, we have been obliged, but yesterday, to prefer an accusation against a judge of the United States, who has been found wanting in his duty to himself and his country. At the last session of Congress, a gentleman from Pennsylvania did, in his place, (on a bill to amend the judicial system of the United States) state certain facts, in relation to the official conduct of an eminent judicial character, which I then thought, and still think, the House bound to notice. But the lateness of the session (for we had, if I mistake not, scarce a fortnight remaining) precluding all possibility of bringing the subject to any efficient result, I did not then think proper to take any steps in the business : Finding my attention, however, thus drawn to a consideration of the character of the officer in question, I made it my business, considering it my duty, as well to myself as those whom I represent, to investigate the charges then made and the official character of the judge, in general. The result having convinced me that there exists ground of impeachment against this officer, I demand an enquiry into his conduct, and therefore submit to the House the following resolution :

Resolved, That a committee be appointed to enquire into the official conduct of SAMUEL CHASE, one of the associate justices of the supreme court of the United States, and to report their opinion, whether the said Samuel Chase hath so acted in his judicial capacity as to require the interposition of the constitutional power of this House."

A short debate immediately arose on this motion, which was advocated by Messrs. J. Randolph, Smilie, and J. Clay ; and opposed by Mr. Elliot. Several members supported a motion to postpone it until the ensuing day, which was superseded by an adjournment of the House.

The House, on the next day, resumed the consideration of Mr. Randolph's motion which was supported by Mr. Smilie, and, on the motion of Mr. Leib, so amended as to embrace an enquiry into the official conduct of Richard Peters, district judge for the district of Pennsylvania. On the motion, thus amended, further debate arose, which occupied the greater part of this and the ensuing day. It was supported by Messrs. Findley, Jackson, Nicholson, Holland, J. Randolph, Eustis, Early, Smilie, and Eppes ; and opposed by Messrs. Lowndes, R. Griswold, Elliot, Dennis, Griffin, Thatcher, Huger, and Dana. Some ineffectual attempts were made to amend the resolution, when the final question was taken on the resolution, as amended, in the following words :

Resolved, That a committee be appointed to enquire into the official conduct of Samuel Chase, one of the associate justices of the supreme court of the United States, and of Richard Peters, district judge of the district of Pennsylvania, and to report their opinion, whether the said Samuel Chase and Richard Peters, or either of them, have so acted in their judicial capacity, as to require the interposition of the constitutional power of this house.

And resolved in the affirmative, Yeas 81....Nays 40 ; as follow :

Those who voted in the affirmative, are,

Willis Alston, junior, Nathaniel Alexander, David Bard, George Michael Bedinger, Phanuel Bishop, William Blackledge, Adam Boyd, John Boyle, Robert Brown, Joseph Bryan, William Butler, Levi Casey, Joseph Clay, John Clopton, Jacob Crowninshield, Richard Cutts, William Dickson, John B. Earle, Peter Early, Ebenezer Elmer, John W. Eppes, William Eustis, William Findley, John Fowler, James Gillespie, Edwin Gray, Andrew Gregg, John A. Hanna, Josiah Hasbrouck, William Hoge, James Holland, David Holmes, John G. Jackson, Walter Jones, William Kennedy, Nehemiah Knight, Michael Leib, John B. C. Lucas, Matthew Lyon, Andrew M'Cord, David Meriwether, Nicholas R. Moore, Thomas Moore, Jeremiah Morrow, Anthony New, Thomas Newton, junior, Joseph H. Nicholson, Gideon Olin, Beriah Palmer, John Patterson, Oliver Phelps, John Randolph, junior, Thomas M. Randolph, John Rea, (of Pennsylvania) John Rhea, (of Tennessee) Jacob Richards, Erastus Root, Thomas Sammons, Thomas Sandford, Ebenezer Seaver, Tompson J. Skinner, James Sloan, John Smilie, John Smith, (of Virginia) Richard Stanford, Joseph Stanton, John Stewart, David Thomas, Philip R. Thompson, Abram Trigg,

John Trigg, Philip Van Cortlandt, Isaac Van Horne, Joseph B. Varnum, Daniel C. Verplank, Matthew Walton, John Whitehill, Marmaduke Williams, Richard Winn, Joseph Winston, and Thomas Wynns.

Those who voted in the negative, are,

Simeon Baldwin, Silas Betton, John Campbell, William Chamberlin, Martin Chittenden, Clifton Claggett, Manasseh Cutler, Samuel W. Dana, John Davenport, John Dennis, Thomas Dwight, James Elliott, Thomas Griffin, Gaylord Griswold, Roger Griswold, Seth Hastings, David Hough, Benjamin Huger, Samuel Hunt, Joseph Lewis, junior, Thomas Lewis, Henry W. Livingston, Thomas Lowndes, Nahum Mitchell, Samuel L. Mitchill, James Mott, Thomas Plater, Samuel D. Purviance, Joshua Sands, John Cotton Smith, John Smith, (of New York) William Stedman, James Stephenson, Samuel Taggart, Samuel Tenney, Samuel Thatcher, George Tibbits, Killian K. Van Rensellaer, Peleg Wadsworth, and Lemuel Williams.

Whereupon, Messrs. J. Randolph, Nicholson,. J. Clay, Early, R. Griswold, Huger, and Boyle, were appointed a committee pursuant to the foregoing resolution.

On the 10th of January, the committee were authorised by the House to send for persons, papers, and records ; and on the 30th day of the same month, they were authorised to cause to be printed such documents and papers, as they might deem necessary, previous to their presentation to the House.

On the 6th day of March, Mr. Randolph, in the name of the committee, made a report, " That in consequence of the evidence collected " by them, in virtue of the powers with which they have been invested " by the House, and which is hereunto subjoined, they are of opinion, " 1st, That Samuel Chase, esquire, an associate justice of the supreme " court of the United States, be impeached of high crimes and misde- " meanors.

" 2d. That Richard Peters, district judge of the district of Pennsyl- " vania, hath not so acted in his judicial capacity as to require the inter- " position of the constitutional power of this House."

This report, accompanied by a great mass of printed documents, em-. bracing various depositions taken before the committee, as well as at a distance, was made the order of the day for the Monday following.

On that day the House took up the report, and after a short debate concurred in the first resolution by the following votes, Yeas 73...Nays 32.

Those who voted in the affirmative, are,

Willis Alston, junior, Isaac Anderson, John Archer, David Bard, George Michael Bedinger, William Blackledge, Walter Bowie, Adam Boyd, John Boyle, Robert Brown, Joseph Bryan, William Butler, Levi Casey, Thomas Claiborne, Joseph Clay, Matthew Clay, John Clopton, Frederick Conrad, Jacob Crowninshield, Richard Cutts, John Dawson, William Dickson, John B. Earle, Peter Early, James Elliott, William Findley, John Fowler, James

Gillespie, Peterson Goodwyn, Andrew Gregg, Samuel Hammond, James Holland, David Holmes, Walter Jones, William Kennedy, Nehemiah Knight, Michael Leib, Matthew Lyon, Andrew M'Cord, William M'Creery, David Meriwether, Andrew Moore, Nicholas R. Moore, Jeremiah Morrow, Anthony New, Thomas Newton, junior, Joseph H. Nicholson, Gideon Olin, John Patterson, John Randolph, Thomas M. Randolph, John Rea, (of Pennsylvania) John Rhea, (of Tennessee) Jacob Richards, Cæsar A. Rodney, Thomas Sammons, Thomas Sandford, Ebenezer Seaver, James Sloan, John Smilie, Henry Southard, Richard Stanford, Joseph Stanton, John Stewart, David Thomas, Philip R. Thompson, Abram Trigg, John Trigg, Isaac Van Horne, Joseph B. Varnum, Marmaduke Williams, Richard Winn, and Joseph Winston.

Those who voted in the negative, are,

Simeon Baldwin, Silas Betton, John Campbell, William Chamberlin, Martin Chittenden, Clifton Claggett, Manasseh Cutler, Samuel W. Dana, John Davenport, Thomas Dwight, Thomas Griffin, Gaylord Griswold, Roger Griswold, Seth Hastings, William Helms, Benjamin Huger, Joseph Lewis, junior, Henry W. Livingston, Thomas Lowndes, Nahum Mitchell, Thomas Plater, Samuel D. Purviance, John Cotton Smith, John Smith, (of Virginia) William Stedman, James Stephenson, Samuel Taggart, Samuel Tenney, Samuel Thatcher, Killian K. Van Rensselaer, Peleg Wadsworth, and Lemuel Williams.

The second resolution was agreed to unanimously.

Whereupon it was ordered, that Mr. John Randolph and Mr. Early, be appointed a committee to go to the Senate, and at the bar thereof, in the name of the House of Representatives, and of all the people of the United States, to impeach Samuel Chase, one of the associate justices of the supreme court of the United States, of high crimes and misdemeanors; and acquaint the Senate, that the House of Representatives will, in due time, exhibit particular articles of impeachment against him, and make good the same. It was also ordered, that the committee do demand, that the Senate take order for the appearance of the said Samuel Chase, to answer to the said impeachment.

On the 13th of March, Messrs. J. Randolph, Nicholson, J. Clay, Early, and Boyle, were appointed a committee to prepare and report articles of impeachment against Samuel Chase, and invested with power to send for persons, papers, and records.

On the 14th, a message was received from the Senate, notifying the House, that they would take proper order on the impeachment, of which due notice should be given to the House.

On the 26th, Mr. Randolph, from the committee appointed for that purpose, reported articles of impeachment against Samuel Chase. No order was taken on the report during the remainder of the session, which terminated the next day.

At the ensuing session of Congress, on the 6th of November, on the motion of Mr. J. Randolph, the articles of impeachment were referred to Messrs. J. Randolph, J. Clay, Early, Boyle, and J. Rhea, of Tennessee.

On the 30th of November, Mr. Randolph reported the following articles of impeachment against Samuel Chase, in substance, not dissimilar from those reported at the last session, with the addition of two new articles:

Articles exhibited by the House of Representatives of the United States, in the name of themselves and of all the people of the United States, against Samuel Chase, one of the associate justices of the supreme court of the United States, in maintenance and support of their impeachment against him, for high crimes and misdemeanors.

ARTICLE I.

That, unmindful of the solemn duties of his office, and contrary to the sacred obligation by which he stood bound to discharge them " faithfully and impartially, and without respect to persons," the said Samuel Chase, on the trial of John Fries, charged with treason, before the circuit court of the United States, held for the district of Pennsylvania, in the city of Philadelphia, during the months of April and May, one thousand eight hundred, whereat the said Samuel Chase presided, did, in his judicial capacity, conduct himself in a manner highly arbitrary, oppressive, and unjust, viz.

1. In delivering an opinion, in writing, on the question of law, on the construction of which the defence of the accused materially depended, tending to prejudice the minds of the jury against the case of the said John Fries, the prisoner, before counsel had been heard in his defence :

2. In restricting the counsel for the said Fries from recurring to such English authorities as they believed apposite, or from citing certain statutes of the United States, which they deemed illustrative of the positions, upon which they intended to rest the defence of their client :

3. In debarring the prisoner from his constitutional privilege of addressing the jury (through his counsel) on the law, as well as on the fact, which was to determine his guilt, or innocence, and at the same time endeavoring to wrest from the jury their indisputable right to hear argument, and determine upon the question of law, as well as the question of fact, involved in the verdict which they were required to give :

In consequence of which irregular conduct of the said Samuel Chase, as dangerous to our liberties, as it is novel to our laws and usages, the said John Fries was deprived of the right, secured to him by the eighth article amendatory of the constitution, and was condemned to death without having been heard by counsel, in his defence, to the disgrace of the character of the American bench, in manifest violation of law and justice, and in open contempt of the rights of juries, on which, ultimately, rest the liberty and safety of the American people.

ARTICLE II.

That, prompted by a similar spirit of persecution and injustice, at a circuit court of the United States, held at Richmond, in the month of May, one thousand eight hundred, for the district of Virginia, whereat the said Samuel Chase presided, and before which a certain James

Thompson Callender was arraigned for a libel on John Adams, then President of the United States, the said Samuel Chase, with intent to oppress, and procure the conviction of, the said Callender, did over-rule the objection of John Basset, one of the jury, who wished to be excused from serving on the said trial, because he had made up his mind, as to the publication from which the words, charged to be libellous, in the indictment, were extracted; and the said Basset was accordingly sworn and did serve on the said jury, by whose verdict the prisoner was subsequently convicted.

ARTICLE III.

That, with intent to oppress and procure the conviction of the prisoner, the evidence of John Taylor, a material witness on behalf of the aforesaid Callender, was not permitted by the said Samuel Chase to be given in, on pretence that the said witness could not prove the truth of the whole of one of the charges, contained in the indictment, although the said charge embraced more than one fact.

ARTICLE IV.

That the conduct of the said Samuel Chase, was marked, during the whole course of the said trial, by manifest injustice, partiality, and intemperance ; viz.

1. In compelling the prisoner's counsel to reduce to writing, and submit to the inspection of the court, for their admission, or rejection, all questions which the said counsel meant to propound to the above named John Taylor, the witness.

2. In refusing to postpone the trial, although an affidavit was regularly filed, stating the absence of material witnesses on behalf of the accused; and although it was manifest, that, with the utmost diligence, the attendance of such witnesses could not have been procured at that term.

3. In the use of unusual, rude, and contemptuous expressions towards the prisoner's counsel; and in falsely insinuating that they wished to excite the public fears and indignation, and to produce that insubordination to law, to which the conduct of the judge did, at the same time, manifestly tend :

4. In repeated and vexatious interruptions of the said counsel, on the part of the said judge, which, at length, induced them to abandon their cause and their client, who was thereupon convicted and condemned to fine and imprisonment :

5. In an indecent solicitude, manifested by the said Samuel Chase, for the conviction of the accused, unbecoming even a public prosecutor, but highly disgraceful to the character of a judge as it was subversive of justice.

ARTICLE V.

And whereas it is provided by the act of Congress, passed on the 24th day of September, 1789, intituled " An act to establish the judicial courts of the United States," that for any crime, or offence, against the United States, the offender may be arrested, imprisoned, or bailed, agreeably to the usual mode of process in the state where such offender may be found: and whereas, it is provided by the laws of Virginia, that, upon presentment by any grand jury of an offence not capital, the court shall order the clerk to issue a summons against the person, or persons offending, to appear and answer such presentment at the next court; yet, the said Samuel Chase did, at the court aforesaid, award a capias against the body of the said James Thompson Callender, indicted for an offence not capital, whereupon the said Callender was arrested and committed to close custody, contrary to law in that case made and provided.

ARTICLE VI.

And whereas it is provided by the 34th section of the aforesaid act, intituled " An act to establish the judicial courts of the United States," that the laws of the several states, except where the constitution, treaties, or statutes of the United States shall otherwise require, or provide, shall be regarded as the rules of decision in trials at common law, in the courts of the United States, in cases where they apply : and whereas, by the laws of Virginia it is provided, that in cases not capital, the offender shall not be held to answer any presentment of a grand jury until the court next succeeding that during which such presentment shall have been made, yet the said Samuel Chase, with intent to oppress and procure the conviction of the said James Thompson Callender, did, at the court aforesaid, rule and adjudge the said Callender to trial, during the term at which he, the said Callender, was presented and indicted, contrary to law in that case made and provided.

ARTICLE VII.

That, at a circuit court of the United States, for the district of Delaware, held at Newcastle, in the month of June, one thousand eight hundred, whereat the said Samuel Chase presided, the said Samuel Chase, disregarding the duties of his office, did descend from the dignity of a judge and stoop to the level of an informer, by refusing to discharge the grand jury, although entreated by several of the said jury so to do ; and after the said grand jury had regularly declared, through their foreman, that they had found no bills of indictment, nor had any presentments to make, by observing to the said grand jury, that he, the said Samuel Chase, understood " that a highly seditious temper had manifested it-
" self in the state of Delaware, among a certain class of people, parti-
" cularly in Newcastle county, and more especially in the town of Wil-
" mington, where lived a most seditious printer, unrestrained by any prin-
" ciple of virtue, and regardless of social order....that the name of this
" printer was"....but checking himself, as if sensible of the indecorum which he was committing, added, " that it might be assuming too much
" to mention the name of this person, but it becomes your duty, gentle-
" men, to enquire diligently into this matter," or words to that effect :

and that with intention to procure the prosecution of the printer in question, the said Samuel Chase did, moreover, authoritatively enjoin on the district attorney of the United States the necessity of procuring a file of the papers to which he alluded, (and which were understood to be those published under the title of "Mirror of the Times and General Advertiser,") and, by a strict examination of them, to find some passage which might furnish the ground-work of a prosecution against the printer of the said paper: thereby degrading his high judicial functions, and tending to impair the public confidence in, and respect for, the tribunals of justice, so essential to the general welfare.

ARTICLE VIII.

And whereas mutual respect and confidence between the government of the United States and those of the individual states, and between the people and those governments, respectively, are highly conducive to that public harmony, without which there can be no public happiness, yet the said Samuel Chase, disregarding the duties and dignity of his judicial character, did, at a circuit court, for the district of Maryland, held at Baltimore, in the month of May, one thousand eight hundred and three, pervert his official right and duty to address the grand jury then and there assembled, on the matters coming within the province of the said jury, for the purpose of delivering to the said grand jury an intemperate and inflammatory political harangue, with intent to excite the fears and resentment of the said grand jury, and of the good people of Maryland against their state government, and constitution, a conduct highly censurable in any, but peculiarly indecent and unbecoming in a judge of the supreme court of the United States: and moreover, that the said Samuel Chase, then and there, under pretence of exercising his judicial right to address the said grand jury, as aforesaid, did, in a manner highly unwarrantable, endeavor to excite the odium of the said grand jury, and of the good people of Maryland, against the government of the United States, by delivering opinions, which, even if the judicial authority were competent to their expression, on a suitable occasion and in a proper manner, were at that time and as delivered by him, highly indecent, extra-judicial, and tending to prostitute the high judicial character with which he was invested, to the low purpose of an electioneering partizan.

And the House of Representatives, by protestation, saving to themselves the liberty of exhibiting, at any time hereafter, any farther articles, or other accusation, or impeachment, against the said Samuel Chase, and also of replying to his answers which he shall make unto the said articles, or any of them, and of offering proof to all and every the aforesaid articles, and to all and every other articles, impeachment, or accusation, which shall be exhibited by them, as the case shall require, do demand that the said Samuel Chase may be put to answer the said crimes and misdemeanors, and that such proceedings, examinations, trials, and judgments may be thereupon had and given, as are agreeable to law and justice.

This report was made the order for the 3d of December. On that and the ensuing day the House took the articles into consideration, to all of which they agreed, according to the following votes :

Article	Yeas.	Nays.		Article	Yeas.	Nays
1	83	34		6 -	73	43
2	83	35		7 -	73	42
3	84	34		8 1st sect.	74	39
4	84	34		8 2d sect.	78	32
5	72	45				

On the 5th the House proceeded to the choice by ballot of seven managers to conduct the impeachment; and on counting the votes, Messrs. J. Randolph, Rodney, Nicholson, Early, Boyle, Nelson, and G. W. Campbell appeared to be elected.

On a subsequent day, Mr. Nelson having declined his appointment, on account of unavoidable absence, Mr. Clarke was chosen in his place.

The following resolution was then adopted :

Resolved, That the articles agreed to by this House, to be exhibited in the name of themselves, and of all the people of the United States, against Samuel Chase, in maintenance of their impeachment against him, for high crimes and misdemeanors, be carried to the Senate by the managers appointed to conduct the said impeachment.

The Senate having appointed the 7th of December for receiving the articles of impeachment, the managers repaired on that day, at 1 o'clock, to the Senate chamber. Having taken seats assigned them within the bar ; and the sergeant at arms having proclaimed silence, Mr. J. Randolph read the foregoing articles ; whereupon the President of the Senate informed the managers that the Senate would take proper order on the subject of the impeachment, of which due notice should be given to the House of Representatives. The managers delivered the articles of impeachment at the table and withdrew.

On the 10th of December, the Senate, sitting as a high court of impeachments, adopted the following resolution :

Resolved, That the secretary be directed to issue a summons to Samuel Chase, one of the associate justices of the supreme court of the United States, to answer certain articles of impeachment exhibited against him by the House of Representatives on Friday last : That the said summons be returnable the 2d day of January, and be served at least fifteen days before the return day thereof.

On the 24th and 31st of December, the Senate adopted the following *rules of proceeding,* to be observed in cases of impeachment.

1. Whensoever the Senate shall receive notice from the House of Representatives, that managers are appointed on their part, to conduct an impeachment against any person, and are directed to carry such articles to the Senate, the secretary of the Senate shall immediately inform the House of Representatives, that the Senate is ready to receive the managers for the purpose of exhibiting such articles of impeachment, agreeably to the said notice.

2. When the managers of an impeachment shall be introduced to the bar of the Senate, and shall have signified that they are ready to exhibit articles of impeachment against any person, the President of the Senate shall direct the sergeant at arms to make proclamation ; who shall, after making proclamation, repeat the following words : " All persons are commanded to keep silence on pain of imprisonment, while the grand inquest of the nation is exhibiting to the Senate of the United States, articles of impeachment against   ;" after which the articles shall be exhibited, and then the President of the Senate shall inform the managers, that the Senate will take proper order on the subject of the impeachment, of which due notice shall be given to the House of Representatives.

3. A summons shall issue, directed to the person impeached, in the form following :

The United States of America, ss.

THE SENATE OF THE UNITED STATES OF AMERICA,

To   *Greeting :*

Whereas, the House of Representatives of the United States of America, did, on the   day of   exhibit to the Senate, articles of impeachment against you, the said   in the words following, viz :

(here recite the articles)

and did demand that you the said   should be put to answer the accusations as set forth in said articles ; and that such proceedings, examinations, trials, and judgments, might be thereupon had, as are agreeable to law and justice. You, the said   are therefore hereby summoned, to be, and appear before the Senate of the United States of America, at their chamber in the City of Washington, on the   day of   then and there to answer to the said articles of impeachment, and then and there to abide by, obey, and perform such orders and judgments as the Senate of the United States shall make in the premises, according to the constitution and laws of the United States. Hereof you are not to fail.

Witness,   Vice President of the United States of America, and President of the Senate thereof, at the City of Washington, this   day of   in the year of our Lord,   and of the independence of the United States, the

Which summons shall be signed by the secretary of the Senate, and sealed with their seal, and served by the sergeant at arms to the Senate, or by such other person as the Senate shall specially appoint for that purpose ; who shall serve the same, pursuant to the directions given in the form next following :

4. A precept shall be endorsed on said writ of summons, in the form following, viz :

United States of America, ss.

THE SENATE OF THE UNITED STATES,

To   Greeting:

You are hereby commanded to deliver to, and leave with   if to be found, a true and attested copy of the within writ of summons, together with a like copy of this precept, shewing him both ; or in case he cannot with convenience be found, you are to leave true and attested copies of the said summons and precept, at his usual place of residence, and in whichsoever way you perform the service, let it be done at least. days before the appearance day mentioned in said writ of summons. Fail not, and make return of this writ of summons and precept, with your proceedings thereon endorsed, on or before the appearance day mentioned in said writ of summons.

Witness,   Vice President of the United States of America, and President of the Senate thereof, at the City of Washington, this   day of   in the year of our Lord   and of the independence of the United States, the

Which precept shall be signed by the secretary of the Senate, and sealed with their seal.

5. Subpœnas shall be issued by the secretary of the Senate, upon the application of the managers of the impeachment, or of the party impeached, or his counsel, in the following form, to wit :

To   Greeting :

You, and each of you, are hereby commanded to appear before the Senate of the United States, on the   day of   at the Senate chamber in the City of Washington, then and there to testify your knowledge in the cause which is before the Senate, in which the House of Representatives have impeached   Fail not.

Witness,   Vice President of the United States of America, and President of the Senate thereof, at the City of Washington, this   day of   in the year of our Lord   and of the independence of the United States, the

Which shall be signed by the secretary of the Senate, and sealed with their seal.

Which subpœnas shall be directed, in every case, to the marshal of the district, where such witnesses respectively reside, to serve and return.

6. The form of direction to the marshal, for the service of the subpœna, shall be as follows :

(SEAL.)

The Senate of the United States of America,

To the marshal of the district of

You are hereby commanded to serve and return the within subpœna, according to law.

Dated at Washington, this   day of   in the year of our Lord   and of the independence of the United States, the

Secretary of the Senate.

7. The President of the Senate shall direct all necessary preparations in the Senate chamber, and all the forms of proceeding, while the Senate are sitting for the purpose of trying an impeachment, and all forms during the trial, not otherwise specially provided for by the Senate.

8. He shall also be authorised to direct the employment of the marshal of the district of Columbia, or any other person or persons, during the trial, to discharge such duties as may be prescribed by him.

9. At twelve o'clock of the day appointed for the return of the summons against the person impeached, the legislative and executive business of the Senate shall be suspended and the secretary of the Senate shall administer an oath to the returning officer, in the form following, viz. " I   do solemnly swear, that the return made and subscribed by me, upon the process issued on the   day of   by the Senate of the United States, against   is truly made, and that I have performed said services as therein described. So help me God." Which oath shall be entered at large on the records.

10. The person impeached shall then be called to appear, and answer the articles of impeachment exhibited against him. If he appears, or any person for him, the appearance shall be recorded, stating particularly, if by himself, or if by agent or attorney ; naming the person appearing, and the capacity in which he appears. If he does not appear, either personally, or by agent or attorney, the same shall be recorded.

11. At twelve o'clock of the day appointed for the trial of an impeachment, the legislative and executive business of the Senate shall be postponed. The secretary shall then administer the following oath or affirmation to the President :

" *You solemnly swear, or affirm, that in all things appertaining to the trial of the impeachment of*   *you will do impartial justice according to the constitution and laws of the United States.*"

12. And the President shall administer the said oath or affirmation to each senator present,

The secretary shall then give notice to the House of Representatives, that the Senate is ready to proceed upon the impeachment of   in the Senate chamber, which chamber is prepared with accommodations for the reception of the House of Representatives.

13. Counsel for the parties shall be admitted to appear, and be heard upon an impeachment.

14. All motions made by the parties, or their counsel, shall be addressed to the President of the Senate, and if he shall require it, shall be committed to writing, and read at the secretary's table ; and all decisions shall be had by ayes and noes, and without debate, which shall be entered on the records.

15. Witnesses shall be sworn in the following form, to wit : " You do swear, (or affirm, as the case may be) that the evidence you shall give in the case now depending between the United States, and   shall be the truth, the whole truth, and nothing but the truth. So help you God." Which oath shall be administered by the secretary.

16. Witnesses shall be examined by the party producing them, and then cross-examined in the usual form.

17. If a Senator is called as a witness, he shall be sworn, and give his testimony standing in his place.

18. If a Senator wishes a question to be put to a witness, it shall be reduced to writing and put by the President.

19. At all times, whilst the Senate is sitting upon the trial of an impeachment, the doors of the Senate chamber shall be kept open.

HIGH COURT OF IMPEACHMENTS.

WEDNESDAY, JANUARY 2d, 1805.

The court having been opened by proclamation,

The return made by the sergeant at arms was read, as follows :

" I James Mathers, sergeant at arms to the Senate of the United States, in obedience to the within summons to me directed, did proceed to the residence of the within named Samuel Chase, on the 12th day of December, 1804, and did then and there leave a true copy of the said writ of summons, together with a true copy of the articles of impeachment annexed, with him the said Samuel Chase.

JAMES MATHERS."

After which the secretary administered to him the oath as follows : " You James Mathers, sergeant at arms to the Senate of the United States, do solemnly swear, that the return made and subscribed by you, upon the process issued on the 10th day of December last, by the Senate of the United States, against Samuel Chase, one of the associate justices of the supreme court, is truly made, and that you have performed said services as therein described. So help you God."

SAMUEL CHASE, having been solemnly called, appeared.

The President of the Senate (Mr. Burr) informed Mr. Chase, that having been summoned to answer to the articles of impeachment exhibited against him by the House of Representatives, the Senate were ready to receive any answer he had to make to them

Mr. Chase requested the indulgence of a chair,* which was immediately furnished.

After being seated for a short time, Mr. Chase rose, and commenced the following address to the Senate, which he read from a paper that he held in his hand.

" *Mr. President,*

" I appear, in obedience to a summons from this honorable court, to answer articles of impeachment exhibited against me, by the honorable the House of Representatives of the United States.

" To these articles, a copy of which was delivered to me with the summons, I say, that I have committed no crime or misdemeanor whatsoever, for which I am subject to impeachment according to the constitution of the United States. I deny, with a few exceptions, the acts with which I am charged; I shall contend, that all acts admitted to have been done by me, were *legal;* and I deny, in every instance, the *improper* intentions with which the acts charged, are alleged to have been done, and in which their supposed criminality altogether consists."

The *President* reminded Mr. Chase, that this was the day appointed to receive any answer he might make to the articles of impeachment.

Mr. *Chase* said his purpose was to request the allowance of further time to put in his answer.

The *President* desired him to proceed.

Mr. *Chase* proceeded in his address :

" But in charges of so heinous a nature, urged by so high an authority, a simple denial is not sufficient. It behoves me, for the legal justification of my conduct, and for the vindication of my character, to meet *each* charge with a full and particular answer ; to explain and refute at length, every principle urged against me ; to state the evidence by which I am to disprove every fact relied on in support of the accusation; and to detail all the facts and arguments on which my defence is to rest. The necessity of an answer embracing all these objects, in cases of impeachment, is obvious ; and the right to make it, is secured by law and sanctioned by uniform practice.

" Such an answer it is my intention to make. It is my purpose to submit the *whole* ground of my defence to the view of this honorable

---

* *We understand, that in correspondence with the parliamentary practise of England, no chair was, previously to the introduction of Mr. Chase, assigned him ; but that an informal intimation was made to him, that, on his requesting it, it would be allowed.*

court, of my country, of the world, and of those who are to conduct the prosecution. So will my judges come to the trial with that full knowledge of the whole matter in dispute, which is essential for enabling them to understand and apply the testimony and the arguments ; and the honorable managers will be better prepared to refute such parts of my defence, as they may think untenable."

The *President* here interrupted Mr. Chase; and asked if the paper he was reading was intended for his answer ; if so, it would be put on file. If it was the prelude to a motion he meant to make, praying to be allowed further time for putting in his answer, he would confine himself strictly to what had relation to that object. From the tenor of what had been urged it had appeared to him as intended for an answer to the articles of impeachment.

Mr. *Chase* said it was not his answer that he was reading ; but that he was assigning reasons, why he could not now answer, in order to shew that he was intitled to further time to prepare and put in his answer.

President. You, who are so conversant in the practice of courts of law, know very well that a motion for time must not be founded on mere suggestions, but must be founded on some facts to prove the propriety of the motion.

Mr. *Chase* said he meant to shew the impracticability of his answering at this time, from the very articles themselves, and it was for that purpose he had made an allusion to them.

The *President* said, with the caution he had given, he might proceed, provided no objection were made by any gentleman of the Senate.

Mr. Chase proceeded in his address:

" But in a case of this kind, where the accusation embraces so great a variety of charges, of principles, and of facts, it is manifest, that preparing such an answer, as I have a right to make and as my duty to myself, my family, my friends and my country, requires at my hand, a considerable time must be necessary.

" Many of the principles involved in this impeachment, are very important, not only to me, but to the liberties of every American citizen, and to the cause of free government in general. These principles ought to be maturely considered, and clearly explained. They present a wide field of legal investigation ; many of them require laborious and extensive research, and although some of them have accompanied the prosecution from its commencement, and have thus been for a considerable time subjected to my consideration ; some, on the other hand, have been very recently introduced.

" Of this description is the principle, whereon the 5th and 6th articles rest: relative to the extent in which the courts of the United States are to be governed, not only in their *decisions*, but in their *proceedings* by the state laws. A principle which was not brought into view until a few weeks ago, and the explanation of which will require a careful consideration, of the conduct and proceedings of the supreme and circuit courts of the United States, from the first establishment of our federal system.

" The same articles involve the construction of two state laws of Virginia, which I am charged with having infringed in the trial of Callender, which were not mentioned on the trial, or during any of the introductory proceedings, and of which I never heard until these articles were reported a few weeks ago. It is manifest that in order to fix the true construction of these laws, about which professional men have differed in opinion, recourse must be had to the decisions of the courts of that state, as explained by their records ; or in case those records should be silent, to the recollection and opinion of professional men, accustomed to preside or attend in the courts where those laws are enforced. It is manifest that such an investigation cannot be accomplished in a short time.

" The facts on which this prosecution rests, except the last article, are alleged to have taken place more than four years ago ; some of them at Philadelphia, some at Wilmington, in the state of Delaware, and some at Richmond, in Virginia. These facts are very numerous, and the greater part of them are of such a nature, as to depend for their criminality or innocence, on minute circumstances, or slight shades of testimony, and often on the different manner in which the same circumstances may affect different spectators, all equally disposed to represent truly what they observed. The most material facts are alleged to have happened in Richmond and Philadelphia. In the former of these places I am an utter stranger, having never been there but once ; and in the latter, I know personally but very few individuals. These circumstances render it very difficult for me, to ascertain the persons who witnessed the various transactions in question, and are able, after this lapse of time, to give accurate testimony concerning them ; and this difficulty is very much increased, by the distance of those places from that of my residence. I assure this honorable court, that from the moment when this prosecution assumed a serious appearance and a definitive form, at the last session of Congress, I have turned my attention to the subject of my defence, and my answer, and have exerted myself in finding out and procuring the requisite testimony ; but the difficulties which I have stated, added to my ill state of health during a great part of the last year, have prevented me from making such progress, as to afford me the hope of being able to obtain the object in a very short time. I have done much, but much, very much, remains to be done, even in those parts of the prosecution where I had some notice by the proceedings of last session. In those very material parts which have originated during the present session, every thing is still to be done.

" It may perhaps be thought, that although these preparations might be necessary for the trial, they are not so for the answer. But such an opinion, I trust, would on examination be found erroneous.

" The answer, in cases of impeachment, must disclose the whole defence, and the defence must be confined to the matters stated in the answer. Otherwise the prosecutors might be surprised at the trial, by objections which with previous notice, it would be in their power to refute or explain. The accused, therefore, before he puts in his answer, ought to have time sufficient for making himself thoroughly master of

his defence, of the grounds on which it rests, and of the facts and evidence by which it is to be supported. He ought to be completely prepared for the trial ; between which and the answer no delay need to take
place, except such as may be necessary for convening the witnesses.

"In so material a part of his preparation for defence, as the drawing
up of his answer, it will not, I presume, be denied that he ought to have
an opportunity of obtaining the best *professional* assistance, which it may
be in his power to procure. This assistance is rendered peculiarly necessary to me, by the very precarious state of my health ; which affords me, at this season of the year especially, but short and uncertain
intervals, of fitness for mental or bodily exertion. Should my answer
be required in a short time, I have no reason to suppose, that I shall be
able to obtain such assistance of this kind as I so much need, and as
probably, I shall otherwise have in my power. Professional gentlemen,
engaged extensively in business, are at all times too liable to interruption, and too much occupied to devote themselves exclusively to an affair of this nature, so as to complete it within a short period ; and at
this season of the year, they are for the most part particularly and in-
dispensably engaged.

"These reasons in favor of a liberal allowance of time for preparing
the answer, derive great additional force from one further consideration,
which I hope that I may, without impropriety, present to the view of
this honorable court. Reputation ought to be more dear to every man,
and is more dear to me than the honors or the emoluments of office. In
cases of impeachment, the facts which appear, the explanations which
are given, and the arguments which are urged, at the trial, are sometimes wholly omitted in the statements given to the public, and often
misrepresented, or stated too indistinctly to be generally understood.
It is to the answer that the world must look for the justification of the
accused. It is by his answer alone, that he can furnish a clear, concise
and authentic explanation of his conduct and his motives, supported by
such a statement of his proofs, as can be extensively read, clearly understood, and easily remembered. He may, therefore, claim from justice, and expect from the high dignity and responsible character of this
honorable tribunal, such time for preparing this very important docu-
ment, as may enable him to bestow on it all the care and labor which
it requires, and to give it all the force of which it may be susceptible.

"In stating these considerations, Mr. President, in support of my
request for a continuance of this case, I disclaim all intention of affected delay. Feeling a consciousness of my integrity, and a just pride of
character, which place me far above the fear of events, I am anxious
to meet this accusation, and I rejoice in an opportunity of refuting it.
I know that my conduct, though liable to a full portion of human error,
has at all times been free from intentional impropriety. I know that
in all the instances selected as the grounds of accusation, I have discharged my official duties, with a sacred and inviolate regard to my oath,
my character, the laws of my country, and the rights of my fellow citizens. I know that I can prove my innocence as to all the matters alleged against me. And acrimonious as are the terms in which many of

the accusations are conceived ; harsh and opprobrious as are the epithets wherewith it has been thought proper to assail my name and character, by those who were ' *puling in their nurse's arms,' whilst I was contributing my utmost aid to lay the ground-work of American liberty ;* I yet thank my accusers, whose functions as members of the government of my country I highly respect, for having at length put their charges into a definitive form, susceptible of refutation ; and for having thereby afforded me an opportunity of vindicating my innocence, in the face of this honorable court, of my country, and of the world."

On using the expressions marked in *italics*,

The *President* interrupted Mr. Chase, and said that observations of censure or recrimination were not admissible ; it would be very improper for him to listen to observations on the statements of the House of Representatives before an answer was filed.

Mr. Chase said he had very few words more to add, which would conclude what he had to say at the present time.

With the permission of the President he proceeded :

" But this vindication, situated as I am, and as this case is, cannot be the work of a few weeks. Much time has been employed in preparing the accusation ; less will be required for the defence ; but a short time will not suffice. I am far from presuming to prescribe to this honorable court, whose sense of justice and disposition to grant every proper indulgence, I cannot doubt ; but it may perhaps be not improper to suggest that by the first day of next session, the answer could be prepared and put in ; and that the trial might then take place as soon afterwards, as the witnesses could be collected. I declare that it will be impossible for me to prepare my answer in such time as to commence the trial during this session with any prospect of bringing it to a close before the session must end ; and were I to omit that full answer which I wish to give, it would be impossible for me, in the course of this session, (only two months of which now remain) to ascertain fully all the facts necessary for my defence ; to find out and bring to this place, the witnesses and written testimony ; or to make arrangements relative to that assistance of counsel which my case requires, my age and infirmities render essential, and a longer time would enable me to procure.

" I hope, Mr. President, I may be permitted to observe, that my *private* and *professional* reputation for probity and honor, has never been called in question. I have sustained a high judicial character for above sixteen years, and during the first six I presided at the trial of more criminals than any other judge within the United States. During this whole period of time my *official* conduct has never been arraigned, except only in the trials of Cooper, Fries, and Callender, above four years ago. For the truth of these assertions I appeal to all who know me ; and particularly to the two honorable senators from Maryland.

" In respect to the present prosecution, I will make but one remark. That I am impeached for giving on the trial of Callender, several judicial opinions, in which judge Griffin, my associate, concurred ; my opinions are held to be criminal, or that they flowed from partiality, and an intention to oppress Callender ; but the *same* opinions given by my associate have been considered perfectly innocent.

" I have now only to solicit this honorable court to allow me until the first day of next session to put in my answer, and to prepare for my trial ; and I submit myself as to the further proceedings in this case to the discretion of this honorable court, in whose integrity, impartiality and independence I repose the highest confidence. I will not for a moment believe that the spirit of party can ever enter and pollute these walls, or that popular prejudice or political motives will be harbored in the bosom of any member in this honorable body.

" On the contrary, I hope and expect, that all its decisions will be governed by the immutable principles of justice, and a sacred regard to the constitution and the law of the land, which every member of this court is bound by duty, and the obligations of a christian judge, to support and observe."

Mr. Chase, having finished his address, was desired by the President, if he had any motion to make, to reduce it to writing, and hand it to the secretary.

Whereupon, Mr. Chase submitted the following motion :

" I solicit this honorable court to allow me until the first day of the next session, to put in my answer, and to prepare for my trial."

The *President* informed Mr. Chase, that the court would take time to consider his motion.*

The Senate withdrew to a private apartment, where debate arose on the question, whether it was not incumbent on the Senators to take the oath required by the constitution, before they took into consideration the motion of Mr. Chase, which issued in the adoption of the following resolution :

Resolved, That on the meeting of the Senate, to-morrow, before they proceed to any business on the articles of impeachment before them, and before any decision of any question, the oath prescribed by the rules, shall be administered to the President and members of the Senate.

On the ensuing day, previously to the entrance of the Senate into the public room, considerable debate took place on the motion of Mr. Chase, without any decision being made.

THURSDAY, JANUARY 3d, 1805.

The court was opened by proclamation about 2 o'clock.

The oath prescribed was administered to the President by the secretary.

The President administered the oath prescribed to the following members :

Messrs. Adams, Anderson, Baldwin, Bradley, Breckenridge, Brown, Condit, Dayton, Ellery, Franklin, Giles, Hillhouse, Howland, Jackson, Mitchill, Moore, Olcott, Pickering, Smith, *(of Maryland,)* Smith, *(of New York,)* Smith, *(of Ohio,)* Smith, *(of Vermont,)* Sumter, Tracy, White, Worthington, Wright.

* *During these proceedings, neither the Managers, or House of Representatives were present.*

And the affirmation was administered to Messrs. Logan, Maclay, and Plumer.

The President stated that he had received a letter from the defendant, enclosing an affidavit that further time was necessary for him to prepare for trial ; which affidavit was read, as follows :

City of Washington, ss.

Samuel Chase made oath on the holy evangels of Almighty God, that it is not in his power to obtain information respecting the facts alleged in the articles of impeachment to have taken place in the city of Philadelphia, in the trial of John Fries ; or of the facts alleged to have taken place in the city of Richmond, in the trial of James T. Callender, in time to prepare and put in his answer, and to proceed to trial, with any probability that the same could be finished on or before the fifth day of March next. And further, that it is not in his power to procure information of the names of the witnesses, whom he thinks it may be proper and necessary for him to summon, in time to obtain their attendance, if his answer could be prepared in time sufficient for the finishing of the said trial, before the said fifth day of March next : and the said Samuel Chase further made oath, that he believes it will not be in his power to obtain the advice of counsel, to prepare his answer, and to give him their assistance on the trial, which he thinks necessary, if the said trial should take place during the present session of Congress ; and that he verily believes, if he had at this time, full information of facts, and of the witnesses proper for him to summon, and if he had also the assistance of counsel, that he could not prepare the answer he thinks he ought to put in, and be ready for his trial, within the space of four or five weeks from this time. And further, that his application to the honorable the Senate, for time to obtain information of facts, in order to prepare his answer, and for time to procure the attendance of necessary witnesses, and to prepare for his defence in the trial, and to obtain the advice and assistance of counsel, is not made for the purpose of delay, but only for the purpose of obtaining a full hearing of the articles of impeachment against him, in their real merits.

SAMUEL CHASE.

Sworn to this third day of January, 1805, before

SAMUEL HAMILTON,

Whereupon, The following motion was made by Mr. Bradley :

Ordered, That Samuel Chase file his answer, with the secretary of the Senate, to the several articles of impeachment exhibited against him, by the House of Representatives, on or before the   day of

A motion was made by Mr. Giles to amend the motion, and to strike out all that follows the word " *Ordered,*" and insert " That   next shall be the day for receiving the answer, and proceeding on the trial of the impeachment against Samuel Chase."

Mr. Hillhouse called for a division of the question. And the yeas and nays being taken on striking out, it passed in the affirmative, yeas 20, nays 10.

Those who voted in the affirmative, are,

Messrs. Anderson, Baldwin, Breckenridge, Brown, Condit, Ellery, Franklin, Giles, Howland, Jackson, Logan, Maclay, Mitchill, Moore, Smith, *(of Maryland,)* Smith, *(of New York,)* Smith, *(of Ohio,)* Smith, *(of Vermont,)* Sumter, Worthington.

Those who voted in the negative, are,

Messrs. Adams, Bradley, Dayton, Hillhouse, Olcott, Pickering, Plumer, Tracy, White, Wright.

On motion, to insert the amendment proposed, the yeas and nays being taken, it passed in the affirmative, yeas 22, nays 8.

Those who voted in the affirmative, are,

Messrs. Anderson, Baldwin, Bradley, Breckenridge, Brown, Condit, Dayton, Ellery, Franklin, Giles, Howland, Jackson, Logan, Maclay, Mitchill, Moore, Smith, *(of Maryland,)* Smith, *(of New York,)* Smith, *(of Ohio,)* Smith, *(of Vermont,)* Sumter, Worthington.

Those who voted in the negative, are,

Messrs. Adams, Hillhouse, Olcott, Pickering, Plumer, Tracy, White, Wright.

On motion, by Mr. Tracy, to fill the blank with the words " the first Monday of December next," the yeas and nays being taken, it passed in the negative, yeas 12, nays 18.

Those who voted in the affirmative, are,

Messrs. Bradley, Dayton, Hillhouse, Logan, Olcott, Pickering, Plumer, Smith, *(of Maryland,)* Smith, *(of Ohio,)* Smith, *(of Vermont,)* Tracy, White,

Those who voted in the negative, are,

Messrs. Adams, Anderson, Baldwin, Breckenridge, Brown, Condit, Ellery, Franklin, Giles, Howland, Jackson, Maclay, Mitchill, Moore, Smith, *(of New York,)* Sumter, Worthington, Wright.

On motion, by Mr. Breckenridge, to fill the blank with the words " the fourth day of February next," the yeas and nays being taken, it passed in the affirmative, yeas 22, nays 8.

Those who voted in the affirmative, are,

Messrs. Adams, Anderson, Baldwin, Breckenridge, Brown, Condit, Ellery, Franklin, Giles, Howland, Jackson, Logan, Maclay, Mitchill, Moore, Smith, *(of Maryland,)* Smith, *(of New-York,)* Smith, *(of Ohio,)* Smith, *(of Vermont,)* Sumter, Worthington, Wright.

Those who voted in the negative, are,

Messrs. Bradley, Dayton, Hillhouse, Olcott, Pickering, Plumer, Tracy, White.

On motion, to agree to the order, as amended, the yeas and nays being taken, it passed in the affirmative, yeas 21, nays 9.

Those who voted in the affirmative, are,

Messrs. Anderson, Baldwin, Breckenridge, Brown, Condit, Ellery, Franklin, Giles, Howland, Jackson, Logan, Maclay, Mitchell, Moore, Smith, *(of Maryland,)* Smith, *(of New-York,)* Smith, *(of Ohio,)* Smith, *(of Vermont,)* Sumter, Worthington, Wright.

Those who voted in the negative, are,

Messrs. Adams, Bradley, Dayton, Hillhouse, Olcott, Pickering, Plumer, Tracy, White.

So it was

Ordered, That the fourth day of February next, shall be the day for receiving the answer, and proceeding on the trial of the impeachment against Samuel Chase.

Ordered, That the secretary notify the House of Representatives, and Samuel Chase thereof.

———

Between this day, and that assigned for receiving the answer of Mr. Chase, the Senate chamber was fitted up in a style of appropriate elegance. Benches, covered with crimson, on each side, and in a line with the chair of the President, were assigned to the members of the Senate. On the right and in front of the chair, a box was assigned to

the Managers, and on the left a similar box to Mr. Chase, and his counsel, and chairs allotted to such friends as he might introduce. The residue of the floor was occupied with chairs for the accommodation of the members of the House of Representatives; and with boxes for the reception of the foreign ministers, and civil and military officers of the United States. On the right and left of the chair, at the termination of the benches of the members of the court, boxes were assigned to stenographers. The permanent gallery was allotted to the indiscriminate admission of spectators. Below this gallery, and above the floor of the House, a new gallery was raised, and fitted up with peculiar elegance, intended primarily for the exclusive accommodation of ladies. But this feature of the arrangement made by the Vice-President, was at an early period of the trial abandoned, it having been found impracticable to separate the sexes! At the termination of this gallery, on each side, boxes were specially assigned to ladies attached to the families of public characters. The preservation of order was devolved on the marshal of the district of Columbia, who was assisted by a number of deputies.

TRIAL

OF

SAMUEL CHASE.

MONDAY, FEBRUARY 4th, 1805.

ABOUT a quarter before ten o'clock the court was opened by proclamation; all the members of the Senate, thirty four, attending.

The chamber of the Senate, which is very extensive, was soon filled with spectators, a large portion of whom consisted of ladies, who continued, with little intermission, to attend during the whole course of the trial.

The oath prescribed was administered to Mr. Bayard, Mr. Cocke, Mr. Gaillard, and Mr. Stone, members of the court, who were not present when it was before administered.

Ordered, that the secretary give notice to the House of Representatives, that the Senate are in their public chamber, and are ready to proceed on the trial of Samuel Chase; and that seats are provided for the accommodation of the members.

In a few minutes the managers, viz: Messrs. J. Randolph, Rodney, Nicholson, Boyle, Early, G. W. Campbell, and Clarke, accompanied by the House of Representatives in committee of the whole, entered and took their seats.

Samuel Chase being called to make answer to the articles of impeachment, exhibited against him by the House of Representatives, appeared, attended by Messrs. Harper, Martin, and Hopkinson, his counsel; to whom seats were assigned.

The President, after stating to Mr. Chase the indulgence of time which had been allowed, enquired if he were prepared to give in his answer.

Mr. Chase said, he had prepared it, as well as circumstances would permit: and submitted the following motion:

" Samuel Chase moves for permission to read his answer, by himself and his counsel, at the bar of this honorable court."

The President asked him if it was the answer on which he meant to rely? to which he replied in the affirmative.

The motion being agreed to by a vote of the Senate, Mr. Chase commenced the reading of his answer, (in which he was assisted by Messrs. Harper, and Hopkinson,) as follows:

THIS respondent, in his proper person, comes into the said court, and protesting that there is no high crime or misdemeanor particularly alleged in the said articles of impeachment, to which he is, or can be bound by law to make answer; and saving to himself now, and at all times hereafter, all benefit of exception to the insufficiency of the said articles, and each of them, and to the defects therein appearing in point of law, or otherwise; and protesting also, that he ought not to be injured in any manner, by any words, or by any want of form in this his answer; he submits the following facts and observations by way of answer to the said articles.

The first article relates to his supposed misconduct in the trial of John Fries, for treason, before the circuit court of the United States, at Philadelphia, in April and May, 1800; and alleges that he presided at that trial, and that " unmindful of the solemn duties of his office, and contrary to the sacred obligation by which he stood bound to discharge them, faithfully and impartially, and without respect to persons," he did then, " in his judicial capacity, conduct himself in a manner highly arbitrary, oppressive, and unjust."

This general accusation, too vague in itself for reply, is supported by three specific charges of misconduct:

1st. " In delivering an opinion, in writing, on the question of law, on the construction of which, the defence of the accused materially depended:" which opinion, it is alleged, tended to prejudice the minds of the jury against the case of the said John Fries, the prisoner, before counsel had been heard in his favor."

2d. " In restricting the counsel for the said John Fries, from recurring to such English authorities, as they believed apposite; or from citing certain statutes of the United States, which they deemed illustrative of the positions, upon which they intended to rest the defence of their client."

3d. " In debarring the prisoner from his constitutional privilege of addressing the jury (through his counsel) on the law, as well as on the fact, which was to determine his guilt or innocence, and at the same time endeavoring to wrest from the jury their indisputable right to hear argument, and determine upon the question of law, as well as the question of fact, involved in the verdict which they were required to give."

This first article then concludes, that in consequence of this irregular conduct of this respondent, " the said John Fries was deprived of the right, secured to him by the *eighth* article, amendatory of the constitution; and was condemned to death, without having been heard, by counsel, in his defence."

By the eighth article amendatory to the constitution, this respondent supposes, is meant the *sixth* amendment to the constitution of the United States; which secures to the accused, in all criminal prosecutions, the right to have the assistance of counsel for his defence.

In answer to these three charges, the respondent admits that the circuit court of the United States, for the district of Pennsylvania, was held at Philadelphia, in that district, in the months of April and May, in the year of our Lord, one thousand eight hundred; at which court John Fries, the person named in the said first article, was brought to trial, on an indictment for treason against the United States; and that this respondent then held a commission, as one of the associate justices of the supreme court of the United States; by virtue of which office, he did, pursuant to the laws of the United States, preside at the above mentioned trial, and was assisted therein by Richard Peters, esq. then, and still district judge of the United States, for the district of Pennsylvania; who, as directed by the laws of the United States, sat as assistant judge at the said trial.

With respect to the opinion, which is alleged to have been delivered by this respondent, at the above-mentioned trial, he begs leave to lay before this honor-able court, the true state of that transaction, and to call its attention to some facts and considerations, by which his conduct on that subject will, he presumes, be fully justified.

The constitution of the United States, in the third section of the third article, declares that " treason against the United States, shall consist *only in levying war against them*, or in adhering to their enemies, giving them aid and comfort."

By two acts of Congress, the first passed on the third day of March, 1791, and the second on the eighth day of May, 1792, a duty was imposed on spirits distilled within the United States, and on stills; and various provisions were made for its collection.

In the year 1794, an insurrection took place in four of the western counties of Pennsylvania, with a view of resisting, and preventing by force the execution of these two statutes; and at a circuit court of the United States, held at Philadelphia, for the district of Pennsyl-vania, in the month of April, in the year 1795, by William Patterson, esq. then one of the associate jus-tices of the supreme court of the United States, and the above mentioned Richard Peters, then district judge of the United States, for the district of Pennsyl-vania, two persons, who had been concerned in the above named insurrection, namely, Philip Vigol and John Mitchel, were indicted for treason, of levying war against the United States, by resisting and preventing by force the execution of the two last mentioned acts of Congress; and were, after a full and very solemn trial, convicted on the indictments and sentenced to death. They were afterwards pardoned by George Washington, then President of the United States.

In the first of these trials, that of Vigol, the defence of the prisoner was conducted by very able counsel, one of whom, William Lewis, esq. is the same person who appeared as counsel for John Fries, in the trial now under consideration. Neither that learned gentleman, nor his able colleague, then thought proper to raise the question of law, " whether resisting and preventing by armed force, the execution of a *particular* law of the United States, be a ' levying of war against the United States," according to the true meaning of the constitution? although a decision of this question in the negative, must have acquitted the prisoner. But in the next trial, that of Mitchell, this question was raised on the part of the prisoner, and was very fully and ably discussed by his counsel; and it was solemnly determined by the court, both the judges concurring, "that to resist or prevent by armed force, the execution of a particular law of the United States, is a levying of war against the United States, and consequently is treason, within the true meaning of the constitution." The decision, according to the best established principles of our jurisprudence, became a precedent for all courts of equal or inferior jurisdiction; a precedent which, although not absolutely obligatory, ought to be viewed with very great respect, especially by the court in which it was made, and ought never to be departed from, but on the fullest and clearest conviction of its incorrectness.

On the 9th of July, 1798, an act of Congress was passed, providing for a valuation of lands and dwelling houses, and an enumeration of slaves throughout the United States; and directing the appointment of commissioners and assessors for carrying it into execution: And on the 4th day of July, in the same year, a direct tax was laid by another act of Congress of that date, on the lands, dwelling houses, and slaves, so to be valued and enumerated.

In the months of February and March, A. D. 1799, an insurrection took place in the counties of Bucks and Northampton, in the state of Pennsylvania, for the purpose of resisting and preventing by force, the execution of the two last mentioned acts of Congress, and particularly that for the valuation of lands and dwelling houses. John Fries, the person mentioned in the article of impeachment now under consideration, was apprehended and committed to prison, as one of the ringleaders of this insurrection; and at a circuit court of the United States, held at Philadelphia, in and for the district of Pennsylvania, in the month of April, A. D. 1799, he was brought to trial for this offence, on an indictment for treason, by levying war against the United States, before James Iredell, esq. then one of the associate justices of the supreme court of the United States, who presided in the said court, according to law, and the above mentioned Richard Peters, then district judge of the United States, for the district of Pennsylvania, who sat in the said circuit court as assistant judge.

In this trial, which was conducted with great solemnity, and occupied nine days, the prisoner was assisted by Wm. Lewis and Alexander James Dallas, esqs. two very able and eminent counsellors; the former of whom, Wm. Lewis, is the person who assisted as above mentioned, in conducting the defence of Vigol, on a similar indictment. These gentlemen, finding that the facts alleged were fully and undeniably proved, by a very minute and elaborate examination of witnesses, thought proper to rest the case of the prisoner, on the question of law which had been determined in the cases of Vigol and Mitchel above mentioned, and had then been acquiesced in, but which they thought proper again to raise. They contended, " that to resist by force of arms a particular law of the United States, does not amount to levying war against the United States, within the true meaning of the constitution, and therefore it is not *treason*, but a *riot* only." This question they argued at great length, and with all the force of their learning and genius; and after a very full discussion at the bar, and the most mature deliberation by the court, the learned and excellent judge who then presided, and who was no less distinguished by his humanity and tenderness towards persons tried before him, than by his extensive knowledge and great talents as a lawyer, pronounced the opinion of himself and his colleague, " that to resist or prevent by force, the execution of a particular law of the United States, does amount to levying war against them, within the true meaning of the constitution, and does therefore constitute the crime of treason:" thereby adding the weight of another and more solemn decision, to the precedent which had been established in the above mentioned cases of Vigol and Mitchel.

Under this opinion of the court on the question of law, the jury, having no doubt as to the facts, found the said John Fries guilty of treason, on the above mentioned indictment. But a new trial was granted by the court, not by reason of any doubt as to the correctness of the decision on the question of law, but solely on the ground, as this respondent hath understood and believes, that one of the jurors of the petit jury, after he was summoned, but before he was sworn on the trial, had made some declaration unfavorable to the prisoner.

The yellow fever having appeared in Philadelphia in the summer of the year 1799, the above mentioned Richard Peters, then district judge of the United States for the district of Pennsylvania, did according to law appoint the next circuit court of that district, to be held at Norris town therein : Pursuant to which appointment, a circuit court was held at Norris town aforesaid, in and for the said district, on the 11th day of October, in the last mentioned year, before Bushrod Washington, esq. then one of the associate justices of the supreme court of the United States, and the above mentioned Richard Peters; at which court no proceedings were had on the aforesaid indictment against John Fries, because, as this respondent hath been informed and believes, the commission of the marshal of the said district had expired, before he summoned the jurors to attend at the said court, and had not been renewed; by reason of which no legal pannel of jurors could be formed.

On the 11th day of April, A. D. 1800, and from that day until the 2d day of May in the same year, a circuit court of the United States was held at Philadelphia, in and for the district of Pennsylvania, before this respondent, then one of the associate justices of the supreme court of the United States, and the above mentioned Richard Peters, then district judge of the United States for the district of Pennsylvania. At this court, the indictment on which the said John Fries had been convicted as above mentioned, was quashed ex officio by William Rawle, esq. then attorney of the United States for the district of Pennsylvania, and a new indictment was by him preferred against the said John Fries, for treason of levying war against the United States, by resisting and preventing by force, in the manner above set forth, the execution of the above mentioned acts of Congress, for the valuation of lands and dwelling houses and the enumeration of slaves, and for levying and collecting a direct tax. This indictment, of which a true copy, marked exhibit No. 1, is herewith exhibited by this respondent, who prays that it may be taken as part of this his answer, being found by the grand jury on the 16th day of April, 1800, the said John Fries was on the same day arraigned thereon, and plead not guilty. William Lewis and Alexander James Dallas, esqrs. the same persons who had conducted his defence at his former trial, were again at his request assigned by the court as his counsel; and his trial was appointed to be had, on Tuesday the 22d day of the last mentioned month of April.

After this indictment was found by the grand jury, this respondent considered it with great care and deliberation, and finding from the three overt acts of treason which it charged, that the question of law arising upon it, was the same question which had already been decided twice in the same court, on so-

lemn argument and deliberation, and once in that very case, he considered the law as settled by those
decisions, with the correctness of which on full consideration he was entirely satisfied; and by the authority of which he should have deemed himself bound,
even had he regarded the question as doubtful in itself. They are moreover in perfect conformity with
the uniform tenor of decisions in the courts of England
and Great Britain, from the revolution, in 1688, to
the present time, which, in his opinion, added greatly
to their weight and authority.

And surely he need not urge to this honorable court,
the correctness, the importance, and the absolute necessity of adhering to principles of law once established, and of considering the law as finally settled, after
repeated and solemn decisions by courts of competent
jurisdiction. A contrary principle would unsettle the
basis of our whole system of jurisprudence, hitherto
our safeguard and our boast; would reduce the law
of the land, and subject the rights of the citizen, to
the arbitrary will, the passions, or the caprice of the
judge in each particular case; and would substitute
the varying opinions of various men, instead of that
fixed, permanent rule, in which the very essence of
law consists. If this respondent erred in regarding
this point as settled, by the repeated and solemn adjudications of his predecessors, in the same court and
in the same case; if he erred in supposing, that a
principle established by two solemn decisions, was
obligatory upon him, sitting in the same court where
those decisions had been made; if he erred in believing that it would be the highest presumption in
him, to set up his opinion and judgment over that of
his colleague, who had twice decided the same question, and of two of his predecessors, who justly rank
among the ablest judges that have ever adorned a
court; if in all this he erred, it is an error of which he
cannot be ashamed, and which he trusts will not be
deemed criminal in the eyes of this honorable court,

of his country, or of that posterity by which he, his accusers, and his judges, must one day be judged.

Under the influence of these considerations, this respondent drew up an opinion on the law, arising from the overt acts stated in the said indictment, which was conformable to the decisions before given as above mentioned, and which he sent to his colleague the said Richard Peters, for his consideration. That gentleman returned it to this respondent, with some amendments affecting the form only, but not in any manner touching the substance.

The opinion thus agreed to, this respondent thought it proper to communicate to the prisoner's counsel.... several reasons concurred in favor of this communication.

In the first place, this respondent considered himself and the court, as bound by the authority of the former decisions ; especially the last of them, which was on the same case. He considered the law as settled, and had every reason to believe that his colleague viewed it in the same light. It was not suggested or understood, that any new evidence was to be offered ; and he knew that if any should be offered, which could vary the case, it would render wholly inapplicable both the opinion and the former decisions on which it was founded. And he could not and did not suppose, that the prisoner's counsel would be desirous of wasting very precious time, in addressing to the court an useless argument, on a point which that court held itself precluded from deciding in their favor. He therefore conceived that it would be rendering the counsel a service and a favor, to apprise them before hand of the view which the court had taken of the subject; so as to let them see in time, the necessity of endeavoring to produce new testimony, which might vary the case, and take it out of the authority of former decisions.

. *Secondly,* There were more than one hundred civil causes then depending in the said court, as appears by the exhibit marked No. 1, which this respondent prays may be taken as part of this, his answer. Many of those causes had already been subjected to great delay, and it was the peculiar duty of this respondent, as presiding judge, to take care, that as little time as possible should be unnecessarily consumed, and that every convenient and proper dispatch should be given to the business of the citizens. He did believe, that an early communication of the court's opinion, might tend to the saving of time, and consequently to the dispatch of business.

Thirdly, As the court held itself bound by the former decisions, and could not therefore alter its opinion in consequence of any argument; and as it was the duty of the court to charge the jury on the law, in all cases submitted to their consideration, he knew that this opinion must not only be made known at some period or other of the trial, but must at the end of the trial be expressly delivered to the jury by him, in a charge from the bench : and he could not suppose and cannot yet imagine, that an opinion, which was to be thus solemnly given in charge to the jury, at the close of the trial, could make any additional impression on their minds, from the circumstance of its being intimated to the counsel before the trial began, in the hearing of those who might be afterwards sworn on the jury.

And, lastly, it was then his opinion, and still is, that it is the duty of every court of this country, and was his duty on the trial now under consideration, to guard the jury against erroneous impressions respecting the laws of the land. He well knows, that it is the right of juries in criminal cases, to give a general verdict of acquittal, which cannot be set aside on account of its being contrary to law, and that hence results the power of juries, to decide on the law as well as on the facts, in all criminal cases. This power he holds to be a sacred part of our legal privileges, which he never has attempted, and never will attempt to abridge or to obstruct. But he also knows, that in the exercise of this power, it is the duty of the jury to govern themselves by the laws of the land, over which they have no dispensing power; and their right to expect and receive from the court, all the assistance which it can give, for rightly understanding the law. To withhold this assistance, in any manner whatever; to forbear to give it in that way, which may be most effectual for preserving the jury from error and mistake; would be an abandonment or forgetfulness of duty, which no judge could justify to his conscience or to the laws. In this case, therefore, where the question of law arising on the indictment, had been finally settled by authoritative decisions, it was the duty of the court, and especially of this respondent as presiding judge, early to apprise the counsel and the jury of these decisions, and their effect, so as to save the former from the danger of making an improper attempt, to mislead the jury in a matter of law, and the jury from having their minds preoccupied by erroneous impressions.

It was for these reasons, that on the 22d day of April, 1800, when the said John Fries was brought into court, and placed in the prisoners' box for trial, but before the petit jury was impannelled to try him, this respondent informed the abovementioned William Lewis, one of his counsel, the aforesaid Alexander James Dallas not being then in court, " that the court had deliberately considered the indictment against John Fries for treason, and the three several overt acts of treason stated therein : That the crime of treason was defined by the constitution of the United States: That the federal legislature had the power to make, alter, or repeal laws, so the judiciary only had the power, and it was their duty, to declare, expound and interpret the constitution and laws of the United States : That it was the duty of the court, in all criminal cases, to state to the petit jury, their opinion of the law arising on the facts; but the petit jury, in all criminal cases, were to decide both the law and the facts, on a consideration of the whole case: That there must be some constructive exposition of the terms used in the constitution, " levying war against the United States:" That the question, what acts amounted to levying war against the United States, or the government thereof, was a question of law, and had been decided by judges Patterson and Peters, in the cases of Vigol and Mitchel, and by judges Iredell and Peters, in the case of John Fries, prisoner at the bar, in April 1799: That judge Peters remained of the same opinion, which he had twice before delivered, and he, this respondent, on long and great consideration, concurred in the opinion of judges Patterson, Iredell, and Peters: That to prevent unnecessary delay, and to save time on the trial of John Fries, and to prevent a delay of justice, in the great number of civil causes depending for trial at that term, the court had drawn up in writing, their opinion of the law, arising on the overt acts, stated in the indictment against John Fries; and had directed David Caldwell their clerk, to make out three copies of their opinion, one to be delivered to the attorney of the district, one to the counsel for the prisoner, and one to the petit jury, after they should have been impannelled and heard the indictment read to them by the clerk, and after the district attorney should have stated to them the law on the overt acts alleged in the indictment, as it appeared to him."

After these observations, this respondent delivered one of the abovementioned copies to the aforesaid William Lewis, then attending as one of the prisoner's counsel; who read part of it, and then laid it down on the table before him. Some observations were then made on the subject, by him and the abovementioned Alexander James Dallas, who had then come into court; but this respondent doth not now recollect those observations, and cannot undertake to state them accurately.

And this respondent further saith, that the paper marked exhibit No. 2, and herewith exhibited, which he prays leave to make part of this his answer, is a true copy of the original opinion, drawn up by him and concurred in by the said Richard Peters, as above set forth, which original opinion is now in the possession of this respondent, ready to be produced to this honorable court. He may have erred in forming this opinion, and in the time and manner of making it known to the counsel for the prisoner. If he erred in forming it, he erred in common with his colleague and with two of his predecessors; and he presumes to hope that an error which has never been deemed criminal in them, will not be imputed as a crime to him, who was led into it by their example and their authority. If he erred in the time and manner of making known this opinion, he feels a just confidence, that when the reasons which he has alleged for his conduct, and by which it seemed to him to be fully justified, shall come to be carefully weighed, they will be sufficient to prove, if not that this conduct was perfectly regular and correct, yet that he might sincerely have considered it as right; and that in a case where so much doubt may exist, to have committed a mistake, is not to have committed a crime.

And this respondent further answering insists, that the opinion thus delivered to the prisoner's counsel, viz. that " any insurrection or rising of any body of people within the United States, for the purpose of resisting or preventing by force or violence, under any pretence whatever, the execution of any statute of the United States, for levying or collecting taxes, or for any other object of a general or national concern, is levying war against the United States, within the contemplation and true meaning of the constitution of the United States," is a legal and correct opinion, supported not only by the two previous decisions abovementioned, but also by the plainest principles of law and reason, and by the uniform tenor of legal adjudications in England and Great Britain, from the revolution in 1688, to this time. It ever was, and now is his opinion, that the peace and safety of the national federal government, must be endangered by any other construction of the terms "levying war against the United States," used by the federal constitution; and he is confident that no judge of the federal government, no judge of a superior state court, nor any gentleman of established reputation for legal knowledge, would or could deliberately give a contrary opinion.

If, however, this opinion were erroneous, this respondent would be far less censurable than his predecessors, by whose example he was led astray, and by whose authority he considered himself bound. Was it an error to consider himself bound by the authority of their previous decisions? If it were, he was led into the error by the uniform course of judicial proceedings, in this country and in England, and is supported in it, by one of the fundamental principles of our jurisprudence. Can such an error be a crime or misdemeanor?

If, on the other hand, the opinion be in itself correct, as he believes and insists that it is, could the expression of a correct opinion on the law, wherever and however made, mislead the jury, infringe their rights, or give an improper bias to their judgments? Could truth excite improper prejudice? Could the jury be less prepared to hear the law discussed, and to decide on it correctly, because it was correctly stated to them by the court? And is not that a new kind of offence, in this country at least, which consists in telling the truth, and giving a correct exposition of the law.

As to the second specific charge adduced in support of the first article of impeachment, which accuses this respondent, " of restricting the counsel for the said Fries, from recurring to such English authorities as they believed apposite, or from citing certain statutes of the United States, which they deemed illustrative of the positions upon which they intended to rest the defence of their client," this respondent admits that he did, on the above mentioned trial, express it as his opinion to the aforesaid counsel for the prisoner, " that the decisions in England, in cases of indictments for treason at common law, against the person of the king, ought not to be read to the jury, on trials for treason under the constitution and statutes of the United States; because such decisions could not inform, but might mislead and deceive the jury: that any decisions on cases of treason, in the courts of England, before the revolution of 1688, ought to have very little influence in the courts of the United States; that he would permit decisions in the courts of England or of Great Britain, since the said revolution, to be read to the court or jury, for the purpose of shewing what acts have been considered by those courts, as a constructive levying of war against the king of that country, in his regal capacity, but not against his person; because levying war against *his government*, was of the same nature as levying war against *the government of the United States:* but that such decisions, nevertheless, were not to be considered as authorities binding on the courts and juries of this country, but merely in the light of opinions entitled to great respect, as having been delivered after full consideration, by men of great legal learning and ability.

These are the opinions which he did, on that occasion, deliver to the counsel for the prisoner, and which he then thought, and still thinks, it was his duty to deliver. The counsellors admitted to practice in any court of justice are, in his opinion, and according to universal practice, to be considered as officers of such courts, and ministers of justice therein, and as such subject to the direction and control of the court, as to their conduct in its presence, and in conducting the defence of criminals on trial before it.—As counsel, they owe to the person accused, diligence, fidelity, and secrecy, and to the court and jury, due and correct information, according to the best of their knowledge and

ability, on every matter of law which they attempt to
adduce in argument. The court, on the other hand,
hath power, and is bound in duty, to decide and direct
what evidence, whether by record or by precedents of
decisions in courts of justice, is proper to be admitted
for the establishment of any matter of law or fact.
Consequently, should counsel attempt to read to a jury,
as a law still in force, a statute which had been repealed, or a decision which had been reversed, or the judgments of courts in counties whose laws have no connection with ours, it would be the duty of the court to inter-
pose, and prevent such an imposition from being practised on the jury. For these reasons, this respondent
thinks that his conduct was correct, in expressing to
the counsel for Fries, the opinions stated above. He
is not bound to answer here for the correctness of those
principles, though he thinks them incontestible; but
merely for the correctness of his motives in delivering them. A contrary opinion would convert this
honorable court, from a court of impeachment into a
court of appeals; and would lead directly to the strange
absurdity, that whenever the judgment of an inferior
court should be reversed on appeal or writ of error, the
judges of that court must be convicted of high crimes
and misdemeanors, and turned out of office: that error
in judgment is a punishable offence, and that crimes
may be committed without any criminal intention.
Against a doctrine so absurd and mischievous, so contrary to every notion of justice hitherto entertained, so
utterly subversive of all that part of our system of jurisprudence, which has been wisely and humanely established for the protection of innocence, this respondent deems it his duty now, and on every fit occasion,
to enter his protest and lift up his voice; and he trusts
that in the discharge of this duty, infinitely more important to his country than to himself, he shall find approbation and support in the heart of every American,
of every man throughout the world, who knows the

blessings of civil liberty, or respects the principles of universal justice.

It is only then, for the correctness of his motives in delivering these opinions, that he can now be called to answer; and this correctness ought to be presumed, unless the contrary appear by some direct proof, or by some violent presumption, arising from his general conduct on the trial, or from the glaring impropriety of the opinion itself. For he admits that cases may be supposed, of an opinion delivered by a judge, so palpably erroneous, unjust and oppressive, as to preclude the possibility of its having proceeded from ignorance or mistake.

Do the opinions now under consideration bear any of these marks? This honorable court need not be informed that there has existed in England, no such thing as treason at common law, since the year 1350, when the statute of the 25th Edward III, chap. 2, declaring what alone should in future be judged treason, was passed. Is it perfectly clear that decisions made before that statute, 450 years ago, when England, together with the rest of Europe, was still wrapped in the deepest gloom of ignorance and barbarism; when the system of English jurisprudence was still in its infancy; when law, justice and reason, were perpetually trampled under foot by feudal oppression and feudal anarchy; when, under an able and vigorous monarch, every thing was adjudged to be treason which he thought fit to call so, and under a weak one, nothing was considered as treason which turbulent, powerful, and rebellious nobles thought fit to perpetrate: is it perfectly clear that decisions, made at such a time, and under such circumstances, ought to be received by the courts of this country as authorities to govern their decisions, or lights to guide the understanding of juries? Is it perfectly clear that decisions made in England, on the subject of treason, before the revolution of 1668, by which alone the balance of the English constitution was adjusted, and the English

liberties were fixt on a firm basis; decisions made
either during the furious civil wars, in which two
rival families contended for the crown; when in the
vicissitudes of war, death and confiscation in the
forms of law, continually walked in the train of the
victors, and actions were treasonable or praise-worthy,
according to the preponderance of the party by whose
adherents they were perpetrated; during the reigns of
three able and arbitrary monarchs, who succeeded this
dreadful conflict, and relaxed or invigorated the law
of treason, according to their anger, their policy or
their caprice; or during those terrible struggles between the principles of liberty, not yet well defined or
understood, on one hand, and arbitrary power, insinuating itself under the forms of the constitution, on
the other; struggles which presented at some times
the wildest anarchy, at others, the extremes of servile
submission, and after having brought one king to the
scaffold, ended in the expulsion of another from his
throne : Is it clear that decisions on the law of treason,
made in times like these, ought not only to be received as authorities in the courts of this country, but also
to have great influence on their decisions? Is it clear
that decisions made in England, as to what acts will
amount to levying war against the king, personally,
and not against his government, are applicable to the
constitution and laws of this country? Is it clear that
such English decisions on the subject of treason, as
are applicable to our constitution and laws, are to be
received in our courts, not merely as the opinions of
learned and able men, which may enlighten their
judgment, but as authorities which ought to govern
absolutely their decisions? Is all this so clear, that
a judge could not honestly and sincerely have thought
the contrary? That he could not have expressed an
opinion to the contrary, without corrupt or improper
motives? If it be not thus clear, then must it be admitted that this respondent, sincerely and honestly,
and in the best of his judgment, considered these de-

cisions as wholly inadmissible, or admissible only for the purposes and to the extent which he pointed out. And if he did so consider them, was it not his duty to prevent them from being read to the jury, except under those restrictions, and for those purposes? Would his duty permit him to sit silently, and see the jury imposed on and misled? To sit silently and hear a book read to them as containing the law, which he knew did not contain the law? Such silence would have rendered him a party to the deception, and would have justly subjected him to all the contumely, which a conscientious and courageous discharge of his duty, has so unmeritedly brought on his name.

With respect to the statutes of the United States, which he is charged with having prevented the prisoner's counsel from citing on the aforesaid trial, he denies that he prevented any act of Congress from being cited, either to the court or jury, on the said trial; or declared at any time, that he would not permit the prisoner's counsel to read to the jury, or to the court, any act of Congress whatever. Nor does he remember or believe, that he expressed on the said trial, any disapprobation of the conduct of the circuit court before whom the said case was first tried, in permitting the act of Congress relating to crimes less than treason, commonly called the *sedition act*, to be read to the jury. He admits indeed that he was then and still is of opinion, that the said act of Congress was wholly irrelevant to the issue, in the trial of John Fries, and therefore ought not to have been read to the jury, or regarded by them. This opinion may be erroneous, but he trusts that the following reasons on which it was founded, will be considered by this honorable court, as sufficiently strong to render it possible, and even probable, that such an opinion might be sincerely held and honestly expressed :...1st, That Congress did not intend by the sedition law, to define the crime of treason by " levying war." Treason and sedition are crimes very distinct in their nature, and subject to very different punishments; the former by death, and the latter by fine and imprisonment. 2dly, The sedition law makes a combination or conspiracy, with intent to impede the operation of any law of the United States, or the advising or attempting to procure any insurrection or riot, a high misdemeanor punishable by fine and imprisonment; but a combination or conspiracy with intent to prevent the execution of a law, or with intent to raise an insurrection for that purpose, or even with intent to commit treason, is not treason by "levying war" against the United States, unless it be followed by an attempt to carry such combination or conspiracy into effect, by actual force or violence. 3dly, The constitution of the United States is the fundamental and supreme law, and having defined the crime of treason, Congress could not give any legislative interpretation or exposition of that crime, or of the part of the constitution by which it is defined. 4thly, The judicial authority of the United States, is alone vested with power to expound their constitution and laws.

And this respondent further answering saith, that after the above mentioned proceedings had taken place in the said trial, it was postponed until the next day, Wednesday, April 23d, 1800; when at the meeting of the court, this respondent told both the above mentioned counsel for the prisoner, "that to prevent any misunderstanding of any thing that had passed the day before, he would inform them, that although the court retained the same opinion of the law, arising on the overt acts charged in the indictment against Fries, yet the counsel would be permitted to offer arguments to the court, for the purpose of shewing them that they were mistaken in the law; and that the court, if satisfied that they had erred in opinion, would correct it : and also that the counsel would be permitted to argue before the petit jury, that the court were mistaken in the law." And this respondent added, that the court had given no opinion as to the facts in the case, about which both the counsel had declared that there would be no controversy. After some observations by the said William Lewis and Alexander James Dallas, they both declared to the court, " that they did not any longer consider themselves as the counsel for John Fries the prisoner." This respondent then asked the said John Fries, whether he wished the court to appoint other counsel for his defence? He refused to have other counsel assigned; in which he acted, as this respondent believes and charges, by the advice of the said William Lewis and Alexander James Dallas: whereupon the court ordered the said trial to be had on the next day, Thursday, the 24th of April, 1800.

On that day the trial was proceeded in; and before the jurors were sworn, they were, by the direction of the court, severally asked on oath, whether they were in any way related to the prisoner, and whether they had ever formed or delivered any opinion as to his guilt or innocence, or that he ought to be punished? Three of them answering in the affirmative, were withdrawn from the pannel. The said John Fries was then informed by the court, that he had a right to challenge thirty-five of the jury, without shewing any cause of challenge against them, and as many more as he could shew cause of challenge against. He did accordingly challenge peremptorily thirty-four of the jury, and the trial proceeded. In the evening, the court adjourned till the next day, Friday, the 25th of April; when after the district attorney had stated the principal facts proved by the witnesses, and had applied the law to those facts, this respondent, with the concurrence of his colleague, the said Richard Peters, delivered to the jury the charge contained and expressed in exhibit marked No. 3, and herewith filed, which he prays may be taken as part of this his answer.

Immediately after the petit jury had delivered their verdict, this respondent informed the said Fries, from the bench, that if he, or any person for him, could shew any legal ground, or sufficient cause to arrest the judgment, ample time would be allowed him for that purpose. But no cause being shewn, sentence of death was passed on the said Fries, on Tuesday the 2d day of May, 1800, the last day of the term; and he was afterwards pardoned by John Adams, then President of the United States.

And this respondent further answering saith, that if the two instances of misconduct, first stated in support of the general charge, contained in the first article of impeachment, were true as alleged, yet the inference drawn from them, viz. " that the said Fries was thereby deprived of the benefit of counsel for his defence," is not true. He insists that the said Fries was deprived of the benefit of counsel, not by any misconduct of this respondent, but by the conduct and advice of the above mentioned William Lewis and Alexander James Dallas, who having been, with their own consent, assigned by the court as counsel for the prisoner, withdrew from his defence, and advised him to refuse other counsel when offered to him by the court, under pretence that the law had been prejudged, and their liberty of conducting the defence, according to their own judgment, improperly restricted by this respondent; but in reality because they knew the law and the facts to be against them, and the case to be desperate, and supposed that their withdrawing themselves under this pretence, might excite odium against the court; might give rise to an opinion that the prisoner had not been fairly tried; and in the event of a conviction, which from their knowledge of the law and the facts they knew to be almost certain, might aid the prisoner in an application to the President for a pardon. That such was the real motive of the said prisoner's counsel, for depriving their client of legal assistance on his trial, this respondent is fully persuaded, and expects to make appear, not only from the circumstances of the case, but from their own frequent and public declarations.

As little can this respondent be justly charged with having by any conduct of his, endeavored to " wrest from the jury their indisputable right to hear argument, and determine upon the question of law as well as the question of fact involved in the verdict which they were required to give." He denies, that he did at any time declare that the aforesaid counsel should not at any time address the jury, or did in any manner hinder them from addressing the jury on the law as well as on the facts arising in the case. It was expressly stated in the copy of his opinion delivered as above set forth to William Lewis, that the jury had a right to determine the law as well as the fact; and the said William Lewis and Alexander James Dallas were expressly informed, before they declared their resolution to abandon the defence, that they were at liberty to argue the law to the jury. This respondent believes that the said William Lewis did not read the opinion delivered to him as aforesaid, except a very small part at the beginning of it, and of course, acted upon it without knowing its contents : and that the said Alexander James Dallas read no part of the said opinion until about a year ago, when he saw a very imperfect copy, made in court by a certain W. S. Biddle.

And this respondent further answering, saith, that according to the constitution of the United States, *civil officers* thereof, and no other persons, are subject to impeachment; and they only for treason, bribery, corruption, or other high crime or misdemeanor, consisting in some act done or omitted, in violation of some law forbidding or commanding it; on conviction of which act, they *must* be removed from office ; and may, after conviction, be indicted and punished therefor, according to law. Hence it clearly results, that no civil officer of the United States can be impeached, except for some offence for which he may be indicted at law ; and that no evidence can be received on an impeachment, except such as on an indictment at law, for the same offence, would be admissible. That a judge cannot be indicted or punished according to law, for any act whatever, done by him in his judicial capacity, and in a matter of which he has jurisdiction, through error of judgment merely, without corrupt motives, however manifest his error may be, is a principle resting on the plainest maxims of reason and justice, supported by the highest legal authority, and sanctioned by the universal sense of mankind. He hath already endeavored to shew, and he hopes with success, that all the opinions delivered by him in the course of the trials now under consideration, were correct in themselves, and in the time and manner of expressing them; and that even admitting them to have been incorrect, there was such strong reason in their favor, as to remove from his conduct every suspicion of improper motives. If these opinions were incorrect, his mistake in adopting them, or in the time or manner of expressing them, cannot be imputed to him as an offence of any kind, much less as a high crime and misdemeanor, for which he ought to be removed from office; unless it can be shewn by clear and legal evidence, that he acted from corrupt motives. Should it be considered that some impropriety is attached to his conduct, in the time and mode of expressing any of these opinions; still he apprehends, that a very wide difference exists between such impropriety, the casual effect of human infirmity, and a high crime and misdemeanor for which he may be impeached, and must on conviction be removed from office.

Finally, this respondent, having thus laid before this honorable court a true state of his case, so far as respects the first article of impeachment, declares, upon the strictest review of his conduct during the whole trial of John Fries for treason, that he was not on that occasion unmindful of the solemn duties of his office as judge; that he faithfully and impartially, and according to the best of his ability and understanding, discharged those duties towards the said John

Fries; and that he did not in any manner, during the said trial, conduct himself arbitrarily, unjustly or oppressively, as he is accused by the honorable the House of Representatives.

And the said Samuel Chase, for plea to the said first article of impeachment, saith, that he is not guilty of any high crime or misdemeanor, as in and by the said first article is alleged; and this he prays may be enquired of by this honorable court, in such manner as law and justice shall seem to them to require.

The second article of impeachment charges, that this respondent, at the trial of James Thompson Callender for a libel, in May 1800, did, " with intent to oppress and procure the conviction of the said Callender, overrule the objection of John Basset, one of the jury, who wished to be excused from serving on the said trial, because he had made up his mind as to the publication from which the words, charged to be libellous in the indictment, were extracted."

In answer to this article, this respondent admits that he did, as one of the associate justices of the supreme court of the United States, hold the circuit court of the United States, for the district of Virginia, at Richmond, on Thursday the 22d day of May, in the year 1800, and from that day, till the 30th of the same month; when Cyrus Griffin, then district judge of the United States for the district of Virginia, took his seat in the said court; and that during the residue of that session of the said court, which continued till the day of June, in the same year, this respondent and the said Cyrus Griffin, held the said court together. But how far any of the other matters charged in this article, are founded in truth or law, will appear from the following statement; which he submits to this honorable court, by way of answer to this part of the accusation.

By an act of Congress passed on the 4th day of May, A. D. 1798, it is among other things enacted, " That if any person shall write, print, utter or publish, or shall knowingly and wittingly assist and aid in writing, printing, uttering or publishing, any false, scandalous, and malicious writing or writings against the President of the United States, with intent to defame or to bring him into contempt or disrepute, such person, being thereof convicted, shall be punished by fine, not exceeding two thousand dollars, and by imprisonment, not exceeding two years:" and " that if any person shall be prosecuted under this act, it shall be lawful for him to give in evidence in his defence, the truth of the matter contained in the publication charged as a libel; and the jury shall have a right to determine the law and the fact, under the direction of the court, as in other cases," as in and by the said act, commonly called the *sedition law*, to which this respondent begs leave to refer this honorable court, will more fully appear.

At the meeting of the last above mentioned circuit court, this respondent, as required by the duties of his office, delivered a charge to the grand jury ; in which, according to his constant practice, and to his duty as a judge, he gave in charge to them, several acts of Congress for the punishment of offences, and among them, the above mentioned act, called the sedition law; and directed the said jury to make particular enquiry, concerning any breaches of these statutes or any of them, within the district of Virginia. On the 24th day of May, 1800, the said jury found an indictment against one James Thompson Callender, for printing and publishing, against the form of the said act of Congress, a false, scandalous, and malicious libel, called " The Prospect before Us," against John Adams, then President of the United States, in his official character as President; as appears by an official copy of the said indictment, marked exhibit No. 4. which this respondent begs leave to make part of this his answer.

On Wednesday, the 28th day of the same month, May, 1800, Philip Norbonne Nicholas, esq. now attorney general of the state of Virginia, and George

Hay, esq. now district attorney of the United States, for the district of Virginia, appeared in the said circuit court as counsel for the said Callender; and on Tuesday the 3d of June following, his trial commenced, before this respondent, and the said Cyrus Griffin, who then sat as assistant judge. The petit jurors being called over, eight of them appeared, namely, Robert Gamble, Bernard Mackham, John Barrell, William Austin, William Richardson, Thomas Tinsley, Matthew Harvey and John Basset; who as they came to the book to be sworn, were severally asked on oath, by direction of the court, " whether they had ever formed and delivered any opinion respecting the subject matter then to be tried, or concerning the charges contained in the indictment?" They all answered in the negative, and were sworn in chief to try the issue. The counsel for the said Callender declaring, that it was unnecessary to put this question to the other four jurymen, William Mayo, James Hayes, Henry S. Shore and John Prior, they also were immediately sworn in chief. No challenge was made by the said Callender or his counsel, to any of these jurors; but the said counsel declared, that they would rely on the answer that should be given by the said jurors, to the question thus put by order of the court.

After the abovementioned John Basset, whom this respondent supposes and admits to be the person mentioned in the article of impeachment now under consideration, had thus answered in the negative to the question put to him by order of the court, as abovementioned, which this respondent states to be the legal and proper question, to be put to jurors on such occasions, he expressed to the court, his wish to be excused from serving on the said trial, because he had made up his mind, or had formed his opinion, " that the publication, called ' The Prospect before Us,' from which the words charged in the indictment as libellous were said to be extracted, but which he had never seen, was, according to the representation of it, which he had received, within the sedition law." But the court did not consider this declaration by the said John Basset, as a sufficient reason for withdrawing him from the jury, and accordingly directed him to be sworn in chief.

In this opinion and decision, as in all the others delivered during the trial in question, this respondent concurred with his colleague, the afore mentioned Cyrus Griffin, in whom none of these opinions have been considered as criminal. He contends that the opinion itself was legal and correct; and he denies that he concurred in it, under the influence of any "spirit of prosecution and injustice," or with any "intent to oppress and procure the conviction of the prisoner;" as is most untruly alleged by the second article of impeachment. His reasons were correct and legal. He will submit them with confidence to this honorable court; which, although it cannot condemn him for an incorrect opinion, proceeding from an honest error in judgment, and ought not to take on itself the power of enquiring into the correctness of his decisions, but merely that of examining the purity of his motives; will, nevertheless, weigh his reasons, for the purpose of judging how far they are of sufficient force, to justify a belief that they might have appeared satisfactory to him. If they might have so appeared, if the opinion which he founded on them be not so palpably and glaringly wrong, as to carry with it internal evidence of corrupt motives, he cannot in delivering it have committed an offence.

This honorable court need not be informed, that it is the duty of courts before which criminal trials take place, to prevent jurors from being excused for light and insufficient causes. If this rule were not observed, it would follow, that as serving on such trials as a juror, is apt to be a very disagreeable business, especially to those best qualified for it, there would be a great difficulty, and often an impossibility, in finding proper juries. The law has therefore established a fixed and general rule on this subject, calculated not to gratify the wishes or the unreasonable scruples of jurors, but to secure to the party accused, as far as in the imperfection of human nature it can be secured, a fair and impartial trial. The criterion established by this rule is, " that the juror stands indifferent between the government and the person accused, as to the matter *in issue*, on the indictment." This indifference is always, according to a well known maxim of law, to be presumed, unless the contrary appear; and the contrary may be alleged by way of excuse by the juror himself, or by the prisoner by way of challenge. Even if not alleged, it may be inquired into by the court of its own mere motion, or on the suggestion of the prisoner, and it may be established by the confession of the juror himself, on oath, or by other testimony.

But in order to shew that a juror does not " stand indifferent between the accuser and the accused, *as to the matter in issue*," it is not sufficient to prove that he has expressed a general opinion, " that such an offence as that charged by the indictment ought to be punished ;" or " that the party accused, if guilty of the offence charged against him, ought to be punished ;" or " that a book, for printing and publishing which the party is indicted, comes within the law on which the indictment is founded." All these are general expressions of opinion, as to the criminality of an act of which the party is accused, and of which he *may* be guilty ; not declarations of an opinion that he actually is guilty of the offence with which he stands charged. It is impossible for any man in society to avoid having, and extremely difficult for him to avoid expressing, an opinion, as to the criminality or innocence of those acts, which for the most part are the subjects of indictments for offences of a public nature ; such as treason, sedition, and libels against the government. Such acts always engage public attention, and become the subject of public conversation; and if to have formed or expressed an opinion, as to the general nature of those acts, were a sufficient ground of challenge to a juror, when alleged against him, or of excuse from serving when alleged by himself, it would be in the power of almost every offender, to prevent a jury from being impannelled to try him, and of almost every man, to exempt himself from the unpleasant task of serving on such juries. The magnitude and heinous nature of an offence, would give it a greater tendency to attract public attention, and to draw forth public expressions of indignation; and would thus increase its chance of impunity.

To the present case this reasoning applies with peculiar force. The " Prospect before Us," is a libel so profligate and atrocious, that it excited disgust and indignation in every breast not wholly depraved. Even those whose interest it was intended to promote, were, as this respondent has understood and believes, either so much ashamed of it, or so apprehensive of its effects, that great pains were taken by them to withdraw it from public and general circulation. Of such a publication, it must have been extremely difficult to find a man of sufficient character and information to serve on a jury, who had not formed an opinion, either from his own knowledge, or from report. The juror in the present case had expressed no opinion. He had formed no opinion, as to the facts. He had never seen the " Prospect before Us," and therefore could have formed no fixed or certain opinion about its nature or contents. They had been reported to him, and he had formed an opinion that if they were such as reported, the book was within the scope and operation of a law for the punishment of " false, scandalous and malicious libels, against the President in his official capacity, written or published with intent to defame him." And who is there, that having either seen the book or heard of it, had not necessarily formed the same opinion?

But this juror had formed no opinion about the guilt or innocence of the party accused ; which depended on four facts wholly distinct from the opinion which he had formed. First, whether the contents of the book were really such as had been represented to him? Secondly, whether they should, on the trial, be proved to be true? Thirdly, whether the party accused was really the author or publisher of this book? And fourthly, whether he wrote or published it "with intent to defame the President, or to bring him into contempt or disrepute, or to excite against him the hatred of the good people of the United States?" On all these questions, the mind of the juror was perfectly at large, notwithstanding the opinion which he had formed. He might, consistently with that opinion, determine them all in the negative; and it was on them that the issue between the United States and James Thompson Callender depended. Consequently, this juror, notwithstanding the opinion which he had thus formed, did stand indifferent as to the matter in issue, in the legal and proper sense, and in the only sense in which such indifference can ever exist ; and therefore his having formed that opinion, was not such an excuse as could have justified the court in discharging him from the jury.

That this juror did not himself consider this opinion as an opinion respecting the "matter in issue," appears clearly from this circumstance, that when called upon to answer on oath, "whether he had expressed any opinion as to the matter in issue?" he answered that he had not. Which clearly proves that he did not regard the circumstance of his having formed this opinion, as a legal excuse, which ought to exempt him of right from serving on the jury; but merely suggested it as a motive of delicacy, which induced him to wish to be excused. To such motives of delicacy, however commendable in the persons who feel them, it is impossible for courts of justice to yield, without putting it in the power of every man, under pretence of such scruples, to exempt himself from those duties which all the citizens are bound to perform. Courts of justice must regulate themselves by legal principles, which are fixed and universal; not by delicate scruples, which admit of endless variety, according to the varying opinions and feelings of men.

Such were the reasons of this respondent, and he presumes of his colleague the said Cyrus Griffin, for refusing to excuse the said John Basset, from serving on the jury above mentioned. These reasons, and the decision founded on them, he insists were legal and valid. But if the reasons should be considered as invalid, and the decision as erroneous, can they be considered as so clearly and flagrantly incorrect, as to justify a conclusion that they were adopted by this respondent, through improper motives? Are not these reasons sufficiently strong, or sufficiently plausible, to justify a candid and liberal mind in believing, that a judge might honestly have regarded them as solid? Has it not been conceded, by the omission to prosecute judge Griffin for this decision, that his error, if he committed one, was an honest error? Whence this distinction between this respondent and his colleague? And why is that opinion imputed to one as a crime, which in the other is considered as innocent?

And the said Samuel Chase, for plea to the said second article of impeachment, saith, that he is not guilty of any high crime or misdemeanor, as in and by the said second article is alleged against him ; and this he prays may be enquired of by this honorable court, in such manner as law and justice shall seem to them to require.

The third article of impeachment alleges that this respondent " with intent to oppress and procure the conviction of the prisoner, did not permit the evidence of John Taylor, a material witness in behalf of the said Callender, to be given in, on pretence that the said witness could not prove the truth of the whole of one of the charges, contained in the indictment, although the said charge embraced more than one fact."

In answer to this charge, this respondent begs leave to submit the following facts and observations.

The indictment against James Thompson Callender, which has been already mentioned, and of which a copy is exhibited with this answer, consisted of two distinct and separate counts, each of which contained twenty distinct and independent charges, or sets of words. Each of those sets of words was charged as a libel against John Adams, as President of the United States, and the twelfth charge embraced the following words, " He (meaning President Adams) was a professed aristocrat; he proved faithful and serviceable to the British interest." The defence set up was confined to this charge, and was rested upon the truth of the words. To the other nineteen charges, no defence of any kind was attempted or spoken of, except such as might arise from the supposed unconstitutionality of the sedition law; which, if solid, applied to the twelfth charge, as well as to the other nineteen. It was to prove the truth of these words, that John Taylor, the person mentioned in the article of impeachment now under consideration, was offered as a witness. It can hardly be necessary to remind this honorable court, that when an indictment for a libel contains several distinct charges, founded on distinct sets of words, the party accused, who in such cases is called the " traverser," must be convicted, unless he makes a sufficient defence against every charge. His innocence on one, does not prove him innocent on the others. If the sedition law should be considered as unconstitutional, the whole indictment, including this twelfth charge, must fall to the ground, whether the words in question were proved to be true or not. If the law should be considered as constitutional, then the traverser, whether the words in the twelfth charge were proved to be true or not, must be convicted on the other nineteen charges, against which no defence was offered. This conviction on nineteen charges, would put the traverser as completely in the power of the court, by which the amount of the fine and the term of the imprisonment were to be fixed, as a conviction upon all the twenty charges. The imprisonment could not exceed two years, nor the fine be more than two thousand dollars. If then this respondent were desirous of procuring the conviction of the traverser, he was sure of his object, without rejecting the testimony of John Taylor. If his temper towards the traverser were so vindictive, as to make him feel anxious to obtain an opportunity and excuse for inflicting on him the whole extent of punishment permitted by the law, still a conviction on nineteen charges afforded this opportunity and excuse, as fully as a conviction on twenty charges. One slander more or less, in such a publication as the " Prospect before Us," could surely be of no moment. To attain this object, therefore, it was not necessary to reject the testimony of John Taylor.

That the court did not feel this vindictive spirit, is clearly evinced by the moderation of the punishment, which actually was inflicted on the traverser, after he was convicted of the whole twenty charges. Instead of two thousand dollars, he was fined only two hundred, and was sentenced to only nine months imprisonment, instead of two years. And this respondent avers, that he never felt or expressed a wish to go further; but that in this decision, as well as in every other given in the course of the trial, he fully and freely concurred with his colleague, judge Griffin.

As a further proof that his rejection of this testimony did not proceed from any improper motive, but from
a conviction in his mind that it was legally inadmissible, and that it was, therefore, his duty to reject it, he
begs leave to state, that he interfered, in order to prevail on the district attorney to withdraw his objection
to those questions, and consent to their being put;
which that officer refused to do, on the ground "that
he did not feel himself at liberty to consent to such a
departure from legal principles."

Hence appears the utter futility of a charge, which
attributes to this respondent a purpose as absurd as it
was wicked; and without the slightest proof, im-
putes to the worst motives in him the same action,
which in his colleague is considered as free from
blame. But this respondent will not content himself
with shewing, that his conduct in concurring with
his colleague in the rejection of John Taylor's testimony, could not have proceeded from the motives
ascribed to him; but he will show that this rejection,
if not strictly legal and proper, as he believes and insists that it is, rests on legal reasons of sufficient force
to satisfy every mind, that a judge might have sincerely considered it as correct.

The words stated as the ground of the twelfth charge
above mentioned, are stated in the indictment as one
entire and indivisible paragraph, constituting one entire offence. This respondent considered them at the
trial, and still considers them, as constituting one
entire charge, and one entire offence; and that they
must be taken together in order to explain and support each other. It is clear that no words are indictable as libellous, except such as expressly, or by
plain implication, charge the person against whom
they are published, with some offence either legal or
moral. To be an " aristocrat," is not in itself an
offence, either legal or moral, even if it were a charge
susceptible of proof; neither was it an offence either

legal or moral, for Mr. Adams to be " faithful and serviceable to the British interest," unless he thereby betrayed or endangered the interests of his own country ; which does not necessarily follow, and is not directly alleged in the publication. These two phrases, therefore, taken separately, charge Mr. Adams with no offence of any kind; and, consequently, could not be indictable as libellous : but taken together, they convey the implication that Mr. Adams, being an " aristocrat," that is, an enemy to the republican government of his own country, had subserved the British interest, against the interest of his own country ; which would, in his situation, have been an offence both moral and legal; to charge him with it was, therefore, libellous.

Admitting, therefore, these two phrases to constitute one distinct charge, and one entire offence, this respondent considers and states it to be law, that no justification which went to part only of the offence, could be received. The plea of justification must always answer the whole charge, or it is bad on the demurrer; for this plain reason, that the object of the plea is to shew the party's innocence ; and he cannot be innocent, if the accusation against him be supported in part. Where the matter of defence may be given in evidence, without being formally pleaded, the same rules prevail. The defence must be of the same nature, and equally complete, in one case as in the other. The only difference is in the manner of bringing it forward. Evidence, therefore, which goes only to justify the charge in part, cannot be received. It is not indeed necessary, that the whole of this evidence should be given by one witness. The justification may consist of several facts, some of which may be proved by one person, and some by another. But proof, in such cases, must be offered as to the whole, or it cannot be received.

In the case under consideration, no proof was offered as to the whole matter contained in the twelfth article. No witness except the above mentioned John Taylor, was produced or mentioned. When a witness is offered to a court and jury, it is the right and duty of the court, to require a statement of the matters intended to be proved by him. This is the invariable practice of all our courts, and was done most properly by this respondent and his colleague, on the occasion in question. From the statement given by the traverser's counsel, of what they expected to prove by the said witness, it appeared that his testimony could have no possible application to any part of the indictment, except the twelfth charge above mentioned, and but a very weak and imperfect application even to that part. The court, therefore, as it was their right and duty, requested that the questions intended to be put to the witness, should be reduced to writing, and submitted to their inspection; so as to enable them to judge more accurately, how far those questions were proper and admissible. This being done, the questions were of the following tenor and effect:

1st. " Did you ever hear Mr. Adams express any sentiments favorable to monarchy, or ' aristocracy,' and what were they?"

2d. " Did you ever hear Mr. Adams, while Vice President, express his disapprobation of the funding system?"

3d. " Do you know whether Mr. Adams did not, in the year 1794, vote against the sequestration of British debts, and also against the bill for suspending intercourse with Great Britain?"

The second question, it is manifest, had nothing to do with the twelfth charge; for Mr. Adams's approbation or disapprobation of the funding system, could not have the most remote tendency to prove that he was an aristocrat, or had proved faithful and serviceable to the British interest. In that part of the publication which furnishes the matter of the thirteenth charge in the indictment, it is indeed stated, that Mr. Adams, "when but in a secondary station, censured the funding system," but these words are in themselves wholly immaterial; and no attempt was made, nor any evidence offered or spoken of, to prove the truth of the other matter contained in the thirteenth charge. It was from their connection with that other matter, that these words could alone derive any importance; and consequently their truth or falsehood was altogether immaterial, while that other matter remained unproved. This question, therefore, which went solely to those immaterial words, was clearly inadmissible. The third question was, in reality, as far as the second from any connection with the matter in issue, although its irrelevancy is not quite so apparent. Mr. Adams's having voted against the two measures alluded to in that question, if he did in fact vote against them, could by no means prove that he was " faithful and serviceable to the British interest," in any sense, much less with those improper and criminal views, with which the publication in question certainly meant to charge him. He might, in the honest and prudent performance of his duty towards his government and his country, incidentally promote the interests of another country; but it was by no means competent for a jury to infer from thence, that he was " faithful" to that other country, or, in other words, that he held the interests of that other country chiefly in view, and was actuated in giving his vote by a desire to promote them, independently of, or without regard to, the interests of his own country. Such an inference could not be made from the fact, admitting it to be true. The fact, if true, was *no* evidence to support such an inference, therefore the fact was immaterial; and as it is the province and duty of the court, in such circumstances, to decide on the materiality of facts offered in evidence, it follows clearly, that it was the right and duty of the court, in this instance, to reject the third question; an affirmative answer to which could have proved nothing in support of the defence.

The first question, therefore, and the only remaining one proposed to be put to this witness, stood alone; and an affirmative answer to it, if it could have proved any thing, could have proved only a part of the charge; namely, that Mr. Adams was an aristocrat. But evidence to prove a part only of an entire and indivisible charge, was inadmissible for the reasons stated above.

If, on the other hand, the phrases in question, "that Mr. Adams was an aristocrat," that "he had proved faithful and serviceable to the British interest," were distinct and divisible, and constituted two distinct charges, which may perhaps be the proper way of considering them, still the above mentioned questions were improper and inadmissible, in that point of view. The first charge in that case is, that Mr. Adams "was an aristocrat." To be an aristocrat, even if any precise and definite meaning could be affixed to the term, is not an offence either legal or moral; consequently, to charge a man with being an aristocrat is not a libel; and such a charge in an indictment for a libel, is wholly immaterial. Nothing is more clear, than that immaterial matters in legal proceedings ought not to be proved, and need not be disproved. In the next place, the term "aristocrat" is one of those vague indefinite terms, which admit not of precise meaning, and are not susceptible of proof. What one person might consider as aristocracy, another would consider as republicanism, and a third as democracy. If indictments could be supported on such grounds, the guilt or innocence of the party accused, must be measured not by any fixed or known rule, but by the opinions which the jurors appointed to try him might happen to entertain, concerning the nature of aristocracy, democracy or republicanism. And, lastly, the question itself was as vague, and as void of precise meaning, as the charge of which it was intended to furnish the proof. The witness was called upon to declare "whether he had heard Mr. Adams express any and what opinions favorable to aristocracy or monarchy?" How was it to be determined, whether an opinion was favorable to aristocracy or monarchy? One man would think it favorable and another not so, according to the opinions which they might respectively entertain, on political subjects. The first question, therefore, was inconclusive, immaterial and inadmissible.

The second, as has already been remarked, was wholly and manifestly foreign from the matter in issue. Mr. Adams's dislike of the funding system, if he did in fact dislike it, had nothing to do with his aristocracy or his faithfulness to the British interest. There is no pretence for saying, that such a question ought to have been admitted.

As to the third, " whether Mr. Adams had not voted against the sequestration of British property, and the suspension of commercial intercourse with Great Britain," it has already been shewn to be altogether improper; on the ground that such votes, if given by Mr. Adams, were no evidence whatever of his having been " faithful and serviceable to the British interest." If he had been so, provided it were, in his opinion, at the same time useful to the interests of his own country, which it well might be, and the contrary of which is not alleged by this part of the publication, taken separately, it was no offence of any kind; and to charge him with it was not a libel. The charge was, therefore, immaterial and futile, and no evidence for or against it could properly be received. And, finally, if the charge had been material, and the giving of these votes had been legal evidence to prove it, that fact was on record in the journals of the Senate, and might have been proved by that record, or an official copy of it. As this evidence was the highest of which the case admitted, no inferior evidence of it, such as oral proof is well known to be, could be admitted.

For these reasons this respondent did concur with his colleague, the said Cyrus Griffin, in rejecting the three above mentioned questions; but not any other testimony that the said John Taylor might have been able to give. In this he insists that he acted legally and properly, according to the best of his ability. If he erred, it is impossible, for the reasons stated by him in the beginning of his answer to this article, to suppose that he erred wilfully : since he could have had no possible motive for a piece of misconduct so shameful, and at the same time so well calculated to give offence. In a point so liable to misapprehension and misrepresentation, and so likely to be used as a means of exciting public odium against him, it is far more probable, that had he been capable of bending his opinion of the law to other motives, he would have admitted illegal testimony; which, taken in its utmost effect, could have had no tendency to thwart those plans of vengeance against the traverser, under the influence of which he is supposed to have acted.

If his error was an honest one, which as his colleague also fell into it, might in charity be supposed; and, as there is not a shadow of evidence to the contrary, must in law be presumed; he cannot, for committing it, be convicted of any offence, much less a high crime and misdemeanor, for which he must, on conviction, be deprived of his office.

And for plea to the said third article of impeachment, the said Samuel Chase, saith, that he is not guilty of any high crime or misdemeanor, as in and by the said third article is alleged against him: and this he prays may be enquired of by this honorable court, in such manner as law and justice shall seem to them to require.

The fourth article of impeachment alleges, that during the whole course of the trial of James Thompson Callender, above mentioned, the conduct of this respondent was marked by " manifest injustice, partiality, and intemperance;" and five particular instances of the " injustice, partiality, and intemperance," are adduced.

The first consists, " in compelling the prisoner's counsel to reduce to writing and submit to the inspection of the court, for their admission or rejection, all questions which the said counsel meant to propound to the above mentioned John Taylor, the witness."

This respondent, in answer to this part of the article now under consideration, admits that the court, consisting of himself and the above mentioned Cyrus Griffin, did require the counsel for the traverser, on the trial of James Thompson Callender, above mentioned, to reduce to writing the questions which they intended to put to the said witness. But he denies that it is more his act than the act of his colleague, who fully concurred in this measure. The measure, as he apprehends and insists, was strictly legal and proper ; his reasons for adopting it, and he presumes those of his colleague, he will submit to this honorable court, in order to shew that if he, in common with his colleague, committed an error, it was an error into which the best and wisest men might have honestly fallen.

It will not be denied, and cannot be doubted, that according to our laws, evidence, whether oral or written, may be rejected and prevented from going before the jury, on various grounds.—1st, For incompetency : where the source from which the evidence is attempted to be drawn, is an improper source : as if a witness were to be called who was infamous, or interested in the event of the suit; or a paper should be offered in evidence, which was not between the same parties, or was not executed in the forms pre-

scribed by law. 2d, For irrelevancy : when the evidence offered is not such, as in law will warrant the
jury to infer the fact intended to be proved ; or where
that fact, if proved, is immaterial to the issue. For
these reasons, and perhaps for others which might be
specified, evidence may properly be rejected, in trials before our courts.

As little can it be doubted, that according to our
laws, the court and not the jury is the proper tribunal for deciding all questions relative to the admissibility of evidence. The effect of the evidence when received, is to be judged of by the jury; but whether it
ought to be received, must be determined by the
court. This arises from the very constitution of the
trial by jury ; one fundamental principle of which is,
that the jury must decide the case, not according to
vague notions, secret impressions or general belief,
but according to legal and proper evidence delivered
in court. So strictly is this rule observed, that if one
juror have any knowledge of the matter in dispute, it
may influence his own judgment, but not that of his
fellow jurors, unless he state it to them on oath, in
open court ; and nothing is more common than for
our courts, after all the evidence which the party can
produce has been offered and received, to tell the jury
that there is no evidence to support the claim, or the
defence ; or when proof is offered of a certain fact, to
determine that such fact is not proper to be given in
evidence.

Hence it results, and is every day's practice, that
when a witness is produced, or a writing is offered
in evidence, the opposite party having a right to object to the evidence if he should think it improper,
requires to be informed what the witness is to prove,
or to see the writing, before the first is examined, or
the second is read to the jury. The court has the
same right, resulting necessarily from its power to decide all questions relative to the admissibility of evi-

dence. This right our courts are in the constant habit of exercising ; not only when objections are made by the parties, but when there being no objection, the court itself has reason to suspect that the testimony is improper. In most cases, but not in all, consent by the opposite party removes all objections to the admissibility of evidence, and courts sometimes infer consent from silence; but as it is their duty to take care, that no improper or illegal evidence goes to the jury, unless the objection to it be removed by consent of parties ; it is consequently their duty, in all cases where they see reason to suspect that the evidence offered is improper, to ascertain whether consent has been given, or whether the seeming acquiescence of the opposite party has proceeded from inattention. This is more particularly their duty in *criminal* cases, where they are bound to be counsel for the government, as well as for the party accused.

It being thus the right and duty of a court before which a trial takes place, to inform itself of the nature of the evidence offered, so as to be able to judge whether such evidence be proper, it results necessarily that they have a right to require, that any question intended to be put to a witness, should be reduced to writing, for that is the form in which their deliberation upon it may be most perfect, and their judgment will be most likely to be correct. In the case now under consideration, the court did exercise this right.— When the testimony of John Taylor was offered, the court enquired of the traverser's counsel, what that witness was to prove. The statement of his testimony given in answer, induced the court to suspect that it was irrelevant and inadmissible. They therefore, that they might have an opportunity for more careful and accurate consideration, called upon the counsel to state in writing, the questions intended to be put to the witness.

This is the act done by the court, but concurred in by the respondent, which has been selected and adduced as one of the proofs and instances of " manifest injustice, partiality, and intemperance" on his part. He owes an apology to this honorable court, for having occupied so much of its time with the refutation of a charge which has no claim to serious consideration, except what it derives from the respect due to the honorable body by which it was made, and the high character of the court where it is preferred.

The next circumstance stated by the article now under consideration, as an instance and proof of " manifest injustice, partiality, and intemperance" in this respondent, is his refusal to postpone the trial of the said James Thompson Callender, " although an affidavit was regularly filed, stating the absence of material witnesses on behalf of the accused, and although it was manifest that with the utmost diligence, the attendance of such witnesses could not have been procured at that term."

This respondent, in answer to this part of the charge, admits, that in the above mentioned trial, the traverser's counsel did move the court, while this respondent sat in it alone, for a continuance of the case until the next term; not merely a postponement of the trial, as the expressions used in this part of the article would seem to import; and did file as the ground work of their motion, an affidavit of the traverser, a true and official copy of which, marked exhibit No. 5, this respondent herewith exhibits, and begs leave to make part of this answer ; but he denies that any sufficient ground for a continuance until the next term, was disclosed by this affidavit ; as he trusts will clearly appear from the following facts and observations.

The trial of an indictment at the term when it is found by the grand jury, is a matter of course, which the prosecutor can claim as a right, unless legal cause can be shewn for a continuance. The prosecutor may consent to a continuance, but if he withholds his consent, the court cannot grant a continuance without legal cause. Of the sufficiency and legality of this cause, as of every other question of law, the court must judge ; but it must decide on this as on every other point, according to the fixed and known rules of law.

One of the legal grounds, and the principal one on which such a continuance may be granted, is the absence of competent and *material* witnesses, whom the party cannot produce at the present term, but has a *reasonable ground* for expecting to be able to produce at the next term. Analagous to this, is the inability to procure at the present term, legal and *material* written testimony, which the party has a *reasonable expectation* of being able to procure at the next term.

These rules are as reasonable and just in themselves, as they are essential to the due administration of justice, to the punishment of offences on the one hand, and to the protection of innocence on the other. If the continuance of a cause, on the application of the party accused, were a matter of right, it is manifest that no indictment would be brought to trial until after a delay of many months. If, on the other hand, the granting of a continuance depended not on fixed rules, but on the arbitrary will of the court, it would follow that weakness or partiality might induce a court, on some occasions, to extend a very improper indulgence to the party accused ; while on others, passion or prejudice might deprive him of the necessary means of making his defence. Hence the necessity of fixed rules, which the judges are bound to expound and apply, under the solemn sanction of their oath of office.

The true and only reason for granting a continuance, is that the party accused may have the best opportunity that the laws can afford to him, of making his defence. But incompetent or immaterial witnesses, could not be examined if they were present; and consequently, their absence can deprive the party of no opportunity which the laws afford to him, of making his defence. Hence the rule, that the witnesses must be competent and material.

Public justice will not permit the trial of offenders to be delayed, on light or unfounded pretences. To wait for testimony which the party really wished for, but did not expect to be able to produce within some definite period, would certainly be a very light pretence; and to make him the judge, how far there was reasonable expectation of obtaining the testimony within the proper time, would put it in his power to delay the trial, on the most unfounded pretences. Hence the rule, that there must be reasonable ground of expectation, in the judgment of the court, that the testimony may be obtained within the proper time.

It is therefore a settled and most necessary rule, that every application for a continuance, on the ground of obtaining testimony, must be supported by an affidavit, disclosing sufficient matter to satisfy the court, that the testimony wanted " is competent and material," and that there is " reasonable expectation of procuring it within the time prescribed." From a comparison of the affidavit in question with the indictment, it will soon appear how far the traverser in this case, brought himself within this rule.

The absent witnesses, mentioned in the affidavit, are William Gardner, of Portsmouth, in New-Hampshire; Tench Coxe, of Philadelphia, in Pennsylvania; Judge Bee, of some place in South-Carolina; Timothy Pickering, lately of Philadelphia, in Pennsylvania, but of what place at that time, the deponent did not know; William B. Giles, of Amelia county, in the state of Virginia; Stephens Thompson Mason, whose place of residence is not mentioned in the affidavit, but was known to be in Loudon county, in the state of Virginia; and General Blackburn, of Bath county, in the said state. The affidavit also states, that the traverser wished to procure, as material to his defence, authentic copies of certain answers made by the President of the United States, Mr. Adams, to addresses from various persons; and also, a book entitled " an Essay on Canon and Feudal Law," or entitled in words *to that purport*, which was ascribed to the President, and which the traverser believed to have been written by him; and also, evidence to prove that the President was in fact the author of that book.

It is not stated, that the traverser had any reasonable ground to expect, or did expect, to procure this book or evidence, or these authentic copies, or the attendance of any one of these witnesses, at the *next* term. Nor does he attempt to shew in what manner the book, or the copies of answers to addresses, were material, so as to enable the court to form a judgment on that point. Here then, the affidavit was clearly defective. His believing the book and copies to be material, was of no weight, unless he shewed to the court, sufficient grounds for entertaining the same opinion. Moreover he does not state, where he supposes that this book, and those authentic copies, may be found: so as to enable the court to judge, how far a reasonable expectation of obtaining them might be entertained. On the ground of this book and these copies, therefore, there was no pretence for a continuance. As to the witnesses, it is manifest, that, from their very distant and dispersed situation, there existed no ground of reasonable expectation, that their attendance could be procured at the *next* term, or at any subsequent time. Indeed, the idea of postponing the trial of an indictment, till witnesses could be convened at Richmond, from South Carolina, New-Hampshire, and the western extremities of Virginia, is too chimerical to be seriously entertained. Accordingly, the traverser, though in his affidavit he stated them to be material, and declared that he could not procure their attendance at that term, could not venture to declare on oath, that he expected to procure it at the next, or at any other time; much less that he had any reasonable ground for such expectation. On this ground, therefore, the affidavit was clearly insufficient; and it was consequently the duty of the court to reject such application.

But the testimony of these witnesses, as stated in the affidavit, was wholly immaterial; and therefore, their absence was no ground for a continuance, had there been reasonable ground for expecting their attendance at the next term.

William Gardner and Tench Coxe, were to prove, that Mr. Adams had turned them out of office, for their political opinions or conduct. This applied to that part of the publication, which constituted the matter of the third charge in the indictment, in these words, " the same system of persecution extended all over the continent. Every person holding an office, must either quit it, or think and vote exactly with Mr. Adams."—Judge Bee was to prove, that Mr. Adams had advised and requested him by letter, in the year 1799, to deliver Thomas Nash, otherwise called Jonathan Robins, to the British consul, in Charleston. This might have had some application to the matter of the seventh charge; which alleged that " the hands of Mr. Adams, were reeking with the blood of the poor, friendless, Connecticut sailor." Timothy Pickering was to prove, that Mr. Adams, while President, and while Congress was in session, was many weeks in possession of important dispatches, from the American minister in France, without communicating them to Congress. This testimony was utterly immaterial; because, admitting the fact to be so, Mr. Adams was not bound, in any respect, to communicate those dispatches to Congress, unless in his discretion, he should think it necessary ; and also, because the fact, if true, had no relation to any part of the indictment. There are, indeed, three charges, on which it might at first sight seem to have some slight bearing. These are the eighth, the words furnishing the matter of which are, " every feature in the administration of Mr. Adams, forms a distinct and additional evidence, that he was determined at all events, to embroil this country with France;" the fourteenth, the words stated in which, allege, that " by sending these ambassadors to Paris. Mr. Adams and his British faction, designed to do nothing but mischief," and the eighteenth, the matter of which states, " that in the midst of such a scene of profligacy and usury, the President persisted as long as he durst, in making his utmost efforts, for provoking a French war." To no other charge in the indictment, had the evidence of Timothy Pickering, as stated in the affidavit, the remotest affinity. And surely it will not be pretended by any man, who shall compare this evidence, with the three charges above mentioned, that the fact intended to be proved by it, furnished any evidence proper to go to a jury, in support of either of those charges, that " every feature of his administration, formed a distinct and additional evidence, of a determination at all events, to embroil this country with France," that " in sending ambassadors to Paris, he intended nothing but mischief." that " in the midst of a scene of profligacy and usury, he persisted, as long as he durst, in making his utmost efforts for provoking a French war," are charges, which surely cannot be supported or justified, by the circumstance of his ' keeping in his possession, for several weeks, while Congress was in session, dispatches from the American minister in France, without communicating them to Congress,' which he was not bound to do, and which it was his duty not to do, if he supposed that the communication, at an earlier period, would be injurious to the public interest. The testimony of William B. Giles and Stephens Thompson Mason, was to prove, that Mr. Adams had uttered in their hearing, certain sentiments, favorable to aristocratic or monarchical principles of government.

This had no application except to a part of the twelfth charge; which has been already shewn to be wholly immaterial if taken separately, and wholly incapable of a separate justification, if considered as part of an entire charge. And, lastly, it was to be proved by general Blackburn, that in his answer to an address, Mr. Adams avowed, " that there was a party in Virginia, which deserved to be humbled into dust and ashes, before the indignant frowns of their injured, insulted, and offended country." There were but two charges in the indictment to which this fact, if true, had the most distant resemblance.— These are the fifteenth and sixteenth, the words forming the matter of which, call Mr. Adams, " an hoary-headed libeller of the governor of Virginia, who with all the fury, but without the propriety or sublimity of Homer's Achilles, bawled out, to arms, then, to arms!" and " who floating on the bladder of popularity, threatened to make Richmond the centre point of a bonfire." It would be an abuse of the patience of this honorable court, to occupy any part of it's time in proving, that the fact intended to be proved by general Blackburn, could not in the slightest degree support or justify such charges as these. This is the account given of the testimony of the absent witnesses, by the affidavit filed as the ground of the motion for a continuance. From a comparison of it with the indictment, it will appear, that out of twenty charges in the indictment, there were but eight, to which any part of the testimony of these witnesses had the most distant allusion ; and that of those eight charges there are five, which the testimony, having some allusions to them, could not in the slightest degree support. Twelve charges, therefore, remained without even an attempt to justify them ; and seventeen were wholly destitute of any legal or sufficient justification. On these seventeen charges, therefore, the traverser must have been convicted ; even if the remaining three had been completely justified by the testimony of the absent witnesses. The conviction on these seventeen charges, or even on one of them, would have put it into the power of the court to fine and imprison the traverser, to the whole extent allowed by the law. If the truth of these three charges, admitting it to be established, could have any effect in mitigating the punishment, which depended on the court and not on the jury, the court in passing sentence might make, and in this case, actually did make, the fullest abatement on that account that the testimony if adduced would warrant.

This testimony, therefore, was in every view immaterial; and had it been material, there existed no ground of reasonable expectation, that it could be obtained at the next term, or any future term. For these reasons, and not from those criminal motives, which without the least shadow of proof are ascribed to him, this respondent did over-rule and reject the motion for a continuance till the next term: as it was his duty to do, since he had no discretion in the case, but was bound by the rules of law.

But in order to afford every accommodation to the traverser and his counsel, which it was in his power to give, this respondent did offer to postpone the trial for a month or more, in order to afford them full time for preparation, and for procuring such testimony as was within their reach. This indulgence they thought proper to refuse.

On Monday, the second, and Tuesday, the third day of June, 1800, when judge Griffin had taken his seat in court, and was on the bench, the counsel for the traverser, renewed their motion for a continuance, founded on the same affidavit; and after a full hearing and consideration of the argument, the court, judge Griffin concurring, overruled the motion, and ordered the trial to proceed.

If this decision be correct, as he believes and insists that it is, no offence could be committed by him in making or concurring in it. It was a proper and legal performance of his duty as a judge. If it be erroneous, still the error, if an honest one, cannot be an offence, much less a high crime and misdemeanor; and as in his colleague it has been considered as an honest error, he confidently trusts it will be considered so in him also.

To the third charge adduced in support of the article now under consideration, the charge of using "unusual, rude, and contemptuous expressions, towards the prisoner's counsel," and of "falsely insinuating, that they wished to excite the public fears and indignation, and to produce that insubordination to law, to which the conduct of this respondent did manifestly tend," he cannot answer otherwise than by a general denial. A charge so vague, admits not of precise or particular refutation. He denies that there was any thing unusual or intentionally rude or contemptuous in his conduct or his expressions towards the prisoner's counsel; that he made any false insinuation whatever against them, or that his own conduct tended in any manner to produce insubordination to law. On the contrary, it was his wish and intention, to treat the counsel with the respect due to their situation and functions, and with the decorum due to his own character. He thought it his duty to restrain such of their attempts as he considered improper, and to overrule motions made by them, which he considered as unfounded in law; but this it was his wish to accomplish in the manner least likely to offend, from which every consideration concurred in dissuading him. He did indeed think at that time, and still remains under the impression, that the conduct of the traverser's counsel, whether from intention or not he will not undertake to say, was disrespectful, irritating, and highly incorrect. That conduct which he viewed in this light, might have produced some irritation in a temper naturally quick and warm, and that this irritation might, notwithstanding his endeavors to suppress it, have appeared in his manner and in his expressions, he thinks not improbable; for he has had occasions of feeling and lamenting the want of sufficient caution and self-command, in things of this nature. But he confidently affirms, that his conduct in this particular was free from intentional impropriety; and this respondent denies, that any part of his conduct was such as ought to have induced the traverser's counsel to " abandon the cause of their client," nor does he believe that any such cause did induce them to take that step. On the contrary, he believes that it was taken by them under the influence of passion or for some motive into which this respondent forbears at this time to enquire. And this respondent admits, that the said traverser was convicted and condemned to fine and imprisonment, but not by reason of the abandonment of his defence by his counsel; but because the charges against him were clearly proved, and no defence was made or attempted against far the greater number of them.

The fourth charge in support of this article, attributes to this respondent, " repeated and vexatious interruptions of the said counsel, which at length induced them to abandon the cause of their client, who was therefore convicted, and condemned to fine and imprisonment." To this charge also, it is impossible to give any other answer but a general denial. He avers that he never interrupted the traverser's counsel vexatiously, or except when he considered it his duty to do so. It cannot be denied that courts have power to interrupt counsel, when in their opinion the correctness of proceeding requires it. In this, as in every thing else, they may err. They may sometimes act under the influence of momentary passion or irritation, to which they in common with other men, are liable. But unless their conduct in such cases, though improper or ill-judged, be clearly shewn to proceed, not from human infirmity, but from improper motives, it cannot be imputed to them as an offence, much less as a crime or misdemeanor.

Lastly, this respondent is charged under this article, with an " indecent solicitude, manifested by him, for the conviction of the accused, unbecoming even a public prosecutor, but highly disgraceful to the character of a judge, as it was subversive of justice." This is another charge of which it is impossible to give a precise refutation, and to a general denial of which, this respondent must therefore confine himself. He denies that he felt any solicitude whatever for the conviction of the traverser ; other than the general wish natural to every friend of truth, decorum, and virtue, that persons guilty of such offences, as that of which the traverser stood indicted, should be brought to punishment, for the sake of example. He has no hesitation to acknowledge, that his indignation was strongly excited, by the atrocious and profligate libel which the traverser was charged with having written and published. This indignation, he believes, was felt by every virtuous and honorable man in the community, of every party, who had read the book in question, or become acquainted with its contents. How properly it was felt, will appear from the book itself, which this respondent has ready to produce to this honorable court ; from the parts of it incorporated into the indictment now under consideration; and from some further extracts contained in the paper marked exhibit No. 6.

which this respondent prays leave to make part of this his answer. He admits, and it can never be to him a subject of self-reproach or a cause of regret, that he partook largely in this general indignation, but he denies that it in any manner influenced his conduct towards the traverser, which was regulated by a conscientious regard to his duty and the laws. He moreover contends, that a solicitude to procure the conviction of the traverser, however unbecoming his character as a judge, would not have been an offence, had he felt it; unless it had given rise to some misconduct on his part. Intentions and feelings, unless accompanied by actions, do not constitute crimes in this country; where the guilt or innocence of men is not judged of by their wishes and solicitudes, but by their conduct and its motives. And this respondent thinks it his duty, on this occasion, to enter his solemn protest against the introduction in this country, of those arbitrary principles, at once the offspring and the instruments of despotism, which would make " high crimes and misdemeanors" to consist in " rude and contemptuous expressions," in " vexatious interruptions of counsel," and in the manifestation of " indecent solicitude" for the conviction of a most notorious offender. Such conduct is no doubt, improper and unbecoming in any person, and much more so in a judge: but it is too vague, too uncertain, and too susceptible of forced interpretations, according to the impulse of passion or the views of policy, to be admitted into the class of punishable offences, under a system of law whose certainty and precision in the definition of crimes, is its greatest glory, and the greatest privilege of those who live under its sway.

In concluding his defence against those charges contained in the fourth article of impeachment, he declares, that his whole conduct in that trial, was regulated by a strict regard to the principles of law, and by an honest desire to do justice between the United

States and the party accused. He felt a sincere wish, on the one hand, that the traverser might establish his innocence, by those fair and sufficient means which the law allows; and a determination, on the other, that he should not, by subterfuges and frivolous pretences, sport with the justice of the country, and evade that punishment of which, if guilty, he was so proper an object. These intentions he is confident, were legal and laudable; and if, in any part of his conduct, he swerved from this line, it was an error of his judgment and not of his heart.

And the said respondent for plea to the said fourth article of impeachment, saith, that he is not guilty of any high crime and misdemeanor, as in and by the said fourth article is alleged against him, and this he prays, may be enquired of by this honorable court, in such manner as law and justice shall seem to require.

The fifth article of impeachment charges this respondent, with having awarded " a capias against the body of the said James Thompson Callender, indicted for an offence *not capital*, whereupon the said Callender was arrested and committed to *close* custody, contrary to law in that case made and provided."

This charge is rested, 1st, on the act of Congress of September 24th, 1789, entitled "an act to establish the judicial courts of the United States," by which it is enacted "that for any crime or offence against the United States, the offender may be arrested, imprisoned, or bailed, agreeably to the usual mode of process, in the state where such offender may be found." And 2dly, on a law of the state of Virginia, which is said to provide "that upon *presentment* by any grand jury, of an offence *not capital*, the court shall order the clerk to issue a *summons* against the person or persons so offending, to appear and answer such presentment at the *next* court." It is contended, in support of this charge, that the act of Congress above mentioned, made the state law the rule of proceeding, and that the state law was violated by issuing a capias against Callender, instead of a summons. The first observation to be made on this part of the case is, that the date of the law of Virginia is not mentioned in the article. A very material omission! For it cannot be contended, that by the act of Congress in question, which was passed for establishing the laws of the United States, and regulating their proceedings; it was intended to render those proceedings dependent on all *future* acts of the state legislatures. The intention certainly was, to adopt, to a certain limited extent, the regulations existing in the states at the time of passing the act. Consequently, a law of Virginia, passed after this act, can have no operation on the proceedings under it. But by referring to the law of Virginia in question, it will be found to bear date on November 13th, 1792, more than three years after this act of Congress, by which it is said to have been adopted. But the omission of the date of this law of Virginia, is not the most material oversight which has been made in citing it. Its title is " An act directing the method of proceeding against free persons, charged with certain crimes," &c. and it enacts, section 28th, " That upon presentment made by the grand jury, of an offence not capital, the court shall order the clerk to issue a summons, or *other proper process*, against the person or persons so presented, to appear and answer at the next court." It will be observed that these words, " or other proper process," which leave it perfectly in the discretion of the court what process shall issue, provided it be such as is proper for bringing the offender to answer to the presentment, are omitted in this article of impeachment.

From these words it is perfectly manifest, that the law of Virginia, admitting it to apply, did not order a summons to be issued, but left it perfectly in the discretion of the court to issue a summons, or such other process as they should judge proper. It is therefore, a sufficient answer to this article to say, that this respondent considered a capias as the proper process, and therefore ordered it to issue; which he admits that he did, immediately after the presentment was found against the said Callender, by the grand jury.

This he is informed, and expects to prove, has been the construction of this law by the courts of Virginia, and their general practice. Indeed it would be most strange, if any other construction or practice had been adopted. There are many offences not capital, which are of a very dangerous tendency, and on which very severe punishment is inflicted by the laws of Virginia; and to enact by law that in all such cases, however notorious or profligate the offenders might be, the courts should be obliged, after a presentment by a grand jury, to proceed against them by summons; would be to enact, that as soon as their guilt was rendered extremely probable, by the presentment of a grand jury, they should receive regular notice, to escape from punishment by flight or concealment.

It will also appear, as this respondent believes, by a reference to the laws and practice of Virginia, into which he has made all the enquiries which circumstances and the shortness of time allowed him for preparing his answer, would permit, that all the cases in which a summons is considered as the only proper process, are cases of petty offences, which on the presentment of a grand jury, are to be tried by the court in a summary way, without the intervention of a petit jury.—Therefore, these provisions had no application to the case of Callender, which could be no otherwise proceeded on than by indictment, and trial on the indictment by a petit jury.

It must be recollected that the act of Congress of September 24th, 1789, enacts, section 14, " that the courts of the United States, shall have power to issue writs of scire facias, habeas corpus, *and all other writs* not specially provided for by statute, which may be necessary for the exercise of their respective jurisdictions, and agreeable to the principles and usages of laws." Consequently, the circuit court, where the proceedings in question took place, had power to issue a capias against the traverser, on the presentment, unless the state law above mentioned governed the case, and contained something to restrain the issuing of that writ in such a case. This respondent contends, for the reasons above stated, that this state law neither applied to the case, nor contained any thing to prevent the issuing of a capias, if it had applied.

Thus it appears that this respondent, in ordering a capias to issue against Callender, decided correctly, as it certainly was his intention to do. But he claims no other merit than that of upright intention in this decision: for when he made the decision, he was utterly ignorant that such a law existed in Virginia; and declares that he never heard of it, till this article was reported by a committee of the House of Representatives, during the present session of Congress. This law was not mentioned on the trial either by the counsel or the traverser or by judge Griffin, who certainly had much better opportunities of knowing it than this respondent, and who, no doubt, would have cited it had they known it and considered it as applicable to the case. This respondent well knows that in a criminal view, ignorance of the law excuses no man in offending against it; but this maxim applies not to the decision of a judge; in whom ignorance of the law in general would certainly be a disqualification for this office, though not a crime; but ignorance of a particular act of assembly, of a state where he was an utter stranger, must be considered as a very pardonable error; especially as the counsel for the prisoner to whose case that law is supposed to have applied, forebore or omitted to cite it; and as a judge of the state, always resident in it, and long conversant with its local laws, either forgot this law, or considered it as inapplicable.

Such is the answer, which this respondent makes to the fifth article of impeachment. If he erred in this case, it was through ignorance of the law, and surely, ignorance under such circumstances, cannot be a crime, much less a high crime and misdemeanor, for which he ought to be removed from his office. If a judge were impeachable for acting against law from ignorance only, it would follow, that he would be punished in the same manner for deciding against law wilfully, and for deciding against it through mistake. In other words, there would be no distinction between ignorance and design, between error and corruption.

And the said respondent, for plea to the said fifth article of impeachment, saith, that he is not guilty of any high crime and misdemeanor, as in and by the said fifth article is alleged against him; and this he prays, may be enquired of, by this honorable court, in such manner, as law and justice shall seem to them to require.

The sixth article of impeachment alleges, that this respondent, " with intent to oppress and procure the conviction of the said James Thompson Callender, did, at the court aforesaid, rule and adjudge the said Callender to trial, during the term at which he, the said Callender was presented and indicted, contrary to the law in that case made and provided."

This charge also, is founded, 1st, on the act of Congress of Sept. 24th, 1789, abovementioned, which enacts, section 34, " that the laws of the several states, except where the constitution, treaties, or statutes of the United States shall otherwise provide, shall be regarded as the rules of decision, in trials at *common law*, in the courts of the United States, in cases where they apply," and 2ndly, on a law of the state of Virginia, which is supposed to provide, " that in cases not capital, the offender shall not be held to answer any presentment of a grand jury, until the court next preceding that, during which such presentment shall have been made." This law, it is contended, is made the rule of decision by the abovementioned act of Congress, and was violated by the refusal to continue the case of Callender till the next term.

In answer to this charge this respondent declares, that he was at the time of making the abovementioned decision, wholly ignorant of any such law of Virginia as that in question, that no such law was adduced or mentioned by the counsel of Callender, in support of their motion for a continuance; neither when they first made it, before this respondent sitting alone; nor when they renewed it, after judge Griffin had taken his seat in court: that no such law was mentioned by judge Griffin; who concurred in overruling the motion for a continuance and ordering on the trial; which he could not have done had he known that such a law existed, or considered it as applicable to the case; and that this respondent never heard of any such law, until the articles of impeachment now under consideration were reported, in the course of the present session of Congress, by a committee of the House of Representatives.

A judge is certainly bound to use all proper and reasonable means of obtaining a knowledge of the laws which he is appointed to administer; but after the use of such means, to overlook, misunderstand, or remain ignorant of some particular law, is at all times a very pardonable error. It is much more so in the case of a judge of the supreme court of the United States, holding a circuit court in a particular state, with which he is a stranger, and with the local laws of which he can have enjoyed but very imperfect opportunities of becoming acquainted. It was foreseen by Congress, in establishing the circuit courts of the United States, that difficulties and inconveniences must frequently arise from this source, and to obviate such difficulties it was provided, that the district judge of each state, who having been a resident of the state and a practitioner in its courts, had all the necessary means of becoming acquainted with its local laws, should form a part of the circuit court in his own state. The judge of the supreme court is expected, with reason, to be well versed in the general laws; but the local laws of the state form the peculiar province of the district judge, who may be justly considered as particularly responsible for their due observance. If in the case in question, this respondent overlooked or misconstrued any local law of the state of Virginia, which ought to have governed the case, it was equally overlooked and misunderstood, not only by the prisoner's counsel who made the motion, and whose peculiar duty it was to know the law and bring it into the view of the court, but also by the district judge, who had the best opportunities of knowing and understanding it, and in whom, nevertheless, this oversight or mistake is considered as a venal error, while in this respondent it is made the ground of a criminal charge.

This respondent further states, that after the most diligent and the most extensive enquiry which the time allowed for preparing this answer would permit, he can find no law of Virginia which expressly enacts, that " in cases not capital, the offender shall not be held to answer any presentment of a grand jury, until the court next succeeding that during which such presentment shall have been made." This principle he supposes to be an inference drawn by the authors of the articles of impeachment, from the law of Virginia mentioned in the answer to the preceding article, the law of November 15th, 1792, which provides

" that upon presentment made by the grand jury of an offence not capital, the court shall order the clerk to issue a summons, or other proper process, against the person or persons so presented, to appear and answer such presentment at the NEXT court." This law he conceives does not warrant the inference so drawn from it, because it speaks of *presentments* and not of *indictments*, which are very different things; and is, as he is informed, confined by practice and construction in the state of Virginia, to cases of small offences, which are to be tried by the court itself upon the presentment, without an indictment or the itervention of a petit jury. But for cases, like that of Callender, where an indictment must follow the presentment, this law made no provision. Further, the state laws are directed by the above mentioned act of Congress, to be the rule of decision in the courts of the United States, only " in cases where they apply." Whether they apply or not to a particular case, is a question of law, to be decided by the court where such case is pending, and an error in making the decision is not a crime, nor even an offence, unless it can be shewn to have proceeded from improper motives. This respondent is of opinion, that the law in question did not apply to the case of Callender, for the reasons stated above; and therefore that it would have been his duty to disregard it, even had it been made known to him by the counsel for the traverser.

And in the last place he contends, that the law of Virginia in question, is not adopted by the above mentioned act of Congress as the rule of decision, in such cases as that now under consideration. That act does indeed provide, " that the laws of the several states, except where the constitution, treaties or statutes of the United States shall otherwise provide, shall be regarded as rules of decision in trials at *common law*, in the courts of the United States, in cases where they apply." But this provision, in his opinion, can relate only to rights acquired under the state laws, which come into question *on* the trial; and not to forms of process or modes of proceeding, anterior or preparatory to the trial. Nor can it, as this respondent apprehends, have any application to indictments for offences against the statutes of the United States, which cannot with any propriety be called " trials at common law." It relates merely, in his opinion, to civil rights acquired under the state laws ; which by virtue of this provision are, when they come in question in the courts of the United States, to be governed by the laws under which they accrued.

If in these opinions this respondent be incorrect, it is an honest error : and he contends that neither such an error in the construction of a law, nor his ignorance of a local state law which he had no opportunity of knowing, and of which the counsel for the party whose case it is supposed to have affected were equally ignorant, can be considered as an offence liable to impeachment, or to any sort of punishment or blame.

And for plea to the said sixth article of impeachment, the said Samuel Chase saith, that he is not guilty of any high crime or misdemeanor as in and by the said article is alleged against him; and this he prays may be enquired of by this honorable court, in such manner as law and justice shall seem to them to require.

The seventh article of impeachment relates to some conduct of this respondent in his judicial capacity, at a circuit court of the United States held at New-Castle, in the state of Delaware, in June 1800. The statement of this conduct made in the article is altogether erroneous ; but if it were true, this respondent denies, that it contains any matter for which he is liable to impeachment. It alleges that " disregarding the duties of his office, he did descend from the dignity of a judge, and stoop to the level of an informer." This high offence consisted, according to the article, 1st, " in refusing to discharge the grand jury although intreated by several of the said jury to do so." 2dly, in " observing to the said grand jury, after the said grand jury had regularly declared through their foreman, that they had found no bills of indictment, and had no presentments to make, that he the said Samuel Chase, understood ' that a highly seditious temper had manifested itself in the state of Delaware, among a certain class of people, particularly in New-Castle county, and more especially in the town of Wilmington, where lived a most seditious printer, unrestrained by any principle of virtue, and regardless of social order, that the name of this printer was —————.' 3dly, " in then checking himself as if sensible of the indecorum which he was committing." 4thly, in adding " that it might be assuming too much, to mention the name of this person; but it becomes your duty, gentlemen, to enquire diligently into this matter," or words to that effect. And 5thly, in authoritatively enjoining on the district attorney of the United States, with intention to procure the prosecution of the printer in question, the necessity of procuring a file of the papers to which he alluded, and by a strict examination of them to find some passage, which might furnish the ground work of a prosecution against the printer."

These charges amount in substance to this; that the respondent refused to discharge a grand jury on their request, which is every day's practice, and which he was bound to do, if he believed that the due administration of justice required their longer attendance; that he directed the attention of the grand jury to an offence against a statute of the United States, which he had been informed was committed in the district; and that he desired the district attorney to aid the grand jury, in their enquiries concerning the existence and nature of this offence. By these three acts, each of which it was his duty to perform, he is

alleged " to have degraded his high judicial functions, and tended to impair the public confidence in,
and respect for, the tribunals of justice, so essential to
the general welfare."

That this honorable court may be able to form correctly its judgment, concerning the transaction mentioned in this article, this respondent submits the following statement of it, which he avers to be true, and
expects to prove.

On the 27th day of June, 1800, this respondent,
as one of the associate justices of the supreme court
of the United States, presided in the circuit court of
the United States, then held at Newcastle, in and for
the district of Delaware, and was assisted by Gunning Bedford, esq. then district judge of the United
States, for that district. At the opening of the court
on that day, this respondent according to his duty
and his uniform practice, delivered a charge to the
grand jury, in which he gave in charge to them several statutes of the United States, and among others,
an act of Congress, passed July 14th, 1798, entitled
" An act in addition to the act for the punishment of
certain crimes against the United States," and commonly called the " sedition law." He directed them
to enquire concerning any breaches of those statutes,
and especially of that commonly called the sedition
law, within the district of Delaware.

On the same day, before the usual hour of adjournment, the grand jury came into court, and informed
the court that they had found no indictment or presentment, and had no business before them, for which
reason they wished to be discharged. This respondent replied, that it was earlier than the usual hour of
discharging a grand jury; and that business might
occur during the sitting of the court. He also asked
them if they had no information of publications within the district, that came under the sedition law, and
added, that he had been informed, that there was a

paper called the "Mirror," published at Wilmington, which contained libellous charges against the government and President of the United States : that he had not seen that paper, but it was their duty to enquire into the subject; and if they had not turned their attention to it, the attorney for the district would be pleased to examine a file of that paper, and if he found any thing that came within the sedition law, would lay it before them."—This is the substance of what the respondent said to the grand jury on that occasion, and he believes nearly his words; on the morning of the *next day*, they came into court and declared that they had no presentments or indictments to make, on which they were immediately discharged. The whole time therefore, for which they were detained, was twenty four hours, far less than is generally required of grand juries.

In these proceedings, this respondent acted according to his sense of what the duties of his office required. It certainly was his duty to give in charge to the grand jury, all such statutes of the United States as provided for the punishment of offences, and among others, that called the sedition act; into all offences against which act, while it continued in force, the grand jury were bound by their oaths to enquire. In giving it in charge, together with the other acts of Congress for the punishment of offences, he followed moreover the example of the other judges of the supreme court, in holding their respective circuit courts. He also contends, and did then believe, that it was his duty, when informed of an offence, which the grand jury had overlooked, to direct their attention towards it, and to request for them, and even to require if necessary, the aid of the district attorney in making their enquiries. In thus discharging what he conceives to be his duty, even if he committed an error in so considering it, he denies that he committed or could commit any offence whatever.

With respect to the remarks which he is charged by this article with having made to the grand jury, relative to " a highly seditious temper, which he had understood to have manifested itself in the state of Delaware, among a certain class of people, particularly in Newcastle county, and more especially in the town of Wilmington," and relative to " a most seditious printer, residing in Wilmington, unrestrained by any principle of virtue, and regardless of social order;" this respondent does not recollect or believe, that he made any such observations. But if he did make them, it could not be improper in him to tell the jury that he had received such information, if in fact he had received it; which was probably the case, though he cannot recollect it with certainty at this distance of time. That this information, if he did receive it, was correct, so far as it regarded the printer in question, will fully appear from a file of the paper called the " Mirror of the Times," &c. published at Wilmington, Delaware, from February 5th, to March 19th, 1800, inclusive, which he has lately obtained, and is ready to produce to this honorable court when necessary, and some extracts from which are contained in the exhibits severally marked No. 7, which he prays leave to make part of this his answer.

And for plea to the said seventh article of impeachment, the said Samuel Chase saith, that he is not guilty of any high crime or misdemeanor, as in and by the said seventh article is alleged against him, and this he prays may be enquired of by this honorable court, in such manner as law and justice shall seem to them to require.

The eighth article of impeachment charges, that this respondent, " disregarding the duties and dignity of his official character did, at a circuit court for the district of Maryland, held at Baltimore, in the month of May, 1803, pervert his official right and duty to address the grand jury then and there assembled, on the matters coming within the province of the said jury, for the purpose of delivering to the said grand jury an intemperate and inflammatory political harangue, with intent to excite the fears and resentment of the said grand jury, and of the good people of Maryland, against their state government and constitution," and also that this respondent, " under pretence of exercising his judicial right to address the grand jury as aforesaid, did endeavor to excite the odium of the said grand jury, and of the good people of Maryland, against the government of the United States, by delivering opinions which were, at that time and as delivered by him, highly indecent, extra judicial, and tending to prostitute the high judicial character with which he was invested, to the low purpose of an electioneering partizan."

In answer to this charge this respondent admits, that he did, as one of the associate justices of the supreme court of the United States, preside in a circuit court held at Baltimore in and for the district of Maryland, in May 1803, and did then deliver a charge to the grand jury, and express in the conclusion of it some opinions as to certain public measures, both of the government of Maryland and of that of the United States. But he denies that in thus acting, he disregarded the duties and dignity of his judicial character, perverted his official right and duty to address the grand jury, or had any intention to excite the fears or resentment of any person whatever, against the government and constitution of the United States or of Maryland. He denies that the sentiments which he thus expressed, were " intemperate and inflammatory," either in themselves or in the manner of delivering; that he did endeavor to excite the odium of any person whatever against the government of the United States, or did deliver any opinions which were in any respect indecent, or which had any tendency to prostitute his judicial character, to any low or improper purpose. He denies that he did any thing that was unusual, improper or unbecoming in a judge, or expressed any opinions, but such as a friend to his country, and a firm supporter of the governments both of the state of Maryland and of the United States, might entertain. For the truth of what he here says, he appeals confidently to the charge itself; which was read from a written paper now in his possession ready to be produced. A true copy of all such parts of this paper as relate to the subject matter of this article of impeachment, is contained in the exhibit marked No. 8, which he prays leave to make part of this his answer. That part of it which relates to the article now under consideration is in these words; " You know, gentlemen, that our state and national institutions were framed to secure to every member of the society *equal* liberty and *equal* rights ; but the late alteration of the federal judiciary, by the abolition of the office of the sixteen circuit judges, and the *recent* change in our state constitution by the establishing *universal* suffrage, *and* the further alteration that is contemplated in our state judiciary, (if adopted) will in my judgment take way *all security for property and personal liberty*. The independence of the national judiciary is already shaken to its foundation ; and the virtue of the people alone can restore it. The independence of the judges of this state will be entirely destroyed, if the bill for the abolishing the two supreme courts, should be ratified by the next general assembly. The change of the state constitution by allowing universal suffrage, will in my opinion certainly and rapidly destroy all protection to property, and all security to personal liberty ; and our republican constitution will sink into a *mobocracy*, the worst of all possible governments.

" I can only lament that the *main pillar* of our state constitution has been thrown down, by the establishment of *universal suffrage*. By this shock *alone*, the whole building totters to its base, and will crumble into ruins before *many* years elapse, unless it be *restored* to its original state. If the independency of your state judges, which your bill of rights wisely declares ' to be essential to the impartial administration of justice, and the great security to the rights and liberties of the people,' shall be taken away, by the ratification of the bill passed for that purpose, it will precipitate the destruction of your whole state constitution, and there will be nothing left in it, worthy the care or support of freemen.''

Admitting these opinions to have been incorrect and unfounded, this respondent denies that there was any law which forbid him to express them, in a charge to a grand jury; and he contends that there can be no offence, without the breach of some law. The very essence of despotism consists, in punishing acts which, at the time when they were done, were forbidden by no law. Admitting the expression of political opinions by a judge, in his charge to a jury, to be improper and dangerous; there are many improper and very dangerous acts, which not being forbidden by law cannot be punished. Hence the necessity of new penal laws; which are from time to time enacted for the prevention of acts not before forbidden, but found by experience to be of dangerous tendency. It has been the practice in this country, ever since the beginning of the revolution, which separated us from Great Britain, for the judges to express from the bench, by way of charge to the grand jury, and to enforce to the utmost of their ability, such political opinions as they thought correct and useful. There have been instances in which the legislative bodies of this country, have recommended this practice to the judges; and it was adopted by the judges of the supreme court of the United States, as soon as the present judicial system was established. If the legislature of the United States considered this practice as mischievous, dangerous, or liable to abuse, they might have forbidden it by law; to the penalties of which, such judges as might afterwards transgress it, would be justly subjected. By not forbidding it, the legislature has given to it an implied sanction; and for that legislature to punish it now by way of impeachment, would be to convert into a crime, by an ex post facto proceeding, an act which when it was done and at all times before, they had themselves virtually declared to be innocent. Such conduct would be utterly subversive of the fundamental principles on which free government rests; and would form a precedent for the most sanguinary and arbitrary persecutions, under the forms of law.

Nor can the incorrectness of the political opinions thus expressed, have any influence in deciding on the guilt or innocence of a judge's conduct in expressing them. For if he should be considered as guilty or innocent, according to the supposed correctness or incorrectness of the opinion, thus expressed by him, it would follow, that error in political opinion however honestly entertained, might be a crime; and that a party in power might, under this pretext, destroy any judge, who might happen in a charge to a grand jury, to say something capable of being construed by them, into a political opinion adverse to their own system.

There might be some pretence for saying, that for a judge to utter seditious sentiments, with intent to excite sedition, would be an impeachable offence: although such a doctrine would be liable to the most dangerous abuses; and is hostile to the fundamental principles of our constitution, and to the best established maxims of our criminal jurisprudence. But admitting this doctrine to be correct, it cannot be denied that the seditious intention must be proved clearly, either by the most necessary implication from the words themselves, or by some overt acts of a seditious nature connected with them. In the present case no

such acts are alleged, but the proof of a seditious intent must rest on the words themselves. By this rule
this respondent is willing to be judged. Let the opinions which he delivered be examined; and if the
members of this honorable court can lay their hands
on their hearts, in the presence of God, and say, that
these opinions are not only erroneous but seditious
also, and carry with them internal evidence of an intention in this respondent to excite sedition, either
against the state or general government, he is content
to be found guilty.

In making this examination, let it be borne in
mind, that to oppose a depending measure, by endeavoring to convince the public that it is improper,
and ought not to be adopted ; or to promote the repeal
of a law already past, by endeavoring to convince the
public, that it ought to be repealed, and that such men
ought to be elected to the legislature as will repeal it;
to attempt in fine, the correction of public measures,
by arguments tending to shew their improper nature,
or destructive tendency ; never has been or can be
considered as sedition, in any country, where the principles of law and liberty are respected ; but is the proper and usual exercise of that right of opinion and
speech, which constitutes the distinguishing feature
of free government. The abuse of this privilege, by
writing and publishing as facts, malicious falsehoods,
with intent to defame, is punishable as libellous, in
the courts having jurisdiction of such offences ; where
the truth or falsehood of the facts alleged, and the malice or correctness of the intention, form the criterion
of guilt and innocence. But the character of libellous,
much less of seditious, has never been applied to the
expression of opinions concerning the tendency of
public measures, or to arguments urged for the purpose of opposing them, or of effecting their repeal.
To apply the doctrine of sedition or of libels to such
cases, would instantly destroy all liberty of speech,

subvert the main pillars of free government, and convert the tribunals of justice into engines of party vengeance. To condemn a public measure, therefore, as pernicious in its tendency; to use arguments for proving it to be so; and to endeavor by these means to prevent its adoption, if still depending, or to procure its repeal in a regular and constitutional way, if it be already adopted; can never be considered as se·dition, or in any way illegal.

The first opinion expressed to the grand jury on the occasion in question, by this respondent, was, that " the late alteration of the federal judiciary, by the abolition of the office of the sixteen circuit judges; and the recent change in our state constitution, by establishing universal suffrage; and the further alter·ation that was then contemplated in our state judicia·ry, if adopted;" would, in the judgment of this re·spondent, " take away all security for property and personal liberty." That is, " these three measures, if the last of them, which is still depending, should be adopted, will, in my opinion, form a system whose pernicious tendency must be, to take away the secu·rity for our property and our personal liberty," which we have hitherto derived from the salutary restrictions laid by the authors of our constitution on the right of suffrage, and from the present constitution of our courts of justice." What is this but an argument to persuade the people of Maryland to reject the altera·tions in their state judiciary which were then pro·posed; which this respondent as a citizen of that state had a right to oppose; and the adoption of which depended on a legislature then to be chosen? If this be sedition, then will it be impossible to express an opi·nion opposite to the views of the ruling party of the moment, or to oppose any of their measures by argu·ment, without becoming subject to such punishment as they may think proper to inflict.

The next opinion is, that " the independence of the national judiciary was already shaken to its foundation, and that the virtue of the people alone could restore it." In other words, " The act of Congress for repealing the late circuit court law, and vacating thereby the offices of the judges, has shaken to its foundation the independence of the national judiciary, and nothing but a change in the representation of Congress, which the return of the people to correct sentiments alone can effect, will be sufficient to produce a repeal of this act, and thereby restore to its former vigor, the part of the federal constitution, which has been thus impaired."

This is the obvious meaning of the expression; and it amounts to nothing more than an argument in favor of that change, which this respondent then thought and still thinks to be very desirable; an argument, the force of which as a patriot he might feel, and which as a free man he had a right to advance.

The next opinion is, that " the independence of the judges of the state of Maryland, would be entirely destroyed if the bill for abolishing the two supreme courts should be ratified by the next general assembly." This opinion, however incorrect it may be, seems to have been adopted by the people of Maryland, to whom this argument against the bill in question was addressed : for at the next session of the legislature this bill, which went to change entirely the constitutional tenure of judicial office in the state, and to render the subsistence of the judges dependent on the legislature, and their continuance in office on the executive, was abandoned by common consent.

All the other opinions expressed by this respondent, as above mentioned, bear the same character with those already considered. They are arguments addressed to the people of Maryland, for the purpose of dissuading them from the adoption of a measure then depending; and of inducing them, if possible, to restore to its original state, that part of their constitution relating to the right of suffrage, by a repeal of the law, which had been made for its alteration.

Such were the objects of this respondent in delivering those opinions, and he contends that they were fair, proper, and legal objects, and that he had a right to pursue them in this way: a right sanctioned by the universal practice of this country, and by the acquiescence of its various legislative authorities. Such, he contends, is the true and obvious meaning of the opinions which he delivered, and which he believes to be correct. It is not now necessary to enquire into their correctness; but, if incorrect, he denies that they contain any thing seditious, or any evidence of those improper intentions which are imputed to him by this article of impeachment. He denies that in delivering them to the grand jury, he committed any offence, infringed any law, or did any thing unusual, or heretofore considered in this country as improper or unbecoming in a judge. If this article of impeachment can be sustained on these grounds, the liberty of speech on national concerns, and the tenure of the judicial office under the government of the United States, must hereafter depend on the arbitrary will of the House of Representatives and the Senate, to be declared on impeachment, after the acts are done, which it may at any time be thought necessary to treat as high crimes and misdemeanors.

And the said Samuel Chase, for plea to the said eighth article of impeachment, saith, that he is not guilty of any high crime and misdemeanor, as in and by the said eighth article is alleged against him, and this he prays may be inquired of by this honorable court, in such manner as law and justice shall seem to them to require.

This respondent has now laid before this honorable court, as well as the time allowed him would permit, all the circumstances of his case, with an humble trust in Providence, and a consciousness that he has discharged all his *official* duties with justice and impartiality, to the best of his knowledge and abilities; and, that intentionally he hath committed no crime or misdemeanor, or any violation of the constitution or laws of his country. Confiding in the impartiality, independence and integrity of his judges, and that they will patiently hear, and conscientiously determine this case, without being influenced by the spirit of party, by popular prejudice, or political motives, he cheerfully submits himself to their decision.

If it shall appear to this honorable court, from the evidence produced, that he hath acted in his *judicial* character with wilful injustice or partiality, he doth not wish any favor; but expects that the whole extent of the punishment permitted in the constitution will be inflicted upon him.

If any part of his official conduct shall appear to this honorable court, *stricti juris*, to have been *illegal*, or to have proceeded from *ignorance* or *error* in judgment; or if any part of his conduct shall appear, although not illegal, to have been irregular or improper, but not to have flown from a depravity of heart, or any unworthy motive, he feels confident that this court will make allowance for the imperfections and frailties incidental to man.

He is satisfied, that every member of this tribunal will observe the principles of humanity and justice, and will presume him innocent, until his guilt shall be established by legal and credible witnesses, and will be governed in his decision, by the moral and christian rule of rendering that justice to this respondent, which he would wish to receive.

This respondent now stands not merely before an earthly tribunal, but also before that awful Being whose presence fills all space, and whose all-seeing eye more especially surveys the temples of justice and religion. In a little time, his accusers, his judges, and himself, must appear at the bar of Omnipotence, where the secrets of all hearts shall be disclosed, and every human being shall answer for his deeds done in the body, and shall be compelled to give evidence against himself, in the presence of an assembled universe. To his Omniscient Judge, at that awful hour, he now appeals for the rectitude and purity of his conduct, as to all the matters of which he is this day accused.

He hath now only to adjure each member of this honorable court, by the living GOD, and in his holy name, to render impartial justice to him, according to the constitution and laws of the United States. He makes this solemn demand of each member, by all his hopes of happiness in the world to come, which he will have voluntarily renounced by the oath he has taken; if he shall wilfully do this respondent injustice, or disregard the constitution or laws of the United States, which he has solemnly sworn to make the rule and standard of his judgment and decision.

Mr. *Randolph*, on behalf of the Managers, requested time to consult the House of Representatives, and likewise to be furnished with a copy of the answer of judge Chase, for the purpose of making a replication to it.

The *President* said the Senate would take the request into consideration, and make known to the House of Representatives such order as should be taken thereon.

Whereupon the Senate, at the suggestion of the President, retired to their legislative apartment.

On *Wednesday*, the 6th instant, the House of Representatives received a copy of the foregoing answer, which was referred to the Managers. On the same day Mr. Randolph reported a replication to the answer, which was immediately taken into consideration. Several motions were made, and rejected, after a short debate, to soften the style; when the replication, as reported, was adopted, Yeas 77, Nays 34. Whereupon, it was resolved that the Managers be instructed to proceed to maintain the said replication at the bar of the Senate, at such time as shall be appointed by the Senate.

THURSDAY, *February* 7, 1805.

The court was opened about 2 o'clock.

Present, the Managers—and Mr. Hopkinson, of counsel for Mr. Chase.

Mr. *Randolph,* on behalf of the Managers, read the replication of the House of Representatives, to the answer of Samuel Chase, as follows:

Replication by the House of Representatives of the United States, to the answer of Samuel Chase, one of the associate justices of the supreme court of the United States, to the articles of impeachment exhibited against him by the said House of Representatives.

The House of Representatives of the United States have considered the answer of Samuel Chase, one of the associate justices of the supreme court of the United States, to the articles of impeachment against him, by them exhibited, in the name of themselves and of all the people of the United States, and observe,

That the said Samuel Chase hath endeavored to cover the high crimes and misdemeanors laid to his charge, by evasive insinuations and misrepresentation of facts; that the said answer does give a gloss and coloring utterly false and untrue, to the various criminal matters contained in the said articles; that the said Samuel Chase did, in fact, commit the numerous acts of oppression, persecution, and injustice, of which he stands accused; and the House of Representatives, in full confidence of the truth and justice of their accusation, and of the necessity of bringing the said Samuel Chase to a speedy and exemplary punishment, and not doubting that the Senate will use all becoming diligence to do justice to the proceedings of the House of Representatives, and to vindicate the honor of the nation, do aver their charge against the said Samuel Chase to be true, and that the said Samuel Chase is guilty in such manner as he stands impeached: and that the House of Representatives will be ready to prove their charges against him, at such convenient time and place as shall be appointed for that purpose.

Signed by order, and in behalf of the said House.

NATH. MACON, *Speaker.*

Attest,

JOHN BECKLEY, *Clerk.*

Mr. *Hopkinson* requested a copy of the replication, which, the President replied, would be furnished by the secretary.

Mr. *Breckenridge* moved a resolution to the following effect:

That the secretary be directed to inform the House of Representatives, that the Senate will to-morrow, at 12 o'clock, proceed with the trial of Samuel Chase; which was agreed to without a dissenting voice....34 members voting for it.

Whereupon, the Senate withdrew to their legislative apartment.

FRIDAY, *February* 8, 1805.

The court opened precisely at 12 o'clock.

Present, the Managers, and House of Representatives, in committee of the whole :—and,

Mr. Chase, attended by his counsel, Messrs. Martin, Harper, Hopkinson, and Key.

The cryer having, agreeably to a prescribed form, notified all those concerned to come forward and make good the charges exhibited against Samuel Chase,

Mr. *Randolph*, the leading Manager, requested that the witnesses on the part of the prosecution, might be called, to ascertain who were present.

They were accordingly called, to the number of twenty-four, as follows : —

Those who answered are marked (*p*)—and those absent (*a.*)

Alexander James Dallas,	*p.* Philip Stewart,	*a.*
William Lewis,	*p.* John Thomſon Maſon,	*p.*
William Rawle,	*p.* Samuel H. Smith,	*p.*
William S. Biddle,	*p.* Thomas Hall,	*a.*
Edward Tilghman,	*p.* John Taylor,	*p.*
George Read,	*p.* George Hay,	*p.*
James Lea,	*a.* Philip Norborne Nicholas,	*a.*
John Crow,	*a.* William Wirt,	*p.*
Risdon Biſhop, .	*a.* John Harvie,	*a.*
John Montgomery,	*p.* Meriwether Jones,	*a.*
John Stephen,	*p.* John Heath,	*p.*
Aquila Hall,	*a.* James Pleaſants,	*a.*

Mr. *Randolph* observed, that various considerations, which it was unnecessary to detail, induced him, on behalf of the Managers, to move a postponement of the trial till to-morrow, when they hoped to be prepared to proceed with it.

Mr. *Harper* said, that on behalf of judge Chase, he would not object to the motion.

The *President* informed the Managers, that the Senate acceded to their request, and added that the Senate would attend to-morrow at 12 o'clock, for the purpose of proceeding with the trial.

At the request of Mr. Harper, the witnesses on the part of judge Chase were called over, to the number of forty, as follows :—

Those present are marked (*p*)—and those absent (*a.*)

William Marſhall,	*a.* John A. Chevalier,	*p.*
David M. Randolph	*p.* Robert Gamble,	*a.*
Edmund Randolph,	*a.* John Marſhall,	*p.*

John Baſſet,	*p.*	Samuel P. Moore,	*p.*
Cyrus Griffin,	*ſick.*	William C. Frazier,	*p.*
David Robertſon,	*p.*	Edward Tilghman,	*p.*
J. C. Barrett,	*dead.*	Wm. Meredith,	*p.*
John Hopkins,	*not found.*	Jared Ingerſoll,	*p.*
Philip Gocch,	*not found.*	Samuel Wheeler,	*not found.*
William Minor,	*not found.*	Samuel Ewing,	*p.*
James Wincheſter,	*p.*	Walter Dorſey,	*p.*
Philip Moore,	*a.*	James P. Boyd,	*p.*
Cornelius Comegys,	*a.*	Nicholas Brice,	*p.*
John Purviance,	*p.*	Wm. M. Mechin,	*p.*
Thomas Chaſe,	*p.*	William H. Wynder,	*p.*
John Stewart,	*a.*	William Gwyn,	*p.*
William Rawle,	*p.*	William J. Govane,	*p.*
Gunning Bedford,	*p.*	Edward J. Coale,	*a.*
Nicholas Vandyke,	*p.*	John Hall, jun.	*p.*
Archibald Hamilton,	*p.*	Thomas Carpenter.	*p.*

Whereupon the court rose.

SATURDAY, *February* 9, 1805.

The court was opened precisely at 12 o'clock.

Present, the Managers, attended by the House of Representatives in committee of the whole; and *Judge Chase,* attended by his counsel, as mentioned in the proceedings of yesterday.

At a quarter after 12 o'clock, Mr. *Randolph,* on behalf of the Managers, opened the impeachment, as follows:

Mr. *President,*

It becomes my duty to open this cause on behalf of the prosecution. From this duty, however incompetent I feel myself to its performance, at all times, and more especially at this time, as well from the very short period which has been allowed us to consider the long and elaborate plea of the respondent, as from the severe pressure of disease, it does not become me to shrink. The station in which I have been placed calls for the discharge of an important public trust at my hands. It shall be performed to the best of my ability, inadequate as I know that ability to be. When I speak of the short period which has been allowed us, I hope not to be understood as expressing, on our part, any dissatisfaction at the course which has been pursued, or any wish to prolong the time which has been allotted for trial. We are sensible of a disposition in this honorable court to grant us every indulgence which we ought to ask, and when their attention is called to the precipitate hurry of our preparation, it is only to offer, on behalf of an individual, perhaps a weak apology for the weak defence which he is about to make of the cause confided to his care. A desire for the furtherance of justice and the avoidance of delay, but, above all, an unshaken conviction that we stand on impregnable ground, induce us on this short notice to declare that we are ready to substantiate our accusation, to prove that the respondent is guilty in such manner as he stands impeached.

It is a painful but indispensible task which we are called upon to perform :—to establish the guilt of a great officer of government, of a man, who, if he had made a just use of those faculties which God and Nature bestowed upon him, would have been the ornament and benefactor of his country, would have rendered her services as eminent and useful as he has inflicted upon her outrages and wrongs deep and deadly. A character endowed by nature with some of her best attributes, cultivated by education, placed by his country in a conspicuous station, invested with authority whose righteous exercise would have rendered him a terror to the wicked, whilst it endeared him to the wise and good :—such a character, presented to the nation in the light in which he now stands, and in which his misdeeds have made it our duty to bring him forward, forms one of the saddest spectacles which can be offered to the public eye. Base is that heart which could triumph over him.

I will now proceed to state the principal points on which we mean to rely, and which we expect to establish by the clearest evidence. In doing this I shall be necessarily led to notice many of the leading statements of the respondent's answer. We will begin with the first article. [Here Mr. R. read that article.] The answer to the first of these charges is by evasive insinuation and misrepresentation, by an attempt to wrest the accusation from its true bearing, the manner and time of delivering the opinion, and the intent with which it was delivered, to the correctness of the opinion itself, which is not the point in issue. And here permit me to remark, that if the Managers of this impeachment were governed only by their own conviction of the course which they ought, necessarily, to pursue, and not by the high sense of duty which they owe to their eminent employers, they would have felt themselves justified in resting their accusation on the admissions of the respondent himself. It is not for the opinion itself, that the respondent is impeached; it is for a daring inroad upon the criminal jurisprudence of his country, by delivering that opinion at a time and in a manner (in writing) before unknown and unheard of. The criminal intent is to be inferred from the boldness of the innovation itself, as well as from other overt acts charged in this article. The admission of the respondent ought to secure his conviction on this charge. He acknowleges that he did deliver an opinion, *in writing*, on the question of law (which it was the right and duty of the jury to determine, as well as the fact) *before* counsel had been heard in defence of John Fries, the prisoner. I must beg the assistance of one of the gentlemen with whom I am associated, to read this part of the answer. [Mr. Clark accordingly read the reply of Mr. Chase to this charge.] We charge the respondent with a gross departure from the forms, and a flagrant outrage upon the substance of criminal justice, in delivering a

written, prejudicated opinion on the case of Fries,
tending to bias the minds of the jury against him
before counsel had been heard in his defence. The respondent (page 33, of the answer) admits the fact, for he
knew that we are prepared to prove it. But he artfully
endeavors to shift the argument from the real point in
contest, to the soundness of the opinion itself, which,
however questionable (and of its incorrectness I entertain no doubt) it is not our object, at this time, to
examine. For the truth of this opinion, and, as it
would seem, for the propriety of this proceeding, the
respondent takes shelter under precedent. He tells
you, sir, this doctrine had been repeatedly decided on
solemn argument and deliberation, twice in the same
court, and once in that very case.—What is this, but a
confession, that he himself hath been the first man to
venture on so daring an innovation on the forms of our
criminal jurisprudence? To justify himself for having
given a written opinion *before* counsel had been heard
for the prisoner, he resorts to the example set by his predecessors, who had delivered the customary verbal
opinion, after solemn argument and deliberation. And
what do these repeated arguments and solemn deli-
berations prove, but that none of his predecessors
ever arrogated to themselves the monstrous privilege
of breaking in upon those sacred institutions, which
guard the life and liberty of the citizen from the rude
inroads of powerful injustice? The learned and eminent judges, to whose example he appeals, for justification, decided *after*, and not *before* a hearing. They
exercised the acknowledged privilege of the bench
in giving an opinion to the jury on the question of
law, after it had been fully argued by counsel, on
both sides. They never attempted, by previous and
written decisions, to wrest from the jury their undeniable right, of deciding upon the law as well as the
fact, necessarily involved in a general verdict, to usurp
this decision to themselves, or to prejudice the minds

of the jurors against the defence. I beg this honorable court never to lose sight of the circumstance, that this was a *criminal* trial, for a *capital* offence, and that the offence charged was *treason*. The respondent also admits, that the counsel for Fries, not meaning to contest the truth of the facts charged in the indictment, rested their defence altogether upon the law, which he declared to have been settled in the cases of Vigol and Mitchel : a decision which, although it might be binding on the court, the jury were not obliged to respect, and which the counsel had a right to controvert before them, the sole judges, in a case of that nature, both of the *law* and the *fact*. I do not deny the right of the court to explain their sense of the law, to the jury, after counsel have been heard ; but I do deny that the jury are bound by such exposition.— If they verily believed that the overt acts charged in the indictment, did not amount to treason, they could not without a surrender of their consciences into the hands of the court, without a flagrant violation of all that is dear and sacred to man, bring in a verdict of Guilty. I repeat that in such a case the jury are not only the sole judges of the law, but that where their verdict is favorable to the prisoner, they are the judges without appeal. In civil cases, indeed, the verdict may be set aside and a new trial granted—but in a criminal prosecution, the verdict, if not guilty, is final and conclusive. It is only when the finding of the jury is unfavorable to the prisoner, that the humane provisions of our law, always jealous of oppression when the life, or liberty of the citizen is at stake, permits the verdict to be set aside, and a new trial granted to the unhappy culprit. When I concede the right of the court to explain the law to the jury in a criminal, and especially in a capital case, I am penetrated with a conviction that it ought to be done, if at all, with great caution and delicacy. I must beg leave to take, before this honorable court, what appears to my unlettered judgment, to be a strong and obvious distinction. There is, in my mind, a material difference between a naked definition of law, the application of which is left to the jury, and the application by the court, of such definition to the particular case, upon which the jury are called upon to find a general verdict. Surely, there is a wide and evident distinction between an abstract opinion upon a point of law, and an opinion applied to the facts admitted by the party accused, or proven against him. But it is alleged, on behalf of the respondent, that the law in this case was settled, and upon this he rests his defence. Will it be pretended by any man that the law of treason is better established than the law of murder? What is treason as defined by the constitution? Levying war against the United States, or adhering to their enemies, giving them aid and comfort. What is murder? Killing with malice aforethought, a definition at least as simple and plain as the other. And because what constitutes murder has been established and settled through a long succession of ages and adjudications, has any judge for that reason, been ever daring enough to assert that counsel should be precluded from endeavoring to convince the jury that the overt acts, charged in the indictment, did not amount to murder? Is a court authorised to say, that because killing with deliberate malice is murder, therefore the act of killing, admitted by the prisoner's counsel, or established by evidence, was a killing with malice prepense, and did constitute murder? I venture to say that an instance cannot be adduced, familiar as the definition of murder is even to the most ignorant, numerous as have been the convictions for that atrocious crime, where counsel have been deprived of their unquestionable right to address the jury on the law, as well as on the fact. Much less can an instance be produced, in any trial for a capital offence, where they have found themselves anticipated in the question of law by a written opini-

on, to be taken by the jury out of court, as the land-
mark by which their verdict is to be directed. I have
always understood, that, even in a civil case, when
the jury carried out with them a written paper, relating to the matter in issue, and which was not offered,
or permitted to be given in evidence to them, it was
sufficient to vitiate their verdict, and good ground for
a new trial. This written opinion of the court delivered previous to a hearing of the cause, is a novelty to our laws and usages. It would be reprehensible
in any case, but in a criminal prosecution, for a capital offence, and that offence *treason*, (where, above all,
oppression and arbitrary proceedings on the part of
courts are most to be dreaded and guarded against)
it cannot be too strongly reprobated, or too severely
punished.

What would be said of a judge who in a trial for
murder, where the facts were admitted (or proved)
should declare from the bench, that whatever argument counsel had to offer, in relation to the facts, may
be addressed to the jury, but that they should not attempt to convince the jury that such facts came not
within the law, did not amount to murder, but that
every thing which they had to say upon the question
of law, should be addressed to the court, and to the
court only. Can you figure to yourselves a spectacle
more horrible?

We are prepared to prove, what the respondent has
in part admitted, that he "restricted the counsel of
Fries from citing such English authorities as they believed apposite, and certain statutes of the United
States, which they deemed material to their defence:"
that the prisoner was debarred by him, from his constitutional privilege of addressing the jury, through
his counsel, on the law, as well as the fact, involved
in the verdict which they were required to give—and
that he attempted to wrest from the jury their undeniable right to hear argument, and, consequently, to

determine upon the question of law which in a criminal case it was their sole and unquestionable province to decide. These last charges (except so far as relates to the laws of the United States) are impliedly admitted by the respondent. He confesses that he would not permit the prisoner's counsel to cite certain cases, " because they could not inform but might deceive and mislead the jury." Mr. President, it is the noblest trait in this inestimable trial, that in criminal prosecutions, where the verdict is general, the jury are the sole judges, and where they acquit the prisoner, the judges, without appeal, both of law and fact. And what is the declaration of the respondent but an admission that he wished to take from the jury their indisputable privilege to hear argument and determine upon the law, and to usurp to himself that power, which belonged to them, and to them only ? It is one of the most glorious attributes of jury trial, that in criminal cases (particularly such as are capital) the pri - soner's counsel may (and they often do) attempt " to deceive and mislead the jury." It is essential to the fairness of the trial, that it should be conducted with perfect freedom. It is congenial to the generous spirit of our institutions to lean to the side of an unhappy fellow creature, put in jeopardy, of limb, or life, or liberty. The free principles of our governments, individual and federal, teach us to make every humane allowance in his favor, to grant him with a liberality, unknown to the narrow and tyrannous maxims of most nations, every indulgence not inconsistent with the due administration of justice. Hence, a greater latitude is allowed to the accused, than is permitted to the prosecutor. The jury, upon whose verdict the event is staked, are presumed to be men capable of understanding what they are called upon to decide, and the attorney for the state, a gentleman learned in his profession, capable of detecting and exposing the attempts of the opposite counsel to mislead and deceive. There is moreover the court, to which, in cases of difficulty, recourse might be had. But what indeed is the difficulty arising from the law in criminal cases, for the most part? What is to hinder an honest jury from deciding, especially after the aid of an able discussion, whether such an act was a killing with malice prepense, or such other overt acts set forth in an indictment, constituted a levying war against the United States—and to what purpose has treason been defined by the constitution itself, if overbearing arbitrary judges are permitted to establish among us the odious and dangerous doctrine of constructive treason? The acts of Congress which had been referred to on the former trial, but which the respondent said he would not suffer to be cited again, tended to shew that the offence committed by Fries did not amount to treason. That it was a misdemeanor, only, already provided for by law and punishable with fine and imprisonment. The respondent indeed denies this part of the charge, but he justifies it even (as he says) if it be proved upon him. And are the laws of our own country (as well as foreign authorities) not to be suffered to be read in our courts, in justification of a man whose life is put in jeopardy!

I now proceed to the second article—the case of Basset, whose objection to serve on Callender's jury was over-ruled by the judge, who stands arraigned before this honorable court. In the 30th page of the respondent's answer it is stated, that a new trial was granted to Fries, " *upon the ground (as this respondent understood and believes) that one of the jurors, after he was summoned, but before he was sworn, had made some declaration unfavorable to the prisoner.*" It will be remembered that both the trials of Fries preceded that of Callender. Upon what principle then, could the respondent declare Basset a good juryman, when he was apprized of the previous decision in the case of Fries, by his brother judge, whom he professes to hold in such high reverence, and by whose decision, on his own principles, he must have held himself bound. For surely the same exception to a juryman, which would furnish ground for a new trial, ought to be a cause of setting aside such juror, if it be taken previous to his being sworn.

From the respondent's own shewing [page 51, of the answer] it appears, that the question put to the jurymen generally, and to Basset among others, was, whether they "had formed *and* delivered any opinion upon the subject matter then to be tried, or concerning the charges contained in the indictment." And here let me refer the court to the question which the respondent put to the jurors in the case of Fries, [page 45.] It was, "whether they had ever formed, *or* delivered any opinion as to his guilt, or innocence, or that he ought to be punished?" How is this departure from the respondent's own practice, this inconsistency with himself to be reconciled? In the one case the question is put in the disjunctive; "have you formed *or* delivered?" In the other, it is in the conjunctive, "formed *and* delivered;" besides other material difference in the terms and import of the two questions. Wherefore, I repeat, this contradiction of himself? But, Mr. President, we shall be prepared to prove that the words "*subject matter then to be tried*" were not comprised in the question propounded to Basset, or to any of the other jurors. The question was, as will be shewn in evidence, "have you ever formed *and* delivered any opinion *concerning the charges contained in the indictment?*" And it is remarkable that the whole argument of the respondent upon this point, goes to justify the question which was *actually* put, and which he probably expected we should prove that he did put, rather than that which he himself declares to have been propounded by him. Such a question must necessarily have been answered in the negative. Basset could never have seen the indictment; and although his mind might have been made

up on the *book*, whatever opinion he might have formed and delivered as to the guilt of Callender, or however desirous he might have been of procuring his
conviction and punishment, still, not having seen the
indictment, he could not divine what passages of the
book were made the subject of the charges, and by the
criterion established by the judge, he was a good jur-
or. But if the juror's mind was thus prejudiced
against the book and the writer, was he, merely because he had not seen the indictment, competent to
pass between him and his country on the charges contained in it, and extracted out of the book? And even
if the question had been such as the respondent states,
yet being put in the conjunctive, the most inveterate
foe of the traverser who was artful, or cautious enough
to forbear the expression of his enmity, would thereby have been admitted as competent to pass between
the traverser and his country in a criminal prosecution.

The 3d article relates to the rejection of John Taylor's testimony. This fact also is admitted, and an
attempt is made to justify it, on the ground of its "*irrelevancy*," on the pretext that the witness could not
prove the whole of a particular charge. By recurring
to "The Prospect before Us," a book, which, with
all its celebrity, I never saw till yesterday, I find this
charge consists of two distinct sentences. Taken separately the respondent asserts that they mean nothing;
taken together, a great deal. And because the respondent undertook to determine (without any authority as far as I can learn) that col. Taylor could
not prove the whole, that is both sentences, he rejected his evidence entirely, for "*irrelevancy.*" Might
not his testimony have been relevant to that of some
other witness, on the same, or on another charge?
I appeal to the learning and good sense of this honorable court, whether it is not an unheard of practice
(until the present instance) in a criminal prosecution,

to declare testimony inadmissible because it is not expected to go tó the entire exculpation of the prisoner? Does it not daily occur in our courts, that a party accused, making out a part of his defence by one witness and establishing other facts by the evidence of other persons; does it not daily occur that the testimony of various witnesses sometimes to the same, and sometimes to different facts, does so *relieve* and support the whole case, as to leave no doubt of the innocence or guilt of the accused, in the minds of the jury, who, it must never be forgotten, are, in such cases, the sole judges both of the law and the fact? Suppose for instance that the testimony of two witnesses would establish all the facts, but that each of those facts are not known by either of them. According to this doctrine the evidence of both might be declared inadmissible, and a man whose innocence, if the testimony in his favor were not rejected, might be clearly proved to the satisfaction of the jury, may thus be subjected by the verdict of that very jury to an ignominious death. Shall principles so palpably cruel and unjust be tolerated in this free country? I am free to declare that the decision of Mr. Chase, in rejecting col. Taylor's testimony, was contrary to the known and established rules of evidence, and this I trust will be shewn by my learned associates, to the full satisfaction of this honorable court, if indeed they can require further satisfaction on a point so clear and indisputable. But this honorable court will be astonished when they are told (and the declaration will be supported by undeniable proof) that at this very time neither the traverser, his counsel, or the court, knew the extent to which col. Taylor's evidence would go. They were apprized, indeed, that he would shew that Mr. Adams was an aristocrat, and that he had proved serviceable to the British interest, in the sense conveyed by the book; but they little dreamt that his evidence, if permitted to have been given in, would have thrown great light upon many other of the charges. There is one ground of defence taken by the respondent, which I did suppose, a gentleman of his discernment would have sedulously avoided. That although the traverser had justified nineteen out of twenty of the charges, contained in the indictment, if he could not prove the truth of the twentieth, it was of little moment, as he was, " thereby, put into the power of the court." Gracious God! Sir, what inference is to be drawn from this horrible insinuation?

In justification of the charges contained in the fourth article, the respondent, unable to deny the fact, confesses (page 61,) that he did require " the questions intended to be put to the witness to be reduced to writing, and submitted to the court," in the first instance (as we shall prove) and before they had been verbally propounded. And this requisition, he contends, it was " the right and duty of the court" to make. It would not become me, elsewhere, or on any other occasion, to dispute the authority of the respondent, on legal questions, but I do aver that such is *not* the *law*, at least in the state in which that trial was held, nor do I believe that it is law any where. I speak of the United States. Sir, in the famous case of Logwood, whereat the chief justice of the United States presided, I was present, being one of the grand jury who found a true bill against him. It must be conceded that the government was as deeply interested in arresting the career of this dangerous and atrocious criminal, who had aimed his blow against the property of every man in society, as it could be in bringing to punishment a weak and worthless scribbler. And yet, although much testimony was offered by the prisoner, which did, by no means, go to his entire exculpation, although much of that testimony was of a very questionable nature, none of it was declared *inadmissible ;* it was suffered to go to the jury, who were left to judge of its weight and credibility, nor were any interrogatories to the witnesses required to be reduced to writing. And I will go farther, and say that it never has been done before, or since Callender's trial, in any court of Virginia, (and I believe I might add in the United States) whether state or federal. No sir, the enlightened man who presided in Logwood's case knew that, although the basest and vilest of criminals, he was entitled to *justice*, equally with the most honorable member of society. He did not avail himself of the previous and great discoveries, in criminal law, of this respondent; he admitted the prisoner's testimony to go to the jury; he never thought it *his right*, or *his duty*, to require questions to be reduced to writing; he gave the accused a *fair trial*, according to law and usage, without any innovation, or departure, from the established rules of criminal jurisprudence, in his country.

The respondent also acknowledges his refusal to postpone the trial of Callender, although an affidavit was regularly filed stating the absence of material witnesses on his behalf; and here again the ground of his defence is, in my estimation, good cause for his conviction. The dispersed situation of the witnesses, which he alleges to have been the motive of his refusal, is, to my mind, one of the most unanswerable reasons for granting a postponement. The other three charges, contained in this article, will be supported by unquestionable evidence. The rude and contemptuous expressions of the judge to the prisoner's counsel; his repeated and vexatious interruptions of them; his indecent solicitude and predetermined resolution to effect the conviction of the accused. This predetermination we shall prove to have been expressed by him, long before, as well as on his journey to Richmond, and whilst the prosecution was pending; besides the proofs which the trial itself afforded.

The 5th article is for the respondent's having " awarded a capias against the body of James Thompson Callender, indicted for an offence not capital, whereupon the said Callender was arrested and committed to close custody, contrary to law in such case made and provided;"—that is, contrary to the act of assembly of Virginia, recognized (by the act of Congress passed in 1789, for the establishment of the judicial courts of the United States) as the rule of decision in the federal courts, to be held in that state, until other provision be made. The defence of the respondent embraces several points: That the act of Virginia was passed posterior to the act of Congress, (viz. in 1792,) and could not be intended, by the latter, to be a rule of decision. Fortunately, there is no necessity to question (which we might well do) the truth of his position. It may be necessary to inform some of the members of this honorable court, that, about twelve or thirteen years ago, the laws of Virginia underwent a revision; all those relating to a particular subject, being condensed into one, and the whole code, thereby, rendered less cumbrous and perplexed. Hence many of our laws, to a casual and superficial observer, would appear to take their date so late as the year 1792, although their provisions were, long before, in force. The 28th section of this very act on which we rely, the court will perceive to have been enacted in 1788, one year *preceding* the act of Congress. (Virg. laws, chap. LXXIV, sec. 28, page 106, note b. Pleasant's edition.) [Here Mr. Randolph read the act referred to.] "Upon presentment made by a grand jury of an offence not capital, the court shall order the clerk to issue a summons, or other proper process, against the person so presented, to appear, and answer such presentment at the next court," &c. But the respondent, aware no doubt of this fact, asserts that the act not being adduced, he was not bound to know of its existence, and that he ought not to be censured for the omissions of the traverser's counsel, whose duty it was to have cited it on behalf of their client; and this objection, with the preceding ones, which I have endeavored to answer, will equally apply to the 6th article. Sir, when the counsel for the traverser were told by the judge at the outset, when they referred to a provision of this very law, "that such may be your local state laws, here in Virginia, but that to suppose them as applying to the courts of the United States, is a *wild notion*," would it not indeed have been a *wild experiment* in them to cite the same law with a view of influencing the opinion of a man, who had scornfully scouted the idea that he was to be governed by it.

Unwilling however to rest himself now, on the ground which he then took, the respondent justifies himself by declaring that he complied, although ignorantly, with this law, by issuing that *other proper process*, of which it speaks, that is, a capias. But that other process must be of the nature of a summons, notifying the party to appear at the *next term;* and will any man pretend to say, that a capias taking him into close custody and obliging him to appear not at the next but at the existing term, is such process as that law describes? Sir, not only the law but the uniform practice under it, as we are prepared to shew by evidence, declares the capias not to be the proper process. But it is said, that this would be nothing more than notice to the party accused to abscond, and therefore *ought not* to be law. Sir, we are not talking about what ought to have been the law; that is no concern of ours—the question is what *was* the law. But the impolicy of this mode of proceeding is far from being ascertained. It is a relief to the innocent who may be in a state of accusation. It saves the expense of imprisoning the guilty, and if they should prefer voluntary exile to standing a trial, is it so very clear that the state is thereby more injured than by holding them to punishment, after which they would remain in her bosom to perpetrate new offences. Remember,—this proceeding is against petty offenders, not felons.—It does not apply to capital cases; to felonies, then, capital, for which our law has, since, commuted the punishment of death, into that of imprisonment at hard labour.

For further defence against the 6th article, the respondent takes shelter under this position: That the provision of the law of the United States establishing the judicial courts relates only to rights acquired under *state* laws, which come into question *on* the trial, and not to forms of process *before* the trial, and can have no application to offences created by statute, which cannot with propriety, be termed trials at " *common law*." We are prepared to shew that the words " trials at common law" are used in that statute, not in their most restricted sense, but to contra-distinguish a certain description of cases from those arising in equity, or under maritime, or civil law.

I will pass over the seventh article of impeachment, as well because I am nearly exhausted, as being content to leave it on the ground where the respondent himself has placed it. It would be impossible for us to put it in a stronger light, than has been thrown upon it by his own admission.

The 8th and last article remains to be considered. [article read.] I ask this honorable court whether the prostitution of the bench of justice to the purposes of an hustings is to be tolerated? We have nothing to do with the politics of the *man*. Let him speak and write and publish as he pleases. This is his right in common with his fellow citizens. The press is free. If he must electioneer and abuse the government under which he lives, I know no law to prevent or punish him, provided he seeks the wonted theatres for his exhibition. But shall a judge declaim on these topics from his seat of office? Shall he not put off the political partizan when he ascends the tribune; or shall we have the pure stream of public justice polluted with the venom of party virulence? In short, does it

follow that a judge carries all the rights of a private
citizen with him upon the bench, and that he may,
there, do every act which, as a freeman, he may do
elsewhere, without being questioned for his conduct?
But, Sir, we are told that this high court is not a
court of errors and appeals, but a court of impeachment, and that however incorrectly the respondent
may have conducted himself, proof must be adduced
of criminal intent, of wilful error, to constitute guilt.
The *quo animo* is to be inferred from the facts themselves; there is no other mode by which in any case
it can be determined, and even the respondent admits
that there are acts of a nature so flagrant that guilt
must be inferred from them, if the party be of sound
mind. But this concession is qualified by the monstrous pretention that an act to be impeachable, must
be indictable. Where? In the federal courts? There
not even robbery and murder are indictable, except in
a few places under our exclusive jurisdiction. It is
not an indictable offence under the laws of the United
States for a judge to go on the bench in a state of in-
toxication—it may not be in all the state courts. But
it is indictable no where, for him to omit to do his
duty, to refuse to hold a court. And who can doubt
that both are impeachable offences, and ought to subject the offender to removal from office? But in this
long and disgusting catalogue of crimes and misde
meanors (which he has in a great measure confessed)
the respondent tells you he had accomplices and that
what was guilt in him could not be innocence in them.
I must beg the court to consider the facts alleged
against the respondent in all their accumulated atroci-
ty;—not to take them, each in an insulated point of
view, but as a chain of evidence indissolubly linked
together, and establishing the indisputable proof of his
guilt. Call to mind his high standing and character,
and his superior age and rank, and then ask yourselves
whether he stands justified in a long course of oppres-

sion and injustice, because men of weak intellect, and yet feebler temper—men of far inferior standing to the respondent, have tamely acquiesced in such acts of violence and outrage? He is charged with various acts of injustice, with a series of misconduct so connected in time and place and circumstance, as to leave no doubt, on my mind at least, of intentional ill. Can this be justified, because his several associates have at several times and occasions barely yielded a faint compliance, which perhaps they dared not withhold? Can they be considered as equally culpable with him whose accumulated crimes are to be divided amongst them, who had given at best but a negative sanction to them? But, sir, would the establishment of their guilt prove his innocence? At most it would only prove that they too ought to be punished. Whenever we behold the respondent sitting in judgment, there do we behold violence and injustice. Before *him* the counsel are always contumacious. The most accomplished advocates of the different states whose demeanor to his brethren is uniformly conciliating and temperate, are to *him*, and him only, obstinate, perverse, rude, and irritating. Contumacy has been found to exist only where he presided.

Mr. President, it appears to me that one great distinction remains yet to be taken. A distinction between a judge zealous to punish and repress crimes generally, and a judge anxious only to enforce a particular law whereby he may recommend himself to power, or to his party. It is this hideous feature of the respondent's judicial character, on which I would fix your attention. We do not charge him with a general zeal in the discharge of his high office, but with an indecent zeal in particular cases, for laws of doubtful and suspicious aspect. It is only in cases of constructive treason and libel, that this zeal breaks out. Through the whole tenor of his judicial conduct runs the spirit of party. I could cite the name and authority of a judge of whom, if I might be permitted to speak, I would say, that he was no less a terror to evil doers than a shield to the oppressed. In a commendable zeal for the faithful execution of the laws, he has never been surpassed, neither in tenderness to the liberty of the citizen, nor the liberty of the press, nor trial by jury. [Here Mr. R. read the following passage from Tucker's Blackstone, vol. 4, page 350.] " But it is not customary nor agreeable to the general course of proceeding (unless by consent of parties, or where the defendant is actually in gaol) to try persons indicted of smaller misdemeanors at the same court in which they have pleaded not guilty, *or traversed the indictment.*" [What follows is subjoined in a note.] And this is the practice in Virginia; but in the case of the United States against Callender, in the federal court at Richmond, May 1800, a different course was pursued, although the act of Congress (First Congress, 1 Sept. chap. 20, sec. 32.) may be interpreted otherwise. This is the very act and section on which we rely.

I have endeavored, Mr. President, in a manner, I am sensible, very lame and inadequate, to discharge the duty incumbent on me; to enumerate the principal points upon which we shall rely, and to repel some of the prominent objections advanced by the respondent. Whilst we confidently expect on his conviction, it is from the strength of our cause, and not from any art or skill, in conducting it. It requires so little support that (thank heaven) it cannot be injured by any weakness of mine. We shall bring forward in proof, such a specimen of judicial tyranny, as, I trust in God, will never be again exhibited in our country.

The respondent hath closed his defence by an appeal to the great Searcher of hearts for the purity of his motives. For his sake, I rejoice, that, by the timely exercise of that mercy, which, for wise purposes, has been reposed in the executive, this appeal is not drowned by the blood of an innocent man crying aloud for vengeance; that the mute agony of widowed despair and the wailing voice of the orphan do not plead to heaven for justice on the oppressor's head. But for that intervention, self accusation before that dread tribunal would have been needless. On that awful day the blood of a poor, ignorant, friendless, unlettered German, murdered under the semblance and color of law, sent without pity to the scaffold, would have risen in judgment at the Throne of Grace, against the unhappy man arraigned at your bar. But the President of the United States by a well timed act, at once of justice and of mercy, (and mercy like charity covereth a multitude of sins,) wrested the victim from his grasp, and saved him from the countless horrors of remorse, by not suffering the pure ermine of justice to be dyed in the innocent blood of John Fries.

The Managers proceeded to the examination of witnesses in support of the prosecution.

WILLIAM LEWIS *affirmed.*

Mr. Dallas, Mr. W. Ewing and I were counfel for John Fries, at his requeft, and I believe by the affignment of the court, on his trial in the year 1799. It was conducted, I believe, in the ufual manner, and we were certainly allowed all the privileges that are cuftomary on fuch occafions. The trial was had before judges Iredell and Peters. He was convicted and a new trial was ordered, becaufe one of the jurors had manifefted a prejudice againft the people in general concerned in the infurrection, and againft Fries in particular. This trial took place partly in April and partly in May, 1799. At October feffion following, Mr. Dallas and I attended at Norristown, expecting the trial would again take place; but it did not. The proceedings on the firft indictment were quafhed by the diftrict attorney, and a new bill was found at April term 1800, at which judges Chase and Peters prefided. Mr.

Dallas and I appeared again as the counfel of Fries, at his re-queft, and I believe we were affigned by the court, but of this I am not certain. On the morning of a certain day, which I do not now recollect, I entered the court room when the judges were on the bench, and if I recollect rightly the prifon-er was in the bar; but if he was not then there, I feel very fure that he foon was. The lift of petit jurors was called over, and many of them anfwered. Whether his trial had been ap-pointed for that day, I do not recollect; nor can I fay whether he was brought up in confequence of fuch appointment or not. I will now ftate as accurately as is in my power what took place on the occafion, premifing that although my memory is a re-markably accurate one for a fhort time, it is far from being fo after a confiderable lapfe of time. I will not, therefore, under-take to ftate the precife words ufed in the altercation which took place; but I am very confident that I fhall not vary from the fubftance. When I fay that I am thus confident, I beg to be underftood as not undertaking to diftinguifh pofitively in all re-fpects between what took place on the firft or on the fecond day.

Almoft immediately after the jurors were called over, judge Chafe began to fpeak. At this time Mr. Dallas had not come into court. Judge Chafe faid, he underftood, or had been informed, that on the former trial or trials, for it was impof-fible for me to know whether he alluded to the cafe of Fries only, or of him and others, there had been a great wafte of time in making long fpeeches on topics which had nothing to do with the bufinefs, and in reading common law cafes on treafon, as well as on treafon under the ftatute of Edward the Third, and alfo certain ftatutes of the United States, refpecting the refifting of procefs, and other offences lefs than treafon. He alfo faid, that to prevent this in future, he or they, I do not precifely recollect which, had confidered the law, had made up their minds, and had reduced their opinion to writing on the fubject, and would not fuffer thefe cafes to be read again; and in order that the counfel (but whether for the prifoner, or the counfel on both fides, I cannot fay) might govern them-felves conformably, he had ordered three copies of that opi-nion to be made out, one to be delivered to the prifoner's counfel, one to the counfel in fupport of the profecution, and the other, as foon as the cafe was fully opened, or gone through, I cannot fay which, to be delivered by the clerk of the court to the jury. I rather think that the expreffion was, fully gone through.

Mr. *Randolph.* And this, Sir, before the counfel had been heard?

Mr. *Lewis.* I have faid Mr. Dallas had not yet come into court, and as to myfelf I had not at this time faid a fingle word. I think it was at or about this time, that judge Chafe handed, or threw down to Mr. Caldwell, clerk of the court, one or more papers; but whether I faw them pafs immediately from the hands of one to the other, I am not certain. Mr. Caldwell reached one of the papers towards me. If I took it in my hand, I did not read a fingle line of it. I remember well that fpeaking aloud, but whether addreffing myfelf to the court or not, I am not pofitive, and either waving my hand, or throwing the paper from me, I ufed this expreffion—" I will never permit my hand to be tainted with a prejudged opinion in any cafe, much lefs in a capital one." If judge Peters made ufe of a fingle expreffion on the firft day, I either did not hear him or do not recollect it.

Judge Chafe, when fpeaking of the authorities at common law, and thofe under the ftatute of Edward the Third, and I believe of the acts of Congrefs, faid he would not fuffer them to be read again. I am fure he faid he would not fuffer the decifions at common law, or under the ftatute of Edward the Third, to be read. I am not altogether certain whether he did or did not fay the fame thing as to the ftatutes of the United States; but I am perfectly fure that he did fay they had nothing to do with the queftion, and that he expreffed himfelf in ftrong terms of difapprobation either at their having been read or permitted to be read on the former trial. I am not certain whether fome parts of this as well as of that which I am about to mention occurred on the firft or the fecond day.

Judge Chafe faid, I think on the firft day, that they were judges of the law, and if they did not underftand it they were unworthy of their feats, or unfit to fit there, and that if the prifoner's counfel had any thing to fay, to fhew that they had miftaken the law, or that they were wrong, the counfel muft addrefs themfelves to the court for that purpofe, and not to the jury. I made fome obfervations in anfwer, which it is impoffible for me in all refpects to particularly recollect, as having paffed at this time, fince fome parts of it may perhaps have taken place in other ftages of the bufinefs. At this time Mr. Dallas was not in court. I was ftruck with what appeared to me to be a great novelty in the proceedings, and as I was ex-

tremely anxious to be of fervice to Fries, I was defirous that
Mr. Dallas might be prefent. I think I went out of the bar to
get fomebody to go for him, and while I was out of the bar,
he entered the room. I briefly ftated to him what had taken
place, or fome parts of it ; but I believe not the whole. We
came forward, and we made fome remarks which I am unable
to repeat. I was early ftruck with the idea, that as the court
had made up their minds, and decided the queftion of law, before the jury was fworn, or the witneffes or counfel heard, it
was not likely we fhould alter that opinion by any thing we
might fay, and that we fhould probably render Fries more fervice by withdrawing from his defence, than by engaging in it.
We told him fo, and earneftly recommended to him to purfue
that courfe. He appeared greatly alarmed and extremely agitated, and much at a lofs what determination to come to. We,
however, told him, that, if he infifted on it, we would proceed
in his defence at every hazard, and contend for what we
deemed our conftitutional rights as his counfel, until ftopped
by the court ; or we ufed expreffions to this effect. His ftate
of alarm and apprehenfion fcarcely left him the power to decide
for himfelf. After fome time he acquiefced in our advice ;
faid he had nobody to depend on but us ; that he was fure we
would do our beft for him, and he would leave us to do for
him as we pleafed. Being very anxious for him, we told him
we would call upon him at the jail, and fatisfy his mind as to
the courfe which we wifhed him to purfue. He finally agreed
to our propofal to withdraw ; but as we were apprehenfive that
the court might affign him other counfel in our place, and that
our views might be defeated by fuch an arrangement, we ad-
vifed him againft accepting any, and I underftood that he afterwards did refufe to accept of any other counfel. I will not
affign my reafons for giving this advice, as it might perhaps
be improper, unlefs I am directed by the court.

Mr. *Martin* afked what thofe reafons were ?

The *Prefident* defired the examination to proceed on the
part of the Houfe of Reprefentatives ; and faid when that was
clofed, the witnefs might be examined by the counfel for Judge
Chafe.

Mr. *Lewis.* It being thus determined that we fhould withdraw, and that Fries fhould not accept any counfel that might
be affigned him, I left the court, expecting to have little or
nothing more to fay, as we were no longer counfel for the

prifoner. The next morning, foon after the court was opened, and, I believe, when the prifoner was in the bar, Judge Chafe addreffed Mr. Dallas and myfelf, and probably Mr. Rawle, and afked us if we were ready to proceed ? I anfwered that I was not, or that we were not any longer counfel for the prifoner. He afked our reafons for this ; and I began to anfwer by mentioning what had taken place the day before ; on which he and Judge Peters certainly manifefted a ftrong difpofition that we fhould proceed in the prifoner's defence, and that they would remove every reftriction, which had been previoufly impofed. I was ftopped in what I was about to fay by Judge Chafe telling us to go on in our own way, and addrefs the jury on the law as well as the facts, as we thought proper; but at the fame time he faid it would be under the direction of the court; and at our own peril, or the rifk of our characters if we conducted ourfelves with impropriety. This had rather a contrary effect on my mind than that of inducing me to proceed, as I did not know that there had been any thing in my conduct fo indecorous as to make it neceffary to remind me, that if I proceeded it fhould be at my own peril and rifk of character; and this expreffion, therefore, rather ftrengthened than leffened the determination which I had taken.

I have faid if judge Peters made ufe of a fingle expreffion on the firft day I did not hear it, or have forgotten it. On the fecond day he fpoke, and joined judge Chafe in urging us to proceed, in the prifoner's defence. He told us we might take as large a fcope as we pleafed; faid he knew the Philadelphia bar would take the ftud; and afked, if they (the judges) had committed an error or got into a fcrape, would we not permit them to get out of it? I mentioned in this or fome other ftage of the bufinefs, that I deemed it the conftitutional right of the prifoner to be heard by himfelf or counfel in his defence. That it was the conftitutional right of the jury to hear counfel on the law as well as the facts; that it was their conftitutional right to pafs between the prifoner and his country on both, and that it was the conftitutional right of counfel to be heard by the jury on the law as well as the facts. If I did not deliver myfelf in thefe precife words, I am confident that the fubftance is the fame, and that there is no material difference in the fenfe. I alfo mentioned that I confidered this a great conftitutional right, which fhould never be furrendered or facrificed by me. Of this expreffion I am fure. And I added that I never had, nor ever would in a criminal profecution addrefs a court either on the law or the facts: In this I find however that I was miftaken; for I fince recollect, though from the hurry of the moment I did not then, an inftance where in a criminal cafe I did addrefs the jury on a point of law, which was feparate and diftinct from the facts. Judge Peters remarked that no harm could arife from the papers, (containing the opinion of the court) as they, or the copies had been called in or collected, and either burnt or deftroyed. To this I anfwered, that although the papers were or might be deftroyed, the opinion which the court had formed, without hearing the prifoner's counfel, ftill remained, and could not be erafed from their minds, and would be as injurious to my client (the jurors being prefent and having heard what had paffed) as if the papers had not been deftroyed.

When judge Chafe faid that we fhould read no common law authorities, or decifions under the ftatute of Edward the third, before the revolution in England, I faid that we meant to contend that what was the law of treafon in England under the head of " levying war," was not in all refpects law here; that we did not mean to cite any cafes before the Englifh revolution to prove what the law of treafon was, or for any other purpofe than to fhew the dangerous lengths that the judges had gone while they were corrupt and dependent on the crown; that although fince the revolution in England the judges had been independent and upright, they had in a variety of particulars held themfelves bound by a train of former decifions which had taken place in bad times; but that the judges in this country in the conftruction of a new inftrument of our own defining the offence of treafon, were not bound by any of the decifions or conftructions which had taken place in England under the ftatute of Edward the third; and that the authorities we meant to cite were intended as a guard againft the dangerous conftructions which had prevailed in that country. It was not therefore to fhew what the law was, but to guard againft the dangers of conftructive treafon; and to fhew that our judges were not bound by the Englifh decifions, that we had read them before and intended to read them again. This principle we contended for before, and meant to contend for again; and we were principally led to it, from Mr. Sitgreaves, who had affifted the diftrict attorney on the former trial, having begun by

ftating " that the words of our conftitution refpecting treafon
are taken from the 25th Edward 3d, and therefore the people
of this country had, by adopting the words of that ftatute,
adopted all judicial determinations under it." This pofition
we could not agree to, and the cafes which had been read were
merely intended to fhew and guard againft the dangerous
lengths to which we fhould be carried, if it were admitted to
be true. Judge Chafe afked if the counfel offered to read cafes
from any foreign country, (mentioning feveral with whom we
had never been connected) was the court to permit them? We
in reply faid that we had not cited fuch cafes on the former occafions, and it was not likely that we fhould attempt it now.

Finding that Mr. Dallas and I were determined not to proceed in the prifoner's defence, judge Chafe faid, if we intended
to embarrafs the court we fhould find ourfelves miftaken, as
they would proceed without us, and by the blefling of God
render the prifoner as much juftice, as if he had the aid of our
counfel or affiftance. Both the judges, therefore, on the fecond
day, even took pains to induce us to proceed in the defence with
liberty to go through the whole queftion as well in relation to
the law as the facts; but we abfolutely refufed, believing it not
likely that any arguments we could urge, would change the
opinion of the court already formed, or deftroy its effects, and
alfo believing that after what had taken place, the life of Fries,
even if he fhould be convicted, would be expofed to lefs jeopardy without our aid than it would be if we fhould engage in
his defence.

Mr. *Nicholfon.* You fay that on the firft trial of Fries you
were allowed the ufual latitude. What do you mean by
ufual latitude?

Mr. *Lewis.* We were allowed to addrefs the jury on the
law as well as on the facts. We were allowed the privilege
of reading to the jury all fuch law authorities as we thought
applicable, and as might, under the direction of the court, tend
to fatisfy them, that the doctrine contended for on the part
of the profecution was not well founded. We met with no
reftraint or interruption, not having that I know of given occafion for either.

Mr. *Nicholfon.* Were you on the firft trial allowed to read
the ftatutes of the United States?

Mr. *Lewis.* Unqueftionably—I have the notes in my pocket from which I fpoke on that occafion, which I can produce
if defired.

Mr. *Nicholfon*. Were you allowed to read cafes before the revolution as well as fince ?

Mr. *Lewis*. We were ; we did it to fhew the extravagant lengths to which conftructive treafon had been carried, and not what the law actually was.

In anfwer to an interrogatory,

Mr. *Lewis* faid that he did not read the opinion of the court which had been handed or thrown down ; that he had never read it in his life.

Mr. *Randolph*. If not the oldeft, are you not an old practitioner at the bar, and have you not been frequently employed in criminal cafes ?

Mr. *Lewis*. I was admitted to practice in the court of common pleas in November 1774, and in the fupreme court in April 1775, and I have been employed in a pretty extenfive practice almoft ever fince. Immediately after the Britifh left Philadelphia in 1778, I was engaged for one hundred and fifty-three perfons charged with treafon or mifprifion of treafon. I defended almoft every man of them that was tried ; and fince that time I have been concerned in perhaps more capital cafes, particularly for treafon, than any other gentleman in Pennfylvania, compared with our bufinefs in other refpects.

Mr. *Randolph*. Did you ever fee fuch a proceeding as that which took place on the bench in the cafe of Fries ; or did you fee any thing before, to induce you to abandon the defence of your client ?

Mr. *Lewis*. This queftion feems to be a pretty general one, but if—

Mr. *Key*. If I underftand this queftion, it is calculated to draw from the witness an opinion, inftead of a narration of facts.

The *Prefident* defired Mr. Randolph to reduce his queftion to writing.

While Mr. Randolph was engaged in penning it,

Mr. *Chafe* faid he had no objection to the queftion being put.

In the mean time the queftion in writing had been handed to the chair, and been read by the clerk.

The *Prefident* faid the objection being withdrawn, the queftion would be put unlefs objected to by any member of the Senate.

No objection being made,

Mr. *Lewis* anfwered. No, I did not.—It was entirely novel to me.

Mr. *Randolph.* And yet you have been prefent at criminal trials, at trials for treafon, when there was a vaft number of civil actions on the docket?

Mr. *Lewis.* Criminal trials for capital offences are generally tried before the court of oyer and terminer in Pennfylvania, where there is feldom much interference with civil fuits.

At the circuit court of the United States in 1794, there were I believe many civil cafes. Judges Iredell and Peters prefided. I do not know, or believe, that the circumftance of their being civil cafes occafioned the leaft variation in the mode of procedure in the criminal cafes.

Mr. *Lewis* faid he had one thing further to ftate, that Mr. Dallas and he withdrew from a defire to fave the life of John Fries, and becaufe they thought it moft likely that it would be effected by doing fo, and not becaufe they were influenced by any other confiderations, and that had it not been for this confideration, he would have perfifted in the exercife of what he deemed his profeffional rights, until he was actually ftopped by the authority of the court.

Mr. *Harper.* Did you not appear for Vigol?

Mr. *Lewis.* I did.

Mr. *Harper.* With what overt acts was he charged?

Mr. *Lewis.* The overt act was levying of war, particularizing the time and place.

Mr. *Harper.* I will afk you whether on the trial of John Fries in 1799, in which Mr. Dallas and you appeared as his counfel, you did not make this point of law—that to refift by force the execution of a particular law of the United States does not amount to treafon, but to riot only? Or what was the point of law?

Mr. *Lewis.* On the firft trial of Fries we made this point of law. Before the trial before judges Chafe and Peters came on, I had confidered the fubject with great deliberation, and my determination was to infift, that, although refifting the laws generally or even a particular law refpecting the regular forces or militia of the nation was treafon, yet that refifting any other particular law was not treafon.

Mr. *Harper.* Was not the fame point made on the firft trial?

Mr. *Lewis.* It was.

Mr. *Harper.* Was it not ruled by the court that fuch acts amounted to treafon ?

Mr. *Lewis.* It was.

Mr. *Harper.* When then the court granted a new trial did they exprefs any doubt on this point, or was it not granted on a collateral point ?

Mr. *Lewis.* The new trial was granted folely on a collateral point.

Mr. *Harper.* How long did the trial laft ?

Mr. *Lewis.* I cannot tell; but it was a very long trial. The point of law was argued to the fulleft extent, and we quoted all the authorities we thought relevant. I was affifted by Mr. Dallas. We fpoke very fully, and were laid under no reftriction. At the laft trial we meant to have alfo taken other ground, and to have contended that the trial could not take place in Philadelphia, but muft be in the county in which the offence had been committed, according to a law of the United States, which provides that in capital cafes trials fhall take place in the county where the crimes are committed, unlefs this cannot be without great inconvenience. This we had before contended; and had been then over-ruled becaufe it was alleged the county in which the offences had been committed was not free from a ftate of infurrection or the effects of it. At the time of the laft trial, there was no infurrection in the county where the offences charged againft Fries had been committed, and we believed him, therefore, entitled to a trial in that county.

Mr. *Harper.* Did any part of judge Chafe's written opinion go to this point ?

Mr. *Lewis.* It was not mentioned to the court, as Mr. Dallas and I determined to have nothing further to do in the cafe.

Mr. *Harper.* Why did you abandon that part of your client's cafe? It was a new point, upon which you might have had the decifion of the court.

Mr. *Lewis.* I did not wifh to have any thing more to do with the cafe, after the manner in which we had been treated by the court.

Mr. *Hopkinfon.* Did not the court afk Fries, whether he would have counfel affigned him ?

Mr. *Lewis.* I believe there is no doubt of the fact.

Mr. *Randolph.* I underftand you to fay that by withdrawing from the defence of Fries, and the not having counfel affigned him, you expected to ferve your client. Wherefore did you think the caufe of your client would thereby be ferved?

Mr. *Lewis.* It appeared to me that the conduct of the court juftified us in withdrawing, after not being fuffered to go on in the ufual manner, and I thought it more probable that a man, thus convicted, would be pardoned by the Prefident, than that we fhould be able, by any thing we could fay, to alter the opinion of the court.

Mr. *Nicholfon.* Were the jurors prefent?

Mr. *Lewis.* They were—they were called over as ufual, but I do not know that they were called for the trial of Fries. It was I believe ufual to call over the lift on the morning of each day.

ALEXANDER J. DALLAS *fworn.*

Mr. *Dallas.* I will endeavor to be correct in the ftatement which it is my duty to give; and I am fure that I fhall be fub-ftantially fo, though I cannot promife to place the facts pre-cifely in the order of time, in which they occurred; nor to re-cite the very words that were ufed by the feveral parties, in the courfe of the tranfaction.

When the Northern Rioters were brought to Philadelphia, in the fpring of 1799, fome of their friends applied to Mr. In-gerfoll and to me, to undertake their defence. Mr. Ingerfoll was then attorney general of Pennfylvania; and on confidera-tion, I believe, declined the tafk. Mr. Lewis, either before or after this application, was alfo requefted to act as counfel for the prifoners; and upon his acquiefcence we repaired to the prifon, to make the neceffary arrangements preparatory to a trial. Mr. Wm. Ewing had been engaged by feveral of the rioters, and we agreed to unite in the defence, as the fame general facts and law, applied to all the cafes.

In April term 1799, the firft trial of Fries took place. It was conducted with great propriety throughout by the court, and by the profecuting officer; and the counfel of the prifon-er were permitted to addrefs the jury at large, on the law and the facts; as well as to cite every authority which they thought proper. Fries was convicted; but on a motion made by Mr. Lewis and me, the verdict was fet afide, and a new trial awarded.

The fecond trial of Fries, upon a new indictment (the firft having been difcontinued by Mr. Rawle) occurred in May, 1800. Mr. Lewis and I had again, at his requeft, been affigned by the court, to defend him. On the morning fixed for the trial, I entered the court-room fome time after the court had been opened. Fries was ftanding in the prifoner's box: The jurors of the general pannel appeared to be in the jury boxes: And the hall was crowded with citizens. On my entrance, I perceived Mr. Lewis and Mr. E. Tilghman engaged eagerly in converfation, and the gentlemen of the bar, generally, feemed to be much agitated. As foon as Mr. Lewis faw me, he haftened towards me, on the outfide of the bar; and told me in effect, " that a very extraordinary incident had occurred; that Mr. Chafe, after fpeaking in terms of great difapprobation of the defence, at the former trial, declared that the court, on mature confideration, had formed, and reduced to writing, an opinion on the law of treafon, involved in the cafe ; and that he fhould direct one copy to be delivered to the attorney of the diftrict, another to the prifoner's counfel, and a third [after the opening for the profecution] to the jury to take out with them."

Here Mr. *Harper* rofe, and faid :—Mr. Prefident, furely it is improper that the witnefs fhould repeat what Mr. Lewis told him, not in court, nor when the judge was prefent.

Mr. *Dallas*, turning to Mr. Harper, obferved " fir, I know the rules of evidence, and I mean to conform to them." Then turning to the Vice-Prefident, he continued ; " If, Mr. Prefident, the counfel's patience had lafted for a minute, he would have heard, that I repeated Mr. Lewis's communication to the court, and that it was not contradicted. What I have faid was neceffary to introduce that fact ; and, furely, it is ftrictly within the rules of evidence.

Mr. Lewis and I exchanged an opinion on the impropriety of the conduct of the court; we determined (as I thought when firft recurring to my memory for the facts and as I ftill think, though I wifh not to fpeak pofitively) to withdraw from the defence ; and we went into the bar together. When there, fomething occurred, which called the attention on our part ; and Mr. Lewis informed the court in effect " that there was little difpute about the facts in the caufe; and that as the court had deliberately prejudged the law, he could not hope to change their opinion, nor to ferve his client ; while a fub-

miſſion to ſuch a proceeding would be degrading to the pro-
feſſion." It was then, I think, that I stated to the court, the
information, which I had received from Mr. Lewis (but certainly it was either then, or, as it has been ſuggeſted to me by
a reſpectable gentleman of the bar, at the opening of the court
on the next day) and I pauſed, to give an opportunity for contradiction, or explanation. For although I had no doubt of
Mr. Lewis's intention to deliver a correct repreſentation of
what had paſſed, it was poſſible, and I might myſelf have miſtaken the import of his communication. I cannot now ſtate
all that Mr. Lewis told me; but, I am confident, that I then
repeated it all to the court. No remark being made, in con-
ſequence of the pauſe, I proceeded to ſtate a few comparative
obſervations on the province and rights of the judge, and the
province and rights of the advocate; and concluded with declining to act any longer as counſel for the priſoner. The
court was ſoon afterwards adjourned.—Theſe are all the material occurrences of the firſt day, which I recollect; except,
perhaps, that ſoon after I came into court, I heard Mr. Peters
remark to Mr. Chaſe: " I told you what would be the conſe-
quence. I knew they would take the ſtud."

On the next day, the court was opened, Fries was placed
in the priſoner's box, the jury attended, and the number of
ſpectators were increaſed. Silence being proclaimed, Mr.
Chaſe aſked, " if the priſoner's counſel were ready to proceed
on the trial;" and Mr. Lewis and I, ſucceſſively, declared, that
we no longer conſidered ourſelves as the counſel of Fries.
Mr. Peters then, as well as at other times, expreſſed a great
deſire that we ſhould overlook what had paſſed; he told us
that the papers delivered the day before had been withdrawn,
and that he did not care what range we took either on the
law, or the fact. Mr. Chaſe alſo ſaid: " The papers are withdrawn; and you may take what courſe in the defence you
pleaſe; but it is at the hazard of your characters." I thought
the expreſſion was in the nature of a menace; that it was un-
kind, improper, and unneceſſary, Mr. Lewis obſerved, in effect: " You have withdrawn the papers; but can you eradi-
cate from your own minds the opinion which you have formed; or the effect of your declaration on the attending jurors,
a part of whom muſt try the priſoner?" Mr. Chaſe ſaid: "If
you think to embarraſs the court, you will find yourſelves miſtaken." He then aſked Fries, if he choſe to have other coun-

fel affigned ? Fries anfwered, that he did not know how to
act, but that he thought he would leave it to the court and
the jury. On which judge Chafe exclaimed ; " Then we will
be your counfel; and, by the blefling of God, do you as much
juftice, as thofe who were affigned to you." Mr. Lewis and
I had vifited Fries in prifon during the preceding afternoon ;
we had told him our determination to withdraw from his defence, unlefs he and his friends wifhed us to refume it; and
we declared it to be, in our view of the cafe, his beft chance
to efcape, as we could entertain no hope of changing the opinion of the court. He, finally, left the matter to us ; and,
I think, Mr. Lewis, in my hearing, with my concurrence, ad-
vifed him not to accept other counfel, if the court fhould offer
to affign them. The reft of the facts, as ftated by Mr. Lewis,
correfpond fo precifely with my recollection, that I prefume,
after this recognition, it is unneceffary to repeat them. I wifh
it, however, to be properly underftood, that on the fecond day,
both the judges were extremely anxious to prevail on us to
proceed in the defence; and, as I underftood, withdrew all
the reftrictions of the preceding day. We perfifted, however,
in our determination ; becaufe after what had happened, we
deemed it the beft chance to fave our client's life ; and not becaufe we wifhed (as has been infinuated) to bring the court
into difgrace or odium. Fries was, accordingly, tried, and
convicted without counfel.

It is, perhaps, proper to ftate, what paffed on the firft trial
of Fries, as it has been much mifunderftood, or mifreprefent-
ed. The general courfe of argument, *on the facts*, was an
endeavor to fhew that the acts of Fries and his companions
amounted to nothing more than a riotous oppofition to the
direct tax officers, or obftruction of the marfhal in the execution of procefs ; and the refcue of a particular defcription
of prifoners, whom the marfhal had arrefted. We drew to
our aid, in this part of the difcuffion, the fections of the penal
law, and the fedition act, which provided for the punifhment
of fuch offences, diftinct from the crime of treafon. The general courfe of our argument, on the law, was an endeavor
to fhew, that the offence did not amount to an act of levying war againft the United States. The conftitution defines
that to be the only treafon that can be committed ; and neither the legiflature, nor the courts, can amplify, or alter, the
definition. The words of the conftitution, however, require

a practical expofition. This expofition can only be obtained by a confideration of the natural, the familiar, and the reafonable import of the words themfelves, or by a reference to the gloffary of the Englifh decifions on the fame branch of treafon, expreffed in the fame terms, in the Englifh ftatute of *Edward* 3. The gloffary of the Englifh decifions ought not to be relied on. It is true, that fince the Englifh revolution of 1688, and, particularly, fince the ftatute of *William* 3, (which firft gave judicial freedom to the Englifh bench) the judges of England have been independent, as well as wife and virtuous ; and implicit confidence may be repofed in their judgments, upon all matters originally fubmitted to their jurifdiction. But the Englifh judges, fince the revolution of 1688, are bound to adminifter the law, according to the precedents eftablifhed by the Englifh judges, before that revolution ; although, either in criminal, or in civil matters, if the queftion were *res integra*, they would themfelves, have decided in a different way. Hence, the counfel of Fries were induced to cite common law authorities, and authorities under the ftatute of Edward 3, to fhew (not what the law of England was or ought to be, not what the law of the United States was, or ought to be, but) what had been the extravagance of dependent judges, in fetting the precedents, which the independent judges of England were bound to follow. Among other books they read Blackftone's commentaries, where, in illuftration of a pofitive or imputed treafon, the commentator cites the cafes (under the ftatute of Edward 3,) of one man being hung as a traitor, for faying that his fon was heir to the crown, becaufe he was himfelf the owner of a tavern, with the fign of the crown ; and of another man's meeting the fame fate, becaufe he wifhed the horn of his buck, which had been killed by the king, in the belly of the monarch. Thefe were, indeed, the illuftrations of Blackftone, and not of Fries's counfel ; but what profeffional man need be afhamed, to be fuppofed capable of reforting to the fame authorities, to enforce an argument, which Blackftone had employed! Though the Englifh judges were thus bound by precedents eftablifhed in very bad times of the juridical hiftory of England, Fries's counfel contended that the American judges were not under the fame obligation ; and that the era of our federal conftitution furnifhed a favorable opportunity to emancipate ourfelves from the trammels of conftructions given to the words of our conftitution by corrupt and dependent courts, before the Englifh revolution. Reforting, then, to the natural, familiar, and reafonable, import of the words, it was urged in defence of Fries, on the firft trial, that it was not a cafe of treafon, but of riot, obftruction of procefs, and refcue of prifoners; that the difcrimination in the offences, was marked by the very diftinct nature of the actions; and that the fedition act having treated the latter cafe, as a cafe of mifdemeanor, it was a legiflative conftruction, that it was not a cafe of treafon. There was ftill ground enough for the conftitutional provifion to occupy (an attempt by force to fubvert the government, to defeat the legitimate operation of its principal departments, to attack, or to refift, its military power, &c.) and, after the paffing of the fedition act, it might be prefumed, fuch ground alone was intended to be occupied.

On this courfe of argument, we could not afcertain the opinion of the court, nor how far the cafe of the Weftern infurrection would be deemed to apply, till the charge was pronounced. But, after hearing the charge, and after a new trial was granted, I confefs the whole force of my mind was bent to fhew, on the new trial, the ftrong diftinction between the cafes of 1794, and thofe of 1799; and that, even in England, there was no authority fince the revolution of 1688, for conftruing the offence of Fries to be treafon, unconnected with the obligation of the judges, to conform to the previous adjudications.

The *Prefident.* Both you and Mr. Lewis have ftated, that the jury were prefent when the written opinions of the court were handed to the clerk: Could they hear what paffed on the occafion?

Mr. *Dallas.* Undoubtedly, fir; I do not mean, however, the jury who tried Fries; but the general pannel of jurors, from whom Fries's jury might have been taken.

The court rofe about 4 o'clock.

MONDAY, *February* 11, 1805.

The court was opened at 12 o'clock.

Prefent, the Managers, attended by the Houfe of Reprefentatives in committee of the whole: and Judge Chafe, attended by his counfel.

Mr. *Randolph* obferved, that it was the wifh of the Managers that there fhould be no departure from the ordinary rules obferved in examining witneffes, and that immediately after their examination on the part of the profecution, they might be crofs examined by the counfel for the accufed.

Mr. *Harper* hoped, that no abfolute rule would be adopted to this effect, as circumftances might arife that would juftify a departure from it. The counfel for the refpondent would without any fpecial rule endeavor to conform to the mode fuggefted. After a few further remarks from Mr. Martin and Mr. Nicholfon, it was agreed to wave any fpecific motion.

Mr. *Lewis* was called in; when

Mr. *Harper* put to him the following queftion :

Did you at the firft trial of Fries make a diftinction between refiftance to a particular law, and the general law of the United States, or fome fpecial laws of a peculiar nature, and ftate your intention to argue that point on the fecond trial.

Mr. *Lewis*. I was not able to anfwer the queftion the other day precifely. But having fince looked at my notes, I find that that diftinction was made and urged.

EDWARD TILGHMAN *fworn.*

I was prefent at the circuit court of the United States, for the diftrict of Pennfylvania, held on the 22d day of April, 1800. A very fhort time after the opening of the court (whether the general pannel of jurors had been called over or not, I do not recollect) judge Chafe declared that the court had maturely confidered the law arifing on the overt acts charged in the indictment againft John Fries ; and that they had reduced their opinion to writing ; he mentioned that he underftood that a great deal of time had been confumed on a former trial, and that in order to fave time, a copy of the opinion of the court would be given to the attorney of the diftrict ; another to the counfel for the prifoner, and that the jury fhould have a third to take out with them. I took no notes of what paffed either on the firft or fecond day. Fries was tried on the third day, and having been appointed with Mr. Levy, counfel for Heany and Getman, indicted for treafon, and who were actually tried on the 27th or 28th, I deemed it my duty to attend the trial of Fries, to take notes of the evidence, the arguments and the charge of the judge. I do not recollect that judge Chafe faid any more on the firft day than what I have mentioned previous to his throwing a paper or papers on the table round which the bar ufually fit. The moment the paper or papers were thrown on the table, judge Chafe expreffed himfelf in thefe words: " Neverthelefs, or notwithftanding this, (I cannot recollect which expreffion he ufed) " counfel will be heard." The throwing of the papers on the table and the addrefs of the judge caufed fome degree of agitation at the bar; in a fhort time after the judge ufed the laft expreffion, I looked round and faw Mr. Lewis walking from under the gallery, towards the bar: I ftepped towards Mr. Lewis, and met him directly oppofite the entrance into the prifoner's bar. The prifoner, as well as I recollect, not being then in court, but being brought into court fome time that morning, I entered into converfation with Mr. Lewis, and as well as I can recollect, during that converfation, Mr. Dallas came into court. Mr. Dallas and Mr. Lewis had fome converfation in my hearing, after which they came forward to the bar; the paper, as well as I can recollect, was then handed by Mr. Caldwell, the clerk of the court, to Mr. Lewis. Mr. Lewis caft his eyes on the outfide of the paper, and looked down, as if he was confidering what to fay. He threw the paper from him, as it appeared to me, without reading it, and the moment he threw the paper down, faid, " my hand fhall never be ftained by receiving a paper containing a prejudged opinion, or an opinion made up without hearing counfel." I cannot recollect which was the expreffion, but this was the fubftance. I have not the leaft recollection that any thing paffed on the firft day, between the counfel for the prifoner and the court; for when Mr. Lewis ufed thefe expreffions, his face was not turned to the court, and he fpoke with a confiderable degree of warmth; the court fat in the fouth part of the room, and Mr. Lewis (I think) turned his face full to the weftward, when he ufed thefe expreffions. The paper lay on the table a confiderable time; after which fome gentlemen of the bar took it up, and I for one copied it. Whether I took the whole of it, and all the authorities cited, I cannot fay. The prifoner having been brought into court, his counfel had a good deal of converfation in my hearing, on the fubject of fupporting or abandoning his defence; that converfation appears to me to have been accurately ftated by Mr. Lewis and Mr. Dallas. I do not recollect why the prifoner was not put on his trial that day, but the court adjourned between 12 and 1 o'clock. I went home, and after taking a walk, on returning, I faw the diftrict attorney on my fteps. He afked me whether I would have any objection to delivering up the copy which I had taken of the opinion of the court. I faid I had no objection, and gave it to him. That paper was not read on the firft, or on any other day by the court, or any thing ftated by the court, as the fubftance of it. On the next morning, to wit: the 23d, the prifoner was brought into court. The court afked the prifoner's counfel, if they were ready to proceed to the trial. Mr. Lewis rofe and uttered a few words, in order to fhew that they did not mean to proceed with it. Judge Chafe here interrupted Mr. Lewis—the particular expreffions of the judge I do not recollect; the fubftance of them was, that the counfel were not to confider themfelves bound by the opinion which the court had reduced to writing the day before; that the counfel were at liberty on both fides to combat that opinion. Judge Chafe as well as judge Peters appeared to be very anxious that the counfel fhould undertake the defence of the prifoner. Judge Chafe faid, the cafes at common law before the ftatute of Edward the Third, ought not to be read to the court: he mentioned the cafe of a man whofe ftag the king had killed, and who faid he wifhed the ftag's horns was in the king's belly; he alfo mentioned the man who kept a public houfe, with the fign of the crown, and faid he would make his fon heir to the crown. He faid fuch cafes as thefe muft not, fhall not be cited; and I think he made ufe of thefe expreffions: " What! cafes from Rome, Turkey and France!" That the counfel fhould go into the law, but muft not cite cafes that were not law. He faid that he had an opinion in point of law as to every cafe that could be brought before the court, or elfe he was not fit to fit there. He faid fomething (but the precife words I do not pretend to recollect) as to the counfel proceeding according to their confciences; he faid that the gentlemen would proceed at the hazard of their character, and when it appeared pretty plain, that the gentlemen would not proceed in defence of the prifoner, he faid you may think to put the court to difficulties; but if you do, you mifs your aim, or words in fubftance to that effect. Judge Peters addreffed the counfel, and faid if an error has been committed, why may it not be redreffed? The paper has been withdrawn—and I think both the judges concurred in exprefling the fentiment that matters were to be confidered as if the paper had never been thrown on the table. When judge Peters mentioned that the paper had been withdrawn, Mr. Lewis anfwered, the paper, it is true, is withdrawn, but how can the court erafe from their minds an opinion formed without hearing counfel. A good deal more paffed which I do not recollect, having taken no notes. Mr. Dallas addreffed the court, but I have no recollection of what he faid. The counfel continued firm in their determination to abandon the prifoner: the court took great pains to induce them to act as counfel for the prifoner, and before Fries was remanded to jail, expreffed their hope that the counfel would think better of it, and appear in his defence. I recollect nothing more of what happened on the fecond day. Should any queftions be put to me, they may awaken a recollection of what does not now occur to me.

On the third day when the prifoner was brought to the bar, he was afked whether he had any counfel (I think on the fecond day, the court had mentioned to him that he might have other counfel) he faid no, he would depend on the court to be his counfel. Judge Chafe faid, the court will be your counfel, and by the blefling of God, will ferve you as effectually as your counfel could have done. The trial proceeded, and after the teftimony was given and a fhort ftatement of the cafe made by the diftrict attorney, the judge charged the jury; he told them they were judges of the law as well as the fact. He ftated to them that cafes determined in England, before their revolution, fhould not be received by the court. I have my notes of the charge; he ftated the law very much in the manner as it was ftated by judge Paterfon in the trial of Mitchell for whom I was counfel. I cannot undertake to recollect any thing further than I have already ftated.

Mr. *Randolph.* I underftood you to have ftated that the written paper thrown or handed down by judge Chafe on the table produced a confiderable degree of agitation at the bar. From what do you conceive that agitation arofe?

Mr. *Harper* faid he would take the opinion of the court, at fome ftage of the bufinefs, as to what was proper teftimony. On Saturday there had been opinion and argument interwoven in the teftimony given. He paid great deference to the opinion of the witnefs, but he fubmitted it to the decifion of the court whether it was proper to require it.

The *Prefident.* The gentleman may vary the queftion, fo as to attain his object, by enquiring as to the facts that took place.

Mr. *Randolph* then faid, I afk, with the permiffion of the court, whether in the courfe of your practice, which I under-ftand to have been long and extenfive, you have ever witneff-ed a fimilar proceeding.

Mr. *Key.* I fhall object to that queftion. I pray the opi-nion of the court, whether, in order to abridge time——

The *Prefident* defired that the queftion might be in the firft inftance reduced to writing.

It was accordingly reduced to writing as follows:

Queftion 1ft. You fay that when the written opinion of the court was thrown on the table, it produced confiderable agita-tion among the gentlemen of the bar. What did you conceive to be the caufe of that agitation?—which being read by the fecretary,

Mr. *Bayard* moved that the Senate fhould withdraw—the motion was loft on a divifion.

The queftion was then taken on receiving the propofed ques-tion, and paffed in the negative by an unanimous vote.

Mr. *Randolph* then fubmitted in writing,

Queftion 2d. In the courfe of your practice, which is un-derftood to have been long and extenfive, did you ever witnefs a fimilar proceeding on the part of the court?

To the putting of this queftion, Mr. *Martin* withdrew the objection which had previoufly been made.

Mr. *Tilghman* anfwered. I have been in the practice of the law for thirty-one years, and have no recollection of a fimilar proceeding.

Mr. *Randolph.* When Mr. Chafe, after throwing or hand-ing down the papers, went on to fay that counfel would be heard, did he go on to fay, or not, that counfel, when heard, muft addrefs themfelves to the court and not to the jury.

Mr. *Tilghman.* I am confident that at that time he faid nothing of the fort, nor do I recollect that he faid any fuch thing at any other time. If he did it efcaped my recollection, which is very ftrong, as to what was faid by the judge when he threw down the paper or papers.

Mr. *Harper.* You have faid that you are perfectly clear, that when the paper was delivered or thrown down, the court did not fay the counfel muft addrefs themfelves to the court and not to the jury, and I underſtand you alſo to ſay that you have no recollection that they ſaid any ſuch thing at any other time.

Mr. *Tilghman*. I have no recollection that they did.

Mr. *Harper*. Have you any recollection that the court at that time prevented the counſel from proceeding?

Mr. *Tilghman*. I have not.

Mr. *Harper*. Did the court forbid them during the proceedings, or on the trial, to cite caſes?

Mr. *Tilghman*. There were no counſel at the trial.

Mr. *Harper*. Did judge Chaſe at any time ſay that they would prohibit their reading the acts of Congreſs to the jury?

Mr. *Tilghman*. I do not recollect that he did.

Mr. *Harper*. Was any thing ſaid about the ſedition law, and the act——

Mr. *Tilghman*. I do not recollect that there was.

Mr. *Harper*. Did judge Chaſe expreſs any diſapprobation of the conduct of the circuit court on a former trial in ſuffering thoſe acts to be read?

Mr. *Tilghman*. I do not recollect that he did.

Mr. *Hopkinſon*. I think you have ſtated that you attended the trial of John Fries throughout?

Mr. *Tilghman*. I did.

Mr. *Hopkinſon*. Did you ſee any diſpoſition, or act, or conduct of the court calculated to oppreſs the priſoner?

Mr. *Nicholſon* objected to this queſtion being put, and Mr. Hopkinſon ſaid, that to avoid all difficulty, he would wave it.

Mr. *Martin*. Has it been the uſual practice in the courts of Pennſylvania for the judges to declare to the jury what is the law in criminal caſes?

Mr. *Tilghman*. They always in their charge to the jury ſtate the law and the evidence, and apply the law to the evidence.

To an interrogatory offered by Mr. Martin,

Mr. *Tilghman* anſwered. The court generally hear the counſel at large on the law, and they are permitted to addreſs the jury on the law and the fact; after which the counſel for the ſtate concludes; the court then ſtates the evidence to the jury, and their opinion of the law, but leaves the deciſion of both law and fact to the jury.

To another interrogatory of Mr. *Martin* as to the practice of the courts, Mr. *Tilghman* replied, that counſel generally take that courſe which they conſider beſt calculated to benefit their clients. In capital cafes, he did not recollect the court ftopping gentlemen of character in any courfe they thought fit to adopt.

Mr. *Nicholfon.* In your practice in Pennfylvania, or Delaware, where I underftand you have practiced, did you ever hear the court undertake to inform the jury of their opinion of the law before the prifoner's counfel had been heard.

Mr. *Tilghman.* I do not recollect I ever did.

In anfwer to a queftion,

Mr. *Tilghman* faid, in the charge to the jury, the contents of the paper containing the opinion of the court, and which had been withdrawn, were never alluded to; nor in the leaft alluded to when it was thrown down or delivered.

Mr. *Nicholfon.* You have ftated that the opinion was not read to the jury. I afk whether when this paper was laid on the table the jury was fworn?

Mr. *Tilghman.* No. They were not fworn till the next day but one.

Mr. *Nicholfon.* Were the general pannel then in court?

Mr. *Tilghman.* According to my recollection the general pannel attended with great punctuality. I this morning looked over my notes and I took down thofe that were challenged by Fries, and thofe that tried him, in order to affift me in making my challenge in the cafe of Heany and Getman. But I do not know that I then faw the face of any of them. It is proper to ftate that the common jury as foon as the court is opened generally walk forward into the jury box, which holds only eleven, a chair being placed for the twelfth—The other jurors take their feats behind thofe in another box, or remain in the hall of the court.

Mr. *Nicholfon.* The judge declared that the counfel for the prifoner might proceed at the hazard of their characters?

Mr. *Tilghman.* I think thofe were the words he ufed.

Mr. *Nicholfon.* Were the general pannel, at this time, in a fituation to hear what was faid?

Mr. *Tilghman.* Certainly, fir, this was on the fecond day.

Mr. *Randolph.* Before the written opinion was handed down, did not Mr. Chafe or the court declare that the queftion of law had been fettled in the cafe of Vigol and Mitchell?

Mr. *Tilghman.* On the trial of Fries they did cite this cafe and rely upon it. If the court will indulge me I can turn to my notes. Judge Chafe ftated the opinion of the court in his charge to the jury to be the fame as in the-cafe of Vigol and Mitchell.

Mr. Randolph. Did he fay that the opinion in the cafe of Vigol and Mitchell was the opinion contained in that paper?

Mr. Tilghman. I do not remember. Many things might have happened, of which I have no recollection as I did not take notes at the time.

Mr. Campbell. How many of thofe papers were thrown down or given to the clerk?

Mr. Tilghman. I cannot fay with perfect certainty. But I ftated before that one was handed to the attorney of the diftrict, another to the counfel for the prifoner, and the third to the jury to take out with them.

Mr. Campbell. Was there fufficient time before the papers were withdrawn, for the jurors or other perfons to have read them?

Mr. Tilghman. I ftated before that the court rofe between twelve and one o'clock. The jury were not in a fituation to have accefs to the bar table. After the paper lay for fome time, feveral of the bar employed themfelves in copying it. I have no recollection that any one of the papers were handed into the jury box.

Prefident. At what hour were they withdrawn?

Mr. Tilghman. I think on the fame day, between one and two o'clock, that the diftrict attorney called on me. I am pretty certain that the papers thrown down were not taken away, but remained in the hands of the court.

Mr. Campbell. Can you fay how many copies were taken?

Mr. Tilghman. Not precifely. I took one, and Mr. Thomas Rofs another. I believe we copied them at the fame time. But I do not know of my own knowledge that any other perfon tranfcribed them. Now I recollect, I think I faw one or two others alfo taking copies.

Mr. Campbell. Do you know whether all thofe taken were withdrawn?

Mr. Tilghman. I do not. I only know that mine was withdrawn.

Mr. Nicholfon. Did you hear the fubject fpoken of generally that day?

Mr. Tilghman. Thofe who copied the paper fpoke on the fubject to each other.

Mr. Nicholfon. I afk whether it was a fubject of general converfation?

Mr. *Tilghman.* Very much fo among the gentlemen of the bar.

Mr. *Nicholfon.* You have faid that it is a ufual thing in the courts of Pennfylvania for the judge to charge the jury after the counfel on both fides have fpoken. Do you recollect to have feen a court reduce their charge to writing, and give it to the jury?

Mr. *Tilghman.* Never.

Wm. S. BIDDLE *fworn.*

Mr. *Randolph.* Were you prefent at the trial of John Fries?

Anfwer. I was.

Mr. *Randolph.* Were you prefent when the written opinion of the court was handed down?

A. From the length of time which has paffed I have not a very diftinct recollection of the circumftances that occurred.

Mr. *Randolph.* Did you take a copy of that opinion, and was that copy the whole or a part of it?

A. I did take a copy in part; I took the fubftance in regard to the point of treafon, but I believe I did not copy the whole.

Mr. *Randolph.* Were there other copies taken?

A. I know of one taken by Mr. Rawle.

Mr. *Randolph.* Was any application ever made to you to deliver up the copy in order to deftroy it?

A. Never.

Mr. *Randolph.* Did you communicate to any perfons the fubftance of the copy?

A. Never, until during the laft feffion of Congrefs, in converfation with Mr. Dallas, I mentioned my being poffeffed of it, and he expreffing a defire to fee it, I ftepped over to my office and brought it.

Mr. *Randolph.* Although you did not take a copy of it verbatim, did you take the fubftance of it?

A. I did.

Mr. *Randolph.* Would you know that copy?

A. I fubfcribed my name to it.

Mr. *Randolph.* Is that the paper? (fhewing him a paper.)

A. Yes, it is.

Mr. *Randolph.* Did you hear much converfation about the paper at that time?

A. I have no diftinct recollection; I attended the trial óf Fries and others for treafon, but I do not recollect any converfation about it.

Mr. *Randolph.* Can you tell whether the contents became known to any of the jurors?

A. I cannot.

Mr. *Harper.* I obferve the paper contains notes and references to authorities; were they taken from the paper handed down by the court, or were they made by yourfelf?

A. I cannot fay as to thofe at the bottom; thofe at the end were all my own.

Mr. *Martin.* Do you know whether the judges or the diftrict attorney knew you had a copy?

A. I do not.

WM. RAWLE *affirmed.*

The circuit court of the United States fat in Philadelphia in April, 1800. As the former proceedings in relation to the prifoners indicted for treafon were confidered at an end, except from the intervention of an act of Congrefs, it appeared to me moft regular to quafh all the previous proceedings. I made a motion to this effect, which was granted. On the fame day the court charged the grand jury, and I fent to them bills againft John Fries, and other perfons charged with treafon and other offences. The bill againft John Fries was returned on the 16th a true bill, and he was immediately brought up, arraigned and pleaded not guilty. Meffrs. Lewis and Dallas appeared as counfel for Fries. Copies of the indictment, and lifts of the jurors and witneffes were furnifhed to Fries as directed by law. The bringing on the trial was poftponed on account of the abfence of George Mitchel, whom I deemed to be a material witnefs. According to my beft recollection it was not intended that John Fries fhould be tried on the 22d, the firft day alluded to. I cannot fay that John Fries was then at the bar. That circumftance does not appear on the minutes of the clerk of the court. It was certainly not my intention that he fhould have been brought up, but he may poffibly have been brought through miftake. Shortly after the court met, judge Chafe obferved, that as much time had been loft on the former trial or trials, the court had determined to exprefs their opinion in writing, on the point of law, that they might not be mifunderftood ; that they had therefore committed that opinion to writing, and that the clerk had made copies of it, one of which fhould be given to the diftrict attorney, one to the counfel for the prifoner ; and one the jury fhould take out with them : as thefe words were pronounced, feveral papers, I think three, were handed down or thrown down, as it were ; my back was to the court, and whether this was done by judge Chafe or the clerk, I know not. I immediately took up the one intended for me and began to read it, but cafting my eyes to the oppofite fide of the table, I faw Mr. Lewis with another copy before him, looking at it, apparently with great indignation, and then throwing it on the table. I am pretty clear that nothing paffed between the court and the counfel in the courfe of that morning. I obferved much agitation among the gentlemen of the bar, who were converfing with each other with apparent warmth; but having at that time, a very great burthen of criminal profecutions on me, my attention was much engaged, and I did not hear diftinctly what was faid, nor did I know, until the court rofe, that there was a probability of the counfel for John Fries declining to act. I think that twenty-one perfons were that day brought before the court charged with feditious combinations, and who fubmitted to the court. The court rofe pretty early in the morning, and intimated that I fhould not call any witneffes in relation to the fubmiffions until the trials for treafon were over. When the court rofe I learnt from feveral gentlemen, that Mr. Lewis and Mr. Dallas were difgufted with the conduct of the court, and meant to decline acting as counfel for Fries, and I have an indiftinct recollection that I heard fomething of this kind drop from Mr. Dallas himfelf. I went home, and had been there but a few minutes, when judge Chafe and judge Peters came in. We went into another room, and judge Peters began by expreffing a good deal of uneafinefs, from an apprehenfion that the gentlemen affigned as counfel for John Fries would not go on. Judge Chafe faid he could not fuppofe that that would be the confequence. I fupported the idea which judge Peters had expreffed; I told him the gentlemen of the Philadelphia bar were men of much independence and character, and that unlefs thofe papers were withdrawn, and the bufinefs conducted as ufual at our bar, they probably would defift from conducting the defence. My recollection at this diftance of time cannot be very diftinct, but I am pretty well fatisfied that judge Chafe expreffed his regret that the conduct of the court fhould be fo taken, and faid, that he did not mean, that any thing which he had done fhould preclude the counfel from making a defence in the ufual manner. Judge Peters afked if I would confent to go out, and undertake to recover the papers. I faid I had no objection, and both the judges concurred in requefting me to do fo. I recollected feeing Mr. Edward Tilghman and Mr. Thomas Rofs engaged in making copies—I did not recollect to have feen any others fo engaged. I went to their houfes and afked for the copies, which were readily given, and took them to Mr. Caldwell, clerk of the court. I afked him if he had noticed any others to have been taken? He faid, he thought a copy had been taken by Mr. William Meredith. I defired him to go to him and endeavor to recall it. I did not know that Mr. Biddle, who was then a ftudent in my office, had taken a copy in part, or I fhould have defired him to give it up. From fome circumftances which I do not recollect, I find that I did not hand my own copy to Mr. Caldwell. I now have it in my poffeffion. The paper was not read, I think, by any but thofe who tranfcribed it, and I entertained an anxious hope, after what had taken place, that the gentlemen would proceed with the defence of the prifoner. I fhall now take the liberty of referring to fome original notes made by me at the time—from which I can ftate what paffed the following morning. So far as they go, I believe them accurate, though they may not enable me to relate all that was faid. On the 23d April, John Fries was brought and put to the bar, Meffrs. Lewis and Dallas attending. The court afked if we were ready to proceed. Mr. Lewis rofe and faid, if employed by the prifoner, I fhould think myfelf bound to proceed, but being affigned—he was here interrupted by judge Chafe, who faid, " you are not bound by the opinion delivered yefterday, you may conteft it on both fides." Mr. Lewis anfwered, I underftood that the court had made up their minds, and as the prifoner's counfel have a right to make a full defence, and addrefs the jury both on the law and the fact, it would place me in too degrading a fituation, and therefore I will not proceed. Judge Chafe anfwered with apparent impatience— " You are at liberty to proceed as you think proper, and addrefs the jury and lay down the law as you think proper." Mr. Lewis anfwered with confiderable emphafis, I will never addrefs the court in a criminal cafe on a queftion of law. He then took a pretty extenfive view on the propriety of going into cafes decided before the revolution, and faid, if he was precluded from fhewing that the judges fince the revolution in England had confidered themfelves bound by the decifions before the revolution, which ought not to be the doctrine in this country, he muft decline acting as counfel for the pri-foner. Judge Chafe anfwered, fir, you muft do as you pleafe. Mr. Dallas then addreffed the court. He contended that the rights of advocates had been encroached upon by the proceedings of the day before. He went into a general view of the ground taken by Mr. Lewis, and concluded with his determination not to proceed as counfel for John Fries.

Judge Chafe then obferved—no opinion has been given as to facts in this cafe. I would not let the witneffes be examined in the combination cafes becaufe I would not let the jury hear them before the trial of Fries came on. As to the law I knew that the trial before had taken nine days—that many common law cafes were cited, fuch as wifhing a ftag's horns in the king's belly, and that of a man's faying he would make his fon heir to the crown; fuch cafes ought not, fhall not go to the jury. No cafe can come before me on which I have not a decided opinion as to the law, otherwife I fhould not be fit to prefide here. I have always conducted myfelf with candor, and I meant, gentlemen, to fave you trouble. It is not refpectful, nor is it the duty of counfel, to fay they have a right to offer any thing they pleafe. What! decifions in Rome, France, Turkey? No lawyer will fay that common law cafes are law under the ftatute of Edward the Third, nor juf-tify thofe judges who overfet the ftatute of William, and over-rule the neceffity of having two witneffes to one overt act, and admit hearfay teftimony to prove matters of fact. It is the duty of counfel to lay down the law, but not to read cafes that are not law. Having thus explained the meaning of the court, you will ftand acquitted or condemned to your own confciences, as you think proper to act. But, gentlemen, do as you pleafe. The courfe will be, the diftrict attorney will open the law, ftate his cafe, and produce his witneffes. You are at liberty to controvert the law as to the matter, but the manner muft be regulated by the court. Judge Peters faid you are to confider every thing done yefterday as withdrawn. Mr. Lewis replied, true, fir, the papers are withdrawn, but the fentiments ftill remain, I fhall not therefore act.

Mr. Dallas expreffed the fame determination, which I did not take down.

A paufe, for a few moments, took place, when judge Chafe faid, you cannot put the court into a difficulty, by this conduct, gentlemen; you do not know me if you think fo; and defiring the perfons between him and the prifoner to ftand afide, and addreffing himfelf to John Fries, he afked, are you defirous of having other counfel affigned you, or will you go on to trial without? John Fries, after a paufe, faid he did not know what to do; he would leave it to the court. Under thefe circumftances I felt a repugnance to go on with the trial, not wifhing to act in a cafe fo extremely fingular. I therefore moved to poftpone the trial to the next day; the court readily concurred, and Fries was remanded to jail.

On the 24th, Fries was brought to the bar again. Judge Chafe afked him if he had any counfel. He told the court that he relied on them as his counfel, and he expreffed himfelf with a degree of firmnefs and compofure that convinced me that his decifion was formed on mature reflection. Then, judge Chafe anfwered, by the bleffing of God we will be your counfel, and do you as much juftice as thofe affigned you.

The jury were then called over, and the court took pains to inform Fries of his right to challenge 35 without caufe; and as many others as he could fhew caufe againft. In every inftance they appeared extremely anxious that he fhould defend himfelf. There were one or two friends near him, I believe, to affift him in his challenges. After the jurors had been feverally paffed by him, and before they were fworn, the court directed that they fhould feverally be afked whether they had delivered an opinion on the fubject. The firft juror faid he had not, and was fworn; the fecond faid he had; he was then fworn to make true anfwers; and he declared that he had in a converfation faid that thefe men ought to be punifhed; the court directed this perfon to be fet afide, and he was not fworn on the trial.

The court afterwards directed the queftion to be fomewhat altered.—" Have you formed *or* delivered an opinion, &c.?" Before this queftion was put to more than three perfons, it was again altered, and put in thefe words: " Have you formed *and* delivered an opinion?" Three, including the one already mentioned, anfwered affirmatively, and were fet afide. The prifoner challenged, without caufe, thirty-four of the pannel. Twelve jurors were then sworn, and I opened the cafe in a very brief manner, laid down the law, and adduced the teftimony. The trial lafted till the afternoon, and till the next day; the court retired twice for refrefhment and repofe. John Fries called no witneffes. But at the end of the examination of each witnefs called on the part of the profecution, judge Chafe reminded him that he had a right to put any queftion to the witnefs that he thought proper, and told him to be cautious not to put any queftion the anfwer to which might injure him. When the evidence on the part of the profecution had clofed, John Fries expreffed his determination to call none on his part. I then addreffed the jury in as brief a manner as I could, confiftent with the duty I had to perform, for I feverely felt the unpleafantnefs of the fituation in which I ftood, acting againft a man tried on a capital charge without profeffional affiftance. The court then charged the jury, who retired, and in about half an hour returned with a verdict of guilty. Thefe are all the general facts I recollect in relation to the trial.

Mr. *Randolph.* Did you on the firft day, the 22d of April, hear Mr. Lewis exprefs in court any fentiments in regard to the paper which you fay he viewed with fuch indignation?

Mr. *Rawle.* I have no recollection of hearing Mr. Lewis fay one word on that day.

Mr. *Randolph.* You ftated that on the next day, Mr. Lewis, when told by the court to proceed as he thought proper, anfwered that he never would addrefs the court in a criminal cafe on a point of law, and urged the propriety of citing cafes before the revolution, to fhew that the Englifh judges fince the revolution thought themfelves bound by cafes before the revolution, which ought not to be the law in this country, and that if he was not permitted to do this, he would be obliged to abandon the defence?

Mr. *Rawle.* Yes fir.

Mr. *Randolph.* Did you hear any opinion given by the court, which warranted Mr. Lewis in the opinion that he was precluded from citing fuch cafes?

Mr. *Rawle.* On the 23d I did underftand the court to fay that fuch cafes fhould not be cited, becaufe they tended to miflead the jury. But at no time did I hear the court fay that counfel were precluded from addreffing the jury on the law, but it was faid that as to the authorities cited, it muft be determined by the court, whether they were admiffible or not.

Mr. *Randolph.* You ftated that both the judges after the adjournment came to your houfe. Was your houfe their place of abode?

Mr. *Rawle.* No fir.

Mr. *Randolph.* At what hour did they call?

Mr. *Rawle.* About ten o'clock.

Mr. *Randolph.* And that judge Peters expreffed an aprehenfion that Meffrs. Lewis and Dallas would not go on?

Mr. *Rawle.* Yes fir.

Mr. *Randolph.* On what grounds did he exprefs this apprehenfion?

Mr. *Rawle.* I do not know.

Mr. *Randolph.* Have you any recollection of any grounds for fuch an apprehenfion, except that which arofe from the general character of the bar.

Mr. *Rawle.* I have already ftated that I underftood there was a meafure of that kind in contemplation. I have a faint recollection of having heard fomething of that kind fall from Mr. Dallas.

Mr. *Randolph.* Did you exprefs to the judges that your opinion was drawn from any other fource than your general knowledge of the bar?

Mr. *Rawle.* I do not recollect that I did.

Mr. *Randolph.* Mr. Chafe expreffed his regret, and faid he did not mean to preclude the counfel from proceeding in the trial in the ufual manner. Was the courfe purfued in the cafe of Fries in the ufual manner?

Mr. *Rawle.* I never faw a fimilar circumftance take place at our bar during the whole courfe of my life.

Mr. *Randolph.* Is it ufual for the court to give a general opinion on the law before counfel are heard?

Mr. *Rawle.* Never, except on their general charge to the grand jury. They fometimes enquire of the gentlemen who profecute, what are the offences likely to be prefented, in order to inform the grand jury what it is their duty to do, and to make their charge more pointed.

Mr. *Randolph.* Did you ever hear of its being done in a particular cafe before the court?

Mr. *Rawle.* Not that I recollect.

Mr. *Randolph.* Do you know whether much converfation took place at the bar on this novel opinion thrown down on the table?

Mr. *Rawle.* I ſtated before that I had a great burthen of criminal caſes to manage; as I was ſituated it was not in my power to keep up the uſual colloquial intercourſe, and I cannot recollect any converſation until that which I have mentioned.

Mr. *Randolph.* Do you ſuppoſe that the act of delivering the opinion in writing was ſo public as to attract the notice of the jurymen that were attending?

Mr. *Rawle.* From the number of the jurymen, and from the conſtruction of the court room, I think that a conſiderable proportion muſt have paid attention to the tranſaction.

Mr. *Randolph.* If you heard Mr. Lewis uſe no language on the opinion of the court, whence do you infer his indignation?

Mr. *Rawle.* From his countenance, and the manner of his throwing down the paper?

Mr. *Randolph.* Was it ſuch as to attract the attention of thoſe in court?

Mr. *Rawle.* If they ſaw him, they muſt have been ſtruck with the manner in which he expreſſed his indignation. It was very ſtrong.

Mr. *Randolph.* Did you hear Mr. Chaſe ſay, that if the priſoner's counſel had any objection as to the law, as laid down by the court, they muſt addreſs the court and not the jury?

Mr. *Rawle.* I have no recollection of hearing ſuch an expreſſion fall from judge Chaſe at any time.

Mr. *Nicholſon.* You ſtated much of your teſtimony from your notes. I would aſk, ſir, were thoſe notes taken at the time, and in the order they ſtand arranged?

Mr. *Rawle.* Preciſely ſo, ſir. I made my notes in court.

Mr. *Nicholſon.* What was there in the conduct of judge Chaſe that induced the counſel to infer that they would be precluded from citing the ſtatutes of the United States which have been referred to?

Mr. *Rawle.* I cannot ſay from what circumſtance, unleſs from a recollection of the ſtrenuous oppoſition made on a former trial on the part of the proſecution to the courſe then adopted.

Mr. *Nicholſon.* Judge Chaſe alſo declared: " No caſe can come before us on which I have not an opinion as to the law, otherwiſe I ſhould not be fit to preſide here." Was there any thing which took place prior to this on which Mr. Lewis founded the opinion that he would be compelled to addrefs the court and not the jury ?

Mr. *Rawle.* It appeared to me that it arofe altogether from mifapprehenfion. Nothing fell from the court in my hearing, either in public, or in private, which tended to control the counfel from fpeaking, or to withdraw the confideration of the law from the jury. There appeared to be much mifapprehenfion ; and I obferved that the court did not fet him right as explicitly as might have prevented part of this mifapprehenfion.

Mr. *Randolph.* I think you faid that you entertained at the time of your conference with the judges, an anxious hope that the gentlemen would be induced to proceed. If there is no impropriety in the queftion, I wifh to know the caufe of the great anxiety you felt on that fubject, which induced you to become the agent of calling in the papers containing the opinion of the court ?

Mr. *Rawle.* My reafons arofe from an anticipation of thofe unpleafant fenfations, which I would never wifh my greateft enemy to feel, that of conducting a trial, in a capital cafe, and ftanding alone againft a man without counfel. It is eafy to conceive that my hopes may have been anxious that I might not be placed in fuch a painful fituation.

Mr. *Nicholfon.* I will afk you whether you took notes of what paffed on the firft day ?

Mr. *Rawle.* I did not.

Mr. *Harper.* Inform the court whether judge Chafe did at any time during the proceedings fay that he would reftrict the counfel of Fries from citing any ftatutes of the United States to the jury, and efpecially the fedition law ?

Mr. *Rawle.* I do not recollect that he did.

Mr. *Harper.* Did he fay that he difapproved of the conduct of the former circuit court in permitting the ftatutes of Congrefs to be read ?

Mr. *Rawle.* He did not. I never heard any fuch expreffion from judge Chafe in relation to the ftatutes.

Mr. *Harper.* Have you the paper in your poffeffion which was thrown down on the table ?

Mr. *Rawle.* I have it in my pocket.

Mr. *Harper.* Will you pleafe to produce it ?

Mr. *Rawle.* This is it, (handing it to Mr. Harper.)

Mr. *Harper.* Do you know in whofe hand writing it is ?

Mr. *Rawle.* In that of the affiftant clerk of the court—
Mr. Bond.

Mr. *Harper.* We will offer this paper in evidence.

Mr. *Harper* then read the paper as follows, being exhibit
No. 2.

"The prifoner, John Fries, ftands indicted for *levying
war* againft the United States.

"This *conftitutional* definition of *treafon* is a queftion of *law.*
Every propofition in any ftatute (whether more or lefs diftinct;
whether eafy or difficult to comprehend) is always a queftion
of *law.*

"What is the true meaning and true import of the ftatute,
and whether the cafe ftated comes within the ftatute, is a
queftion of *law* and not of *fact.* The queftion in an indictment for *levying war* againft (or adhering to the enemies of)
the United States, is "whether the *facts* ftated, do or do not
amount to *levying war.*"

"It is the duty of the court in this, and in all *criminal*
cafes, to ftate to the jury, their opinion of the law arifing on
the facts; but the jury are to decide on the prefent, and in
all criminal cafes, *both the law and the facts,* on their confideration of the *whole* cafe.

"The court heard the indictment read on the arraignment
of the prifoner, fome days paft, and juft now on his trial,
and they attended to the *overt acts* ftated in the indictment.

"It is the opinion of the court that any infurrection or
rifing of any body of people, within the United States, to attain or effect, by *force* or *violence,* any object of a great public
nature, or of public and general (or national) concern, is a
levying war againft the United States, within the contemplation and conftruction of the conftitution of the United States.

"On this general pofition, the court are of opinion, that
any fuch infurrection or rifing to refift or to prevent by force
or violence, the execution of any ftatute of the United States,
for levying or collecting taxes, duties, impofts or excifes; or
for calling forth the militia to execute the laws of the union,
or for any other purpofe (under any pretence, as that the ftatute was unequal, burthenfome, oppreffive, or unconftitutional) is a levying war againft the United States, within the
conftitution.

"The reafon for this opinion is, that an infurrection to
refift or prevent by force the execution of any ftatute, has a

direct tendency to diffolve all the bonds of fociety, to deftroy all order, and all laws, and alfo all fecurity for the lives, liberties, and property of the citizens of the United States.

" The court are of opinion that military weapons (as guns, and fwords, mentioned in the indictment) are not neceffary to make fuch infurrection or rifing amount to levying war, becaufe numbers may fupply the want of military weapons; and other inftruments may effect the intended mifchief. The legal guilt of levying war may be incurred without the ufe of military weapons or military array.

" The court are of opinion that the affembling bodies of men, armed and arrayed in a warlike manner, for purpofes only of a private nature, is not treafon; although the judges and peace officers fhould be infulted, or refifted; or even great outrage committed to the perfons and property of our citizens.

" The true criterion to determine whether acts committed are a treafon or a lefs offence (as a riot) is the *quo animo* the people did affemble. When the intention is univerfal or general, as to effect fome object of a general public nature, it will be treafon, and cannot be confidered, conftrued, or reduced to a riot. The commiffion of any number of felonies, riots, or other mifdemeanors, cannot alter their nature, fo as to make them amount to treafon; and on the other hand, if the intention and acts combined amount to treafon, they cannot be funk down to a felony or riot. The intention with which any acts (as felonies, the deftruction of houfes, or the like) are done, will fhew to what clafs of crimes the cafe belongs.

" The court are of opinion that if a body of people confpire and meditate an infurrection, to refift or oppofe the execution of any ftatute of the United States by force, that they are only guilty of a high mifdemeanor; but if they proceed to carry fuch intention into execution by force, that they are guilty of the treafon of levying war, and the quantum of the force employed, neither leffens nor increafes the crime; whether by one hundred or one thoufand perfons is wholly immaterial.

" The court are of opinion, that a combination or confpiracy to levy war againft the United States is not treafon, unlefs combined with an attempt to carry fuch combination or confpiracy into execution; fome actual force or violence muft be ufed in purfuance of fuch defign to levy war, but that it is altogether immaterial whether the force ufed is fufficient to effectuate the object; any force, connected with the intention, will conftitute the crime of levying war."

Mr. *Harper.* I will afk you one queftion. Do you recollect whether, after the verdict of guilty was brought in againft John Fries, the court gave him information of his right to make a motion for an arreft of judgment.

Mr. *Rawle.* When the verdict was brought in, the court briefly told him he might be heard then or at a future day. When he was afterwards brought up for fentence, they told him, if he, or any perfon for him could point out any error or irregularity in the courfe of the proceedings, they fhould be patiently heard; and in like manner judge Chafe addreffed the other prifoners; the fame queftion was put to all that were found guilty. They anfwered, that they had nothing to fay.

Mr. *Hay* being called, and not immediately appearing—

Mr. *Harper* obferved that this witnefs was called on an article fubfequent to that on which the witneffes already examined had teftified. He would fubmit a propofition to the honorable Managers, to go through at one time the whole of the teftimony on each article. It might not be the regular courfe, but if gentlemen affent to it, faid Mr. H. we fhall prefer it; it will be convenient to the witneffes, many of whom may be difcharged before the whole of the teftimony is gone through.

Mr. *Randolph.* Though this mode may have its advantages, it is attended with its difficulties. A witnefs may be found to fupport more than one article. With regard to the firft article, I have no objection to this courfe; but with regard to the fubfequent articles I have.

Prefident. If the gentlemen are agreed, I will take the fenfe of the Senate on the courfe to be purfued.

Mr. *Randolph.* It is the wifh of the Managers not to depart from the ufual courfe.

Mr. *Harper.* We do not claim it as a right.

GEORGE HAY *fworn.*

The greater part of the evidence I am to deliver relates to what was faid by me as counfel for J. T. Callender, who was indicted for a libel on the Prefident of the United States, and what was faid by *one* of the judges; for I do not recollect to have heard the voice of judge Griffin at any time during the trial. In order to make this ftatement as accurate as poffible, as my memory is not ftrong, it is neceffary to refort to a ftatement made by myfelf and the counfel affociated with me in the defence of J. T. Callender, which I now hold in my hand, and every part of which according to my beft recollection is correct.

Mr. *Harper* here interrupted Mr. Hay, and faid, the witnefs may refer to any thing done by himfelf at the time the occurrences happened, which he relates. But I fubmit it to the court how correct it is to refer to what was not done by him, or done at the time.

The *Prefident* afked Mr. Hay whether the notes were taken by him.

Mr. *Hay.* The ftatement was made by different perfons. Some parts were made by myfelf, perhaps the greater part ; the reft by Mr. Nicholas and Mr. Wirt. I believe I fhall be able to ftate from it every material occurrence which took place at the time. With regard to thofe parts of the ftatement not made by me, a reference to them will call to my recollection the facts mentioned in fuch parts. If I ftate any thing, which I do not diftinctly recollect, upon adverting to the ftatement, I will explain the actual fituation of my mind on that point.

Mr. *Nicholfon.* If I underftand the witnefs, it is not his intention to give the paper in his hand as evidence ; but merely to refer to it for the purpofe of refrefhing his memory.

Mr. *Harper.* I do not underftand the way in which it is meant to ufe the paper. I apprehend that it is a rule of evidence that nothing but notes made at the time of the tranfactions related can be received as evidence. I therefore am of opinion that a reference to this ftatement is inadmiffible, becaufe a part of it is made by others, and none of it made at the time.

Mr. *Rodney.* When we advert to what has been ftated by the witnefs, who fays he does not mean to ftate in evidence any thing in the paper, of which he has not independently of it, a diftinct recollection, I think it is within the law to admit him to avail himfelf of it. I apprehend that had I attended the trial of Callender, and taken minutes, and others had attended and not taken notes, if by recurring to my notes there should be recalled to their recollection facts so diftinctly, that they could fwear to them before a court, it would be competent to admit their reference to fuch notes.

Mr. *Campbell* enquired whether the objection were not confined to that part of the ftatement not made by the witnefs.

Mr. *Harper* faid the objection related to the whole of it.

Mr. *Campbell* believed that a witnefs might ufe any memorandum to refrefh his memory; and that it was not neceffary that it fhould be made at the point of time when the events happened. It is fufficient if made at a time when his remembrance of the facts was correct. With regard to that part not taken by himfelf, if he perufed it at a time fo fhortly after the events related as to be able to determine it to be accurate, and now recognifes the memorandum to be the fame, it is fufficient.

Mr. *Martin* faid, he had been many years in the practice of the law. The rules of evidence were probably different in different ftates. But he had always fuppofed that a witnefs could not be permitted to ufe any memorandum not made by himfelf, or at the time of the events related, or near it. He may before he comes into court confult any memorandum for the purpofe of refrefhing his memory, but not in court.

The *Prefident*. The witnefs propofes to make ufe of a memorandum under the circumftances which he has ftated. The queftion is, fhall the witnefs be permitted to make ufe of it?

Mr. *Adams*. I am not prepared to anfwer that queftion at prefent, not knowing the nature of the minutes the witnefs propofes to ufe. I therefore move that the Senate retire before the queftion is taken.

The queftion on retiring was taken, and, on a divifion, loft.

Mr. *Adams* faid he wifhed to fee the paper before he voted.

The *Prefident* afked Mr. Hay whether it was in his own hand writing?

Mr. *Hay* replied that it was not; but that it was written by a clerk from a printed ftatement.

Prefident. Have you the parts made by yourfelf feparate?

Mr. *Hay* faid he had not.

The *Prefident* then put the queftion, whether the witnefs fhould be permitted to ufe the paper?—and the queftion being taken by Yeas and Nays, paffed in the negative—Yeas 16. Nays 18.

Mr. *Randolph* afked the witnefs, to ftate to the court the cir-cumftances which took place during the trial of J. T. Callender, and particularly what refpected the excufe and teftimony of John Baffet.

Mr. *Hay.* I will ftate as well as I can, what fell from the judge, and which appeared to me to be material. After fome previous obfervations, the counfel for the traverfer claimed for their client his conftitutional right to be tried by an impartial jury. I cannot pretend to relate precifely either the courfe of proceeding, or the exact words which were ufed, fince I am deprived of the aid of thofe notes which I know to be correct. I fhall not, therefore, recite the precife words, but I fhall give the fubftance of them, and the words themfelves as nearly as poffible. According to my beft recollection judge Chafe's declaration on that point was, that he would fee juftice done to the prifoner in that refpect. In order to attain the object which the counfel for Callender had in view, we purfued this courfe. Believing that a majority of the petit jury, if not all of them, were men decidedly oppofed to J. T. Callender, in political fentiments, and thinking it probable from the ftate of parties at that time, that they had made up their minds, we wifhed to afk every juror before he was fworn, whether he had ever formed an opinion with refpect to the book called the Profpect before Us. According to my beft recollection, judge Chafe interfered, and told us it was not the proper queftion; he faid he would tell us what the proper queftion was. He then went on to ftate that the proper queftion was this: " Have you ever formed and delivered an opinion concerning the charges in this indictment?" Though I have but little dependence on my memory in general, yet in this I am certain, that I not only give the fubftance, but the identical words ufed. To this queftion an anfwer was neceffarily given in the negative.

Mr. *Key.* Who anfwered?

Mr. *Hay.* A juror.

Mr. *Key.* The whole, or what jurors. Was it the anfwer of John Baffet, no other juror is mentioned in the fecond article. The moment any attempt is made to extend the enquiry beyond the precife object of the fecond article I will object to it.

Mr. *Randolph.* We have no objection to that courfe being purfued; as we can get all we want under the 4th article.

Mr. *Rodney.* We are examining a witnefs, who may be able to give teftimony on the 2d, 3rd, or 4th articles.

Prefident. Will the gentleman read the article on which the witnefs is called.

Mr. *Randolph.* I do not know that we are bound to do fo.

Prefident. The Senate defire it.

Mr. *Randolph.* I beg pardon. I thought it was defired on the other fide.

Mr. *Rodney* then read the 2d, 3rd, 4th, 5th and 6th articles.

Mr. *Harper.* Our wifh is to confine the witnefs to the *matter* charged. We only objeĉt to the *opinion* of the witnefs being given.

Prefident. It is probable, gentlemen, that nothing will arife in what the witnefs ftates, that will occafion difficulty. He will pleafe to proceed.

Mr. *Hay.* What I was about to mention was not fo much opinion as faĉt. I was proceeding to relate the faĉts which conftitute the bafis of the fecond article. When Mr. Baffet was called by the marfhal, he manifefted fome repugnance to ferving on the jury. He faid, according to my beft recolleĉtion, that he was unwilling to ferve, becaufe he had made up his mind as to that book. I do not pretend to fay that the words ufed were precifely thofe I ftate. He may have expreffed himfelf in the words afcribed to him by the ftenographical ftatement given of the trial. The objeĉtion, thus made by **Mr.** Baffet, was over-ruled by judge Chafe, who afked him whether he had ever formed and delivered an opinion concerning the charges in the indiĉtment. He was fworn to anfwer this queftion. Like the other jurors he anfwered in the negative, and the judge ordered him, like the other jurors, to be fworn on the jury: he was fworn, and did ferve.

Mr. *Harper.* Was the word, ufed by the judge, *and* or *or* ?

Mr. *Hay.* I am perfeĉtly clear it was *and*, and not *or*.

In the ftate of things at that time, and feeing the temper that was manifefted on the trial, I would not, and did not, afk the juror a fingle queftion without fubmitting it to the court, and foliciting their permiffion to afk it. I folicited the leave of the court to afk a queftion. The reply of the judge was this——
The difficulty I experience at this moment in ftating the precife words, furnifhes the reafon I had for wifhing to have recourfe to the ftatement I had in my hand. Since I am denied that indulgence, I will not pretend to ftate literally what was

ſaid, but I will ſtate the ſubſtance. I told the judge I wiſhed
to aſk a queſtion. What, ſaid the judge, is the queſtion you
want to put?—State it. If I think it a proper queſtion, or if
I chooſe it, you may put it. Come, what is your queſtion?
Notwithſtanding the humiliation I felt at being addreſſed in
ſuch a way before a crowded audience, I aſked " have you formed (leaving out " *and delivered*,") an opinion concerning the
book from which the charges in the indictment are taken."—
The reply of judge Chaſe was, " no, ſir, no, you ſhall aſk no
ſuch queſtion." And the queſtion was not aſked. This is all I
recollect at this moment reſpecting Mr. Baſſet, and the occurrences connected with that part of the trial.

It was ſtated by Callender in his affidavit that colonel Taylor, of Caroline, was a material witneſs; but of this I am not
certain, becauſe I have not read the affidavit ſince the trial.
In the interval that elapſed between the day, on which the
firſt motion was made, and that on which the trial took place,
Tueſday, colonel Taylor was ſummoned. When he came to
town I know not. I have no recollection of having ſeen him
until he came into court. I had therefore no opportunity of
aſcertaining whether it would be in his power to furniſh the
accuſed with the evidence he expected to derive from him.
After the witneſſes on the part of the United States had been
adduced to prove the fact of publication, and after the attorney of the United States had opened the caſe, and ſtated the
law ariſing upon the evidence, colonel Taylor was offered to
the court as a witneſs. He was ſworn; and immediately after, or probably while he was ſwearing, Mr. Chaſe aſked the
counſel of Callender, what they expected to prove by him.
If I recollect rightly, Mr. Nicholas, one of my aſſociates, obſerved that we did not know diſtinctly what could be proved
by colonel Taylor; but that we expected to prove what would
amount to a juſtification of one of the counts in the indictment; that we expected to prove that Mr. Adams, the then
Preſident of the United States, had avowed in converſation
with colonel Taylor, ſentiments hoſtile to a republican government; and that he had voted in the Senate of the United
States againſt the law for ſequeſtering Britiſh property in this
country, and againſt the law for ſuſpending commercial intercourſe between the United States, and the kingdom of Great
Britain. I do not recollect preciſely the words which were
uſed by Mr. Nicholas in making the obſervations that accom-

panied this ftatement; but I think he faid, he hoped that it
would be underftood that he was not tied down to thefe particular points, faying that probably the anfwers given by colonel Taylor, might fuggeft other queftions proper to be put.
Nor do I ufe the precife words in which judge Chafe made
an objection; but I do remember that the objection was
made. The principle upon which he founded his objection
was this; that colonel Taylor's evidence did not go to a juftification of any one entire charge; and he declared colonel
Taylor's evidence to be inadmiffible on that ground. The
judge was then afked by Mr. Nicholas, whether we might not
prove part of a charge by one witnefs, and the other part by
another. The judge anfwered him, that he defired him to
underftand the law as he had propounded it; and the law
was this; that this could not be done; that colonel Taylor's
evidence related only to one part of a charge, and that he
could not prove one part by one evidence, and one part by
another. I then obferved to the judge, that I thought colonel Taylor's evidence admiffible even on the principle laid
down by the court; that I thought his teftimony would go to
prove both members of the fentence; the one afferted that
Mr. Adams was an ariftocrat; the other that he had proved
faithful and ferviceable to the Britifh intereft; and that he
could prove that he had heard Mr. Adams make the remarks
already ftated; and that he had proved ferviceable to Great
Britain in the way meant by the author, that is, in giving
the two votes in the Senate alluded to in the work. The judge
did not fay in exprefs terms that the pofition taken at the bar
was wrong, but he faid that the evidence of colonel Taylor
was inadmiffible, and that the counfel knew it to be fo; and
I believe it was at the fame moment of time, he faid that our
object was to deceive and miflead the populace. I remember
thefe expreffions as well as if I heard them yefterday. Finding that the attempt I had made to render a fervice, not to the
man, but to the caufe, inftead of affording fervice to the caufe,
only brought on me the obloquy of the court, I felt myfelf
difgufted, and faid no more on the fubject.

I recollect that we were requefted by the judge to reduce
to writing the queftions that we wifhed to propound to colonel Taylor. I thought the meafure fo novel and unprecedented
that I was not difpofed to comply with this defire. The queftions were, however, ftated in writing by Mr. Nicholas, who

obferved that he hoped we would not be confined in the examination of the witnefs to the queftions thus ftated in writing.
If I miftake not, before the queftions were reduced to writing,
Mr. Nicholas made fome obfervations about the mode purfued
by the court in reference to the attorney for the United States,
and that exercifed towards the counfel for the prifoner; that
the attorney for the United States had not been required to
ftate in writing the queftions he wifhed to afk. When this
remark was made to the judge, he faid that the attorney for
the United States had ftated in the opening of the cafe all
that he expected to prove; " but though this were done, we
were not bound to do it." My impreffion is that that word
efcaped the judge feveral times.

Mr. *Nicholfon*. What word?

Mr. *Hay*. The word " we."

————————Did it refer to the court as well as the attorney?

Mr. *Hay*. So, fir, I underftood it.

The fourth article relates to the refufal of the judge to poftpone the trial on the affidavit of Callender; on which I can
only fay that the affidavit was filed, but whether regularly
drawn or not I do not know. This affidavit, according to
my beft recollection, ftated the abfence of material witneffes.

The next article relates to a fubject, that it is very unpleafant to me to make any remarks upon, becaufe I feel myfelf to be a party concerned. The judge is charged with—

[Mr. *Hay* here read the 3d, 4th, and 5th claufes of the
fourth article.]

There were many expreffions ufed by judge Chafe during
the trial which were uncommon, and which I thought, and
ftill think to be fo. With refpect to the afperity with which
he cenfured me, I fhall not—

Mr. *Harper* interrupted the witnefs, and defired him to
ftate the expreffions, and let the court judge for themfelves.

Mr. *Hay*. The firft expreffion, which made a very ftrong
impreffion on my mind, was this: In the courfe of the argument, urged by me in fupport of the motion for a continuance to the next term, I affumed it as a clear pofition, that the
law of the ftate of Virginia, which directs that the jury fhall
affefs the fine, would govern in this cafe. As foon as I got to
that part of the argument the judge interrupted me, and gave
me to underftand that I was miftaken in the law, and added,
the affefsment of the fine by the jury may be conformable to

your local and ftate laws, but when applied to the federal courts, it is a " *wild notion.*" In the cafe of col. Taylor's evidence, which I have already ftated, the judge faid that we knew the evidence to be inadmiffible, though we preffed it upon the court, and then the expreffion followed which has been already mentioned, that we were endeavoring to miflead and deceive the populace. At another time he was pleafed to obferve, gentlemen, you have all along been in error in this caufe, and you perfift in preffing your miftakes on the court. On more occafions than one he charged the counfel with advancing doctrines they knew to be wrong. I endeavored in one part of the caufe to fatisfy the court that the book called the Profpect before Us, could not be given in evidence in fupport of the indictment, becaufe the title of the book was not mentioned in the indictment. In fupport of my argument, I obferved to the court that if the indictment mentioned the book from which the charges were formed, and any fubfequent profecution fhould afterwards be inftituted, the traverfer would have nothing more to do than to produce a copy of the record, and plead it in bar of a fubfequent profecution ; but that according to the opinion of the court, the fituation of the traverfer would be more precarious than according to the doctrines for which I contended ; for that the traverfer, if he fhould plead a former profecution in bar, would not be able to prove the fact by comparing the record with the indictment; but muft refort to extraneous evidence to prove that the fubfequent profecution was founded on the fame publication that gave rife to the firft. The judge was pleafed to obferve, without feeming to underftand the diftinction that I had endeavored to draw, that I knew the prefent profecution could be pleaded in bar. I certainly did know it, and was endeavoring at that very time to fhew by my argument that the better mode of proving the truth of the plea would be by a copy of the record, rather than by an appeal to parole teftimony. Judge Chafe again interrupted me, and faid, I knew that this profecution might be pleaded in bar.

In the courfe of the fame argument, which I addreffed to the judge, for the purpofe of fhewing the truth of the pofitions we had ftated, I obferved that according to the eftablifhed doctrine, the words " tenor and effect," in an indictment for a libel, bound the party to the literal recital of the parts charged as libellous. In fupport of that opinion I quoted feveral authorities that fatisfied my mind. The judge was pleafed to tell me, I was miftaken in my application of them ; but I do not remember his precife words. He faid the words " tenor and effect" did not oblige the profecutor to give more than the fubftance of the paper meant to be recited. It is contended, faid he, that the book ought to be copied *verbatim et literatim*, I wonder, he continued, *they* do not contend for *punctuatim* too. Mr. *Nicholfon*. Was this obfervation addreffed to the bar ?

Mr. *Hay*. It appeared to me to be intended for the people; for he looked round the room when he faid with a farcaftic fmile, I wonder they do not contend for *punctuatim* too. I recollect alfo, that when Mr. Wirt, who was affociated with me as counfel for the traverfer, was addreffing the court, he was ordered by judge Chafe, to fit down—in this precife language, *fit down*. The judge alfo declared that the counfel on the part of Callender fhould not addrefs any obfervations to the jury concerning the unconftitutionality of the fecond fection of the fedition law, in refpect to profecutions for libellous publications.

Mr. *S. Smith*, at this ftage of the examination of the witnefs, moved an adjournment of the Senate to their legiflative apartment.

The motion not being agreed to;

Mr. *Hay* proceeded.—When Mr. Wirt was arguing from a propofition he had laid down, he faid the conclufion which followed was perfectly fyllogiftical. The judge bowed to him in a manner I cannot defcribe, and faid " *A non fequitur, fir.*" I do not remember any other expreffions ufed by the judge calculated to deter the counfel from proceeding in the defence of J T. Callender. But I do remember that I was more frequently interrupted by judge Chafe on that trial, than I have ever been interrupted during the 16 years I have practiced at the bar. I do not ftate how often I was interrupted, becaufe I do not recollect; but I know the interruptions were frequent, and I believed them to be very unneceffary, not only as they regarded myfelf, but the counfel who were affociated with me in the defence.

Mr. *Randolph*. In your teftimony you have faid that during the whole courfe of the trial you never once heard the voice of judge Griffin. Were thofe replies and thofe decifions, which you have detailed, given by judge Chafe apparently without any confultation with judge Griffin?

Mr. *Hay.* I ftated that I did not hear the voice of judge Griffin; but I by no means meant it to be inferred that judge Griffin was not heard by any other perfon. Judge Chafe's manner of delivering the opinion of the court was generally this:—after having ftopped or interrupted the counfel for the traverfer by telling them to fit down, or that they were miftaken in the law, fometimes, but not every time, he would look at judge Griffin, who fat upon his left hand; and turning to the bar, and to the audience, he would fay, fuch is the opinion of the court. I think alfo, that I faw them fpeaking to each other, but not in fuch a manner as if they were confulting upon a queftion of law.

Mr. *Randolph.* You faid that the question propounded to Mr. Baffet, and the other jurors, was, " Have you formed and delivered an opinion as to the charges contained in the indictment?"—Are you certain that the expreffion was " formed *and* delivered ?"

Mr. *Hay.* I am as clear on that point as I am of any thing that ever occurred in the courfe of my life. I have faid that my memory at beft is not a good one; but fome of the occurrences on this trial were fo fingular and novel, that they made an unufual impreffion on my mind.

Mr. *Randolph.* When it was decided by the court that the queftion, " Have you ever formed and delivered an opinion on the charges contained in the indictment;" was the only proper queftion, was it ftated by the court, or requefted by the counfel for the accufed, that the indictment might be read ?

Mr. *Hay.* It was requefted by the counfel that the indictment might be read, that the juror might have an opportunity of afcertaining whether he had made up his mind on the particular charges it contained.

Mr. *Randolph.* Was the indictment then read?

Mr. *Hay.* It was not then read, nor until after the jurors were fworn,

Mr. *Randolph.* You have been, you have ftated, a practitioner of the law for fixteen years. Has it been the practice of the courts in Virginia, or have you ever heard of, or feen, an inftance, where the queftions propounded by counfel, were required by the court to be reduced to writing, and fubmitted to their infpection, before they were permitted to be put?

Mr. *Hay.* I never knew of a fingle inftance; nor do I remember to have even heard or read of fuch an inftance. I acted as the profecutor in the trial of Logwood, charged with counterfeiting notes of the bank of the United States. The chief juftice of the United States, who prefided at the trial, made no fuch requifition, nor did it ever occur to me, that fuch a thing ought to be, or could be done.

Mr. *Nicholfon.* When you were required to reduce the queftions to writing, was it at the inftance of the attorney of the diftrict, (Mr. Nelfon,) or was it by the court?

Mr. *Hay.* I do not remember that Mr. Nelfon made any objection to putting the queftion. The objection was made only on the part of the court. I recollect that Mr. Nelfon made one remark as to the witnefs giving teftimony on what took place in the Senate of the United States.

Mr. *Randolph.* Upon what ground did the counfel for the accufed affume the right of proving the vote which was given in the Senate by parole teftimony? to prove facts done in the Senate you fhould have reference to their journal.

Mr. *Hay.* It will be recollected that I ftated that colonel Taylor came into court at the time the jury was about to be fworn; and that the counfel for the traverfer was called upon to ftate in writing the queftions that were to be put. Thofe queftions were written without any reflection on my part, as to the propriety or legality of proving the vote of the Senate by parole teftimony.

The court rofe at 5 P. M.

TUESDAY, *February* 12, 1805.

The court met at 12 o'clock.

Present, the Managers, attended by the House of Representatives in committee of the whole: and Judge Chase, attended by his counsel.

MR. HAY, *in continuation.*

A very fhort ftatement will clofe the detail which I have to make. It was the intention of the counfel, who appeared in behalf of the traverfer, to have defended him on the ground of the unconftitutionality of that fection of the law, commonly called the fedition law, on which the indictment was founded. The gentlemen affociated with me in the defence proceeded to argue this point. They were not permitted to addrefs the jury refpecting it. The treatment experienced by Mr. Wirt on this occafion, I have already in fome degree ftated. I recollect he was interrupted by judge Chafe at feveral times, and particularly at one of thofe times, for the purpofe of telling him that the doctrine he contended for was true, that the jury had the right to determine on the law as well as the fact. Mr. Wirt then went on to ftate that the conftitution of the United States was the law of the land. Judge Chafe interrupted him, and faid there was no neceffity for proving that point, it was the *fupreme* law of the land. Mr. Wirt then went on to argue that if the jury had a right to determine the law in this cafe, and if the conftitution was the fupreme law, the conclufion was perfectly fyllogiftical, that the jury had a right to determine on the conftitutionality of the law. It was at that time that judge Chafe addreffed him in the words that I have mentioned. According to my beft recollection he bowed, and with an air of derifion, addreffing him, faid, " a non fequitur, fir." Whether Mr. Wirt faid any thing more after this in behalf of his client, I do not recollect ; he did not, however, fay much. After Mr. Wirt fat down, I rofe, addreffed myfelf to the court, and ftated that I addreffed myfelf to the court exclufively. I obferved that I did not wifh to be heard by the jury, or by the very numerous affemblage that furrounded me. This obfervation was intended by me as a fort of reply to the obfervation made by the judge that our defence was intended for the people. I did not attempt to fpeak to the jury on the queftion, which I wifhed to argue before them, but I addreffed myfelf to the court for the purpofe of fatisfying them. After I had gone on for a fhort time, I was interrupted by the judge, by a queftion which I thought an unneceffary one. I will endeavor to ftate it. I ftated to the court, in terms as diftinct as my knowledge of the Englifh language enabled me to ufe, the fpecific propofition for which I meant to contend ; which was, that the jury had, according to the laws of the land, a right to determine every queftion neceffary to the decifion of the queftion of guilty or not guilty. Judge Chafe afked me whether I laid down that propofition as true in civil as well as criminal cafes—becaufe, if you do, faid he, you are wrong. My reply was that I believed the propofition univerfally true; but it was fufficient for my purpofe if it were true as applied to criminal cafes. I went on, as well as I could, in the argument I intended to urge. I was again interrupted by the judge. What the circumftances were that gave rife to that interruption, my *unaided* memory will not enable me to tell, nor do I recollect what expreffions were ufed by him. I have not, fince yefterday, taken the liberty of looking at the ftatement, which I have in my pocket, of the circumftances that took place on the trial; but I know that I was interrupted more than once, and I believe more than twice; but the impreffion on my mind was, that to get through the argument, I fhould be fubjected to more humiliation than any man vindicating another in a court of juftice was bound on any principle to encounter, and I declined proceeding in my argument.

When the judge perceived from the movements I was making with my papers, that I was about to retire, he afked me to go on. I told him I fhould not go on. He faid there was no occafion for me to be captious. I told him I was not captious. He then faid, go on, go on—you will not be interrupted. I, however, retired from the bar, and, I believe, from the room where the court was held.

Mr. *Randolph.* Did any circumftances occur, in relation to a witnefs brought forward on the part of the profecution, of an unufual nature, were any obfervations made by the court to that witnefs, and what were thofe obfervations?

Mr. *Hay.* I do not know whether the circumftance I am about to ftate is an anfwer to the queftion which has been put to me. But I recollect diftinctly that a circumftance did occur, which I thought extraordinary. A witnefs was brought forward, to prove the publication of the Profpect before Us, who was the very man employed by Callender to print the work. Whether the publication could be proved by any other perfon than Callender's agents, I do not now recollect. But I ftated to the court that this witnefs was about to do what the conftitution authorized him to refufe to do, and what he was not required to do by the eftablifhed rules of law in criminal profecutions, which was that no man was bound to deliver teftimony that would go to criminate himfelf; and if any thing done by him, implicated him in the tranfaction charged againft Callender as libellous, he was not bound to anfwer, nor could he be required to anfwer by the court. Mr.

Chafe faid that the opinion I had expreffed was correct; but the witnefs, who had come forward to give evidence of the publication, might reft affured that he fhould not be molefted for any part which he might have taken in the publication. I do not recollect that the diftrict attorney faid a word on the occafion. Every thing that was faid on that head was faid by myfelf, and anfwered by the court, as I have ftated. The witnefs was fworn, and gave in his teftimony, in which he ftated that he was employed by Callender to print the work called the Profpect Before Us.

Mr. *Randolph.* The counfel for the accufed feemed to have confidered in this cafe, as well as in all the others, that the proceedings would be governed by the act of the ftate of Virginia, which in virtue of the act of Congrefs of 1789, was the rule of procedure. It appears that procefs was iffued, fuch as the laws of Virginia did not authorife. Was there no reference made by the counfel for the accufed to the act of Virginia, to fhew that the procefs was illegal, or that it was contrary to law, to rule the party to trial at the fame term the indictment was found?

Mr. *Hay.* There was a general, but not a fpecific reference to that circumftance. In making the motion for a continuance, I ftated that in conformity to the law and ufage of Virginia, when a prefentment was found, the ordinary procefs was by fummons to the next term, and that during the interval between ferving the procefs, and the time at which it was returnable, the accufed was enabled to prepare and collect matter for his defence. It is extremely probable that fome other motion would have been made, but for an obfervation that fell from the judge, on another part of my argument. I ftated that the jury were to affefs the fine according to law; this opinion was oppofed and denounced as a wild notion. Finding that the judge had made up his mind on that fubject, and that the law of Virginia was not confidered as obligatory, I had no idea of making any motion to the court founded on the doctrine which he had thus denounced. My opinion before, at that time, and at the prefent time, the opinion which I expreffed officially on a late occafion, is, that where the laws of the United States do not otherwife require or provide——

Mr. *Martin* faid that he apprehended this teftimony was of no kind of confequence.

Mr. *Hay.* I was only about to ftate the reafons, why nothing more was faid on that fubject, or a motion founded on it.

The *Prefident.* The Senate object to that fort of teftimony. You will pleafe to confine yourfelf as much as poffible to facts.

Mr. *Hay.* I only meant to have ftated a fact, that the exprefs declaration made by the court to the counfel for the accufed, in relation to the doctrine juft mentioned, put a ftop to my mentioning any idea, or making any motion founded on that doctrine.

Mr. *Randolph.* I wifh to afk the witnefs, who tells us he has been fixteen years a practitioner at the bar, whether he ever knew an inftance, in which, in a cafe fimilar to that of Callender, punifhable only by fine and imprifonment, a capias was iffued.

Mr. *Hay.* I ought to premife, that this queftion relates to a branch of jurifprudence which I have not much attended to, although fome time fince I acted as a profecutor for the ftate for one of its counties. I have never known a fingle inftance, in which a capias has been awarded in the firft inftance. I believe the invariable practice is to iffue a fummons, and I believe it is not cuftomary in Virginia to try a caufe at the fecond term, when the party appears and pleads.

Mr. *Randolph.* If it is not the practice at the fecond term, do you mean that it is at the firft?

Mr. *Hay,* No fir, the prefentment is found at the firft term; the fummons iffues returnable to the next; at the fecond term the iffue is made up and the trial comes on at the fubfequent term. This I believe is the ordinary mode of proceeding in Virginia.

Mr. *Randolph.* Finding that the law of Virginia was not confidered as applicable, did you move, and fupport the motion by argument, for a continuance, founded on the affidavit filed by the accufed, and what were thofe arguments?

Mr. *Hay.* I do not know whether I can ftate accurately all the arguments urged for a continuance. The argument was certainly in part founded on the affidavit of the traverfer. He ftated that he wanted documents which he could not inftantaneoufly procure, and material witneffes who refided at a great diftance. If I recollect rightly, I ftated when Callender was firft carried into court, that I was not prepared to difcufs the important queftion whether a jury had a right to determine on the conftitutionality of a law. I alfo ftated the cafe to be a new one, that a profecution for a libel had never before occurred in Virginia, and that the gentlemen of the bar were not mafters of the fubject; and that therefore I wifhed time to look into it.

Mr. *Charles Lee* was here introduced into court as counfel for judge Chafe.

Mr. *Harper.* In your examination in chief you ftated that you defended the caufe and not the man. We are not capable of underftanding your meaning, and beg you to explain it. Was it the caufe of Callender, or was it fome other caufe?

Mr. *Hay.* It was the caufe of the conftitution, and I did not mean to defend Callender farther than he was connected with that caufe.

Mr. *Harper.* Your object appears to have been to fhew that the law under which he was indicted was unconftitutional?

Mr. *Hay.* That was one great caufe.

Mr. *Harper.* Not the fole one?

Mr. *Hay.* I had previoufly made up my mind, that if a profecution fhould take place in Virginia under that law, I for one would ftep forward and offer my fervices to the perfon who fhould be felected as its firft victim.

Mr. *Harper.* You faid that you referred, when making a motion for a continuance, generally to the law, but not fpecifically to the law of Virginia?

Mr. *Hay.* My meaning was, that I did not quote the precife title of the act, but made a general reference to it.

Mr. *Harper.* Without citing the particular law?

Mr. *Hay.* Without citing it, I made no other than a general reference to the law.

Mr. *Harper.* Do you recollect, whether on the fubject of col. Taylor's teftimony, judge Chafe applied to Mr. Nelfon, the attorney of the diftrict, to determine whether the teftimony fhould be admitted?

Mr. *Hay.* I have fome indiftinct recollection of fome fuch thing.

Mr. *Harper.* Did not judge Chafe offer to poftpone the caufe for a month or more?

Mr. *Hay.* I have no recollection of fuch an offer; it would have been the wifh of the counfel for the accufed to have obtained that delay. I know that, in confequence of an impreffion on my mind, that a poftponement could not be obtained, I devoted my days and nights to make myfelf acquainted with the fubject, previous to the day when the trial came on.

I have no recollection of fuch an offer; if I had fo underftood it at the time, I fhould have avaled myfelf of it.

Mr. *Harper.* Did the counfel of Callender afk for a poftponement, independently of a continuance to the next term?

Mr. *Hay.* I do not recollect that they did.

The *Prefident.* You fay fome converfation appeared to pafs between judge Chafe and judge Griffin; did you hear fo much as to underftand the fubftance of it?

Mr. *Hay.* No, fir.

Prefident. How then did you draw the inference?

Mr. *Hay.* From the bufinefs then before them.

Prefident. You fpoke of a witnefs called by the name of Rind. Did he appear willing to give teftimony?

Mr. *Hay.* He did not appear unwilling. The objection to his teftimony was made by myfelf.

JOHN TAYLOR *fworn.*

Mr. *Randolph.* The witnefs will pleafe to ftate the circumftances that paffed in the rejection of his teftimony, and other circumftances which have any relation to the conduct of judge Chafe on the trial of Callender?

Mr. *Taylor.* I was fummoned as a witnefs on that trial on the part of Callender. I attended and was fworn. On being fworn, judge Chafe enquired what it was intended to prove by my teftimony? I do not recollect the expreffions of judge Chafe, nor do I recollect precifely the anfwer made to this enquiry; but judge Chafe defired the counfel for the accufed to reduce their queftions to writing. They did fo.

[Col. Taylor's teftimony was here fo indiftinctly heard, that we could not collect his words.]

I had come into court very near the hour when the court met, nor had I previoufly given any intimation of the teftimony I could give either to Callender or his counfel. I fhould have added that after, I think, the judge had declared the witnefs could not be examined, he applied to the diftrict judge for his opinion; who replied in fo low a voice, that I could not tell what he faid. But this was after he had given his own opinion that my teftimony could not be received.

Mr. *Randolph.* You ftate that neither the accufed nor his counfel knew the extent to which your teftimony would go. Would your teftimony, according to your belief, have had a material bearing on the charges againft Callender?

Mr. *Martin* objecting to this queftion, Mr. Randolph faid he would withdraw it.

Mr. *Randolph.* Did you obferve any thing unufual in con-ducting the trial?

Mr. *Taylor.* One or more motions were made by the coun-fel for Callender, who was interrupted by judge Chafe re-peatedly. The words in which thefe interruptions were couch-ed, I cannot recollect, though I formed an opinion of the ftyle and manner of them; the effect of which was ·to pro-duce laughter in the audience at the expenfe of the counfel. If I am required to declare the character in which I conceiv-ed them to be made, I am ready to do fo.

There was here a fhort paufe, when judge Chafe rofe and faid he had no objection to the opinion of the witnefs being delivered.

Mr. *Taylor.* I thought the interruptions were in a very high degree imperative, fatirical, and witty.

Mr. *Randolph.* Did there appear to you any thing unufu-al in the manner of the counfel for the accufed towards the court?

Mr. *Taylor.* I neither difcovered the leaft degree of pro-vocation given by the counfel, nor perceived any anger ex-preffed by the court. Judge Griffin was filent, nor were judge Chafe's interruptions accompanied by the indication of any anger as far as I could perceive.

To an interrogatory made, Mr. Taylor faid the interrup-tions of the court were extremely well calculated to abafh and difconcert counfel.

Mr. *Randolph.* Do you recollect any thing in relation to the objection taken by John Baffet to ferving as a juror?

Mr. *Taylor.* I by no means recollect the circumftances with precifion, but the impreffion on my mind is ftrong, that Baffet faid that he had entertained fome prepoffeffion againft the book called The Profpect before Us, or againft Callender, and that the judge enquired whether he had any prepoffeffion in regard to the charges in the indictment. He faid no: and it was alfo faid by him or by fome other perfon brought for-ward as a juror, that he had not read the indictment. Judge Chafe ordered him to be fworn.

Mr. *Randolph.* You were, I believe, a long time a prac-titioner of the law in the courts of Virgina?

Mr. *Taylor.* For a few years—about feven I practifed the law.

Mr. *Randolph*. I will afk you if you have ever known a capias iffued againft a perfon indicted for an offence not capital, or a perfon, prefented for fuch an offence, tried at the fame term the prefentment was made ?

Mr. *Taylor*. I muft anfwer in the negative, but it is proper to remark that, as I never turned my attention to the practice of the criminal law, no great reliance ought on this point to be placed on my anfwer.

Mr. *Randolph*. Has it ever been the practice in the courts of Virginia for counfel to be compelled to reduce to writing, queftions which they wifh to propound, and fubmit them previoufly to the court ?

Mr. *Taylor*. I have never feen fuch a practice in a cafe like that of Callender.

Mr. *Randolph*. Do you remember a queftion put by Mr. Chafe to the counfel on the part of the United States with regard to permitting your teftimony to be received ?

Mr. *Taylor*. After the decifion of the court, I do recollect Mr. Chafe did exprefs fome fuch idea as that intimated in the queftion. The attorney for the diftrict inftantly expreffed his diffent to what I conceived to have been in a very feeble manner recommended by the judge.

Mr. *Randolph*. This intimation was after the pofitive rejection by the court ?

Mr. *Taylor*. I think fo, although I will not be pofitive, as I made no memorandum of what occurred.

Mr. *Randolph*. Was you prefent when a motion for a continuance was made, and do you recollect the grounds of it ?

Mr. *Taylor*. I only recollect that it was founded on the affidavit of Callender : I have no recollection of the arguments ufed.

Mr. *Nicholfon*. Do you recollect the grounds of the court for rejecting your teftimony ?

Mr. *Taylor*. I think on the ground that though it were admitted, it would not acquit the accufed.

Mr. *Randolph*. Was any obfervation made perfonally to you after the teftimony was rejected ?

Mr. *Taylor*. None, fir.

Mr. *Harper*. You have faid, you confidered the interruptions of the court as highly calculated to abafh the counfel ; did you mean thereby to give your opinion that they were fo intended, or that fuch was their tendency ?

Mr. *Taylor.* I thought they were fo intended, and they had their full effect. They were followed by a great deal of mirth in the audience. The audience laughed, but the counfel never laughed at all.

PHILIP N. NICHOLAS, *fworn.*

In the year 1800, in the month of May, the circuit court of the United States fat at Richmond. Of this court Mr. Chafe and Mr. Griffin were the judges. I believe Mr. Chafe fat alone for fome time, for how long I do not recollect. Mr. Griffin did not, I believe, take his feat until the motion to continue the caufe was renewed. On the firft day of the court judge Chafe delivered a charge to the grand jury, and called their attention in a particular manner to infractions of the fedition law. The grand jury returned with a prefentment againft James Thompfon Callender, for a libel againft the Prefident by the publication of a work entitled " The Profpect before Us." On this prefentment the attorney for the diftrict filed an indictment which the grand jury found a true bill.

Procefs was immediately iffued on the indictment. My impreffion at the time and until very lately was that the procefs iffued was a bench warrant. I have lately heard that it was a capias. For feveral days it was believed that Callender, who refided at Peterfburg, could not be found, but the marfhal at length arrefted him and brought him into court. Mr. Hay and myfelf undertook his defence. My motive was that I believed the fedition law unconftitutional, and of courfe oppreffive to any perfon profecuted under it.

Mr. Hay and myfelf had an interview with Callender, in order to afcertain the grounds on which he expected to make his defence. Callender informed us that his witneffes were confiderably difperfed, and that there were many documents which it would be neceffary for him to obtain before he could be prepared for his trial. An affidavit was drawn, ftating the abfence of Callender's witneffes, the want of the documents, and that the counfel could not be prepared during that term. On this affidavit was founded the motion to continue the caufe. This motion was urged with great earneftnefs and zeal, as we were convinced that juftice could not be done, if the cafe was tried during that term. The arguments princi-

pally urged by us were, that the defendant had a conftitutional
right to compulfory procefs for his witneffes, and to counfel,
but that thefe privileges would be nugatory, if the court would
not allow time to fummon the witneffes, and for counfel to
prepare for the defence.

When the motion was firft made, Mr. Chafe fat alone ; he
did not abfolutely reject the motion for a continuance, but he
intimated in pretty ftrong terms his opinion that the affidavit
did not afford a fufficient ground to continue the caufe. Mr.
Chafe obferved that the evidence of Mr. Giles, as ftated in the
affidavit, was of a ferious nature, that he would let the caufe
lie over till Monday, and in the mean time we might fummon
fuch of our witneffes as were acceffible to us. On Monday
Mr. Giles did not attend. Mr. Hay ftated to the court that
the badnefs of the weather during the preceding day had probably prevented Mr. Giles's attendance, and afked that the
caufe might lie over a few hours. The judge faid we might
either let it lie a few hours, or until next day at our option :
the latter was preferred. On Tuefday the motion was renewed to continue the caufe. Amongft other arguments ufed in
fupport of this motion, Mr. Hay obferved, that by the laws of
Virginia a perfon indicted for a mifdemeanor was never tried
at the term at which the indictment was found ; but that a
fummons iffued againft him returnable to the next term.

Mr. Hay farther ftated, that as the fedition law gave the
party accufed the right to give the truth of the matter charged
as libellous in evidence, it refulted that the law meant only
to include the cafe of facts falfely recited, and not the cafe of
abufe or erroneous opinions ; becaufe they are not fufceptible
of proof, and their verity or falfehood would depend on the
particular courfe of thinking of thofe who were to judge in
the cafe. Mr. Hay faid he wifhed time to deliberate maturely
on this view of the fedition law, and faid that if his conftruction was correct, the jury in affeffing the fine ought not to
regard fuch parts of the indictment as related to mere matters of opinion. Here judge Chafe interrupted Mr. Hay, and
told him he was miftaken in fuppofing the jury were to affefs
the fine ; this may be the cafe, faid he, by your local ftate
laws, but as applied to the courts of the United States, it is
a wild notion. Mr. Chafe faid the caufe muft come on, that
the traverfer had not ftated in his affidavit that he could prove
all the charges in the indictment to be true, that it was ne-

ceffary for him to prove the truth of all to obtain his acquittal, and that as the abfent witneffes were to give evidence as to part of the charges only, their abfence afforded no good rea-fon for a continuance. The motion to continue the cafe was over-ruled, and judge Chafe directed the jury to be called. When the jury came to the book, I ftated to the court that I believed there was ground of challenge to the pannel, in con-fequence of one of the jurors who were returned having ex-preffed opinions very hoftile to the traverfer. Mr. Chafe, af-ter looking into an authority which I quoted, and alfo into Coke Littleton, faid the law was clear, that our objection did not apply to the pannel, but to the individual juror; he further faid we muft proceed regularly, that we might either intro-duce teftimony to prove that a particular juror had expreffed an opinion on the cafe, or we might examine the jurors as they came to the book. We preferred the latter mode, and Mr. Hay afked if he might afk a queftion of the firft juror who was fworn. Mr. Chafe faid that Mr. Hay muft fubmit the quef-tion to his previous infpection, and that if he thought it a pro-per queftion it might be afked. Mr. Hay ftated that the queftion, which he wifhed to afk, was, have you ever formed an opinion on the work, entitled " The Profpect Before Us," from which the charges in the indictment were extracted? Judge Chafe faid that the counfel fhould not afk that queftion, that the only proper queftion was, have you ever formed and de-livered an opinion on the charges in the indictment? I fay (con-tinued the judge,) formed and delivered; for it is not only necef-fary that he fhould have formed, but alfo delivered an opnion, to exclude the juror. The judge propounded the laft mention-ed queftion to the firft juror, and he replied that he had never feen the indictment, or heard it read. The judge faid he was a good juror, and defired he might be fworn. Mr. Hay re-quefted that the indictment might be read to the juror, that he might be thereby enabled to fay whether he had formed and delivered an opinion on the indictment. The judge replied, that he had already indulged the counfel as much as he could and they ought to be fatisfied; he refufed to let the indictment be read to the juror. The clerk then called the jury and fwore them, till he came to John Baffet, who in reply to the previ-ous queftion faid, that he had never feen the indictment, or heard it read. But Mr. Baffet feemed to have confiderable fcruple at ferving, and faid he had formed and delivered an opinion that the book called the Profpeдt before Us, came within the fedition law. Judge Chafe, however, faid he was a good juror, and he was fworn and ferved as fuch. The witneffes on the part of the profecution were called and fworn, and amongft others Mr. Rind was examined to prove the publication of the Profpeдt before Us. Mr. Hay obferved that no witnefs, who was any way concerned in the printing of the profpeдt, was bound to criminate himfelf. Mr. Chafe admitted this to be correдt, but declared that the witneffes might reft affured that no perfon would be profecuted in confequence of any evidence given in the cafe then before the court. Under thefe circumftances Mr. Rind proved that he had printed part of the profpeдt for Callender, and took out of his pocket fome of the original fheets from which he had printed parts of the work. Judge Chafe himfelf compared thefe fheets with the work as publifhed, and they were found to correfpond. After the teftimony on the part of the profecution was finifhed, Col. Taylor of Caroline was called on the part of the traverfer, and after he was fworn, judge Chafe afked with apparent hafte and earneftnefs of manner, what we expeдted to prove by that witnefs. We faid we expeдted to prove that Mr. Adams had avowed in the prefence of the witnefs fentiments favorable to monarchy or ariftocracy, and that he had voted in the Senate againft the fequeftration of Britifh debts, and the fufpenfion of commercial intercourfe with Great Britain. Judge Chafe then faid that we muft reduce the queftions to writing. This I objeдted to, and ftated that it was a thing very unufual in our courts, that it had not been required by the court of the diftriдt attorney, when he examined witneffes againft Callender, that it involved a dangerous principle, and was calculated to fubjeдt every queftion of faдt to the controul of the court; befides I added that I did not know the extent to which col. Taylor's evidence would go, that I wifhed him to ftate all he knew, and that very probably the examination would point out new queftions proper to be afked. I then ftated that if the court infifted on the queftions being reduced to writing, I would comply with their direдtion, but that I hoped it would not be confidered as precluding us from afking any additional queftions. The queftions were then reduced to writing, and are as follow, viz:

1. Did you ever hear Mr. Adams exprefs any fentiments favorable to monarchy or ariftocracy, and what were they?

2. Did you ever hear Mr. Adams, whilft Vice-Prefident, exprefs his difapprobation of the funding fyftem ?

3. Do you know whether Mr. Adams did not in the year 1794, vote againft the fequeftration of Britifh debts, and the fufpenfion of intercourfe with Great Britain ?

Judge Chafe, after examining the queftions, declared col. Taylor's evidence inadmiffible. No evidence can be received, faid the judge, which does not go to juftify the whole charge ; the charge is, that the Prefident is a profeffed ariftocrat, and has proved faithful and ferviceable to the Britifh intereft. Now, you muft prove both thefe points, or you prove nothing, and as your evidence relates to one only, it cannot be received; you muft prove all or none. Thefe, I believe, were the precife words of the judge. I think it right here to ftate that after Mr. Chafe had declared colonel Taylor's evidence inadmiffible, he faid to the diftrict attorney, that although the queftions were improper, he wifhed the attorney would confent to let them be afked of the witnefs. The attorney faid, he could not confent. The evidence of colonel Taylor being excluded, the attorney for the United States addreffed the jury, and commented at confiderable length on the indictment. After that, Mr. Wirt addreffed the jury for the defendant. He premifed that the counfel for the traverfer were placed in a very embarraffed fituation ; that the prifoner during the fame term was prefented, indicted, arrefted, arraigned, tried ; and that this precipitation precluded the poffibility of obtaining witneffes or making the neceffary preparations for arguing a caufe of fo much magnitude. Here judge Chafe interrupted Mr. Wirt, and told him, that he would not fuffer any thing to be faid which reflected on the court. Mr. Wirt faid he did not mean to reflect on the court, his object was only to apologize to the jury for the lamenefs of the defence. Mr. Chafe replied that his apology contained the very reflection he difclaimed, and defired him to go on with the caufe. Mr. Wirt then faid, that an act of affembly had adopted the common law of England as a part of the laws of Virginia, that an act of Congrefs had directed the United States courts fitting in Virginia to conform to the laws of the ftate in which fuch court might happen to fit, that by the common law the jury had a right to decide on the law as well as the fact; he then faid, that if the jury upon enquiry fhould find the fedition law unconftitutional, they would not confider it as law, and if they did, they would violate their oaths. Here Mr. Chafe faid to Mr. Wirt, fit down fir. Mr. Wirt endeavored to explain, and faid I am going on, fir, to— No fir, faid Mr. Chafe, you are not going on, I am going on. Judge Chafe then read from a paper, which he held in his hand, an inftruction to the counfel that they fhould not addrefs the jury on the conftitutionality of the act of Congrefs, but that arguments might be addreffed to the court to prove the right of the jury to confider the conftitutionality. Mr. Wirt then addreffed the court. He faid he had not confidered the cafe elaborately, that it appeared to him fo clearly that the jury had the right contended for, that he did not imagine it required any great refearch to prove it. He then proceeded to ftate that it was certainly the right of the jury to confider of and determine both law and fact. Mr. Chafe here remarked that Mr. Wirt need not give himfelf trouble on that point ; we all know, faid he, that the jury have a right to decide the law. Mr. Wirt then faid he fuppofed it equally clear that the conftitution is the law. Yes, fir, faid Mr. Chafe, the fupreme law. If then, faid Mr. Wirt, the jury have a right to decide on the law, and if the conftitution is law, it follows fyllogiftically that they have a right to decide on the conftitutionality of the law in queftion. *A non fequitur*, fir, faid judge Chafe. Here Mr. Wirt fat down.

I followed Mr. Wirt, and fpoke concifely to prove the right of the jury to decide on the conftitutionality of the fedition act. I believe I was not interrupted.

Mr. Hay followed on the fame fide, and in the courfe of the difcuffion laid down the pofition, that the jury had a right to decide the law as well as the fact. Mr. Chafe interrupted him, to afk whether he meant to extend his pofition to civil as well as criminal cafes ; for if you do, fir, faid the judge, you are wrong ; it is not law. Mr. Hay faid he believed the pofition to be univerfally true, but it was fufficient for his purpofe if it was true in criminal cafes. Mr. Hay proceeded a very little way further, before he was again interrupted by judge Chafe. Mr. Hay, who had been during the caufe frequently interrupted, then folded up his papers, and appeared to be retiring from the bar. Mr. Chafe, addreffing him, faid, go on fir. No fir, faid Mr. Hay, I will not go. What, fir, faid Mr. Chafe, will not you proceed with your caufe? No, fir, faid Mr. Hay : my mind is made up, and I will not proceed. The judge told Mr. Hay he need not be captious. Mr. Hay replied, he was not captious. The judge faid, go on, fir; proceed, and you fhall not again be interrupted, you may fay what you pleafe.

Mr. Hay, Mr. Wirt, and myfelf left the bar at the fame moment, and I cannot ftate what happened after with any degree of certainty; Callender was however convicted.

Mr. *Randolph*. When you obferved to the court, at the time you were directed to reduce your queftions to writing, that the attorney for the United States had not been required to do the fame, was there any reply made by judge Chafe?

Mr. *Nicholas*. It was, I believe, ftated by judge Chafe that the attorney for the United States had at the opening ftated what he expected to prove by his witneffes.

Mr. *Randolph*. Did you hear any offer made by the court to poftpone the trial of Callender for a month?

Mr. *Nicholas*. No fir, I did not hear fuch an offer, and I never heard it fuggefted until within a week or two, that fuch an offer was alleged to have been made. If fuch an offer had been made, I am fure we fhould have accepted it, as I know very well that a poftponement would have been the moft acceptable thing to us, except a continuance until the next term.

Mr. *Randolph*. Did the opinion of the court appear to be given after confulting with the diftrict judge?

Mr. *Nicholas*. I never faw judge Chafe confult judge Griffin but once, and that was after he had declared colonel Taylor's evidence inadmiffible; he turned to judge Griffin, and afked whether his brother judge agreed with him, to which judge Griffin affented.

Mr. *Randolph*. Did judge Chafe make ufe of any rude, unufual, and contemptuous expreffions to the counfel, and what were they?

Mr. *Nicholas*. I recollect when he over-ruled colonel Taylor's evidence, he faid, my country has made me a judge, and it is my duty to pronounce the law, the evidence of the witnefs is inadmiffible, the counfel for the traverfer know it to be fo, but they wifh to deceive and miflead the populace. I take the refponfibility of this decifion on myfelf, and fay the evidence cannot be received.

At another time, Mr. Chafe told the counfel, that they had

all along miſtaken this buſineſs, and kept preſſing their miſtakes on the court; and ſaid repeatedly that what we urged as
law, we knew not to be law. Many remarks of a ſimilar nature
were made, and in many inſtances the judge ſeemed to endeavor to throw ridicule on the counſel. When Mr. Hay
was endeavoring to prove that the declaration in the indiĉtment, that the libel was of the tenor and effeĉt following,
held the proſecutor to a ſtriĉt and literal recital, Mr. Chaſe
ſaid that it was not law; the counſel have contended, ſaid he,
that the recital ought to have been *verbatim et literatim;* I
wonder, continued he, that they have not contended for *punctuatim* alſo. In another inſtance, when Mr. Hay was adducing authorities to ſhew that the title of the book ought
to have been ſtated in the indiĉtment, Mr. Chaſe obſerved he
knew there were caſes in which the title was recited. I remember one, continued he, in the caſe called the Nun in her
Smock; but though it was recited in that caſe, it was not neceſſary, nor is it ſo in any caſe. It is difficult in language to
convey an adequate idea of Mr. Chaſe's manner; but in theſe
and ſimilar inſtances, from the ſarcaſtic way in which he expreſſed himſelf, it was evidently his intention to throw ridicule on the counſel.

Mr. *Randolph.* You ſay that on the rejection of colonel
Taylor's evidence, judge Griffin was conſulted by judge
Chaſe; was he conſulted before, or after the opinion of the
court was pronounced?

Mr. *Nicholas.* It was after.

Mr. *Randolph.* In ſpeaking of the diſtriĉt attorney, who,
he ſaid, had in opening the caſe ſtated the purpoſe for which
he meant to introduce the witneſſes, do you recolleĉt that he
ſaid *we* were not bound to do this, and by the word *we* iden-
tifying himſelf with the public proſecutor?

Mr. *Nicholas.* I recolleĉt that judge Chaſe in the courſe of
the trial uſed the term *we* in the manner alluded to; but I do
not recolleĉt with certainty in what part of the trial it was.

Mr. *Randolph.* Were you attorney general of the ſtate of
Virginia at that time?

Mr. *Nicholas.* I was, ſir.

Mr. *Randolph.* Did judge Chaſe apply the epithet young
men or young gentlemen, to you and the other counſel for the
traverſer?

Mr. *Nicholas.* I do not perfectly recollect whether he said young men or young gentlemen. I believe the latter, and as applied to me, it was true, for I was then a very young man.

Mr. *Randolph.* Is it the practice in Virginia to issue a capias to take the body of the party on presentments for misdemeanors at the term when the presentment is made, or the indictment found ?

Mr. *Nicholas.* By our act of assembly the proceedings on an indictment or information for a misdemeanor, is by summons returnable to the next term, and if the summons is returned executed, and the party does not appear, a capias is awarded returnable to the succeeding term. If the party comes in and pleads, his plea is received, and the cause stands over to the next term.

Mr. *Randolph.* Did you ever know the party in such case ruled to trial the same term the presentment was made ?

Mr. *Nicholas.* Never.

Mr. *Randolph.* Did the counsel for the traverser refer to the act of assembly, by which a summons is declared to be the proper process ?

Mr. *Nicholas.* Mr. Hay mentioned it in his argument for a continuance ; he said that as the laws of Virginia pointed out a summons as the proper process, and there was no act of Congress directing a different procedure, he thought the United States courts should allow the same time which the state laws did.

Mr. *Harper.* When you say that Mr. Hay referred to the law in question, do you mean he cited the particular act of assembly ?

Mr. *Nicholas.* No, sir, he referred generally to the Virginia laws, and said such was the process pointed out by them.

Mr. *Harper.* You said that the term *we* was used by Mr. Chase ; how did you understand him to apply the expression ?

Mr. *Nicholas.* I thought he identified himself with the prosecution.

Mr. *Harper.* In what part of the trial did this take place ?

Mr. *Nicholas.* I do not particularly recollect, but I am sure he used the term *we* in the sense stated.

Mr. *Harper.* Is it unusual to give testimony by a person concerned in the commission of the offence for which another is indicted, and do you not as attorney general of Virginia confider it your duty to promife a witnefs in fuch cafe that he fhall not be profecuted for any thing he may then teftify?

Mr. *Nicholas.* No cafe has occurred fince I have been in office in which fuch promife was made.

Mr. *Harper.* Are you correct, fir—do you particularly remember whether you was attorney general of Virginia at the time of the trial?

Mr. *Nicholas.* I certainly was—I had been a fhort time before the trial appointed by the executive, fubject to the approbation, or rejection of the next legiflature.

Mr. *Nicholfon.* You fay the counfel were frequently interrupted, pray how frequently?

Mr. *Nicholas.* The counfel were frequently interrupted during the trial; and as a general character of the trial, I can fay that, on moft of the points which were made, not many fentences were uttered by the counfel at a time without interruption.

The *Prefident.* Were you prefent when the procefs was ruled againft Callender?

Mr. *Nicholas.* I believe procefs was awarded whilft the court was fitting, but my impreffion at the time was that it was a bench warrant.

The *Prefident.* Was any thing faid in court againft its being iffued?

Mr. *Nicholas.* There was not.

The *Prefident.* By whom was the procefs made out?

Mr. *Nicholas.* I do not pofitively know. I fuppofe it was made out by the clerk, but whether by the particular direction of the court, or under an idea that it was of courfe, I do not know.

JOHN THOMSON MASON *fworn.*

Mr. *Randolph.* It has been contended on the part of the refpondent, that the *quo animo* determines the guilt or innocence of an action; now, if the *quo animo* with which he went down to Richmond to execute the fedition law, can be fhown, it will have an important bearing on his conduct. I wifh therefore to afk the witnefs this queftion: Did you ever hear judge Chafe, previous to the trial of Callender, utter any expreffion, and if any, what was it, on the fubject of Callender's profecution, or refpecting the book called the Profpect

Before Us; did he fay that the counfel at the Virginia bar were afraid to prefs the execution of any law, and particularly the fedition law; did he fay he had a copy of that book, or what did he fay? State the circumftances particularly.

Mr. *Mafon*. The queftion refers to circumftances of which I have but an indiftinct recollection, and which happened in a way, which renders it extremely unpleafant on my part to relate them. Judge Chafe prefided in the circuit court held at Annapolis in the fpring of the year 1800; during the term a man by the name of Saunders, was tried for larceny and found guilty. After fentence was paffed upon him, he was taken out of court to receive it. The prefs of the people being very great, the judges and myfelf were detained within the room. Judge Winchefter, judge Chafe and myfelf had a converfation, altogether of a jocular complexion. I think it was juft after he delivered his valedictory, but how to connect the circumftances at this time, I do not know. I remember, however, that he afked me my opinion of the book called the Profpect Before Us; I told him I had not feen it, and from the character I had heard of it, I never wifhed to fee it. He told me in reply, that Mr. Luther Martin had fent a copy to him, and had fcored the parts that were libellous, and that he would carry it to Richmond with him as a proper fubject for profecution. There was a good deal of converfation befides, but I do not recollect it. There was one expreffion, however, that he ufed, which juft occurs to my memory, and which I will repeat, that before he left Richmond, he would teach the people to diftinguifh between the liberty and licentioufnefs of the prefs. He faid that he was as fincere a friend to the liberty, as he was an enemy to the licentioufnefs of the prefs. There was a fentiment he expreffed, which I cannot undertake to give in his precife words, that if the commonwealth or its inhabitants were not too depraved to furnifh a jury of good and refpectable men, he would certainly punifh Callender. I do not precifely recollect the words: I never repeated this converfation before, and feldom or ever after it occurred, thought of it.

JOHN HEATH *fworn.*

During the trial of J. T. Callender, I attended at the court in Richmond as one of the bar. I had occafion to apply to the court for an injunction. The motion not having been decided upon, I went round to Crouch's, where judge Chafe lodged, and found him in his chamber alone, in which I thought myfelf very fortunate. We then talked over the application I had made the day before for an injunction; while talking on it, Mr. David M. Randolph, the then marfhal, ftepped in with a paper in his hand. The judge accofted him, and afked what he had in his hand. He faid that he had the pannel of the petit jury fummoned for the trial of Callender. This was after the indictment was found by the grand jury. After Mr. Randolph had mentioned that it was the pannel of the petit jury that he had in his hand, judge Chafe immediately replied, have you any of thofe creatures called democrats on the pannel. Mr. Randolph hefitated for a moment, and then faid that he had not made any difcrimination in fummoning the petit jury. Jude Chafe faid, look it over, fir, and if there are any of that defcription, ftrike them off. This is all I know of this affair.

The court rofe at 4 o'clock.

WEDNESDAY, *February* 13.

The court was opened at half paft 2 o'clock.
Prefent, the Managers, attended by the Houfe of Reprefentatives in committee of the whole ; and Judge Chafe, attended by his counfel.

JAMES TRIPLETT *fworn.*

Mr. *Randolph.* I wifh to know whether you ever heard previous to, or during the trial of Callender any expreffions ufed by the refpondent judge Chafe, manifefting an hoftility towards J. T. Callender, and what were thofe expreffions ?

Mr. *Triplett.* I recollect to have had a converfation with judge Chafe on our paffage in the ftage down to Richmond. A book was handed to me by him, and I was afked if I had read it. I was afked whether I had ever feen him (Callender). I told him, I never had feen him. There was a ftory recited about the arreft of Callender by a warrant of a magiftrate under the vagrant act of Virginia—I recollect that the judge's reply was " it is a pity you have not hanged the rafcal."

Mr. *Randolph.* Was there any other expreffions of this nature ufed, after you got to Richmond?

Mr. Triplett. I did not hear any thing particular; but I think the judge did fay fomething about the government of the United States fhewing too much lenity towards fuch renegadoes. I do not recollect any other converfation paffing between us at that time, until after the court was fitting, when judge Chafe was the firft who informed me of the prefentment being made by the grand jury againft Callender. At the fame time he informed me that he expected I would have the pleafure of feeing Callender next day before fun-down, that the marfhal had that day ftarted after him for Peterfburg.

Mr. Randolph. We wifh you as well as your memory ferves, to ftate not only the fubftance, but the exact expreffions ufed by the judge.

Mr. Triplett. I will ftate them as well as my memory ferves me. Some time after this converfation, I met the judge at the place where he boarded; he faid that the marfhal had returned without Callender, and ufed this expreffion, I am afraid we fhall not be able to get the damned rafcal at this court.

Mr. Randolph. You fay a copy of this book was handed to you by judge Chafe. Did you read it, fir?

Mr. Triplett. I read feveral paffages of it.

Mr. Randolph. Were they marked?

Mr. Triplett. I faw feveral paffages marked; but by whom I do not know.

Mr. Randolph. Do you remember any particular paffages that were marked?

Mr. Triplett. I do not. I have ftated every thing I recollect; but if the gentlemen have any queftions to afk I am ready to give them an anfwer.

Mr. Martin. I will afk how many days you refided at the fame houfe with the judge?

Mr. Triplett. I think, fix days.

Mr. Martin. Do you recollect whether my name was not marked on the book, which judge Chafe handed to you?

Mr. Triplett. I do not.

Mr. Harper. Can you ftate the day of the month, or of the week, when the laft converfation paffed?

Mr. Triplett. I think it was Sunday, but I am not pofitive. I made no minutes, as I never expected to be called upon to anfwer enquiries of this kind.

Mr. Harper. How long was it after the firft converfation with the judge, when he mentioned that the marfhal had gone after Callender?

Mr. *Triplett.* I do not precifely recollect. It was not, I think, fo much as three days. I do not think it was fo much as two days; but I cannot be pofitive, after fo great a length of time has elapfed.

Mr. *Harper.* Do you recollect who travelled with you in the ftage from Dumfries to Richmond?

Mr. *Triplett.* I cannot recollect.—The ftage was much crouded from Dumfries to Frederickfburg; and there was a paffenger taken in at Stafford court-houfe.

Mr. *Harper.* Well, fir, how was it from Fredericksburg to Richmond?

Mr. *Triplett.* I do not particularly recollect; but there were paffengers repeatedly getting in all the way.

Mr. *Harper.* Did this converfation take place before you reached Stafford court-houfe?

Mr. *Triplett.* It was after.

Mr. *Harper.* Was it between Frederickfburg and Richmond?

Mr. *Triplett.* Yes, fir.

Prefident. Had you any converfation with judge Chafe previous to this interview?

Mr. *Triplett.* No, fir.

Prefident. Did you fit together in the ftage?

Mr. *Triplett.* We did the fecond day, and it was then the converfation paffed.

Mr. *Hopkinfon.* When was it, that for the firft time, you mentioned this converfation to any body?

Mr. *Triplett.* I do not recollect when I mentioned it the firft time; but I remember to have communicated it to general Mafon on my return to Dumfries.

Mr. *Nicholfon.* Have you fince mentioned it to others?

Mr. *Triplett.* Frequently.

On the fuggeftion of Mr. Randolph, that Mr. Triplett had fractured his wrift, from which he apprehended ferious confequences, he was difmiffed with the confent of the counfel for the refpondent, from further attendance on the court.

At the inftance of Mr. Lee, JOHN HEATH, examined yefterday, was again called in.

Mr. *Lee.* You mentioned yefterday that you made two applications for an injunction. Were they made at the judge's chambers, or in court?

Mr. *Heath.* I mentioned that I made the application to the court, and that it was not then granted. I then ftated that

I went to the judge's chambers the next day before the court met.

Mr. *Lee.* Who compofed the court when the injunction was moved in the firft inftance?

Mr. *Heath.* I think, but I cannot be particular, that judge Griffin was there. He was, however, there the next day.

Mr. *Lee.* At what time of the day was it that you went to the judge's chambers refpecting your application for the injunction?

Mr. *Heath.* It was immediately after breakfaft. We generally breakfafted early. Immediately after I waited upon him. I think it was between 8 and 9 o'clock.

Mr. *Lee.* What fpace of time were you there?

Mr. *Heath.* I do not think I was there quite half an hour.

Mr. *Lee.* Was the bill read by yourfelf, or put into the hands of the judge to read it, at the time you made the application at his chambers?

Mr. *Heath.* I do not recollect to have prefented the bill to the judge. I am not pofitive that I had the bill with me. I called upon him for the purpofe of learning the reafons, why he did not grant the application. [Here the witnefs related fome remarks of judge Chafe on the application for an injunction, which were too indiftinctly heard to be reported.]

Mr. *Lee.* Who were prefent at the judge's chambers at the time you ftate the converfation took place between judge Chafe and Mr. David M. Randolph refpecting the pannel of the jury?

Mr. *Heath.* No other perfon was prefent but myfelf. When I came in I found the judge alone, and I thought myfelf fortunate in fo finding him. We had been in converfation by ourfelves for 8 or 10 minutes before Mr. Randolph came in.

Mr. *Lee.* Was any perfon prefent at the door, or was the door open at the time?

Mr. *Heath.* I do not recollect that there was; but it appeared to me that as I was going into the houfe, fomebody was coming out; and I found the judge alone, I am pofitive when I entered; and we continued alone until Mr. Randolph ftepped in. It ftruck me there might have been fomebody that came in at the main door of the houfe between the time I was there and Mr. Randolph's coming in; but I am not certain.

Mr. *Lee.* You fay fomebody was coming out, when you went into the room. Was it Mr. Randolph?

Mr. *Heath.* No, fir, I faid there might be fomebody coming out, but whether out of his chamber, or out of another room, I am not certain; but when I entered his chamber I found him alone, and I thought myfelf fortunate in fo finding him.

Mr. *Lee.* On what day of the week was this?

Mr. *Heath.* I do not recollect.

Mr. *Lee.* How many days was it after your motion to the court before you went to the judge's chambers?

Mr. *Heath.* I do not recollect; but I think it was a few days after the bill againft Callender had been found, and he had been arrefted; but as to days, hours and minutes, I do not pretend to recollect them.

Mr. *Lee.* Am I to underftand that it was after Callender appeared in court?

Mr. *Heath.* I do not fay fo. It was after Callender was brought forward by the marfhal, and a true bill found. I think it was immediately after; but I do not recollect whether a day or two after.

Mr. *Lee.* Did you go to judge Chafe's chambers on any bufinefs more than that one time?

Mr. *Heath.* No—I never did more than that one time.

Mr. *Chafe.* It was with the motion.

Mr. *Heath.* Yes, fir, it was with the motion.

Mr. *Randolph.* Did you at any, and at what time, mention this circumftance, and to whom did you mention it?

Mr. *Heath.* As foon as it happened, I confidered the converfation improper, and I thought I had a right to relate it, as I did not vifit Mr. Chafe as a friend, but as a judge in his judicial character to perform the duties of his office, and on bufinefs which might have been done in open court as well as at his chambers. I mentioned it to Mr. Hugh Holmes, alfo to Mr. Meriwether Jones.

Mr. *Randolph.* Do you mean Mr. Holmes, the prefent fpeaker of the Houfe of Delegates of Virginia?

Mr. *Heath.* Yes, fir.

Mr. *Randolph.* You ftate that you mentioned it to Mr. Holmes and Mr. Jones—did you mention it to any body elfe?

Mr. *Heath.* I was fo much imprefied with it, that I mentioned it to feveral others.

Mr. *Nicholfon*. Did you fay that you made this communication to thofe gentlemen immediately after the converfation occurred?

Mr. *Heath*. On the very day, and within an hour afterwards ; and I have fince mentioned it frequently to others— I never kept it a fecret.

Mr. *Hopkinfon*. Was this converfation on the day of the trial of Callender, or how many days before ?

Mr. *Heath*. I do not recollect whether Callender was tried that day; I mentioned yefterday that I did not attend the trial.

Queftion. Did you make your motion at the fame term that Callender was tried ?

Mr. *Heath*. Yes, fir—There were intervals in which motions were made by counfel. During one of thefe intervals I made my motion for an injunction. Callender had not then been tried ; I do not know that when I made the motion the marfhal had returned with Callender, but I made it the day before I went to the judge's chambers.

Mr. *Nicholfon*. Was the converfation before the impannelling of the jury in the cafe of Callender ?

Mr. *Heath*. Yes, fir—The marfhal came in during the time I was in converfation with the judge, it appeared to me, to fhew the judge what kind of a pannel he had.

At the requeft of Mr. Harper, and with the confent of the managers, JOHN BASSET, a witnefs on the part of judge Chafe, was fworn and examined, in confequence of the peculiar fituation of his family requiring his immediate return home.

Mr. *Harper*. Relate the circumftances that took place relative to your being fworn on the jury, on the trial of Callender, and what the application to the court was on your behalf ?

Mr. *Baffet*. The circuit court of the United States at which James T. Callender was prefented and indicted for a libel, was held on Monday the 2d or 3d of June. I left home in the morning and arrived in Richmond as early as might be expected. On my arrival I faw David M. Randolph, who was ftanding at a corner of a ftreet ; perceiving me, he came towards me; before I alighted from my horfe, he informed me that I had been fummoned as a grand juror, and that for not appearing, had been croffed, that it was my duty to go to the court and juftify myfelf for my abfence ; that he fummoned me on the petit jury for the trial of Callender, and that my ferving in that capacity would be an apology for my previous abfence. I prefented myfelf to the court, but the trial did not come on that day. The fecond day I attended alfo. I knew very well that the law under which the traverfer was to be tried, was odious to my fellow citizens ; I knew it was conceived to be a great oppreffion to the liberty of the fubject, and I believed that great umbrage would be given to the mafs of the people by thofe who fhould undertake to execute that law. I was weak or wicked enough to be among that clafs of people called federalifts, and I did believe that the law [fedition law] was conftitutional. I felt myfelf bound when called on to be a jury man, to make a declaration of my political fentiments. I made this delaration to relieve the impreffion on my own mind, and not in order that it fhould be confidered that I declined, in confequence of my political opinions, to ferve on Callender's trial, or in any other cafe. I thought it poffible that I might be excufed ; but if I were found by the court to ftand in a proper relation between my country and the traverfer, I would cheerfully ferve. My object was to juftify my own conduct to myfelf, and to the whole world. I made ufe of thefe expreffions, and I believe I repeat the very words, but I am well affured that I fhall exprefs the force and efficacy of what I faid. I declared to the judge that my politics were federal ; that I had never feen the book called the Profpect Before Us, but I had feen in a newfpaper fome extracts from it ; that if the extracts were correctly taken from the book, and if the traverfer was the author or publifher of that work, it appeared to me that it was a feditious act, that I had formed and expreffed an unequivocal opinion, that the book was a feditious act, that I had never formed an opinion in refpect to the indictment, for I had neither feen it nor heard it read. The court confidered me a good juror, and I was fworn accordingly. After the trial had been gone through, the jury retired to their room. I informed the jury that I thought we fhould have the book read through.

The *Prefident* here ftopped the witnefs, and informed him that it was a ufelefs wafte of time to relate what took place in the room of the jury.

The witnefs, however, continuing the ftatement he had previoufly begun, the *Prefident* defired him to go on, if it were neceſſary for the purpoſe of connecting the teſtimony he had to give; but to paſs over what occurred among the jury as briefly as poſſible.

Mr. *Baſſet*. I told the jury that I thought the book ſhould be read. The jury did not at firſt agree, but the greater part of it was afterwards read. In reſpect to the general progreſs, I will ſtate one point that makes a great impreſſion on my mind; I do not pretend, however, to a ſuperior recollection, eſpecially after a lapſe of five years, during which I never dreamt it would be the ſubject of diſcuſſion; but I will give my impreſſions. The judge, addreſſing the counſel for the traverſer ſaid, when my country inveſted me with my ſacred office, it placed me under an obligation to adminiſter juſtice according to law; this I am determined to do, and I have done it. I have decided what the law is, but this deciſion is not concluſive againſt the traverſer. If any exceptions are made by his counſel to my deciſion, they may be reduced to writing, and if I have committed errors, a ſuperior tribunal ſhall correct them.

Mr. *Randolph*. You ſtated that you had read extracts from the Proſpect Before Us in newſpapers, before you were impannelled on the jury, which impreſſed you with the opinion that it was a ſeditious publication. After reading over the book, did it appear to you to anſwer that deſcription?

Mr. *Baſſet*. I thought it was more libellous than the extracts I had ſeen.

Mr. *Randolph*. The extracts and the book did not then correſpond.

Mr. *Baſſet*. I cannot ſay. I could not ſay the extracts were the ſame with what I read in the book; I only recollect that my impreſſion was that they were the ſame. I could not then, nor can I now ſay they were conformable to the book, but my impreſſion is, that they were the ſame in ſubſtance.

Mr. *Harper*. Did you mean to ſay that the contents of the book were more libellous than the extracts?

Mr. *Baſſet*. I meant to ſay, that after I had read the book, my impreſſions were that it was more libellous than I conceived it to be when I read the extracts.

Mr. *Nicholſon*. Do you recollect at what time you arrived in town?

Mr. *Baffet.* I cannot recollect, but I believe foon after the court met: that morning I rofe early and rode 22 miles, about four hours riding.

Mr. *Nicholfon.* Was the book given by the court to the jury?

Mr. *Baffet.* I underftood that it was delivered by the court to the jury for their infpection, and to compare the extracts from the book, and fee whether they were correctly taken, but I do not recollect that the judge particularly called our attention to the book, and directed us what was to be done with it; but my recollection is that the book was delivered to us.

Mr. *Rodney.* Was the indictment read after all the jury were fworn?

Mr. *Baffet.* I do not recollect that the indictment was read till after the jury was fworn.

Mr. *Rodney.* Had the book given to the jury any paffages fcored?

Mr. *Baffet.* I think it had.

Mr. *Rodney.* Do you know whether the paffages marked formed any part of the indictment?

Mr. *Baffet.* I cannot fay that I recollect.

Mr. *Campbell.* When you were fworn did you underftand that the charges in the indictment were taken from the book called the Profpect Before Us?

Mr. *Baffet.* It was a fubject of general notoriety, that the indictment was drawn from the Profpect Before Us.

Mr. *Campbell.* What authority had you for fuppofing that the extracts you had read were taken from the Profpect Before Us?

Mr. *Baffet.* I had no authority but the newfpapers, they purported that the extracts were taken from the book called the Profpect Before Us.

Mr. *Randolph.* Have you any reafon to believe that the extracts in the newfpapers were not taken from the book?

Mr. *Baffet.* I firmly believe they were taken from it.

Mr. *Hopkinfon.* Was the book which you took out that which was given in evidence during the trial?

Mr. *Baffet.* Whether it was the book which was furnifhed by the profecutor and handed to us by the agent of the court, I cannot tell.

Mr. *Hopkinfon.* At what hour did the court meet?

Mr. *Baſſet.* I believe about 10 o'clock.

The *Preſident.* I underſtand you as ſaying that you never ſaw the book, until you ſaw it in court?

Mr. *Baſſet.* I am firmly and fully ſo impreſſed.

The *Preſident.* When you were queſtioned as a juror, I underſtand you to have ſaid, that if the extracts you had read were correctly given, the matter was libellous; did you ſay that you had formed an opinion?

Mr. *Baſſet.* No, ſir, nor that I had delivered an opinion, but I ſaid that if the traverſer was the author of thoſe extracts, he was guilty of a breach of the ſedition law. I repeat every expreſſion that is now remaining on my memory. I anſwered ſo far as to the fact. The enquiries extended no farther than to making up my opinion on the extracts contained in the newſpapers. It had no connection whatever with the book. I do not know that I ſtated to the court that I had expreſſed an opinion.

Mr. *Harper.* Did you make an application to the court to be excuſed, or did your obſervations ariſe from motives of delicacy?

Mr. *Baſſet.* If my memory does not fail me I did not ſolicit the judge to excuſe me; the office of a juryman is no doubt always an unpleaſant one, but when I am called upon to perform a duty, I do not ſhrink from the taſk. I had ſome doubts whether my mind was in a proper ſtate to paſs between my country and the traverſer. It was to remove theſe doubts that I made the declaration and for no other purpoſe.

Mr. *Lee.* On what day of the week was Callender tried?

Mr. *Baſſet.* I arrived about 10 o'clock on Monday, and the next day the jury were ſworn at the uſual time.

Mr. *Bayard.* What was the general deportment of the judge to the counſel, and of the counſel to the court?

Mr. *Baſſet.* The different coloring through which the ſame things are ſeen make ſome men ſee things differently from others. My own opinion is that the judge conducted himſelf with deciſion unmixed with ſeverity, and that he was witty without being ſarcaſtic. It was my impreſſion that the judge wiſhed the priſoner to have a full hearing, that he might be acquitted, if innocent, and found guilty, if really guilty. It appeared to me that the ſole point on which the counſel hoped to ſave their client was by proving the unconſtitutionality of the ſedition law, and it appeared to me that they could not form a reafonable expectation of acquitting him on any other ground. I believe his counfel believed the law unconftitutional, and thought they had eloquence and argument enough to convince the jury of it. I believe they thought the judge deprived them of their right to addrefs the jury on that point ; and that having the caufe very much at heart, they were vaftly mortified that the court did not permit them to take the courfe they wifhed. They appeared to confider themfelves as advocating the caufe of an oppreffed citizen, and they felt hurt at not being allowed the mode of defence which in their opinion the law authorifed. In all their arguments they travelled but little way before they came to the point that went to prove the law unconftitutional, and the judge declared, at every fuch time, that they had no right to addrefs the jury on that point ; that the conftitution had made the court the fole judges of the law as far as it refpected its conftitutionality. From thefe circumftances, it is my impreffion that the altercation between the bar and the court arofe folely from the fenfibility of the counfel to this particular fubject, and from being deprived, as they fuppofed, of their rights.

The *Prefident.* What were the particular caufes of irritation between the judge and the counfel ?

Mr. *Baffet.* I have ftated what I confidered the caufes. They arofe from the counfel adverting to that particular point, and their fo frequently doing it occafioned the judge to elevate his voice, and to pronounce over and over again what he conceived to be the law.

Mr. *Rodney.* Was the queftion put by the court, whether you had formed and delivered an opinion on the charges contained in the indictment ?

Mr. *Baffet.* My memory on the particular form of the queftion is imperfect, but I will ftate my idea of it. I at firft thought the queftion had been put in the disjunctive, or— but I am now perfuaded that I was miftaken, fo many gentlemen concurring in recollecting that the word *and* was ufed, I muft believe I was miftaken.

Mr. *Rodney.* When the queftion was put, did you not fay that you had formed an opinion on the extracts, and did you not exprefs the very opinion which you had formed ?

Mr. *Baffet.* I did, and I faid that if the book anfwered to the extracts, I had formed an unequivocal opinion that it was libellous.

Mr. *Rodney.* And this before you was fworn?

Mr. *Baffet.* Yes, fir.

The witnefs was then, from the peculiar circumftances already ftated, excufed with the confent of the parties from any further attendance on the court; the *Prefident* obferving that although the indulgence was granted in this inftance, he hoped it would not be made a precedent for a general practice.

The court rofe at 4 o'clock.

THURSDAY, *February* 14, 1805.

The court was opened at 12 o'clock.

Present, the Managers, attended by the House of Representatives in committee of the whole: and

Judge Chase, attended by his counsel.

On the requeft of Mr. Harper, and with the confent of the managers, EDMUND RANDOLPH, a witnefs on behalf of the refpondent, was *fworn.*

Mr. *Hopkinfon.* Were you prefent at the trial of Callender?

Mr. *Randolph.* I was prefent during a fhort part of the time.

Mr. *Harper.* What was the general conduct and demeanor of the court towards the counfel. Was it harfh, rough, and irritating; or was it mild and facetious?

Mr. *J. Randolph.* I wifh to fubmit to the court, whether it is proper to put this queftion in the form propofed. I wifh the witnefs may, in ftating the conduct of the court, confine himfelf to fpecific facts, as much as poffible.

Mr. *Harper.* The general conduct of the court is a matter of fact, and the particular acts of the court go to fhew what that was.

The *Prefident* here defired the anfwer to be reduced to writing, when Mr. Harper faid that he had no objection to withdrawing the queftion—Mr. J. Randolph, however, waving any objection to it, the Prefident defired Mr. Randolph to proceed.

Mr. *Randolph.* The anfwer I have to make is very fhort. Having been abfent the greater part of the time, I do not confider myfelf competent to fay what the general conduct of the court was. I recollect that shortly after the trial commenced, I came into court, and sat very near the bench on which the judges sat. I continued there some time, while a portion of the very lengthy indictment was reading. I then went out, and returned to my own house, where I continued until the time when I supposed the reading of the indictment would be finished. Just on my entrance into the lobby of the court, I saw the counsel for the traverser folding up their papers, and retiring from the bar.

Mr. *Harper*. Were you in court during the time when the previous motions were made?

Mr. *Randolph.* Shortly after the indictment was found against Callender, I was in court. The only incident which I recollect to have taken place at that time, was seeing the clerk or the attorney of the district hand up to judge Chase a paper, about which I made enquiry of somebody near me, and learnt that it was a warrant for process for apprehending Callender. This is all I recollect previous to the arrest of Callender. When Callender was brought into the court, I stood outside of the croud, at some distance from the court. I heard a great deal said, but I do not recollect what I did hear. I am therefore satisfied that I am incapable of giving a connected statement of what passed at that time. On the succeeding day the trial commenced ; but I was not present when the motion was made for a continuance. I have stated already how far I was a witness from that time to the conclusion of the trial.*

Mr. *Harper*. What was the demeanor of the court when you saw the counsel folding up their papers?

Mr. *Randolph*. I do not recollect any specific facts.

Mr. *Harper*. What was their general demeanor during the trial?

Mr. *Randolph*. From the causes I have stated, I am not able to answer this question.

Mr. *Harper*. Have you no general impression?

Mr. *Randolph*. I cannot say I have.

Mr. *Harper*. Was there any thing which struck you as remarkable, improper, or otherwise?

* The introduction of Mr. Randolph's testimony was delivered in so low a voice as not be heard by the reporter. But it is understood that, in the part not heard, nothing relevant to the charges in the articles of impeachment, was said.

Mr. Randolph. I have no hefitation in faying that I faw nothing that conveyed the idea of corruption.

Mr. Harper. What do you mean by corruption?

Mr. Randolph. I mean an evil intention to opprefs the traverfer. I fpeak only of thofe parts of the trial which I witneffed myfelf, and I muft be underftood as knowing little of what paffed from my own obfervation.

Mr. Harper. You fay you perceived no evil intent to opprefs the traverfer?

Mr. Randolph. I had no idea of the fort.

Mr. Lee. Do you recollect nothing that was faid by the court to the counfel, when they were putting up their papers and retiring?

Mr. Randolph. No, fir, I was at a confiderable diftance, at the door of the lobby at the time. I have no further anfwers to make to the queftions propofed; I do not think it incumbent on me to relate matters that are irrelevant, or to go into conjectures.

Mr. Harper. We are ready to hear any thing from a gentleman fo well fkilled——

Mr. Randolph. The reafon of my remark is my having underftood that I was fummoned in relation to opinions delivered by me at the time of the trial.

Mr. Harper. We are fenfible that we cannot require them.

Mr. Randolph was, by confent of both parties, excufed from further attendance as a witnefs.

GEORGE READ *fworn.*

Mr. Randolph. The witnefs will pleafe to ftate what he knows in relation to certain proceedings at a circuit court of the United States, held at New Caftle, in the ftate of Delaware, in the month of June, 1800.

Mr. Read. It is incumbent on me to ftate that feveral years have elapfed fince the tranfactions, which I am now about to relate, occurred; of courfe I cannot pretend to fay that the language I fhall ufe to convey the fentiments delivered by Mr. Chafe is precifely according to what occurred at the time; but the fubftance of what I relate will be correct. The tranfactions, to which I prefume I am called to teftify, took place at a feffion of the circuit court, held in New Caftle, for Delaware diftrict, in June, 1800. The court fat two days, viz.

on the 27th and 28th days of the month. At that court, Samuel Chafe, one of the affociate juftices, prefided, and Gunning Bedford, diftrict judge, was affociated with him. Judge Chafe, as ufual, delivered a charge to the grand jury, on the firft day of the term. The grand jury, after hearing the charge, retired to their chamber ; after remaining there for fome time, they returned into court, and on being afked whether they had found any bills, or had any prefentments to make, they anfwered, they had found no bills of indictment, and had no prefentments to make. After receiving this anfwer, judge Chafe proceeded to obferve, as nearly as I can recollect, addreffing himfelf to the grand jury, that he had been informed, or heard, that a highly feditious temper had manifefted itfelf in the ftate of Delaware, among a certain clafs of people, efpecially in New Caftle county, and more efpecially in the town of Wilmington, where lived a moft feditious printer, unreftrained by any principle of virtue, and regardlefs of focial order ; that the name of this printer was ———, the judge here paufed, and faid, perhaps it might be affuming, or taking upon himfelf too much to mention the name of this perfon ; but, gentlemen, it becomes your fpecial duty, and you muft enquire diligently into this matter. Several of the jurors, I believe, made a requeft to the court to difmifs them, and affigned as the reafons for their requeft, that fome of them were farmers, and as it was about the time of harveft, they were anxious to be on their farms. The judge obferved that the bufinefs to which he had called their attention was of a very urgent and preffing nature, and muft be attended to ; that he could not, therefore, difcharge them before the next day, when further information fhould be communicated to them on the fubject he had referred to. The judge then addreffing himfelf to me as diftrict attorney, afked me, as I believe is ufual on fuch occafions, whether I had any criminal charges to fubmit to the grand jury. I faid that none fuch had yet occurred, and I believed none were likely to occur during that term. Judge Chafe continuing his addrefs to me, obferved, you might, by profecuting proper refearches, make fome difcoveries. Have you not heard of fome perfons in this ftate, who have been guilty of libelling the government, or the adminiftration of the government of the United States. I am told, and the general circulation of the report induces me to believe it, that there is a certain printer in the town of Wilmington, who publifhes a moft fcandalous newfpaper ; but it will not do to mention names. Have you not two printers in that town ? I anfwered that I believed there were. Judge Chafe obferved that one of them was a feditious printer, adding, he fhall be taken notice of, and it is your duty, Mr. attorney, to examine unremittingly and minutely into affairs of that nature ; times like thefe require that this feditious temper or fpirit which pervades too many of our prefles fhould be difcouraged or reprefled. Can you not find a file of thefe newfpapers between this time and to-morrow morning, and examine them, and difcover whether this printer is not guilty of libelling the government of the United States ? This I fay, fir, muft be done ; I think it is your duty. I obferved, as this fubject was prefled by the honorable judge, I believed I was acquainted with the duties of my office, and was willing to difcharge them. I mentioned that I had not in my poffeffion the papers alluded to by the judge, nor had read them. But that if a file of them were procured and handed to me, I had no objection to examine them, and communicate with the grand jury on the fubject. The judge then faid he was fatisfied, and turning to the grand jury, obferved, that he could not difcharge them, however inconvenient their ftay ; they muft attend the enfuing day, at the ufual hour. The judge then directed that a file of the papers fhould be procured for me ; I underftood him to mean the paper called the Mirror of the Times, and General Advertifer, though I do not recollect to have heard the title of the paper mentioned during the proceedings. A file of thofe papers was brought to me in the afternoon, after the adjournment of the court; by whom they were brought I do not recollect. I examined them, but in a curfory manner, as I was very much interrupted by perfons calling upon me. I did not difcover during the courfe of this examination, any libellous matter coming within the provifions of the fedition act. According to what I underftood to be the wifh of the judge, I fent this file of papers to the grand jury. Soon after the meeting of the court on the fecond day, and at the requeft of the grand jury, I attended them in their room. On entering, the foreman of the jury addrefled me, and directed my attention to a paragraph in a publication contained in the Mirror of the 21ft June, 1800, republifhed from the Aurora, reflecting, perhaps in ftrong and pointed language, on the former conduct of judge Chafe.

He obferved that there was a difference of opinion among the jurors as to the nature of the paragraph—fome doubted whether it was a libel or not, and if libellous, whether they had a right to prefent it to the circuit court. I obferved that it was not neceffary for me to be very particular in my opinion of the publication, as I did not confider it as coming under the fedition law, though it might be confidered as an offence at common law, becaufe judge Chafe had decided that the circuit court could not take cognizance of cafes arifing at common law. I returned into court; after fome time the file was placed before the judge. Judge Chafe afked me what had been done, and whether the grand jury had made any difcoveries of libellous matter. I anfwered none, unlefs it were the paragraph which related to judge Chafe, which I fhewed him, obferving that it did not appear to me to come under the fedition law. Judge Chafe acquiefced ; and the bufinefs was paffed over on his part in a very polite and affable manner. I do not recollect any thing further to have paffed. I have, however, an indiftinct recollection of a converfation between judge Chafe and myfelf, in the room of a tavern, before we went into court ; in which I underftood him to have made a general declaration of hoftility againft feditious printers.

Mr. *Randolph.* You faid the judge gave orders to fomebody to procure a file of newfpapers. Do you recollect to whom he addreffed himfelf ?

Mr. *Read.* I do not; but I underftood to the bailiff or marfhal, or fome other officer.

JAMES LEA *affirmed.*

Mr. *Rodney.* Pleafe to relate to the court, the occurrences which took place at a circuit court of the United States at New Caftle, and whether you were fummoned as a grand juror at that court.

Mr. *Lea.* I was fummoned by the marfhal of the diftrict of Delaware, as a grand juror at the circuit court held in the month of June, 1800. I attended agreeably to that fummons and was qualified as a grand juror. After receiving a charge from judge Chafe we retired to our room, and remained there for fome time. There appearing to be no bufinefs for us, we returned into our box. The ufual queftion was put to us whether we had found any bills. We faid that we had not. After fome time judge Chafe addreffed the grand jury, and obferved that a very feditious difpofition had manifefted itfelf in the ftate of Delaware; in the county of New Caftle, and particularly in the town of Wilmington: that a feditious printer lived in that place, who edited a paper called the Mirror of the Times, and the General Advertifer, who was in the habit of libelling the government of the United States, and that his name was————he faid he would not mention his name ; but that it was our duty to enquire if any feditious publications had been made ; that he would not difcharge us that day, nor until we had made the enquiry. Several of the jurors addreffed the judge for leave to return home, ftating that they were farmers, and were extremely anxious to be on their farms as it was harveft time. Some converfation paffed between judge Chafe and the attorney of the diftrict, after which he faid he could not difcharge us until the next day. We returned the next day into court, and after fitting fome time in our box we retired to the jury room. A file of newf-papers was produced by fome perfons, and we examined them. We found nothing in them of a libellous nature in our opinion, excepting fomething relative to judge Chafe ; which fome of the jury thought came under the fedition law. We fent for the attorney of the diftrict, to inform us, as to the nature of that paragraph. He told us it did not come under the fedition law. We went into the jury box ; when a con-verfation of fome length took place between judge Chafe and the attorney of the diftrict, after which we were difcharged.

Mr. *Martin.* What time did you come down on the firft day?

Mr. *Lea.* We were up a very fhort time ; perhaps an hour.

Mr. *Martin.* What time the fecond day ?

Mr. *Lea.* A good while.

Mr. *Martin.* What time is the harveft in Delaware ?

Mr. *Lea.* It was the time of hay harveft.

Mr. *Randolph.* I will afk you, whether you recollect the judge to have quoted the title of the paper ?

Mr. *Lea.* I recollect that he did.

Mr. *Randolph.* Was it the fame paper that was fent you by the attorney ?

Mr. *Lea.* It was.

JOHN CROW *sworn.*

Mr. *Rodney.* Pleafe to ftate what occurred in the circuit court held at New Caftle.

Mr. *Crow.* I was not in the court houfe the firft day. On the fecond day, I went into court juft after it was opened. I recollect there was fome converfation that took place between judge Chafe and the diftrict attorney. The judge afked the attorney of the diftrict if there were any prefentments likely to be made that day. The attorney anfwered, there were none; that on examining the file of newfpapers, there was nothing found libellous, unlefs it were fome ftrictures on the judge himfelf. If that is all, the judge replied, we will take no notice of it. I recollect nothing further. The judge fhortly after difcharged the grand jury.

JOHN MONTGOMERY *sworn.*

Mr. *Randolph.* The fubject on which it is underftood you are capable of giving fome information to the court, is the conduct of judge Chafe at a circuit court of the United States held for the diftrict of Maryland, at Baltimore, in May 1803, or about that time.

Mr. *Montgomery.* The point I prefume, on which I am called to give teftimony, relates to a charge to a grand jury delivered by judge Chafe, at a circuit court where he prefided, and judge Winchefter was affociated with him. It will not, from the nature of the fubject, be expected that I fhall be able to detail in the precife language of the judge, the whole of the charge which was delivered in 1803, at the May term. Though not one of the bar, I was prefent at the court, and took a chair among the gentlemen of the bar. After the grand jury were impannelled, judge Chafe addreffed them. He appeared to addrefs them from a written paper that lay before him. He proceeded in the ufual manner to charge the jury as to the duties expected to be performed by them. After he had thus far proceeded in his charge, he mentioned that before the jury retired to their chamber, he would make fome obfervations, and that they would be confidered as flowing from a wifh for the happinefs or welfare of the community. He ftated that it was important that the people fhould be fully informed, particularly at fuch a crifis; that falfehood was more eafily difleminated than truth; and that the latter was reluctantly attended to, when oppofed to popular prejudice. I cannot pretend to ftate the fentiments delivered by the judge in the order in which they were delivered. I can undertake to ftate from my recollection, the fubftance of thofe he delivered. To the beft of my recollection the judge ftated that the adminiftration was weak, relaxed, and inadequate to the duties devolved on it, and that its acts proceeded not from a view to promote the general happinefs, but from a defire for the continuance of unfairly acquired power. The language unfairly acquired power, made a ftrong impreflion on my mind at the time, and when the judge called the attention of the jury to the obfervations he was about to make, I was prepared to expect fomething extraordinary from him, as I was at Annapolis, when he pronounced the valedictory addrefs, which Mr. Mafon in his teftimony took occafion to mention. The judge ftated the violation of the conftitution that had taken place by the act of Congrefs repealing the judiciary act of 1800, and the confequent removal of fixteen judges; that it had made a violent attack on the independency of the judiciary. He alfo found fault with a law paffed by the legiflature of Maryland in 1801, the effect of which was the removal of all the judges on the county court eftablifhment; he ftated that thofe acts were a fevere blow againft the independence of the judiciary; he ftated that fince the year 1776, he had been an advocate for a reprefentative or republican form of government; that it was his wifh that freemen fhould be governed by reprefentatives chofen by that clafs of citizens who had a property in, a common intereft with, and an attachment to the community; the language might have been in the words of our conftitution; he found fault with the law paffed by the legiflature of Maryland, which he ftiled the univerfal fuffrage law. He ftated, that that alfo affected the independence of the judiciary, and to the beft of my recollection, he explained his ideas in this manner. That every free white male citizen, in the language of the conftitution, having the qualification of age and refidence, though he had not a property in, an intereft with, and an attachment to the community, being fuffered to choofe thofe who conftituted the legiflature, and the judiciary being dependent on the legiflature for their fupport and continuance in office, few characters of integrity and ability, who are competent to difcharge the duties of judges, would be found to accept of appointments held on fuch a tenure. He ftated that thefe meafures were deftructive of the happinefs and welfare of the community ; that they would have a tendency to fink our republican government into what he called a mobocracy, the worft of all poffible governments. When on the fubject of the alteration of the ftate conftitution, he ftated that the framers of that conftitution were men of ability and patriotifm ; the names of fome of whom were honorably enrolled on the journals of Congrefs, and alfo, I think he faid on the journals of the convention of Maryland; that he had to obferve, that the fons of fome of thofe characters, which he regretted, were the chief fupporters of thefe deftructive meafures. He ftated that where there were equal laws and equal rights, viz. laws equally adminiftered, between the rich and the poor, in that country there was freedom. But where the adminiftration of the laws was partial and uncertain, the people were not free, and he was apprehenfive we were faft approaching to that ftate of things. He ftated that there was but one act remaining to be done, mentioning the act paffed by the legiflature of Maryland, for the trial of facts and for abolifhing the general and appellate court ; if that fhould be adopted, the conftitution would not be worthy of further care or prefervation. At the clofe of the judge's charge, he, in an impreffive manner, called on the jury to paufe, to reflect, and when they returned to their homes, to ufe their endeavors to prevent thefe impending evils, and fave their country. He faid that the people had been mifled by mifreprefentation, falfehood, art and cunning ; that by correcting thefe errors, the threatened evils might be prevented, or words to that effect. With regard to a part of the anfwer of judge Chafe which has been publifhed, and which I have read, perhaps it will not be improper for, and may be expected of me, to mention a fact contradictory to what is ftated therein. It is ftated in the anfwer, " The next opinion is, that " the independence of the judges of the ftate of Maryland, would be entirely deftroyed if the bill for abolifhing the two fupreme courts fhould be ratified by the next general affembly." This opinion, however incorrect it may be, feems to have been adopted by the people of Maryland, to whom this argument againft the bill in queftion was addreffed : for at the next feffion of the legiflature this bill, which went to change entirely the conftitutional tenure of judicial office in the ftate, and to render the fubfiftence of the judges dependent on the legiflature, and their continuance in office on the executive, was abandoned by common confent."

It is true it was abandoned by common confent, but not for the reafons affigned by the judge in this part of his anfwer.

Mr. *Nicholfon*. Was the provifion for eftablifhing univerfal fuffrage a part of the conftitution, at the time judge Chafe delivered the charge?

Mr. *Montgomery*. It was.

Mr. *Randolph*. You ftate that the charge appeared to have been delivered from a written paper which lay before the judge. Do you mean to be underftood, that after going through the firft part of the charge on the ordinary duties of a grand jury, the latter part appeared to be delivered from a written paper?

Mr. *Montgomery*. It appeared to me that the latter, as well as the former part, was delivered in the fame manner; the judge keeping his eyes on the paper before him.

Mr. *Nicholfon*. Do you recollect whether the very laft part of the charge, when he defired the jury to paufe and reflect, &c. was delivered from the written paper?

Mr. *Montgomery*. It appeared to me as if he confined himfelf throughout to the written paper.

JOHN T. MASON was again called.

Mr. *Randolph*. You will pleafe to mention fuch circumftances, as came under your obfervation, at a circuit court of the United States held at Baltimore in May 1803, in relation to a charge delivered to a grand jury.

Mr. *Mafon*. I was prefent when fuch a charge was delivered; I was prefent when it commenced and continued in court until it ended. I have, however, a very imperfect recollection of the greater part of it, and of a great part of it, perhaps, I have no recollection at all. I had not been in Baltimore for two years previous; the court room was very full; and while I was there a number of perfons came up to falute me. I felt no particular intereft in it, and I only attended to thofe parts of the charge, during the delivery of which I was not interrupted by interchanging the civilities of my friends and acquaintance. I do not think I can charge my recollection with more than three great points in the charge; nor am

I certain that I can give them in the order in which the judge delivered them. The firft contained pretty ftrong and cenfuring animadverfions on the act of Congrefs which repealed the law paffed in February 1801, for the new organization of the courts of the United States, by which the fixteen new judges of the circuit court were removed from office. He fpoke of it as an event which had wounded the independence of the judiciary, and as calculated to produce great mifchief. I do not however pretend to give the words, but only to embrace the idea.

With regard to the fecond point which I recollect, it will perhaps be neceffary for me to explain that according to the provifion in the conftitution of Maryland, for altering that inftrument, amendments may be made by a legiflative act paffed by two fucceffive legiflatures. Under the conftitution, before a late amendment was made, no man was permitted to vote unlefs poffeffed of property to the value of thirty pounds. That part of the conftitution had been altered by two fucceffive legiflatures by confining the qualifications of voters, to age, refidence, and color. This amendment Mr. Chafe fpoke of as one calculated to fap the foundations of our government, as injurious, and as leading to a great many evils.

The third ground arofe on this circumftance. An effort had been made to alter the conftitution by a confiderable change in the judiciary fyftem, and which had fo far progreffed as to have obtained the fanction of one legiflative vote. He fpoke of this as a meafure extremely dangerous in its nature, and which, if carried into effect, was calculated to deform and injure one of the moft beautiful features of the conftitution, and fo to affect it as to leave nothing or little in it worth preferving. He concluded his remarks on this point by an earneft recommendation to thofe perfons to whom he addreffed himfelf, to make the neceffary exertions to prevent the paffage of this act, which would have made it a part of the conftitution. There were at leaft two gentlemen in the room, who were members of the legiflature, and whofe fathers, as I underftood, were members of the convention, which formed the conftitution of Maryland. Judge Chafe obferved that it was a matter of peculiar mortification, or concern, to look at, to fee, or to know (ufing fome fuch expreffion) fome gentlemen engaged in thoughtlefsly demolifhing the fair fabric, which their fathers had toiled with him in erecting.

There is one point of fact in which I differ from the witnefs laft examined. Judge Chafe delivered the charge from a written paper, which he had before him. He wore his fpectacles at the time, and though he turned over leaf by leaf, he occafionally threw up his head, and fometimes raifed his fpectacles on his forehead, and fpoke as if he was making what I confidered an enlargement of the original charge, by extemporary obfervations in addition to what he had written. I cannot charge my memory with any thing further.

SAMUEL H. SMITH *fworn.*

Mr. *Nicholfon.* Pleafe to ftate what you know of the charge delivered by judge Chafe at Baltimore.

Mr. *Smith.* The charge of judge Chafe having been publifhed, I did not expect to be called upon to ftate in detail its general contents; fuppofing that the only enquiry made would be on the correfpondence of my recollection with the contents of the publifhed charge. I do not know that I fhould be able, under thefe circumftances, to give a particular ftatement, from memory, of its contents. On the evening fubfequent to the delivery of the charge, I committed to paper the moft important features of it, which were publifhed in the National Intelligencer, and which form part of the printed teftimony received by the committee of enquiry. If I could be indulged with accefs to it, I fhould be enabled to ftate more correctly my knowledge of the charge.

[Mr. Smith here, with permiffion, read the following (extracted from the National Intelligencer of May 20, 1803.]

After a definition of the offences cognizable by the grand jury, judge Chafe faid he hoped he fhould be pardoned for making a few additional obfervations. He had, he remarked, been uniformly attached to a free republican government, and had actively participated in our revolutionary ftruggle to obtain it. He ftill remained warmly attached to the principles of government then eftablifhed. Since that period, however, certain opinions had fprung up which threatened with ruin the fair fabric then raifed. It had been contended that all men had equal rights derived from nature, of which fociety could not rightfully deprive them. This he denied. He could conceive of no rights in a ftate of nature, which was in fact entirely a creature of the imagination, as there was no condition of man in which he was not, under fome modification, fubject to a particular leader or particular fpecies of government. True liberty did not, in his opinion, confift in the poffeffion of equal rights, but in the protection by the law of the perfon and property of every member of fociety, however various the grade in fociety he filled.—Nor did it confift in the form of government in any country. A monarchy might be free, and a republic in flavery. Wherever the laws protected the perfon and property of every man, there liberty exifted, whatever the government was. Such, faid he, is our prefent fituation. But much I fear that foon, very foon, our fituation will be changed. The great bulwark of an independent judiciary has been broken down by the legiflature of the United States, and a wound inflicted upon the liberties of the people which nothing but their good fenfe can cure.

[Judge Chafe here went into an affertion of the right of the judiciary to decide on the conftitutionality of laws.]

He then adverted to the proceedings of the legiflature of Maryland. He commented on the wifdom and patriotifm of thofe who had framed the conftitution of that ftate. That wifdom and patriotifm had never conceived liberty to confift in every man poffeffing equal political rights. To fecure property the right of fuffrage had been limited. The convention had not imagined, according to the new doctrine, that property would be beft protected by thofe who had themfelves no property. The great rampart eftablifhed in the limitation of fuffrage was now demolifhed by the principle of univerfal fuffrage engrafted in the conftitution. In addition to this, a propofition was now fubmitted, whofe ratification depended upon the next legiflature, and which, if ratified, would deftroy the independence and refpectability of the judiciary, and make the adminiftration of juftice dependent upon legiflative difcretion. If this fhall, in addition to that which eftablifhes univerfal fuffrage, become part of the conftitution, nothing will remain that will be worth protecting. Inftead of being ruled by a regular and refpectable government, we fhall be governed by an ignorant mobocracy. When he reflected on the ruinous effects of thefe meafures, he could not but blufh at the degeneracy of fons, who deftroyed the fair fabric raifed by the patriotifm of their fathers.

Prefident. Did you hear any reflections caft on the adminiftration ?

Mr. *Smith.* I do not recollect any other befide thofe contained in the ftatement I have read.

JOHN STEPHEN *sworn*.

I was at Baltimore when the charge was delivered by judge Chafe. My recollection of its contents is extremely vague. But with regard to fome parts of it, it coincides with that of Mr. Montgomery, Mr. Mafon, and Mr. Smith. He fpoke of the repeal of the judiciary law, and faid that it was injurious to the independence of the judges. He alfo mentioned the general fuffrage law as injurious ; and faid no man ought to be permitted to vote unlefs he had a property in, a common intereft with, and an attachment to the community ; that the act violated this principle, and would be attended with very injurious confequences ; he denied the doctrine of natural rights ; and faid that they were altogether derived from con-vention ; and at the end of the charge he exhorted the jury to ufe their efforts to prevent the injury likely to refult from the temper of the times. I cannot fay whether judge Chafe confined himfelf to a written paper, or not. He declared that the independence of the judiciary of the United States had been injured by the repeal of the judiciary fyftem ; and that the bill, then pending before the legiflature of Maryland, if adopted, would have the fame effect upon the judiciary of that ftate.

Mr. *Nicholfon* ftated that all the witneffes prefent on the part of the profecution had been examined ; the Managers would therefore proceed to offer certain records ; but as fe-veral material witneffes were abfent, he hoped they would not be precluded from calling them, fhould they attend, at a future ftage of the trial.

Mr. *Randolph* offered in evidence a copy of the record in the cafe of J. T. Callender ; alfo in the cafe of Fries.

Mr. *Randolph* then ftated that the Managers had fubmitted all the evidence they were prepared to adduce. Whereupon the court rofe.

FRIDAY, *February* 15, 1805.

The court was opened at 10 a. m.

Present, the Managers, accompanied by the House of Representatives in committee of the whole : and Judge Chase, attended by his counfel.

The evidence being closed on the part of the prosecution, Mr. HARPER, of counsel' for the respondent, addressed the court to this effect.

Mr. President—We feel so strong a reliance on the
justice, impartiality, and discernment of this honorable court, that nothing but an anxious regard for the
character and feelings of the honorable gentleman who
is the object of this prosecution, and a solicitude to
remove even the slightest imputation of impropriety
or incorrectness that may rest on his conduct, could
induce us to occupy any portion of that time which
we know to be so precious, by the introduction of
testimony on his part. We believe the charges to be
utterly unsupported, by the testimony adduced on the
part of the prosecution ; and had we no other object
than a mere legal acquittal, we should cheerfully rest
the case on that testimony. But we are aware that
some parts of the honorable judge's conduct, though
not criminal nor punishable by impeachment, may, if
left without explanation, appear in an unfavorable
light. We are prepared with testimony to give this
explanation ; to shew that through all the transactions
which form the matter of this prosecution, he has
been governed by the purest motives, and that whatever errors he may have committed, are trivial in
themselves, are imputable to human infirmity alone,
and were instantly corrected by himself. This testimony we request the permission of this honorable
court to produce. But a consciousness of the strong
ground on which we stand, and a recollection of the
very important public business which now presses on
the attention of this honorable court, in its legislative
capacity, have determined us to wave our right to a
general opening of our case ; and to confine ourselves,
in this stage of the cause, to a brief statement of the
points to which our testimony will be directed.

On the first article, which relates to the conduct of
judge Chase in the trial of John Fries for treason, we

shall produce testimony to shew, that the opinion contained in the paper which the judge delivered to the prisoner's counsel was not only legal, but had been twice expressly decided, and once admitted in the same court, and had before that trial been laid down as a general principle of law, in a charge delivered to a grand jury in the same court, by one of judge Chase's predecessors.

[Here Mr. Harper sat down, while the committee of the whole were entering and taking their seats.]

Mr. Harper then rose and proceeded. He stated that the counsel for the respondent had begun to open their defence, and were stating the ground which they should take in opposition to the first article of impeachment. We shall shew, said he, by the most indisputable testimony, that the point of law respecting treason in levying war against the United States, which was stated in the paper delivered to the counsel of Fries, had been once informally decided by the same court, in a prior case, and twice after solemn argument, and full discussion, and that one of those decisions was made in the case of John Fries himself, on an indictment for the same offence. We shall shew that judge Chase's predecessor had, before counsel was heard, and before an indictment was found, delivered the same opinion in a charge to the grand jury. We shall proceed to prove in a more particular manner the contents of the paper thus delivered to the counsel. We shall produce the original paper itself; and shall prove that delivered to the prisoner's counsel to be a true copy of it; and we shall conclude by shewing that when the counsel of Fries had refused to proceed in his defence, and were informed by the judge that they might go on, and conduct the case as they thought proper, he employed no menacing expression, and uttered no such words as " proceed at the hazard of your characters:" but merely informed them that they should be under no other restriction, but that which a regard to their professional character would impose. That far from threatening, he did all in his power to sooth ; and instead of restricting, gave the utmost latitude of indulgence.

Proceeding then to the second general head of accusation, the conduct of the respondent relative to the trial of Callender, which furnishes the matter of the second article, and embraces in the whole five articles, we shall shew that the copy of the " Prospect Before Us," which the respondent carried with him to Richmond, was marked not by him, but by another person, without any view to a prosecution of the author, and was given to him by that person without any request on his part, as a performance which might amuse him on the road.

As to the private conversation at Annapolis, we shall prove that it was a mere jest between the respondent and the gentleman, who, after treasuring it up for five years, has this day brought it forward to support an impeachment; and whose recollection of it we shall shew to be far less accurate than ought to be required of a man, who after so great a lapse of time adduces a private, confidential and jocular conversation, to aid a criminal prosecution.

We shall then follow judge Chase to Richmond, where we shall shew, that far from having formed a corrupt determination to oppress Callender, he felt solicitous for the escape of that unfortunate wretch; that far from entering into a combination with the marshal to pack a jury for the conviction of Callender, judge Chase expressed a wish that he might be tried by men of that political party, whose cause his book was intended to support. We shall prove, by testimony not to be doubted, that no conversation whatever took place between the judge and the marshal, relative to striking any persons from the pannel, much less such a conversation as has been sworn to by one witness for the prosecution. We shall shew that no pannel of the jury actually summoned was formed, until the opening of the court on the day when the trial of Callender was to have commenced; that it was completed in open court, and was never seen by the judge. And we shall prove, that the marshal, not by the direction of the judge, from whom he was bound to receive no directions on that subject, but with his entire approbation and according to his advice, took the utmost pains to select a jury of the most impartial, considerate, and respectable men; that in this selection no attention was paid to party distinctions; and that if no persons of Callender's political opinion actually did serve on the jury, it was because, after being summoned, they made excuses, which were admitted by the court, or refused to attend.

Thus much respecting the conduct of the judge previous to the trial. Proceeding then to the particular matter of the second article, which relates to the supposed rejection of John Basset's application to serve on the jury, we shall prove, more fully than we have already done, that the nature of this application has been wholly misunderstood by the witnesses on the part of the prosecution; that the juror did not offer an excuse, or apply to be discharged, but merely suggested some scruples of delicacy, and was willing to serve if those scruples were not sufficient to constitute a legal disqualification. We shall fully corroborate the testimony which the juror himself has given on this head, and shall shew clearly that his scruples were not of such a nature, as to furnish a legal or proper ground of objection to his competence as a juror.

As to the refusal of a continuance, which has been so much relied on as a criminal violation of the law, with intent to oppress the party, we shall prove, that although no legal grounds for a continuance were shewn, and it was therefore not in the power of the court to grant it, judge Chase did offer to postpone the trial for a month or six weeks, in order to accommodate Callender and his counsel, and to enable them to prepare; an offer which they thought proper to reject. And we shall also shew, that when this motion for a continuance was made, the law of Virginia, by which it is now contended that the court ought to have been governed, was not cited, nor even mentioned.

With respect to the conduct of judge Chase towards Callender's counsel, we shall prove that it was free from any appearance of harshness, or desire to intimidate, abash or oppress: that the irritation which took place proceeded from the counsel themselves, and that the conduct of the court was far more mild and forbearing than from those irritations could have been expected. That every decision on the law was the joint opinion of judge Chase and his colleague, delivered after consultation between them. That every interruption of the counsel, arose from their pertinacity in pressing points which had been decided, and on which propriety and duty required them to be silent; and that after the respondent had delivered the opinion of the court on these points of law, he offered to assist the counsel for the traverser in framing a case for the opinion of all the judges of the supreme court, and thus to give them an opportunity of correcting any errors which he and his colleague might have committed in those decisions. And finally, we shall produce a witness who having attended the trial and taken down all the proceedings in short hand, will lay before this honorable court an exact detail of all that passed.

Passing then to the matter of the fifth and sixth articles, we shall prove, by a rule solemnly made by the supreme court of the United States, that they never considered the state laws as regulating *process*, by virtue of the act of Congress which is relied on in support of these articles; but merely as governing the decision of rights acquired under them, when such rights should come into question in the courts of the United States; that the practice in the courts of Virginia, under the state law in question, has been and is conformable to our construction, and not to that contended for on the other side. And as a proof how little the recollection of men, even the most correct, can be relied on, in cases where their feelings have been strongly excited, we shall produce a record, in which the learned gentleman who, though very young, was attorney-general of Virginia in 1800, and who has delivered his testimony with the greatest candor and propriety, did himself order a capias, on a presentment, in a case not capital. We shall produce evidence to prove that the capias is the proper process, in all cases of presentments, except those of petty offences, which are tried by the court, without an indictment, and are punishable by fine only, but not imprisonment. And to remove every possible doubt on this head of accusation, we shall prove that when the presentment against Callender was made, and it became necessary to issue process against him, judge Chase applied to the district attorney for information what was the proper process, who answered a capias; and that the capias which actually was issued was drawn up by the clerk, inspected and approved by the district attorney, and issued on his suggestion.

Respecting the transactions at Newcastle, in the state of Delaware, which constitute the matter of the seventh article, we shall prove that those offensive and improper expressions which are attributed to the respondent, relative to a seditious temper in the state of Delaware, and especially in the county of Newcastle and the town of Wilmington, never were uttered by him; that the witnesses who have deposed to those expressions are under a mistake; and that nothing was said or done by judge Chase on that occasion, but what he has admitted in his answer; but what propriety justifies, and his duty required. To this end we shall offer the testimony of persons who were in a situation to remark every occurrence; to listen to every expression, and on whom such expressions, had they been uttered, could not have failed to make a strong impression.

We shall then proceed to the charge delivered to the grand jury at Baltimore, which furnishes the eighth and last ground of accusation; and then we shall prove that the respondent said nothing of a political nature to the jury, except that which he has stated in his answer, and which he hopes to satisfy this honorable court he had a right to say, however indiscreet or unnecessary the exercise of that right in this instance may have been. We shall produce an host of witnesses to prove that he never uttered such sentiments as are attributed to him by one witness, relative to the present administration, its character, views and manner of obtaining its power; sentiments which he admits would have been in the highest degree reprehensible on such an occasion; that the charge which was delivered was read from a book; and that he spoke nothing extemporary, as another witness for the prosecution has supposed. And finally we shall produce this book to speak for itself; shall prove it to be the same from which the charge was delivered; and shall conclude with the examination of witnesses who stood round the respondent while he read it, sat by his side, and almost looked over him while he delivered the charge which it contains.

This, Mr. President, will be the general bearing of our testimony; which we shall now, with the permission of this honorable court, proceed to adduce, in the order in which it has been stated.

SAMUEL EWING *sworn.*

Mr. *Hopkinson* (producing a paper)—Be pleased to inform the court whether that is your hand writing.

Mr. *Ewing.* It is in my hand writing fo far as the paragraph, at which I have figned my name; it was written by me at the time, and my name figned to it—the remainder is not in my hand writing, and I do not know by whom it is written.

Mr. *Hopkinfon.* At what time and from what paper did you make it out?

Mr. *Ewing.* I made it out from the opinion of the court which was thrown down by judge Peters or Chafe, and within about half an hour after it was thrown down from the bench. I took the copy home with me, to Mr. Lewis's office, where I was at that time a ftudent. In the afternoon of the fame day, Mr. Caldwell, the clerk of the court, called on me, and at the defire of judge Chafe and judge Peters, requefted that it might be returned; and I gave it to Mr. Caldwell. I made out only one copy, and this is it.

Mr. *Hopkinfon.* The paper being proved, I will read it in evidence.

Mr. *Rodney* obferved that the original paper was the beft evidence, and as one of the copies thrown down from the bench was already before the court, he prefumed that ought to be confidered as the beft evidence.

Mr. *Hopkinfon* faid he was defirous to read it merely to fhew that it correfponded with the copy in the poffeffion of the attorney of the diftrict.

Mr. *Hopkinfon* then read the copy in the hand writing of Mr. Ewing (containing the opinion of the court in the cafe of Fries) which appeared to correfpond precifely with the copy adduced by Mr. Rawle.

Mr. *Hopkinfon.* Pleafe to ftate whether you were in the court the day fubfequent to that on which the opinion was delivered by the court, and what you recollect occurred at that time?

Mr. *Ewing.* I attended at the court the day fucceeding, and I remember that judges Chafe and Peters, addreffing Meffrs. Lewis and Dallas, faid they were not to confider any thing which took place the day before as a reftriction on the courfe they wifhed to purfue; judge Peters faid that every thing done yefterday was withdrawn. Judge Chafe afked them if they would go on in the caufe; fome converfation enfued, which ended in the determination of Meffrs. Lewis and Dallas not to proceed in the defence of Fries. Judge Chafe then made this obfervation—that if, after the court had expreffed their opinion on the law, they perſiſted in ſtating to the jury their ſentiments on the law, they muſt do it at the hazard of their legal reputations. I did not underſtand this as a menace, but as a declaration to the counſel that they muſt do it on their ſtanding at the bar, and from a regard to their reputations. If I ſtate any thing further, it will be only a recapitulation of the teſtimony already given.

EDWARD I. COALE *ſworn.*

Mr. *Hopkinſon.* Will you examine that paper, and ſay what you know reſpecting it ?

Mr. *Coale.* It is a copy of the paper handed down by judge Chaſe on the trial of Fries, made at the inſtance of judge Chaſe, from a paper in his hand writing ; there were ſome words in the original which I could not aſcertain ; I left blanks for them, and they were filled up by judge Chaſe ; the other parts are written by me. It was made out before the trial of Fries. When in the office of judge Chaſe I was frequently in the habit of tranſcribing papers from his hand writing. After I left him I went to Philadelphia, and lived there when Fries was tried. The judge occaſionally, during my reſidence there, ſent for me to tranſcribe his opinions ; and on that occaſion he called on me to tranſcribe this paper from the original hand writing of himſelf.

Mr. *Hopkinſon.* Was there a converſation between you and judge Chaſe, in which he aſſigned his reaſons, and what were they, for making out this opinion ?

Mr. *Nicholſon* objected to the putting of this queſtion.

The *Preſident* deſired Mr. Hopkinſon to reduce it to writing.

Mr. *Nicholſon* ſaid he would withdraw his objection rather than occaſion delay. Some objection, however, ariſing on the part of the court,

Mr. *Hopkinſon* ſubmitted, in writing, the following queſtion :

At the time judge Chaſe deſired you to make the copy in your hand, did he, or did he not, explain to you his reaſons or motives for drawing up the paper, from which this copy was made ? If yes, what were they ?

Mr. *Hopkinſon* ſaid he thought ſuch queſtions perfectly legal, when they went to ſhew the intention of the accuſed. We have heard, faid he, much of the *quo animo*; and it is perfect-ly clear, that the intention conftitutes the guilt of the of-fence.

Mr. *Nicholfon.* The *quo animo* is to be collected from the acts of the party. The evidence of his declaration may be fhewn to prove the *quo animo.* But I do not confider it to be correct that judge Chafe fhall be permitted to give in evidence declarations made at any other time than that when we have ftated he made them; otherwife it will always lay in the difcretion of the party accufed to ftate declarations made at another time by him for the purpofe of juftifying any acts he may have committed.

Mr. *Martin* faid he had ever confidered the declaration of the party at the time he was charged with committing a cri-minal act, as competent evidence to fhew his innocence.

Mr. *Nicholfon* faid there was no doubt of it; but that he was not charged with drawing out the paper as a criminal act. Any declaration made by judge Chafe at the time he delivered the opinion of the court, may be given in evidence ; but any other declarations have nothing to do with the cafe.

The *Prefident.* Where was the converfation between the judge and yourfelf ?

Mr. *Coale.* At the judge's lodgings.

The queftion was then taken on permitting the queftion to be put, and paffed in the negative.—Yeas 9—Nays 25.

Mr. *Hopkinfon* next offered a certificate of the clerk of the circuit court of Pennfylvania, to fhew that at the trial of Fries in 1799, there were 86 civil fuits depending.

Alfo a copy of the indictment on the firft trial of Fries.

Alfo a part of a charge delivered by judge Iredell at the term when Fries was tried, taken from Carpenter's report of that trial, page 14.

Mr. *Campbell* intimating fome objection to receiving this paper in evidence,

The *Prefident* faid it might be read as a report of the cafe ; but what credit it would deferve, it would be for the court to determine.

Mr. RAWLE was again called in.

Mr. *Hopkinfon.* You were diftrict attorney at the trial of Fries. I will afk you whether the reftriction of the court as to arguing the point of law was not applied to the counfel of the United States, as well as to thofe of the prifoner ?

Mr. *Rawle.* I certainly did confider the reftriction as im-pofed upon us both.

Mr. *Hopkinfon* fubmitted extracts from 2d Dallas, pages 346, 348, to fhew that in the cafes of Vigol and Mitchell the crime of high treafon was completely fettled by. the court, and was the fame as defined by judge Chafe in the trial of Fries.

WILLIAM MEREDITH *fworn.*

Mr. *Hopkinfon.* Were you prefent at the trial of Fries ?

Mr. *Meredith.* On the 22d day of April, 1800, I went to the court houfe for the purpofe of attending the trial. It was rather at a late hour ; I think after eleven o'clock, before I reached the court houfe, I met feveral perfons coming from the court room ; I thought therefore that the court had ad-journed, but not feeing any of the gentlemen of the bar, or the judges, I went on ; when I came into court, I faw judge Chafe holding a paper in his hand, and he faid that the court had with great deliberation confidered the overt acts in the indictment againft Fries, that they had made up their minds on the extent of the conftitutional definition of treafon, and that to prevent their being mifunderftood, they had committed their opinion to writing, one copy of which was intended to be given to the diftrict attorney, another to the counfel for the prifoner, and a third to be given to the jury ; perhaps fomething elfe might have been faid, but I do not recollect it. The paper was then thrown down by him to the bar, and a fentiment of this kind was exprefled by judge Chafe—that this opinion was not intended by the court to prevent the counfel from proceeding in the ufual manner. I felt a defire to take a copy of the paper—I do not recollect whether more than one was thrown down. I had not, however, an opportunity of doing it. The paper was fo fully occupied till the adjournment of the court, that although I made two or three attempts to obtain it, I could not fucceed. The court adjourned a fhort time afterwards. After I went home I re-collect that an application was made to me by the clerk of the court to return the copy, which he underftood I had taken.— I informed him I had not taken a copy. On the following day I was in the court room at the opening of the court.— Fries was put to the bar, and the judge then enquired whether the counfel were ready to proceed on the trial. I remember Mr. Lewis addreffing himfelf to the court, and objecting to proceed in the defence, becaufe the counfel had been reftrained by the court from proceeding in the manner which they deemed moft beneficial to their client. I remember alfo that judge Chafe told him that he ought not to refer to the opinion which had been delivered on the preceding day ; that the counfel were not to be bound by that opinion, as it had been withdrawn. Mr. Lewis referring to that opinion, however, confidered it as the formed and decided opinion of the court, and that although the court had withdrawn it, it ftill would have an operation upon their minds ; that while the court was under its influence, they could not expect to be heard in any of their arguments to effect. Judge Peters replied that the opinion was withdrawn, and I think judge Chafe repeated the opinion before expreffed, that the counfel were not to be bound by that opinion, might enter fully into the cafe and argue as well on the law as on the fact before the jury. I recollect Mr. Lewis ftating to the court his opinion of the appofitenefs of cafes decided at common law in England. I remember judge Chafe's expreffing his opinion and belief that they were perfectly inapplicable ; and, afterwards remarking, that if, however, the counfel would go on, it was not the intention of the court to circumfcribe them, or to take from the jury the decifion of the law as well as the fact. He further added, that the counfel might manage the defence in fuch way as they thought proper, having a regard to their own characters. I am the more particular and pofitive of thefe expreffions, becaufe very fhortly after the trial I made a fummary of the proceedings. I find it ftated as coming from the mouth of judge Chafe, and that he repeated that the counfel for the prifoner might go on in their own way, having a regard to their own characters. Judge Peters made a remark which I thought was calculated to put the counfel into good humor, but they perfifted in their refufal to proceed. Thus far the court manifefted, in my opinion, a defire that the caufe might progrefs, and a perfuafive and conciliatory temper ; but Mr. Lewis having again decidedly faid that he would not proceed, judge Chafe faid, if you fuppofe by conduct like this, to put the court into a difficulty, you are miftaken. After a paufe, judge Chafe addreffed himfelf to the prifoner, and afked him, if he was ready to proceed on his trial, or whether he would have other counfel affigned to him. Fries replied he did not know what was beft for him to do, but he would leave his cafe to the court. Mr. Rawle ftated that from the peculiarity of the circumftances of the cafe, and the prifoner being left without the affiftance of counfel, his wifh was that the trial might be poftponed for a day, and the poftponement took place by order of the court. The following morning when the court was affembled, Fries was again put to the bar, and judge Chafe enquired of him whether he wifhed the court to affign him counfel ? His reply was, that he would truft himfelf to the court and jury. Judge Chafe replied, then by the bleffing of God, the court will be your counfel, and will do you as much juftice as could be done by the counfel that were affigned you, or nearly in thofe words. The trial proceeded, but I was not prefent during the whole of it.

Mr. *Hopkinfon.* Do you recollect whether judge Chafe guarded the prifoner againft putting any improper queftions to the witneffes, &c.

Mr. *Meredith.* Judge Chafe feemed to me to perform his promife. He told him he had a right to put any queftions he pleafed, and guarded him againft putting improper ones.

Mr. *Harper* faid he would next proceed to the cafe of Callender.

LUTHER MARTIN *fworn.*

Mr. *Harper.* Did you furnifh judge Chafe with a copy of the book, entitled the Profpect Before Us, and at what time did you furnifh him with it ?

Mr. *Martin.* It is not a pleafing thing for me to be a witnefs on this point, as I may be confidered as a party concerned, and efpecially from being one of the counfel for judge Chafe. Yet, as it is required from me, I will proceed to ftate what I know. When I was in New York, I obferved in a newfpaper which I took up at a barber's fhop an advertifement for the fale of the Profpect Before Us. I mentioned it to judge Wafhington, and he fent his fervant to procure a copy; and I defired him to purchafe two copies. I read it, and as was ufual with me with refpect to books any wife interefting, I fcored fuch paffages as were remarkable either for their merit or demerit; and I did fcore a great portion of the book. But I did not fcore them with the leaft idea of an indictment being founded upon them. When I fcored the book I did not know that judge Chafe was going on the circuit of Virginia. My fcoring was for my own amufement, and for that of my friends. Afterwards I faw judge Chafe. I afked him if he was going down to Richmond ; he anfwered yes. I afked if he had feen the book called the Profpect Before Us; he faid he had not. I then told him, I will put it into your hands, you may amufe yourfelf with it as you are going down, and make what ufe of it you pleafe. There was a great deal more fcored than was contained in the indictment. I moft folemnly declare that I had no view to a profecution in fcoring it; though I have no hefitation in faying that in common with every worthy inhabitant of America I detefted the book.

Mr. Nicholfon. What do you mean by deteft?

Mr. Martin. I am ready candidly to acknowledge that I did think it a book that ought to be profecuted ; and I did not think that judge Chafe would have an opportunity of feeing it unlefs I gave him a copy of it. Having fince heard it fuggefted that I had fome fhare in drawing up the indictment againft Callender, I moft folemnly declare I did not put pen to paper on the fubject.

Mr. Harper. Was not your name written on the book?

Mr. Martin. It was.

Prefident. Did you exprefs the view you had in putting it into his hands?

Mr. Martin. I faid what I have already ftated; that he might take it down with him, and make fuch ufe of it as he pleafed.

JAMES WINCHESTER *fworn.*

Mr. Harper. Will you pleafe to ftate whether you were in Annapolis in 1800, in court with judge Chafe, and Mr. John T. Mafon ; and what was the converfation which then took place?

Mr. Winchefter. I attended a circuit court held at Annapolis in 1800. I do not recollect either the day the court commenced or ended. I think on the laft day of the term fentence was paffed on —— Saunders for ftealing in his character of poft-mafter the contents of a letter. A crowd gathered round the door, and retarded our paffage out of court. I do not remember what perfons remained; but Mr. Mafon came up, and addreffed himfelf to judge Chafe. My recollection is at beft but imperfect; and of this converfation neceffarily indiftinct. In the account of it therefore I fhall ufe my own language. I may occafionally ufe the language of judge Chafe and Mr. Mafon. According to the impreffion on my mind, the converfation commenced in this way. Judge Chafe had delivered a charge to the grand jury. Mr. Mafon came up, and in a laughing manner jocofely afked in what light are we to confider the charge, as moral, political, judicial, or religious? Thefe are the words, I believe; but of this I am not certain. The judge replied in the fame ftile and manner, I believe, that it was a little of all. I cannot be certain, but I think Mr. Mafon intimated to the judge, that he would not deliver fuch fentiments in Virginia. It appeared to me that the language of Mr. Mafon conveyed to judge Chafe the idea that he was afraid to deliver fuch fentiments in Virginia, though I am not myfelf confident that fuch was his meaning. The judge replied that he would, and that he would at all times and in all places execute the laws in the manner he had declared. The converfation then turned on the book called the Profpect Before Us; as well as I remember it was fpoken of as a book written by Callender. The converfation which paffed on the fubject I cannot pretend to relate at all, more than that I have a ftrong impreffion on my mind that judge Chafe mentioned that Mr. Martin had put the book into his hands, that he would take it with him to Richmond, and lay it before the grand jury, and have it prefented. I heard Mr. Mafon's teftimony, and my recollection correfponds with his, that the whole converfation was jocular. I do not remember the particular expreffions which Mr. Mafon relates; but I cannot fay that they were or were not made. Becaufe my attention was not very pointedly directed to the converfation, and at the time, from the laughing which took place, I might not have heard the expreffions though they had been ufed.

Mr. *Harper*. What is the expreffion you do not recollect?

Mr. *Winchefter*. That if the whole ftate of Virginia was not depraved, he would carry the book down with him, and have the fellow indicted.

WILLIAM MARSHALL *sworn.*

Mr. Harper. Inform the court how foon you faw judge Chafe after his arrival at Richmond, what paffed between you, &c.?
Mr. Marshall. Judge Chafe arrived in Richmond, but whether on the 21ft or 22d of May, I do not recollect; but my impreffion is that it was Tuesday. I waited on him, as was ufual with me, and gave him information refpecting the ftate of the docket. The affociate judge did not attend on the 22d, when the court was opened and the grand jury received their charge. They went to their room, and did not return till Saturday the 24th of May, when they returned a prefentment againft James T. Callender, which I have. [The original prefentment was produced by the witnefs, read, and delivered to the Secretary.]

As foon as I had read the prefentment, at the requeft of the attorney of the diftrict the jury were taken back to their chamber, and progrefs was made in preparing the indictment. There was fome converfation between judge Chafe and Mr. Nelfon, which lafted for a few minutes. Judge Chafe enquired what was the proper procefs on the prefentment. The anfwer which the diftrict attorney made, was, that he fuppofed a capias was the proper procefs. I recollect that judge Chafe faid fomething of a bench warrant, which was a practice unknown to us. Judge Chafe afked me to draw the warrant. I faid I could not. He then faid he would endeavor to draw it. Afterwards judge Chafe defired the diftrict attorney to draw out the form of a capias; the judge faid he would draw one himfelf, and that I might draw out another; and he faid he would take the moft approved of the three. I recollect mine was drawn firft; but whether before judge Chafe and Mr. Nelfon had finifhed theirs, I do not recollect. On looking over mine, he faid he was better fatisfied with mine than his own; and he requefted me to fign, feal and deliver it to the marfhal.

[Mr. Marfhall here produced and read the original capias.]

On Saturday the 24th of May, in the afternoon, the grand jury brought in the indictment. I have taken thefe circumftances from a copy of the minutes of my office, which if the court wifh to fee, I can produce, as I have them with me. Judge Chafe alone formed the court from the 22d to the 29th of May, inclufive. On the 27th of May the marfhal brought

Callender into court, judge Chafe being at that time the only member of the court. A chair was handed to him, and he remained in court while the court proceeded with the docket in the ufual way, until near evening, when judge Chafe obferved that as the traverfer was in court, he might perhaps have fome application to make. I do not recolleĉt whether the counfel afterwards employed for the defence of Callender were then in court; but if they were they made no obfervations. But Mr. Meriwether Jones, with whom Callender refided, faid that Callender was not then prepared to make any application; but that perhaps to-morrow he would move a continuance. Then judge Chafe applied to Callender, and afked if he could give bail. Mr. Jones replied that he could give bail in a moderate fum. Judge Chafe afked Callender what were his circumftances; that in fixing the fum, he would be governed by that circumftance. Callender faid they were nearly equal. The judge repeated the queftion; and then Callender faid he was indebted about two hundred dollars, and there was about as much due to him which he expeĉted to receive; and therefore he did not confider himfelf worth any thing. Judge Chafe then afked if he could give bail, himfelf in two hundred dollars, and another in a like fum. The reply made by Mr. Callender, or Mr. Jones was, that he could find bail to that amount; and he accordingly gave bail. On the 28th May, an application was made by Mr. Hay; this was the firft inftance in which Mr. Callender took any fteps for his defence. Mr. Hay ftated that he was not well acquainted with the praĉtice in fuch cafes; that he had an affidavit, of a general nature, ftating the impoffibility of going into the trial, with any profpeĉt of fuccefs, without the attendance of a number of witneffes who lived at a great diftance. Mr. Hay alfo enquired whether a general affidavit was fufficient, or whether a fpecial affidavit, ftating the names of the witneffes and the faĉts they were expeĉted to prove, would be required. Judge Chafe faid that the ftriĉt praĉtice of the law required a fpecial affidavit; but they might take till to-morrow to prepare a fpecial affidavit, fubmitting it to their difcretion to manage the caufe as they thought proper. I beg pardon for being a little too hafty in my narrative. When Mr. Hay offered his motion for a continuance, the court faid that before they could hear the motion it was neceffary that the traverfer fhould plead to the indiĉtment. For if he pleaded guilty, there would be no neceffity for fuch an application. Mr. Hay affured the court that the traverfer would not plead guilty. Mr. Callender was arraigned and he pleaded not guilty; and then the converfation, which I have ftated, took place. The reply of judge Chafe was, after a general affidavit is made, it muft be relied on, but you may withdraw the general, and file a fpecial affidavit. Nothing further paffed on the 28th. On the 29th in the morning, Mr. Hay produced a fpecial affidavit; I have the original here. It is ftated therein that there were a number of witneffes; one from New-Hampfhire; one from Maffachufetts; fome from Pennfylvania, and fome from South-Carolina, abfent; who were material witneffes for his defence; that there were alfo fundry documents neceffary to be procured; and an effay written by Mr. Adams on canon and feudal law, which the traverfer fuppofed it important to have for his defence. Mr. Hay on thefe grounds moved for a continuance to the next term, in a pretty long fpeech. Judge Chafe obferved that every perfon before he made a publication, if he meant to juftify it, ought to know the names of his witneffes, and if he meant to juftify it by documents, they ought to have been within his reach. It was not to be prefumed, indeed, that he could calculate upon being able to procure his witneffes in a few days. That in this cafe it was alleged that one witnefs refided in New-Hampfhire, which was a great way off. He faid that the ordinary fittings of the court would be too fhort for him to obtain witneffes from fo great a diftance. He faid that the prifoner fhould have time, and he fhould have a fair trial; but he could not allow him to the next term. He faid he might have two weeks—but that might be too fhort a time—you may have three weeks, a month, nay fix weeks. We cannot fit fo long, becaufe we are obliged to hold a court in the diftrict of Delaware; but I will adjourn this court, to go to Delaware, and will return in fix weeks. In the courfe of the obfervations offered by Mr. Hay to the court, as well as I can recollect, he faid if the documents and witneffes were here, he did not think he would be prepared during that term to inveftigate all the facts and the law arifing on them; but he would be prepared againft the next term, if the court would indulge him with a continuance. After judge Chafe had made this offer of a poftponement, I do not diftinctly remember that Mr. Hay or Mr. Nicholas made any reply. After a fhort interval judge

Chafe faid, as they did not feem difpofed to take the time I have offered, the trial fhall come on within the time the teftimony of the witneffes refiding in Virginia, deemed material, can be procured. He afked the marfhal what was the diftance of the refidence of Mr. Giles and general Mafon; and at what time they could conveniently come to Richmond; and whether his deputy marfhals could go for them. The reply of the marfhal was that his deputies were prepared to execute any orders of the court. Judge Chafe then directed me to make out the fubpœnas for Monday the 2d of June; and I iffued fubpœnas for Meffrs. Giles, Mafon, and Taylor; but colonel Taylor's name does not appear in the affidavit. The deputy marfhals were directed to ufe all poffible expedition in ferving the fubpœnas: they were all returned executed on Monday the 2d of June, endorfed with the hour of the day on which they were executed.

[Here Mr. Marfhall offered the originals with the endorfments of the time of fervice.]

On Monday the 2d day of June, colonel Taylor appeared in court. The other witneffes were called, but they did not appear. A poftponement was afked by one of the gentlemen for two hours, who ftated that it had rained on Sunday preceding, which might have impeded travelling, and it was granted. Some time in the courfe of the day judge Chafe obferved that he might have till to-morrow, which was accepted.

On Tuefday morning foon after the opening of the court, the motion for a continuance was renewed, founded on the affidavit of Callender, which gave rife to the firft motion.— Judge Griffin was then in court, having arrived on the 30th of May, and continued during the remainder of the term. It was argued much at length, and received the fame decifion as on the 29th. The marfhal was then ordered to call the petit jury; twelve jurors appeared; there were fome objections, which I do not precifely recollect, to the pannel of the jury; and a motion made to quafh the array; an argument was made and fome authorities quoted. Judge Chafe faid they were not to be relied on, and he afked for Coke upon Lyttleton. I brought it from the library in the capitol; judge Chafe looked into it, and faid the array fhould not be quafhed; but I do not know the principle on which he decided. When the jury had all anfwered, the gentlemen propofed to propound a queftion to the jurors as they came to the book. I do not recollect what the queftion was ; but judge Chafe faid he would propound the proper queftion himfelf. The queftion which judge Chafe faid it was proper to propound was, have you formed and delivered an opinion (for he faid it was neceffary to have delivered as well as formed it) on the indictment ? The anfwer of the firft juror was that he had never feen or heard the indictment, and could not fay that he had formed an opinion refpecting it. Eight or nine of the jurors were afked the fame queftion, and gave a like anfwer. The gentlemen who defended the traverfer then faid it was unneceffary to afk the other jurors that queftion ; the reft were fworn, and the trial proceeded. The courfe it took was pretty lengthy, and I cannot ftate all the circumftances that took place. I recollect that the teftimony of colonel Taylor was refufed, but I do not recollect the particular circumftances attending it.

Mr. *Harper.* Did any thing pafs between you and judge Chafe, refpecting the jury fummoned to try Callender ?

Mr. *Nicholfon* made fome objection to this queftion.

Mr. *Harper* replied in fupport of it.

The objection was then withdrawn by the Managers ; but further objection being made by a member of the court,

The *Prefident* defired the queftion to be reduced to writing, which was accordingly done by Mr. Harper, as follows :

Teftimony on the part of the profecution, tending to fhew from the declarations of the refpondent, that he had a corrupt intention to pack a jury for the trial of Callender, having been given ; he offers in evidence other declarations of his, made during the proceedings, but on a different day, for the purpofe of rebutting the former teftimony, and of fhewing that his intentions, in that refpect, were pure, and even favorable to Callender.

When the Senate decided that it fhould be put.—Yeas 32 —Nays 2.

Mr. *Marfhall.* Mr. Giles was on a jury in the circuit court, on, I think, the 27th of May, the day Callender was brought into court by the marfhal. When Mr. Giles's name was called, judge Chafe afked me whether that was the celebrated Mr. Giles, member of Congrefs. I faid that it was. He faid that he had never feen him before. Nothing more paffed at that time. In the evening I was at judge Chafe's lodgings. He afked me whether I fuppofed Mr. Giles would remain in Richmond until the trial of Callender. I faid it was uncertain, that it was not cuftomary for Mr. Giles to remain any length of time when he came to town. Judge Chafe faid he wifhed he would remain, and ferve in Callender's cafe; nay he wifhed that Callender might be tried by a jury of his own politics. He faid that if his fituation as a judge would permit him to drop a hint to the marfhal with refpect to the jury, he would intimate his wifh that Callender fhould be thus tried ; but in his fituation it would be improper for him to interfere with the duty of the marfhal.

Mr. *Harper.* Inform the court at what time, if any, you were at judge Chafe's chambers, when a certain Mr. John Heath was there, what paffed, and what did not pafs.

Mr. *Marfhall.* Judge Chafe was, as he informed me, a total ftranger at Richmond, and had never been there until he held the court in 1800. He afked me if I would call upon him from time to time. When I knew he was at home, I ufed to go in an evening, and fpend an hour or two with him at his lodgings. I alfo generally went in the morning, about an hour before the meeting of the court. I recollect about ten o'clock, going to Mr. Chafe's lodgings. I went, I think, but of this I am not pofitive, with Mr. Randolph. I found Mr. Heath in judge Chafe's chamber, or in the paffage. Mr. Heath was, I think, in the act of leaving the room, he had his hat in his hand, and I met him either in his way out of the room, or in the paffage.

Prefident. Can you ftate the day of the month ?

Mr. *Marfhall.* I cannot, but I think it was the day before judge Griffin arrived. I recollect very well, on that day Mr. D. Randolph and myfelf walked up to the court room. I was furprifed at feeing Mr. Heath at judge Chafe's, and afked Mr. Randolph what could have brought him there.

Mr. *Harper.* Was Mr. Heath in the act of going out when you entered ?

Mr. *Marfhall.* Yes, fir, he was on the floor, he had taken his leave, as I fuppofed, of judge Chafe, and was either out of the room, or in the act of coming out of it. I do not recollect pofitively whether Mr. Randolph went with me. I recollect going with Mr. Randolph to court, and that it was the ufual practice of Mr. Randolph and myfelf to go to judge Chafe's chambers in the morning and attend him to court. I do not certainly recollect whether that morning we went together to the judge's chambers, but I am pofitive we left the chamber together. The court met generally at 11 o'clock. I had fomething particular to do that morning, and it was from 10 to half paft 10 when I went to the judge's chambers—it may have been about 10 ; the time I faw Mr. Heath muft have been about 10 o'clock.

Mr. *Harper.* Did any converfation take place between the judge and Mr. Heath while you were there ?

Mr. *Marfhall.* I believe I met Mr. Heath outfide of the door. There was not a word of converfation at any rate.

Mr. *Harper.* Did any incident take place refpecting a paper handed from Mr. Randolph to Mr. Chafe ?

Mr. *Marfhall.* There did not.

Mr. *Harper.* Did you hear any thing about creatures called democrats ?

Mr. *Marfhall.* I never heard any thing pafs between them. I never heard the judge fay any thing about the jury, except what occurred either at the judge's lodgings or at court, which I took to be inftructions to fummon 24 jurors above twenty five years of age, and free-holders ; that there fhould be enough to fupply the juries required at that court.

Mr. *Harper.* Did he direct them to be fummoned from the country or the town ?

Mr. *Marfhall.* I have ftated all that I remember relative to the fummoning of the jury.

Mr. *Harper.* Did he fay any thing of the defcription of perfons, relative to parties ?

Mr. *Marfhall.* I do not recollect that he faid a word.

Mr. *Harper.* Did you make it a practice to go with the judge to court every day from his lodgings ?

Mr. *Marfhall.* I walked every day with him, I made it an uniform practice. The judge's lodgings were on my way to court, not more than twenty yards out of my way.

Mr. *Key.* When the fubpœnas were returned on the 2d of June, and neither Mr. Giles nor general Mafon appeared, was there an application made to the court to allow a further time for their appearance ?

Mr. *Marfhall.* There were fome obfervations made, but I do not recollect whether I attended to them at the time or not ; but I think judge Chafe offered to iffue an attachment for them, and left it to the pleafure of the traverfer to fay whether he would have compulfory procefs iffued.

Mr. *Key.* Do you recollect, fir, whether that was applied

for by the counfel, or whether it was a voluntary offer on the part of the court ?

Mr. *Marſhall*. I underſtood that it was a voluntary offer on the part of the court.

Mr. *Harper*. Did judge Chaſe confer with judge Griffin upon the motion for a continuance, and upon the rejeﬅion of colonel Taylor's teﬅimony ?

Mr. *Marſhall*. I ſat very near them, and I frequently heard them in converſation in a ſort of whiſper.

Mr. *Harper*. Did you ever hear any part of the converſation between them ?

Mr. *Marſhall*. I did not hear any thing diﬅinﬅly, but when Mr. Baﬅet was ſworn, after having ﬅated the ſituation in which he ﬅood, judge Chaſe aſked him whether he had formed an opinion who was the author of the Proſpeﬅ Before Us ; he replied that he had not formed an opinion of the author, but he had formed an opinion of the book, and had ſaid that the author ought to be puniſhed. Judge Chaſe then turned to judge Griffin, and ſaid that the queﬅion propounded by the counſel would prevent the formation of a jury with reſpeﬅ to a notorious murder, as every man in the county where it had been committed might have declared that the perpetration ought to be puniſhed. In that caſe there would not be in the whole county a competent jury. Judge Chaſe then ſaid, let him be ſworn. I do not know poſitively that judge Griffin concurred in that opinion ; but I think, from what I heard, that he did.

Mr. *Harper*. Did this converſation take place prior to the declaration of the opinion of the court by judge Chaſe ?

Mr. *Marſhall*. I cannot ſay with certainty, becauſe judge Chaſe ſometimes ſpoke without conſulting judge Griffin.— I do not recolleﬅ any caſe in which they held a conſultation, but that on the rejeﬅion of the teﬅimony of colonel Taylor, and the direﬅion that Mr. Baﬅet ſhould be ſworn on the jury. He was conſulted as to the teﬅimony of colonel Taylor, but I did not hear him declare his aﬀent aloud, but I took it for granted, as it was not denied.

Mr. *Harper*. With reſpeﬅ to the motion for a continuance, do you know whether the deciſion was made after a conſultation with judge Griffin ?

Mr. *Marſhall*. I do not recolleﬅ that any thing was ſaid on the part of judge Griffin ; but I underſtood that it was aſſented to, as it was delivered as the opinion of the court.

Mr. *Harper*. Was there any expreſſion on the part of judge Griffin of diſapprobation of what was delivered by judge Chaſe as the opinion of the court ?

Mr. *Marſhall*. None, ſir.

Mr. *Nicholſon*. At the time of the trial of Callender, was it not the cuſtom of the judges to chooſe their circuits ?

Mr. *Marſhall*. I believe it was, ſir.

Mr. *Nicholſon*. At that time, the Virginia diſtrict was with-in judge Chaſe's circuit, and do you recollect that he ſaid he would not continue the cauſe till the next term ?

Mr. *Marſhall*. I recollect that judge Chaſe ſaid he would not continue it till the next term.

Mr. *Nicholſon*. Who preſided at the next term ?

Mr. *Marſhall*. Judge Paterſon.

Mr. *Randolph*. You have ſaid that on the morning when you found Mr. Heath about retiring from judge Chaſe's cham-ber, you did not recollect whether the marſhal accompanied you there or not ?

Mr. *Marſhall*. I do not recollect whether he did or not, but the probability, as reſting on my mind, is that he did.

Mr. *Randolph*. Did he accompany you from the lodgings of judge Chaſe to the court ?

Mr. *Marſhall*. Yes, I am certain of that, becauſe I had the converſation with him which I have mentioned.

Mr. *Randolph*. You mentioned a converſation you had with judge Chaſe on the ſubject of the political characters ſerving on the jury; that he wiſhed that Mr. Giles, and other gentlemen of the ſame political character, might ſerve on the trial of Callender; did you mention that converſation to the marſhal ?

Mr. *Marſhall*. I do not remember to have converſed with him on that ſubject ?

Mr. *Randolph*. Were you acquainted with the gentlemen who ſerved as petit jurors on Callender's trial ?

Mr. *Marſhall*. Yes ſir.

Mr. *Randolph*. Is there any one of them that comes under the deſcription of being of the ſame political character with Mr. Giles ?

Mr. *Marſhall*. I believe not, ſir. At the time of the trial, I was not fully acquainted with the political characters of the gentlemen that ſerved on the jury; but ſince I have learned, as I then conceived, that none of them were of the ſame politics with Mr. Giles.

Mr. *Randolph.* If I underſtood you right, ſir, you ſtated that a capias was ordered to be iſſued before the grand jury returned the indictment a true bill.

Mr. *Marſhall.* I ſaid on the preſentment a capias was iſſued for the arreſt of Callender, which was before the indictment was found.

Mr. *Nicholſon.* The indictment was found on the 24th of May, was it not ſir ?

Mr. *Marſhall.* The preſentment was made on the morning of that day. The court ſat longer than uſual, and I remember that the jury wiſhed to be diſcharged, but they were not, and it was five or ſix o'clock before they brought in the bill of indictment.

Mr. *Nicholſon.* Do you recollect whether the attorney of the diſtrict had commenced drawing the indictment before the preſentment was made ?

Mr. *Marſhall.* I remember that the diſtrict attorney was drawing up the indictment before the preſentment was made ; he had made however very little progreſs in it at that time, it was finiſhed afterwards as ſoon as convenient, and tranſmitted to the grand jury.

Mr. *Randolph.* During the courſe of that trial, pray, ſir, tell the court were the interruptions of the counſel for the traverſer more frequent than you have been in the habit of witneſſing ?

Mr. *Marſhall.* I have rarely ſeen a trial where the interruptions were ſo frequent.

Mr. *Randolph.* Do you remember a ſingle inſtance ?

Mr. *Marſhall.* I think in a trial where judge Iredell preſided there were interruptions which were as frequent, if not more frequent than took place in the courſe of this trial.

Mr. *Randolph.* Do you recollect any thing diſreſpectful on the part of the counſel towards the court on the trial of Callender ?

Mr. *Marſhall.* One of the counſel, Mr. Hay, appeared to be under a great deal of irritation during a great part of the trial.

Mr. *Randolph.* Did you perceive any cauſe for this ?

Mr. *Marſhall.* The court were very poſitive that the jury ſhould not be addreſſed by the traverſer's counſel on the conſtitutionality of the ſedition law, and whenever that point was touched by the counſel, there was as much deciſion ſhown by the court as I ever witneſſed.

Mr. Randolph. Was there much mirth among the bye-ftanders?

Mr. Marſhall. There was a good deal. I cannot ſay what gave riſe to it, but it was kept up during the courſe of the trial. The court was extremely facetious during that part of the trial which I particularly attended to, but I was not very attentive to the trial till that morning.

Mr. Martin. What was the cauſe of the interruptions?

Mr. Marſhall. It was the counſel perſiſting in addreſſing the jury on the unconſtitutionality of the ſedition law after the court had declared what was their opinion of the law on that point.

Mr. Randolph. Do you recollect any particular expreſſions uſed by the court on this ſubject?

Mr. Marſhall. I heard judge Chaſe ſay that the counſel for the traverſer were miſtaken in their expoſition of the law, and they kept preſſing their miſtakes upon the court; he ſaid ſo once, if not oftener.

Mr. Harper. You ſay, ſir, that there was no gentleman on the petit jury of the ſame political opinion with Mr. Callender or Mr. Giles. Do you mean on the jury that tried Callender, or on the pannel?

Mr. Marſhall. On the jury that tried Callender.

Mr. Harper. Were there any on the pannel?

Mr. Marſhall. There were colonel Harvie, Mr. Radford, and Mr. Marks Vanderval. Mr. Harvie was called very early, and Mr. Marks Vanderval; but it appeared to me that there was a great unwillingneſs on the part of thoſe gentlemen to be on the jury to try this cauſe, and ſeveral applications were made to have them excuſed.

Mr. Harper. How did it happen that none of thoſe gentlemen ſerved?

Mr. Marſhall. Mr. Harvie ſuggeſted that he was ſheriff of Henrico county, and that the county court was ſitting at the time; that his preſence was required, and on that ground the court excuſed him from ſerving on the jury. The other two gentlemen did not attend at all.

Mr. Harper. When you ſaid that the confuſion on this trial took place, from the counſel's preſſing their opinion on the jury, do I underſtand you as ſaying that it was after they (the counſel) had been over-ruled by the court?

Mr. Marſhall. I ſo underſtood it, I did not perceive any other cauſe.

Mr. *Harper*. What took place on the motion for a continuance? The affidavit filed, ftated, that the traverfer could not produce his witneffes; did it ftate that he could prove a juftification as to all the charges in the indiatment?

Mr. *Marfhall*. No, fir, not that I remember, but the affidavit is here on file. It was ftated by judge Chafe, that there were 19 charges in the indiatment, and that it was neceffary for the traverfer, in order to procure his acquittal, to prove the truth of the matter in the whole; it was not fufficient to prove a dozen or more of them to be true, if he could not prove them all. It was not fufficient to prove a part inftead of the whole of any one charge; for example, fuppofe a man fhould charge me with being a great fcoundrel, a rogue, and a very ugly fellow, and he fhould prove that I was a very ugly fellow, would that go to acquit him for having called me a fcoundrel or a rogue? Can a part proven in this way be faid to be a juftification?

Mr. *Harper*. Was this remark made by judge Chafe in good humour?

Mr. *Marfhall*. I thought him in a remarkable good humour.

Mr. *Harper*. You fay judge Chafe was pofitive. Was he harfh towards the counfel of the traverfer?

Mr. *Marfhall*. I did not think fo. I remember that he faid, his country had made him a judge, and he would be the judge on the bufinefs of that day, and whatever was tranfacted fhould be under the direction of the court. He faid alfo that he was a frail and feeble man, and that it was poffible he was in an error, in refpect to the opinion which he entertained of the law. If the gentlemen who diffented from his opinions would form a bill of exceptions, he would be the firft man to allow them a writ of error to go into the fupreme court of the United States, a fuperior tribunal, and have there his opinions tefted.

Mr. *Harper*. Did the counfel for the traverfer ftate a cafe on this offer of the judge?

Mr. *Marfhall*. Thofe were the obfervations of the court, but I do not recollect that the counfel faid any thing in reply.

Mr. *Randolph*. You mentioned that no perfon of Mr. Giles's politics was on the jury; did I underftand you, when fpeaking of Mr. John Harvie as being of thofe politics, as meaning Mr. Harvie of Belvidere?

Mr. *Marfhall*. Yes, fir.

Mr. *Randolph.* What do you conceive to have been his po-litics at that time ?

Mr. *Marſhall.* I thought, from his opinion on the ſedi-tion law, which I had underſtood was, that it was unconſti-tutional, he might have been of the ſame politics as Mr. Giles.

Mr. *Randolph.* What was your opinion of Mr. Radford ?

Mr. *Marſhall.* I underſtood his politics to have been of the ſame kind.

Mr. *Randolph.* Did you ever hear that Mr. Marks Vander-val had denied that he was ſummoned on the jury for the trial of Callender ?

Mr. *Marſhall.* I have underſtood that he denied ever hav-ing been ſummoned.

Mr. *Randolph.* Did Mr. Harvie anſwer to his name when called on the jury liſt ?

Mr. *Marſhall.* Yes, ſir, and he was excuſed as being high ſheriff of the county of Henrico.

Mr. *Randolph.* Did Mr. Radford anſwer to his name ?

Mr. *Marſhall.* I believe not, ſir. Mr. Vanderval I am cer-tain did not.

Mr. *Randolph.* Were you well acquainted at the time with Mr. Radford and Mr. Harvie ?

Mr. *Marſhall.* I was with Mr. Harvie, and tolerably well with Mr. Radford.

Mr. *Randolph.* Were you well acquainted with Mr. Marks Vanderval ?

Mr. *Marſhall.* Not very intimately.

Mr. *Randolph.* Do you know, or believe, that at the elec-tion for members of the Houſe of Repreſentatives in the ſpring of the year 1799, whether Mr. Vanderval did vote for your brother, the preſent chief juſtice ?

Mr. *Marſhall.* I believe he did not vote at all, but if he had voted, I believe it would have been for him.

Mr. *Harper.* Colonel Tinſley appears upon this pannel, I would aſk you if his political opinions were at that time the ſame as they are now ?

Mr. *Marſhall.* I do not know what were his political ſen-timents at the time ; but I remember that he had been hoſtile to the adoption of the federal conſtitution.

Mr. *Martin.* The pannel of the petit jury is never return-ed, if I underſtood you right, by the marſhal, until the jury appears in court, and the clerk of the court knows nothing of it. Did you learn any thing of the pannel that had been summoned by the marshal on the morning you were with him at judge Chase's lodgings ?

Mr. *Marshall.* I did not.

The *President.* Did you know whether Mr. D. Randolph had or had not made out his pannel ?

Mr. *Marshall.* I knew nothing of it.

Mr. *Wright.* When was it that the conversation took place at judge Chase's lodgings, when you met Mr. Heath there ?

Mr. *Marshall.* I do not recollect the precise day, but I think it was the 27th or 28th of May.

The court rose at 3 o'clock.

SATURDAY, *February* 16, 1805.

The court was opened at 10 o'clock.

Present, the Managers, accompanied by the House of Representatives ; and

Judge Chase, attended by his counsel.

DAVID M. RANDOLPH *sworn.*

Mr. *Harper.* Were you marshal of the United States for the district of Virginia in 1800 ?

Answer. I was, sir.

Mr. *Harper.* Did you attend the circuit court held in May of that year, as marshal ?

A. I did, sir.

Mr. *Harper.* Did you summon the pannel of the jury that served on the trial of Callender ?

A. I did.

Mr. *Harper.* Had you any conversation with judge Chase on the forming that pannel ?

A. I had no conversation with him on that subject. There was a conversation offered to me by judge Chase.

Mr. *Harper.* What was it ?

A. The judge recommended to me that I should get persons generally from the country ; represented that they should be twenty-five years of age, of fair characters, untainted by party prejudices.

Mr. *Harper.* What were his reasons for taking them from the country ?

A. I do not know.

Mr. *Harper.* If at that period you had been difpofed to form a jury of the political opinion of thofe then in power, would you have taken them from the town or country ?

A. I knew very little of the political fentiments of the citizens. There were, however, in town a great majority of thofe whofe politics were called federal.

Mr. *Harper.* Was that the cafe in the country ?

A. I cannot fay. I never meddled with politics in any way except in private converfation. Not attending at public meetings, I had but little acquaintance with the politics of individuals.

Mr. *Harper.* Did you, in forming the pannel, fummon any perfons you knew to be oppofed to the then adminiftration ?

A. I believe I did feveral. I fummoned the beft and faireft characters, without refpect to their political opinions. I employed two deputies.

Mr. *Harper.* Did you fummon colonel Vanderval ?

A. I did by my deputy.

Mr. *Harper.* On what day was he fummoned ?

A. I received directions from the bench on Friday, to be prepared with two juries of 24 each on the Monday following.

Mr. *Harper.* When did you proceed to form the jury ?

A. I proceeded the moment I was directed. I fummoned feveral in perfon while in court.

Mr. *Harper.* When did you complete the pannel ?

A. I completed it on Monday morning following while the court was fitting.

Mr. *Harper.* Did you complete the pannel before ?

A. Never. It might have been confidered as in an incomplete ftate at that period.

Mr. *Harper.* Why fo ?

A. It is never the practice in Virginia for the jury fummoned to confift of any precife number of perfons.

Mr. *Harper.* Did you ever fhew the pannel to judge Chafe?

A. Never at any time or place. The lift was handed to the clerk of the court on Monday after the court was in feffion.

Mr. *Harper.* Did Mr. Chafe ever fay any thing to you

about ftriking off any perfons, of any particular defcription, from the pannel?

A. Never at any time or any place, I am very confident.

Mr. *Harper.* You are very confident of that?

A. Perfectly fo.

Mr. *Harper.* You fay the pannel was not compleated till Monday?

A. It was not finifhed till that day when the court was in feffion—and the lift was never fhewn by me to any perfon.

Mr. *Harper.* It was not the practice then to prefent a lift to the clerk?

A. Never, except as the jurors are fworn.

Mr. *Harper.* Were the jurors called and fworn on that day?

A. There were twelve of them fworn on that day.

Mr. *Harper.* Did any gentlemen fummoned apply to you to be difcharged?

A. Several. At the moment I received orders to have two juries ready by Monday, I called on my two deputies, and defired them to take down on diftinct papers the names I mentioned to them. I obferved that I chofe to take the refponfibility on myfelf. While they were taking down the names, I fummoned feveral perfons whofe names were not put down till Monday. On Monday finding my two deputies had not fummoned a fufficient number, I went in queft of them. I found them at the end of the town in the act of executing my orders. Mr. Mofeby, one of my deputies, was ftanding with colonel Vanderval, I think in converfation with him. I called him acrofs the ftreet, and afked him how they fucceeded. At this time I faw my other deputy. They told me they wanted but one or two jurors. I told them they muft make hafte. About this time I faw Mr. Baffet entering town on horfe-back. I told him that he had been croffed as a grand juror for non-attendance—that he muft ferve as a petit juror, which would give him an opportunity of offering his apology. I took out my watch, and told him that I allowed him five minutes. We arrived at the capitol, and my deputies there gave me their memorandums, from which, and my own, I made up the lift of the jury. Two gentlemen, Mr. Lewis and Mr. Blakely, offered fomething like excufes. I looked at Mr. Blakely and faid there was only one excufe that I would admit, to wit: his being under 25 years of age. He faid he was under that age, and I difmiffed him. Mr. Lewis faid he might make the fame excufe. I faid I doubted it, but I let him off. As I went into the paffage, I met Mr. Samuel Myers, who alfo defired to be let off. I told him I could not and would not. He faid I would excufe him for a reafon which he could affign. He whifpered, and faid that he was prejudiced againft Callender. I permitted him to go, but begged him to keep that reafon to himfelf. Another juror fummoned, was very warm and importunate to be excufed. I told him there was only one ground on which I would excufe him. He afked me what it was? I anfwered that if it applied to him, he already knew it. I begged him to go to the court, and he would learn what it was. He did fo.— Colonel Harvie ftopped me in the paffage in a hafty manner, and with great warmth and friendlinefs urged me to let him off. He faid he was fheriff of Henrico county. I faid I knew it, but that I alfo knew that his duties were generally performed by deputies. I did not let him off. He applied to the court, and was excufed.

Mr. *Harper.* Were there any other gentlemen who applied to be excufed?

A. Yes, fir, Mr. Radford. He was in court at the time I commenced making out the lift. He urged as an objection to ferving that he differed in politics from myfelf. This I confidered evafive, and I told him I fhould call him. When called he did not anfwer. I believe he went immediately home.

Mr. *Harper.* Did you go in perfon to execute the procefs againft Callender?

A. I did.

Mr. *Harper.* Did you meet any perfon at Peterfburg, with whom you had a converfation refpecting the arreft of Callender?

A. The firft perfon I had any converfation with was Mr. George Hay.

Mr. *Harper.* Did any thing pafs in that converfation tending to diffuade you from fearching for Callender?

A. I had fruitlefsly gone in purfuit of Callender fome diftance from Peterfburg: on my return about funfet, at a tavern nearly oppofite the refidence of Mr. Hay, he came up, and entered into converfation with me with regard to Callender. I faid I had been on a wild goofe chafe, and had found myfelf foiled ; but that I was determined to find whether he was not in town. Mr. Hay appeared to intereft himfelf very much, in diffuading me from the purfuit. He faid that Callender would not be taken, and that it was in vain to purfue him. I replied, that I would do my duty, and, if poffible, apprehend him. I afked him if he knew where Callender was. He faid he knew not where he was, and if he did, he would not tell me. He invited me to take a bed at his houfe ; which I declined, as I was going to fpend the evening down town.

Mr. *Harper.* Did Mr. Hay affign any reafons why Callender ought not to be arrefted ?

A. I cannot ftate the language he ufed. He urged a great many things. Among others, he obferved that as Callender could not be defended this term, he would be found guilty and imprifoned, and faid that if he was not then arrefted, he might in the fall furrender himfelf.

Mr. *Harper.* You underftood Mr. Hay to fay, that if Callender was not arrefted till the next term, he would furrender himfelf ?

A. He fo intimated to me. Thefe were not his very words, but that was my underftanding of them.

Mr. *Harper.* You fay you completed the pannel after the court met on Monday.

A. I did.

Mr. *Harper.* And that you never fubmitted it to judge Chafe, or fpoke to him about it ?

A. I did not at any time or place whatever.

Mr. *Harper.* And that you had no converfation with the judge about forming it, except that you have mentioned?

A. None other, and that was at his lodgings in a familiar converfation.

Mr. *Randolph.* I underftand you to have faid you did not fummon Marks Vanderval yourfelf ?

A. I faid fo—but he was fummoned by my order.

Mr. *Randolph.* Were you prefent when the order was executed.

A. I was on the oppofite fide of the ftreet, and faw my deputy Mofeby in converfation with him. He croffed the ftreet, and faid that colonel Vanderval expreffed a repugnance to ferving. I told him it lay with him to releafe him, and if he departed from the general rule, he muft anfwer for it.

Mr. *Randolph.* Do you know whether Mr. Vanderval has denied that he was ever fummoned?

A. I do not, except feeing it fo ftated in the public papers.

Mr. *Randolph.* Have you ever at any time had any converfation with judge Chafe on the fubject of the grand jury?

A. Not that I recollect.

Mr. *Randolph.* Was the William Radford, who was fummoned and expreffed his unwillingnefs to ferve on the jury, the fame who keeps the Eagle tavern?

A. The fame.

Mr. *Randolph.* Did he keep the Eagle tavern at that time?

A. I believe not.

Mr. *Randolph.* Did he fay his politics differed from yours?

A. I do not know that he ufed thofe words—but fuch was my impreffion, at the time, of his meaning.

Mr. *Randolph.* Did you underftand his opinions to be of that political character?

A. I cannot fay pofitively. I have fome indiftinct recollection that he was claffed among that defcription of men.

Mr. *Nicholfon.* What party?

A. The democratic party, as they are called.

Mr. *Randolph.* Did I underftand you to fay you were not pofitive to which party he belonged?

A. I was not pofitive at that time.

Mr. *Campbell.* I wifh you to ftate when you fhewed the pannel of the grand jury to the judge?

A. On the firft day of the court after it was formed.

Mr. *Campbell.* Had he never feen it before?

A. Never, fir—I had never feen it before myfelf. The practice is for the returns to be handed in by the deputies, and a lift formed and given to the clerk, who hands it to the court.

Mr. *Campbell.* Have you any recollection of feeing Mr. Heath at the judge's lodgings, and when?

A. I have no recollection of feeing him at the judge's chambers at any time, or of feeing him in Richmond during that feffion of the court, until it was called to my mind by Mr. Marfhall's teftimony.

Mr. *Nicholfon.* Then you recollect by prefumption that he was there—did you fee him?

A. I rather think I faw him—but I have no recollection of feeing him in judge Chafe's chamber, or with judge Chafe alone.

Mr. *Randolph.* Did judge Chafe lodge at Crouch's—is it not a tavern?

A. It is a boarding houfe, and no wife diftinguifhed from a tavern. I had never been in the houfe before judge Chafe's arrival.

Mr. *Randolph.* Did you ever receive any inftructions verbal, or by letter, from judge Chafe in relation to the grand jury?

A. Never.

JOHN MARSHALL *fworn.*

Mr. *Harper.* Pleafe to inform this honorable court whether you did, or did not, on the part of colonel Harvie, make an application for his difcharge from the jury; and on what ground that application was made?

Mr. *Marfhall.* I was at the bar, when colonel Harvie, with whom I was intimately acquainted, informed me that he was fummoned on the jury. Some converfation paffed, in which he expreffed his unwillingnefs to ferve, and ftated that he was an unfit perfon; for that his mind was completely made up, that he thought the (fedition) law unconftitutional, and that whatever the evidence might be, he fhould find the traverfer not guilty; and requefted me on that ground to apply to the marfhal for his difcharge. I told the marfhal that colonel Harvie was extremely defirous of being difcharged, and on his difcovering great repugnance to his difcharge, I informed him that he was predetermined, and that no teftimony could alter his opinion. The marfhal faid that colonel Harvie might make his excufe to the court; he obferved that he was watched, and to prevent any charge of improper conduct from being brought againft him, he fhould not interfere in difcharging any of the jurors who had been fummoned. I informed col. Harvie of this converfation, and it was then agreed that I fhould apply to the court for his difcharge upon the ground of his being fheriff of Henrico county, that his attendance was neceffary as that court was then in feffion; I moved the difcharge of the juror on that ground, and he was difcharged by the court.

Mr. *Harper.* Did you communicate to judge Chafe, or to the court, the reafons which firft induced colonel Harvie to make this application ?

Mr. *Marfhall.* I only ftated that he was fheriff of Henrico county, and that it was unufual to require the attendance of fheriffs on juries. I believe the marfhal was at that time obtaining jurymen, he had at that time a paper in his hand, and appeared to be fetting down the names of perfons within his view.

Mr. *Randolph.* Were you in court during a part of the trial, or during the whole of the trial ?

Mr. *Marfhall.* I think I was there only during a part of the time.

Mr. *Randolph.* Did you obferve any thing unufual in the conduct on the part of the counfel towards the court, or the court towards the counfel, and what ?

Mr. *Marfhall.* There were feveral circumftances that took place on that trial, on the part both of the bar and the bench, which do not always occur in trials. I would probably be better able to anfwer the queftion, if it were made more determinate.

Mr. *Randolph.* Then I will make the queftion more particular by afking whether the interruptions of counfel were much more frequent than ufual ?

Mr. *Marshall.* The counfel appeared to me to wifh to bring before the jury arguments to prove that the fedition law was unconftitutional, and Mr. Chafe faid that that was not a proper queftion to go to the jury ; and whenever any attempt was made to bring that point before the jury, the counfel for the traverfer were ftopped. After this there was an argument commenced (I think) by Mr. Hay, but I do not recollect pofitively, to prove to the judge that the opinion which he had given was not correct in point of law, and that the conftitutionality of the law ought to go before the jury ; whatever the argument was which Mr. Hay advanced, there was fomething in it which judge Chafe did not believe to be law, and he ftopped him on that point. Mr. Hay ftill went on, and made fome political obfervations, Judge Chafe ftopped him again, and the collifion ended, by Mr. Hay fitting down, and folding up his papers as if he intended to retire.

Mr. *Randolph.* There were many preliminary queftions, fuch as, with refpect to the continuance of the caufe, the admiffibility of teftimony, &c. Did the interruptions take place on the part of the court only when the counfel preffed the point of the unconftitutionality of the fedition law?

Mr. *Marfhall.* I believe that it was only at thofe times, but I do not recollect precifely. I do not remember correctly what paffed between the bench and bar ; but it appeared to me that whenever judge Chafe thought the counfel incorrect in their points, he immediately told them fo, and ftopped them fhort ; but what were the particular expreffions that he ufed, my recollection is too indiftinct to enable me to ftate precifely ; what I do ftate is merely from a general impreffion which remains on my mind.

Mr. *Randolph.* Was there any mifunderftanding between the counfel and the court, and what was the caufe of that mifunderftanding, or what was your opinion as to the caufe, or did you form one?

Mr. *Marfhall.* It is impoffible for me to affign the particular caufe. It began early in the proceedings and increafed as the trial progreffed. On the part of the judge it feemed to be a difguft with regard to the mode adopted by the traverfer's counfel, at leaft I fpeak as to the part which Mr. Hay took on the trial, and it feemed to increafe alfo with him as he went on.

Mr. *Randolph.* When the court decided the point that the jury had not a right to decide upon the conftitutionality of a law, did the counfel for the traverfer begin an argument to convince judge Chafe that the opinion which he had delivered on that point was not well founded? Is it the practice in courts when counfel object to the legality of an opinion given by the court, to hear the arguments of counfel againft fuch opinion?

Mr. *Marfhall.* If the counfel have not been already heard, it is ufual to hear them, in order that they may change or confirm the opinion of the court, when there is any doubt entertained. There is however no pofitive rule on this fubject, and the courfe purfued by the court will depend upon circumftances ; where a judge believes that the point is perfectly clear and fettled, he will fcarcely permit the queftion to be agitated. However it is confidered as decorous on the part of the judge to liften while the counfel abftain from urging unimportant arguments.

Mr. *Randolph.* In the circuit courts of the United States, after a court is opened for any diftrict, is it the practice of fuch courts to adjourn over from time to time, in order to hold a court in another diftrict in the intermediate time, and then to return back; or is not the uniform practice to poftpone caufes when they cannot be conveniently tried, to the next term?

Mr. *Marfhall.* I can only fpeak of courts where I have attended, in which the practice is, that the bufinefs of one term fhall be gone through as far as poffible, before any other court is held.

Mr. *Randolph.* Was it ever the practice of any court, in which you have practiced or prefided, to compel counfel to reduce to writing the queftions which they meant to propound to their witneffes?

Mr. *Marshall.* It has not been ufual; but in cafes of the kind, the conduct of the court will depend upon circumftances. If a queftion relates to a point of law, and is underftood to be an important queftion, it might be proper to require that it be reduced to writing. Unlefs there is fome fpecial reafon which appears to the court, or on the requeft of the adverfe counfel, queftions are not commonly reduced to writing, but when there is a fpecial reafon in the mind of the court, or it is required by the oppofite counfel, queftions may be directed to be committed to writing.

Mr. *Randolph.* When thefe queftions are reduced to writing, it is for a fpecial reafon, after the court have heard the queftion, and not before they have been propounded?

Mr. *Marfhall.* I never knew it requefted that a queftion fhould be reduced to writing in the firft inftance in the whole courfe of my practice.

Mr. *Randolph.* I am aware of the delicacy of the queftion I am about to put, and nothing but duty would induce me to propound it. Did it appear to you, fir, that during the courfe of the trial, the conduct of judge Chafe was mild and conciliatory?

Mr. *Marfhall.* Perhaps the queftion you propound to me would be more correct, if I were afked what his conduct was during the courfe of the trial; for I feel fome difficulty in ftating in a manner fatisfactory to my own mind, any opinion which I might have formed; but the fact was, that in the progrefs of the trial, there appeared fome——

Mr. *Cocke,* (a Senator) here interrupted Mr. Marfhall, by obferving that he thought the queftion an improper one.

Mr. *Randolph* faid he would not prefs it, if there were any objection to it.

Mr. *Harper.* We, fir, have no objection ; we are willing to abide in this trial by the opinion of the chief juftice.

Mr. *Randolph.* Did you ever, fir, in a criminal profecution, know a witnefs deemed inadmiffible, becaufe he could not go a particular length in his teftimony—becaufe he could not narrate all the circumftances of the crime charged in an indictment, or in the cafe of a libel ; and could only prove a part of a particular charge, and not the whole of it ?

Mr. *Marfhall.* I never did hear that objection made by the court except in this particular cafe.

[Some enquiry was here made relative to the above queftion put by Mr. Randolph, and objected to by Mr. Cocke, which Mr. R. anfwered by obferving that he withdrew it.]

Mr. *Harper.* Pleafe to inform this honorable court, fir, whether you recollect that judge Chafe during any part of the proceedings made an offer to poftpone the trial of Callender, and if you do, to what time ?

Mr. *Marfhall.* I recollect at the time a motion was made for the continuance till the next term, that judge Chafe declared, as his opinion, that it ought to be tried at the prefent term. A good deal of converfation took place on the fubject. The counfel for the traverfer ftated feveral circumftances in favor of their client, particularly relative to the abfence of his witneffes ; but the whole terminated at that time by a poftponement for a few days; fo many days as, I thought at the time, were fufficient for obtaining the witneffes refiding in Virginia. I do not now recollect what the time was, nor do I fay it was fufficient. I fimply recollect that I thought it was. When the caufe came on again, there was no propofition that I recollect on the part of the traverfer's counfel for a continuance, but a defire was expreffed of a poftponement for a few hours in order to give their witneffes time to arrive at Richmond, as it was poffible they had been impeded by the badnefs of the roads ; a confiderable quantity of rain having fallen the preceding day. There was a declaration on the part of the court that they might take until the next day, and they went on to fay that they might have a longer time, if they thought it was neceffary, but the precife length of time offered I do not recollect ; but I do remember that they faid the trial muft come on before the prefent term clofed.

Mr. *Harper.* Is it the practice of the circuit courts to hold an adjourned court, and is it not in the power of the circuit court to adjourn the jury, and direct them to meet again at some subsequent time?

Mr. *Marshall.* That is a question of law I have never turned my mind to.

Mr. *Harper.* Do you know an instance in which it has been done?

Mr. *Marshall.* I do not know any instance in which it has ever been done.

The President. Do you recollect whether the conduct of the judge on this trial was tyrannical, overbearing, and oppressive?

Mr. *Marshall.* I will state the facts. The counsel for the traverser persisted in arguing the question of the constitutionality of the sedition law, in which they were constantly repressed by judge Chase. Judge Chase checked Mr. Hay whenever he came to that point, and after having resisted repeated checks, Mr. Hay appeared to be determined to abandon the cause, when he was desired by the judge to proceed with his argument, and informed that he should not be interrupted thereafter. If this is not considered tyrannical, oppressive, and overbearing, I know nothing else that was so.

Mr. *Randolph.* Was the check given to the traverser's counsel more than once?

Mr. *Marshall.* There were several interruptions, as I have stated, for whenever the counsel attempted to shew the unconstitutionality of the sedition law, judge Chase observed that it was a point which should not go before the jury, and he would not permit a discussion upon it.

Mr. *Randolph.* Then it was these checks that induced the counsel to abandon the cause of the traverser. I understood that the counsel were endeavoring to shew, without any regard to the jury, that the opinion of the court was incorrect.

Mr. *Marshall.* That was my impression.

Mr. *Randolph.* Is it not usual when the opinion of the court is not solemnly pronounced, to hear counsel?

Mr. *Marshall.* Yes, sir.

President. Is it usual for a trial to take place on the same term that the presentment is made?

Mr. *Marshall.* My practice, while I was at the bar, was very limited in criminal cases, but I believe it is by no means ufual in Virginia to try a man for an offence at the fame term at which he is prefented.

Mr. *Randolph.* Did you hear judge Chafe apply any unufual epithets ; fuch as young men, or young gentlemen, to the counfel ?

Mr. *Marshall.* I have heard it fo frequently fpoken of fince the trial, that I cannot poffibly tell whether my recollection of the terms is derived from the expreffions ufed in court, or from the frequent mention fince made of them ; but I am rather inclined to think that I did hear them from the judge.

Mr. *Randolph.* Are you acquainted with Mr. Wirt ; was he a young man at that time ; was he fingle, married, or a widower ?

Mr. *Marshall.* I am pretty well acquainted with him ; he is about thirty years of age, and a widower.

Mr. *Randolph.* Do you know Mr. Norborne Nicholas, and Mr. Hay ; they practiced with you at the bar ; did you obferve any thing in their conduct that required the interpofition of the court to check or prevent its confequences ?

Mr. *Lee* objecting to this queftion——

Mr. *Randolph*, faid he would decline putting it.

Mr. *Marshall* then withdrew.

Mr. *Randolph.* The Managers think themfelves entitled to put to any witnefs, however refpectable his ftanding in life, any queftions which they deem neceffary to bring out the whole facts.

The *Prefident.* If it is not objected to by the counfel for the refpondent, nor decided by the court to be irrelevant or improper, the Managers will be gratified by having their queftions anfwered.

At the inftance of Mr. *Randolph,* chief juftice *Marshall* was again called.

Mr. *Randolph.* Is it the practice of the courts in Virginia to proceed againft a perfon when indicted for an offence lefs than felony, fay for a mifdemeanor, by iffuing a capias in the firft inftance ?

Mr. *Marshall.* My practice, I before ftated, had not taken this courfe ; I therefore cannot well fay what the ufual practice is.

Mr. *Harper.* I will afk you a queftion, fir. When Mr. Hay was interrupted by the court at the commencement of his argument to fhew to the jury that they were the judges of the conftitutionality of the law, was the interruption that took place one which went to the argument, or barely reminding them of fome erroneous opinion delivered?

Mr. *Marfhall.* I believe it was the latter; though I am not certain.

Mr. *Randolph.* Do you recollect, fir, whether it was as to the matter, or whether the impreffion has not been made on your mind by fome converfations which you have heard fince?

Mr. *Marfhall.* My impreffions are, fir, that Mr. Hay preff-ed the matter of the conftitutionality of the law in the manner I have heretofore ftated.

EDMUND J. LEE *fworn.*

Mr. *Harper.* Were you at the circuit court in the fpring of 1800, held at Richmond, at which judge Chafe prefided.

Mr. *Lee.* I was not in court when Callender was prefented by the grand jury; but I was when application was made for a continuance, and I remember that judge Chafe, on an application made for a continuance, on account of the abfence of fome of the witneffes, informed the counfel, that he could not continue the caufe, but if they would fix upon any determinate time, within which they could obtain their witneffes, without its going over to the next term, the court would poftpone the trial. Judge Chafe alfo added that he had no objection to poftpone it for a fortnight or a month; I am not certain whether he did not fay he would poftpone it for a longer time, I do not know but he faid for fix weeks, but he faid pofitively he would not poftpone it to the next term. He added, if the counfel conceived they could obtain the evidence within the time mentioned, they might have it.

Mr. *Nicholfon.* At what ftage of the bufinefs was this propofition made?

Mr. *Lee.* I think it was made after the affidavit was read.

Mr. *Nicholfon.* On what day was it made?

Mr. *Lee.* I believe it was the firft day. I do not recollect when the application for a continuance was firft made, it poffibly had been before, but I was not in court.

Mr. *Nicholfon.* There was no fubfequent application?

Mr. *Lee.* None, fir.

Mr. *Nicholfon.* How long was it before the jury were fworn?

Mr. *Lee.* I do not recollect the day of the week on which the jury were fworn, but I remember the offer was made at the time the application for a continuance was made.

Mr. *Randolph.* Do you recollect whether the court offered to poftpone the trial until all the witneffes could be procured, or whether the offer related alone to thofe who refided in the ftate of Virginia?

Mr. *Lee.* I do not recollect whether the court faid any thing on that point; but I recollect perfectly that they made the offer to poftpone the trial for fome length of time, fuch as I have juft mentioned, a fortnight, month, or more.

Mr. *Randolph.* How far did you underftand that more to extend?

Mr. *Lee.* Not beyond fix weeks.

Mr. *Campbell.* Were the counfel for the traverfer prefent, and did judge Chafe addrefs himfelf to them?

Mr. *Lee.* The counfel were prefent, and I think the judge did addrefs himfelf to them.

Mr. *Campbell.* What then was their reply?

Mr. *Lee.* I do not recollect, if they did fay any thing, what they faid.

JOHN A. CHEVALIER *fworn.*

Mr. *Harper.* Were you prefent at the circuit court held at Richmond, in Virginia, in the fpring of 1800, on the trial of James Thompfon Callender?

Mr. *Chevalier.* I was at Richmond at the time.

Mr. *Harper.* Do you recollect what took place on the trial of Mr. Callender?

Mr. *Chevalier.* I was in the court room fome few minutes during the trial, but I do not recollect any thing that occurred.

Mr. *Harper.* Why not, fir?

Mr. *Chevalier.* Becaufe I was too far off to hear any thing which was faid, and my mind was otherwife occupied.

Mr. *Randolph.* Pray how long have you refided in the United States?

Mr. *Chevalier.* About 20 years.

Mr. *Randolph.* Have you been much in courts ?

Mr. *Chevalier.* I have had very little to do with court bufinefs. I had a fuit, and it was on that account that I happened to be in court.

Mr. *Randolph.* Do you recollect any thing remarkable in
the conduct of the court while you happened to be prefent ?

Mr. *Chevalier.* Why, fir, I recollect Mr. Hay's fhutting up
his books and putting away his papers, and that judge Chafe
faid to him, when he obferved it, fir, you may go on with
your fpeech as long as you pleafe, and I fhall not interrupt
you any more.

ROBERT GAMBLE *fworn.*

Mr. *Harper.* Were you at the circuit court of the United
States for the Virginia diftrict, in the month of May or June
1800, held at Richmond ?

Mr. *Gamble.* I was one of the jurors, fir, and I was in court
when a motion was made for continuing the caufe of Callender to the next term.

Mr. *Harper.* Do you recollect whether an offer was made
by the court to poftpone that caufe ?

Mr. *Gamble.* Yes, fir, judge Chafe faid he would poftpone
it for a week, a fortnight, a month, or more, and I think he
mentioned he would poftpone it for fix weeks, or as long as
the term would admit, without its going over to the next term.

Mr. *Harper.* Do you recollect what Mr. Baffet's fcruples
were againft ferving on the jury ?

Mr. *Gamble.* I recollect that he ftated to the court that
he had feen extracts in the newfpapers that were alleged to
be taken from the book called the Profpect Before Us, and
upon that circumftance he had made a declaration that if the
extracts were faithfully copied from the work, he was fatisfied that it would come under the operation of the fedition law.
The judge afked him whether he had made up and delivered
an opinion on the articles contained in the indictment, and he
anfwered that he had neither feen the indictment, nor heard
it read ; he therefore could not declare that he had formed
any opinion upon it. The judge faid in that cafe he was a
good juror and muft be fworn.

Mr. *Harper.* What was underftood to have been the fubject of the indictment ?

Mr. *Gamble.* It was pretty well underftood that the indictment was for libellous matter contained in the book called the Profpect Before Us. I did not know it myfelf, I was taken that morning to ferve as a juror, without any previous intimation. I had not feen either the book or the extracts alluded to, but I had heard them fpoken of as being within the fedition law ; yet I faid nothing to the court after having heard judge Chafe declare, that Mr. Baffet's objection would not excufe him.

Mr. *Harper.* Did you underftand that Mr. Baffet urged it as an objection to ferve on the jury ?

Mr. *Gamble.* No, fir, he merely fuggefted it to the court.

Mr. *Harper.* Then he did not afk to be excufed on that account ?

Mr. *Gamble.* No, fir.

Mr. *Randolph.* You fay that Mr. Baffet and yourfelf informed the court that you had not made up your mind on the charges in the indictment, becaufe you had not read it, and did not know its contents ?

Mr. *Gamble.* I had never read or feen the indictment, of courfe I had not made up my mind in refpect to any thing it contained.

Mr. *Randolph.* Had you made up your mind on the publication of the book called the Profpect Before Us, from which you believed the charges were extracted ?

Mr. *Gamble.* Sir, I never read the " Examiner," that contained thofe extracts, nor had I then feen the book called the Profpect Before Us, although after the jury retired, in order to determine on our verdict, we were compelled in fome degree to read it nearly through.

Mr. *Randolph.* What induced you to read the book after you retired ?

Mr. *Gamble.* Mr. Baffet wifhed it to be read. The whole book confifted in defamation of the government.

Mr. *Randolph.* As that book is a lengthy production, fuppofe you had read it before inftead of after the indictment was read, might it not fo have happened that you might have made up your mind as to the publication, and not as to the indictment ?

An objection having been made to this queftion by Mr. Martin,

Mr. *Randolph* faid he would withdraw it, but would afk the witnefs another queftion. Do you recollect any thing of an offer made to poftpone the trial of Callender on the part of the court ?

Mr. *Gamble.* I remember there was a fhort adjournment of the caufe in the firft inftance, and that an offer was made by the court to poftpone the trial for a month or more.

Mr. *Randolph.* Do you recollect what that *more* was ?

Mr. *Gamble.* I do not recollect.

Mr. *Nicholfon.* Was the offer to poftpone the caufe made before the jury was fworn or after ?

Mr. *Gamble.* I do not recollect at what time it was made.

Mr. *Randolph.* Did you underftand that an objection was to be made againft you, fir, as a juror on this trial ?

Mr. *Gamble.* I had underftood that I might be objected to, becaufe I had fpoken words difrefpectful of Callender.

Mr. *Randolph.* Was evidence offered to fhew that you had done fo ?

Mr. *Gamble.* I acknowledged it myfelf, and the judge faid, notwithftanding, I was a good juror.

Mr. *Randolph.* Did you fpeak difrefpectfully of Callender, and fo declare it to the court, and what had you faid ?

Mr. *Gamble.* I had faid that I thought him to be a very unworthy character.

Mr. *Randolph.* How did you underftand that you were to be objected to ?

Mr. *Gamble.* I had heard that Mr. ——— had heard me ufe this expreffion, and that it was intended to bring him forward as a witnefs to prove the fact ; this was on the morning of the day of the trial, and juft before I was fworn.

PHILIP GOOCH *fworn.*

Mr. *Harper.* Pleafe to inform this honorable court whether you were prefent at the trial of James Thompfon Callender, at a circuit court, holden at Richmond, in the year 1800 ?

Mr. *Gooch.* I was in court during a part of the time of that trial—I did not get in until the jury were called, and juft before they were fworn, I believe I was not prefent at the whole of the trial.

Mr. *Harper.* What was the nature of that trial ?

Mr. *Gooch.* I underftood it to be an indictment for a libel upon the Prefident, under the fedition law, and I went on purpofe from Amherft county, where I refide, to be prefent at it.

Mr. *Harper.* What did you obferve relative to the conduct of the court and counfel on that day ? ftate what happened.

Mr. *Gooch.* When Mr. Baffet fuggefted to the court his wifh to be informed whether it was their opinion that he was a proper perfon to ferve on the jury, becaufe he had formed and expreffed an opinion on the extracts which he had feen, and declared that if correctly copied from the work called the Profpect Before Us, the author was within the pale of the fedition law; on that fuggeftion, I recollect, the court decided, and laid it down as law, that he muft not only have formed an opinion but delivered it alfo, and the judge gave fome reafons why he muft not only have formed, but delivered an opinion. I think he faid that if a notorious murder was committed in the body of a county, which every man believed ought to be punifhed with death, and had fo formed his opinion, it would in that cafe be impoffible to get a jury to try fuch an offender, if it were an objection, that a man had formed an opinion. I underftood that he had confulted judge Griffin on this point. The court was very crowded, but I had obtained a fituation juft behind the judges, and had an opportunity of hearing in fome degree what paffed between them, though not diftinctly. Mr. Baffet was eventually fworn upon the jury. The caufe proceeded. Mr. Nelfon (the diftrict attorney) then opened the cafe. I am unable to detail all his obfervations, nor is it material that I fhould do fo; however, he faid that the intention of the traverfer was to be underftood from the matter which had been extracted from the Profpect Before Us, and laid in the indictment with inuendoes. He examined the witneffes on the part of the profecution, but I do not recollect that any queftion was put on the part of the counfel for the traverfer in objection to the teftimony; but I remember that when colonel Taylor was called to give teftimony on the part of the traverfer, the court required his counfel to ftate what they intended to prove by him, and that judge Chafe required the queftions to be reduced to writing; after that was done, I remember that he determined that as this teftimony did not go to prove the whole of a charge, it fhould not be received. He turned to judge Griffin, and afked him if that alfo was his opinion; judge Griffin faid it was. Judge Chafe added afterwards, in a pleafant manner, to the counfel for the traverfer, " you fhow yourfelves to be clever young men, and I believe you know that teftimony of this kind ought not to be adduced, but perhaps you do it to blind the people and to work up their minds to a ftate of oppofition ;" he then turned to the attorney for the diftrict, and faid he was prefied by the counfel to admit the teftimony of colonel Taylor, and that he wifhed him to give his confent that it fhould be received. The diftrict attorney told him that he could not ; judge Chafe afked him a fecond time to accede to the reception of the teftimony of colonel Taylor ; the diftrict attorney replied he would not, it being inconfiftent with his duty.

Mr. Wirt then opened the caufe on the part of the traverfer; he made fome allufion to the court's prohibiting the mode of defence, which the counfel for the traverfer had adopted, but he was interrupted by the court, and was told that the decifion of the court muft be binding for the prefent, that if they objected, they might file their bill of error, and it fhould be allowed.

Mr. Wirt proceeded in the caufe, and was endeavoring to fhew that the fedition law was unconftitutional; the court interrupted him, and told him that what he had to fay muft be addreffed to the court, but if he was going on that point, he muft again be informed that the court would not fuffer it to be urged. Mr. Wirt appeared to be in fome agitation, but continued his argument, and when he came up to that point a fecond time, he was again interrupted by the court. Mr. Wirt refumed his argument, and faid he was going on.— Judge Chafe again interrupted him and faid " no, fir, you are not going on, I am going on ; fit down." I recollect alfo after the judge had made fome obfervations, Mr. Wirt again proceeded, and having obferved that as the jury had a right to confider the law, and as the conftitution was law, it followed fyllogiftically that the jury had a right to decide on the conftitutionality of a law. Judge Chafe replied to him, *a non fequitur*, fir, and at the fame time made him a bow. Whether thefe circumftances took place exactly in the order in which I have mentioned them, I am not pofitive, but I believe they did. Mr. Wirt fat down, and the judge delivered a lengthy opinion. He ftated that the counfel muft argue the law before the court, and not before the jury, for it was not competent for the jury to decide that point, or that the jury were competent to decide, whether the fedition law embraced this cafe or not, but that they were not competent to decide whether the fedition law was conftitutional or not, and that he would not fuffer that point to be argued.

Mr. *Harper*. What was the effect produced by the reply of judge Chafe to Mr. Wirt's fyllogifm—*a non fequitur ?*

Mr. *Gooch*. It appeared to me as if it was intended to excite merriment, and if it was fo intended, it certainly had that effect, and the fame appeared to me to be the motive of the judge in adding the word *punctuatim* after the words *verbatim et literatim*. I thought thefe circumftances were calculated to difplay his wit. After this, Mr. Hay addreffed the court on behalf of Callender, and I recollect, he met with fome interruptions in the courfe of his argument, which ended in his folding up his papers, and moving as if he was about to quit the bar. The judge perceiving it, faid to him, fir, fince you are fo captious, you may go on and fay what you pleafe, you fhall not be again interrupted.

Mr. *Harper*. When the judge told Mr. Wirt to fit down, did you conceive the conduct of the court to be rude, and peremptory, or was there any thing like it in his application of the term " young gentlemen ?"

Mr. *Gooch*. I did not perceive any thing rude or intemperate in his conduct, unlefs it can be inferred from the words themfelves, when he faid you fhow yourfelves clever young gentlemen, but the law is, neverthelefs, not as you have ftated it.

Mr. *Harper*. Was this allufion made to a particular point of law, which had been agitated, or was it general ?

Mr. *Gooch*. I do not know, fir, to what point of law it applied.

Mr. *Harper*. Did judge Chafe confult his brother judge Griffin on the feveral decifions which were made, and did judge Griffin concur in them all ?

Mr. *Gooch*. I think he privately converfed with judge Griffin on all the points which he decided ; I do not mean that he confulted him at every time at which he ftopped or interrupted the counfel.

Mr. *Harper*. Pray, did judge Chafe fay to Mr. Wirt, fit down, or pleafe to take your feat, fir ?

Mr. *Gooch*. I think it was pleafe to fit down, fir. I think on that occafion the judge was proceeding to deliver an opinion of the court, and that Mr. Wirt was ftanding at the time, and that the judge fpoke with a view of letting him have an opportunity of being eafy in his feat.

DAVID ROBERTSON *fworn.*

Mr. *Harper.* Did you attend the trial of James Thompfon Callender, at the circuit court of the United States, held in Richmond, Virginia, in May or June, 1800?

Mr. *Robertfon.* I attended during a part of the trial, and I took down what occurred in fhort hand. I have my original notes with me, as well as a printed copy. I muft however obferve that the printed copy does not exactly correfpond with my fhort hand notes. There are four inftances of a variation, which I have difcovered by comparing it recently with my notes. If I may be permitted to have recourfe to thofe papers, I can give as faithful a narrative, perhaps a more correct one, than when depending altogether on my own recollection. The notes were taken at the time, for my own amufement, and without an idea of their being made public. However, at the requeft of fome of my friends, they were publifhed I think in July following.

Mr. *Randolph.* We have no objection to take the printed ftatement as evidence on this occafion.

Mr. *Robertfon* then read the printed ftatement.

[As this ftatement was publifhed foon after the trial, in the newfpapers, and was republifhed by the committee of enquiry of the Houfe of Reprefentatives, its infertion on this occafion has been deemed unneceffary. The variations in the printed ftatement from the original notes are entirely verbal.]

Mr. *Randolph.* An obfervation has been made in your depofition, that judge Chafe confulted with his brother judge (Griffin) in the opinions which he gave as the opinions of the court; did you fee him in the act of confultation, or did you hear him?

Mr. *Robertfon.* I was too bufily engaged in writing to have leifure for obferving the attitudes or motions of the judges on the bench, but I underftood at the time, and my impreffion is, that they held thofe mutual confultations.

M. *Randolph.* I obferve in this printed depofition, that judge Chafe always fpeaks in the firft perfon fingular, was that his manner of expreffing himfelf?

Mr. *Robertson.* He fpoke in that manner on all thofe occafions on which I cited him.

Mr. *Randolph.* How long, fir, have you been in the practice of the law in Virginia?

Mr. *Robertson.* I have been a practitioner of the law for 17 or 18 years in Virginia. I have been a practitioner on the part of the public for feveral years. I am now a practitioner in two diftricts, having criminal jurifdiction, as public profecutor. I have been twelve years employed in the one, and ever fince the year 1788 employed in the other.

Mr. *Randolph.* What is the mode of proceeding in criminal cafes lefs than capital; I mean lefs than felonies, fuch as mifdemeanors, affaults and batteries, &c?

Mr. *Robertson.* I will explain, fir. Mifdemeanors, (fhort of felony) fuch as affaults and batteries, are the only offences in which it is the practice to iffue a fummons, and upon the return of the fummons, if the party does not appear, a capias is directed to be iffued by the court; but I never knew, in offences of that nature, that a capias was ever iffued in the firft inftance. When I fay, I do not recollect a capias to have iffued in the firft inftance, I mean to be underftood as faying, that I never knew it to be iffued, although there are two cafes within my knowledge in which offenders, for crimes lefs than felony, were indicted and tried at the fame term. The one was a confpiracy to poifon, and the perfon was bound, under recognizance, to attend at the court which was then fitting. Bail was given in a confiderable fum, the trial came on fhortly after, and a fentence of fine and three years imprifonment was pronounced. The other was a confpiracy to fet fire to the town of Peterfburg. It was examined in the county court, and fent to the court above, the diftrict court. There they obtained a new indictment againft the prifoner, and upon that indictment, which was tried at the fame term, the perfon was found guilty, and fentenced alfo to fine and imprifonment. It was from the heinoufnefs of thefe offences, I think, that bail was required.

Mr. *Randolph.* Then in cafes of mifdemeanor, not fo heinous as to poifon a perfon, or to burn a town, I underftand it is your practice, under the laws of Virginia, to iffue a fummons?

Mr. *Robertson.* Yes, fir.

Mr. *Randolph.* Well, fir, at what time is your fummons made returnable?

Mr. *Robertfon*. Always to the next term.

Mr. *Randolph*. Does the trial take place at the next term, fir.

Mr. *Robertfon*. If the party appears he pleads, and the trial goes off until the next term ; if he does not appear, a capias may be awarded, and he is brought in to anfwer at the next term.

Mr. *Randolph*. Did you ever know a capias to iffue in the firft inftance for a mifdemeanor, and the party ruled to trial at the firft court at which he was prefented ?

Mr. *Robertfon*. No, fir, not in cafes of that fort which I have defcribed.

Mr. *Randolph*. Did you ever afk a man to be ruled to trial for a mifdemeanor at the firft term ?

Mr. *Robertfon*. I never did, fir, if I underftand your queftion.

Mr. *Randolph*. Did you ever hear of an offer made by the court to poftpone the trial of Callender ?

Mr. *Robertfon*. I have heard of it out of doors, but I have ftated that I was not prefent the firft day, it was only the two laft days that I was there.

To an interrogatory,

Mr. *Robertfon* anfwered. In all thofe cafes of mifdemeanor to which I have alluded, the punifhment is fine and not imprifonment.

The *Prefident*. When the party comes in on a fummons, and the trial does not proceed, is bail required for his further appearance ?

Mr. *Robertfon*. I never knew an inftance unlefs it was in a flagitious cafe. In one of thofe which I have mentioned, the party was imprifoned, and it was confidered as a favor to him, to bring on the trial in order to avoid the imprifonment which muft have taken place till the next term. It was however confidered within the power of the court either to poftpone the caufe or to bring it on, but I felt it a duty on my part, as public profecutor, to urge it forward; but I have always thought it in the power of the court, in cafes of high mifdemeanor or flagitious offences, that the party might not efcape the punifhment of the law upon conviction, to iffue a capias and require bail.

Mr. *Randolph*. The 83d chapter of the revifed code of Virginia has this claufe refpecting the mode of proceeding upon prefentment. (Mr. R. here read the paffage.)

Mr. *Robertfon.* That is one law on this point : but there is another refpecting proceedings upon information, which I will turn to if indulged with the volume. The book being handed to him—after fome time he difcovered and read fome paffages from the 24th, 25th, 26th, and 28th fections, page 305, directing the mode of proceeding on informations.

Mr. *Campbell.* In the two cafes which you have mentioned in refpect to arfon and poifoning, was there an application made for the continuance of either of them ?

Mr. *Robertfon.* I do not recollect that there was ; I believe there was not.

Mr. *Nicholfon.* Were they proceeded againft by indictment or information ?

Mr. *Robertfon.* One by information, the other upon indictment. In one cafe it was impoffible to obtain an acquittal, becaufe the facts and the law came up to a conviction, and that notorioufly ; but in both cafes, if they had been continued, the imprifonment would have been for fix months longer, the period of the court being half yearly. As the accufed could not procure bail, they would have been confined for fix months longer than the period for which they were condemned.

Mr. *Ropkinfon.* Then if I underftand you right, fir, you would have kept thofe perfons in prifon, till next term, if they could not furnifh bail ?

Mr. *Robertfon.* Yes, fir.

MONDAY, *February* 18, 1805.

The court was opened at 10 A. M.

Prefent, the Managers, attended by the House of Representatives in committee of the whole : and Judge Chase, attended by his counsel.

WILLIAM MARSHALL *called in.*

Mr. *Randolph.* Have you not been clerk of the federal court ever fince its eftablifhment ?

A. Yes, fir.

Mr. *Randolph.* Have you ever known an inftance of the circuit court adjourning from one time to another, and in the interim holding another court ?

A. I knew it once to adjourn from Tuefday to Friday. I have never known it hold another court in the interim.

Mr. *Randolph.* Was that in relation to a particular cafe?

A. Yes, fir. The adjournment took place to give the gentlemen of the bar an opportunity of qualifying in the fuperior court.

Mr. *Harper.* We have heard in this cafe much about political opinions, and of the effects they were intended to have on the trial of Callender. What was the political character of Mr. Nelfon, diftrict attorney, at that time?

A. I confidered his politics as violently oppofed to the then adminiftration of the general government.

Mr. *Harper.* Was he in ftrong and decided oppofition to it?

A. He was at that time.

Mr. *Harper.* Do you know any inftances that occurred before judge Chafe went to Richmond, of a decifion in the circuit court that the ftate law of Virginia refpecting the affeffing the fine by the jury did not apply in that court, and what were they?

A. There had been two inftances of indictment in the circuit court at Richmond. In one cafe judge Iredell prefided, and in the other judge Wilfon. In both it was decided that the jury fhould not affefs the fine, but the court. The indictment in one cafe was quafhed; and in the other the judgment was arrefted, fo that the decifions were not final.

Mr. *Nicholfon.* In what manner did the court decide that the jury fhould not affefs the fine?

A. In one cafe the jury was about to be fworn—when the court faid they would certainly affefs the fine.

Mr. *Nicholfon.* Was any queftion made of the right of the jury to affefs the fine?

A. It was mentioned; but was not, I think, difcuffed.

To an interrogatory put,

Mr. *Marshall* anfwered—that he knew a cafe in which a capias iffued; it was a cafe in which a felon was refcued from the civil authority.

Mr. *Martin.* Was he tried the fame term he was arrefted?

A. Not in that cafe; but I have known repeated trials the fame term; and in fome inftances trials have been had the fame day the indictment was found.

Mr. Randolph. Have you known motions to be made for a continuance, and what was the decifion ?

A. I have generally agreed to them ; but not as a matter of right.

Mr. Nicholfon. In what courts were you public profecutor ?

A. In the court of Huftings for the city of Richmond.

Mr. Nicholfon. Was that court created by a law of the corporation ?

A. No, fir, by an act of the affembly.

Mr. Nicholfon. You ftated that in going to judge Chafe's lodgings you met Mr. Heath, I think in the paffage ?

A. I ftated that I was uncertain whether I met him within or without the houfe.

Mr. Nicholfon. Are you rather inclined to think that you met him in the paffage ?

A. I cannot fpeak with certainty.

Mr. Nicholfon. How is the door of judge Chafe's chamber fituated as to the other parts of the houfe ?

A. As well as I recollect there is but one door in a narrow paffage leading to judge Chafe's room.

Mr. Nicholfon. Are there other doors leading to the paffage ?

A. I believe there are ; but I am not certain, as I have not been at the houfe fince judge Chafe lodged there, and had not been there before.

Mr. Clark. Did I underftand you to fay that mifdemeanors are tried on the fame term that the indictment is found ?

A. Yes, fir.

Mr. Clark. How was the defendant got into court ?

A. He was bound in a recognizance.

Mr. Randolph. Was it at Crouch's tavern that judge Chafe lodged ?

A. I do not know where he lodged. His fitting room was in the upper end of the houfe.

Mr. Randolph. The houfe ftands on the fide of a hill, and may be faid to have two ground floors ; was his room on the upper or lower floor ?

A. He fat in a room on the upper floor.

Mr. Harper. Do you recollect inftances of motions for poftponement which you oppofed ?

A. Yes, fir. I recollect one fuch inftance in which a man was charged with receiving a hogfhead of tobacco, and was imprifoned fix months and fined one hundred dollars.

Prefident. I underftand that you were profecutor for the commonwealth of Virginia ?

A. I was, fir. I was appointed to profecute for Richmond, while colonel Innes was attorney general. I applied to him, and to his fucceffor, Mr. Brooks, for information as to the practice; but I could never find that there was a fixed practice. I therefore acted according to my beft judgment.

Mr. *Harper* faid that before he proceeded in the examination of other witneffes he would correct a mifapprehenfion which had arifen with regard to the teftimony of Mr. D. M. Randolph. For the purpofe of correcting it he would read a letter he had juft received from that gentleman.

[Mr. *Harper* here read the letter to fhew that though Mr. Hay had in converfation with Mr. Randolph ftated his opinion that it would be either impoffible, or extremely difficult to find Callender, and his belief that he would furrender next term, yet it was not the impreffion of Mr. Randolph that this was done to influence him in the difcharge of his official duty.]

Mr. *Nicholfon* obferved that he wifhed, at this ftage of the trial, to fuggeft a queftion which had arifen in his mind; Some of the witneffes on the part of the profecution were abfent. He did not know whether the court confidered itfelf authorized to iffue attachments for abfent witneffes. There were fome witneffes abfent whofe teftimony the managers were extremely anxious to obtain. If the court deemed itfelf authorized to iffue attachments, he would make a motion to that effect.

Prefident. The court cannot take order on hypothetical cafes. If any witneffes fummoned have difobeyed the orders of the court, the court will take proper order for fecuring their attendance on a propofition being made to that effect.

Mr. *Harper.* I will proceed to fhew the practice of the circuit court in the ftate of Maryland, where judge Chafe refides, and alfo in Delaware. It has been a common practice in Maryland ever fince the federal courts were organized, to adjourn, whenever a neceffity for it appeared to the court to exift. In the ftate of Maryland there is no limitation to the feffion of the ftate courts.

JAMES WINCHESTER *called in.*

Mr. *Harper.* Do you at an adjourned court try caufes?

A. No doubt. We progrefs with caufes at an adjourned court, in the fame manner as at an original court.

Mr. *Harper.* Do you not try criminal as well as civil actions ?

A. I do not recollect any inftances of criminal cafes. We have very few inftances of criminal cafes in the circuit court.

Mr. *Harper.* Has this practice exifted as long as the court has exifted ?

A. It has been the conftant practice ever fince I was on the bench. A poftponement often takes place for the convenience of the bar—to allow time for making up the iffues, which cannot be done during the hurry of bufinefs.

Mr. *Harper.* Has judge Chafe ever adjourned the circuit court for Baltimore, and after holding a court in Delaware, opened the adjourned court at Baltimore ?

A. I do not recollect. I think there was one cafe of an adjournment, during the interval of which he went to Delaware.

Mr. *Key.* The circuit meets at Baltimore on the firft Monday of May, and the general court of Maryland at Annapolis on the firft Tuefday of the fame month. Do you recollect an inftance of the circuit court adjourning the firft week in May to September, and that a circuit court was in the mean time held by judge Chafe in Delaware ?

A. I do not recollect this precifely. But I recollect the circuit court having adjourned from May to September; and I believe judge Chafe held a court in Delaware in the mean time.

Mr. *Randolph.* Have you ever known any other judge to make a fimilar adjournment ?

A. I do not recollect. There is very little bufinefs in the circuit court, and generally all the bufinefs is tranfacted without a neceffity for an adjournment.

Mr. *Key.* It has been the invariable practice of the circuit court to adjourn to intervening periods between the ftated terms, at the difcretion of the court—alfo in the ftate courts ?

A. It has.

WILLIAM RAWLE *called.*

Mr. *Harper.* Pleafe to ftate what you know of the practice of the circuit court for Pennfylvania as to adjournments and meeting in the intervening time ?

A. The firft time I recollect the fubject to have been dif-cuffed in the Pennfylvania diftrict, was when Mr. Jay pre-fided. On fome occafion, which I do not remember, it ac-corded with the views of the court to adjourn for a few days, or perhaps a week. At firft I was inclined to doubt whether this could be done. Mr. Jay and Mr. Peters called upon me to ftate my ideas, and defired me to confider the cafe and look at the acts of Congrefs. The next day I gave it as my opinion that the court had a right to adjourn as the length of their feffion was not limited by law. Mr. Jay and Mr. Peters were of the fame opinion; but what took place I do not recollect.

I recollect in 1795, at the trials arifing out of the weftern infurrection, many of the trials lafted till 3 or 4 o'clock in the morning, and that in one inftance the court adjourned from the 16th to the 18th of the month. I recollect another inftance, when judge Chafe prefided, where at the inftance of the bar, an adjournment took place until the firft Monday in Auguft, and that the court met that day, and did fome chancery bufinefs.

Another inftance in which the queftion was difcuffed was during the trials before judge Iredell arifing out of the northern infurrection. Mr. Iredell then thought it the fafeft way for him to come to the court at 10 o'clock, and adjourn the court from day to day, ftating, however, that he did not know that this was neceffary.

The next inftance I recollect, was in the year 1804, when judge Wafhington prefided, when, at my inftance, in confe-quence of large bodies of land having been ordered to be fold, the court adjourned from May to fome day in July. I do not recollect any other inftances.

Mr. *Harper.* Do you recollect an adjourned court being contemplated to be held in January?

A. I do. Judge Wafhington agreed with judge Peters, if the yellow fever fhould occur at the ufual time of holding the court, that the latter fhould open and adjourn the court. But the calamity not occurring that year, there was no necef-fity for the adjournment.

Mr. *Randolph.* Did not the firft cafe you mentioned arife from Mr. Jay having been appointed an envoy extraordinary?

A. I do not recollect.

Mr. *Hopkinfon.* Is it not the invariable practice of the court of common pleas to do every fpecies of common bufinefs at an adjourned court?

A. Unqueftionably. The period of the adjourned court is regularly fixed; and all the jury trials take place at an adjourned court.

Mr. *Harper* faid that he confidered it his duty to do juftice to a gentleman (Mr. Nicholas) to whofe teftimony he had alluded in his remarks on opening the defence. He had ftated that it could be proved, contrary to his teftimony, that he had himfelf iffued a capias in a particular cafe. He had fince infpected the record, and found that it did not warrant the inference.

Mr. *Harper* then faid that to fhew what was the practice in Virginia he would call Mr. E. Lee.

EDMUND J. LEE *called.*

Mr. *Harper.* Pleafe to inform the court whether you are acquainted with the criminal practice in any and what parts of Virginia.

A. I have been a practitioner of the law for about nine years. My practice has been confined to the upper court in three counties, and to one diftrict court. I have never appeared in the character of a public profecutor; but generally in defence of the accufed. In the county courts of Virginia, the ufual practice on prefentments for offences not capital, and not profecuted by way of indictment, is to iffue a fummons. There are fome offences, which according to the laws of Virginia, are tried folely by the court without the intervention of a jury: fuch as neglect of duty on the highway, profane fwearing, fabbath breaking. When the grand jury prefent offences of this fort, the penalty attached to a number of which does not exceed five dollars, a fummons iffues againft the party to appear at the next court, and on his appearance the court examine him and proceed to judgment.

There are alfo fome offences which may be profecuted before the diftrict court, when the penalty does not exceed ———. In thefe cafes the court alfo proceeds to judgment without the intervention of a jury.

There are other offences folely profecuted by way of information. On a prefentment by a grand jury, a fummons iffues.

But in the courts in which I have practised, I have never known a summons against a person to answer an indictment for any offence. The practice in the courts in which I have had occasion to attend is this; when the party is proceeded against by indictment, the attorney for the state sends the indictment to the same grand jury that found the presentment—they return it a true bill; and a capias is then issued.

Mr. *Harper.* Then the distinction is between indictable offences, and those founded on presentment or information.

A. Yes, sir.

Mr. *Harper.* I understand you to say that it is the practice to issue a capias in cases as low as assault and battery.

A. In the county courts.

Mr. *Harper.* Do you recollect a question lately made under the law of Virginia in the district of Columbia?

A. Yes, sir. In the district court for Alexandria it has been determined on argument that a capias is the proper process on all indictments; and Mr. Mason, who has for some years prosecuted on the part of the United States has in all cases for assault and battery issued a capias.

Mr. *Harper.* And this under the law of Virginia?

A. Yes, sir. The laws of Virginia are by act of Congress made the law for Alexandria.

Mr. *Lee.* Is a capias the mode of process for misdemeanors used in Virginia?

A. That is either used, or a warrant.

Mr. *Randolph.* I wish to know whether it is regular to take the professional opinions of witnesses?

President. Gentlemen are enquiring into the practice.

Mr. *Lee.* Is not a capias the usual mode of process for arresting offenders for misdemeanors?

A. I never new any other mode.

Mr. *Randolph.* You have mentioned that it is usual for a capias to issue on an indictment. Did you ever know a capias to issue on a presentment?

A. I have not when the punishment is only fine.

Mr. *Randolph.* When a capias issued in the cases you have mentioned, when was it returnable?

A. To the next court.

Mr. *Clark.* Where bail is required, is it not the practice to take the engagement of the attorney instead of security?

A. I have never known an instance.

Mr. *Randolph.* I think you faid you have not been much engaged in this kind of practice ?

A. Except in the diftrict court, and fome counties of Virginia.

Mr. *Harper.* You have ftated that in cafes where indictments have been found you have known a capias ordered, but not on a prefentment. Have you ever known a man for an offence of an indictable nature taken on a magiftrate's warrant, and held to bail ?

A. Yes, fir, in a cafe of affault and battery, a magiftrate brought the man before him, and compelled him to give fecurity to appear at the next court.

Mr. *Harper.* In cafes of prefentment for indictable offences before the indictment was found, have you ever known a fummons iffued ?

A. No, I do not recollect an inftance of any procefs iffued before the finding the indictment.

Mr. *Harper.* Suppofe procefs fhould iffue before, what do you conceive it would be ?

A. I do not know.

Mr. *Harper.* I will examine one witnefs more as to this *very variable and doubtful practice.*

PHILIP GOOCH *called.*

Mr. *Gooch* faid that he had practifed thirteen or fourteen years in the diftrict court of Charlotte, and in the county courts, and obferved that when the punifhment was only pecuniary, it was ufual to iffue a fummons ; and if the party did not appear on the return day, a capias was iffued. If the cafe were important, the general practice was to apply to a magiftrate for a warrant, or for the bye-ftanders to carry the offender before a magiftrate.

Mr. *Harper.* It is not then an object in your part of the country that offenders fhould efcape ?

A. No, fir. A magiftrate may iffue his warrant, and apprehend perfons punifhable for mifdemeanors. I do not recollect any inftance of the kind on a prefentment. But at the diftrict court, where judge Tucker prefided, I underftood that a capias iffued againft a perfon for throwing a ftone at the court.

Mr. *Harper.* Was it on an indictment or prefentment ?

A. Neither. It was for a contempt of the court.

Mr. *Harper.* They do then punifh for contempts in Virginia ?

A. Certainly.

Mr. *Harper.* I will afk you a queftion relative to another part of this cafe. Have you ever known an inftance in Virginia in which a queftion was propofed to a juror of this kind—" Have you ever formed and delivered an opinion refpecting the matter in iffue ?"

A. In the county where I refided, the Britifh merchants had a great many claims againft the citizens, called Britifh debts, fome of which I was employed to profecute. It was found that it would be impoffible to get a jury, if the having formed an opinion was admitted as an excufe, as every man had formed an opinion. The court determined that unlefs a man had delivered as well as formed an opinion he was a good juror.

Mr. *Harper.* As the Virginia practice is extremely unfettled, I will proceed to fhew what the practice of Maryland is, in which ftate judge Chafe was brought up.

Mr. *Randolph.* I am of opinion that the counfel might as well adduce the law in Turkey. The article only charges the refpondent with a breach of the Virginia law.

Mr. *Lee.* I hold it as undeniable that when a high officer is brought before this high tribunal, charged with high crimes and mifdemeanors, he may produce evidence from any fource whatever that reprobates the evil intention wherewith he is charged. When teftimony is produced by the managers to fhew what the judge faid in the prefence of ftrangers, jocofely, and with unfufpicious freedom, to prove an evil intent, how comes it, when we attempt to fhew by indifputable evidence that there was no evil intent, that we are denied the right ? This high court, which I have the honor of addreffing, is, I apprehend, a court of impeachment, and not of errors. When an error is alleged to have been committed by the judge, fhall we be denied the right of adducing evidence to fhew, that if it was an error, it was common to the judicial tribunals before he was raifed to the high place he now holds ; that during the whole courfe of his profeffional career he retained the opinion, now charged as an error ; that in all cafes he held and fupported this opinion, and that he ever acted under the conviction that he was faithfully difcharging his duty; that he fat as a judge in criminal cafes for fix years; and that it was his uniform practice to have the capias returned to the fame term on which it iffued, and that it was his practice to try for offences at the fame term that they were indicted. Will the court deny this right? If the conduct of the judge fhall be deemed an error, will not this be confidered as fome excufe?

Mr. *Randolph* faid, had he known that his remark would have occafioned fo long an argument, he would not have faid a word. He was ready to admit as proven that for which the gentlemen meant to produce teftimony—that the practice was fuch as they ftated it to be in Maryland.

Mr. *Key*. I underftand then that it is admitted to be the univerfal practice in Maryland in criminal cafes, before the indictment is found, to iffue a capias or bench warrant.

Mr. *Randolph*. I admit it.

Mr. *Key*. And that in all cafes where there is a prefentment, a capias or bench warrant iffues *inftanter*.

Mr. *Randolph*. I admit that it is the *general* practice.

Mr. *Key*. That is fufficient.

Mr. *Martin*. And that it is the general practice to try the firft term.

Mr. *Nicholfon*. I admit that this is the cafe in capital cafes; but not in lighter cafes, if the party accufed oppofe it.

Mr. *Martin*. The reverfe is the cafe. The court will rather avoid preffing a trial in capital cafes, where the life of the party is involved.

Mr. *Wright* faid he wifhed to put a queftion to Mr. Martin in his capacity of a witnefs. In what cafes have you ever known a bench warrant to iffue?

Mr. MARTIN. I have practiced for twenty-feven years: and the invariable practice is to iffue a bench warrant immediately on the prefentment; in all cafes from the loweft to the higheft offences.

Prefident. Is there any difference between a capias and a warrant?

Mr. *Martin*. They are the fame, except that one is iffued by a magiftrate, and the other by the court.

Mr. *Lee* here adduced a number of authorities, (the greater part of which he barely referred to,) for the purpofe of exhibiting fully the grounds of the defence. As thefe were again introduced in the arguments of counfel, we fhall only, in this place, refer to them. He referred to the 14th and 34th fections of the judicial act of the United States; to 2d Dallas, 411—Gilbert's law of evidence, page 307, 308—alfo page 333—2d Dallas 235, 341.

Mr. *Harper* faid they would proceed to adduce teftimony relative to the 7th article.

GUNNING BEDFORD *fworn.*

Mr. *Harper.* Pleafe to ftate to the court whether you were prefent in your judicial character at a circuit court held at Wilmington in 1800, and relate the circumftances which occurred?

A. I attended that court on the 27th of June. Judge Chafe prefided. I arrived in the morning about half an hour before judge Chafe. We went into court about 11 o'clock. The grand jury was called and empannelled. The judge delivered a charge; they retired to their box; after an abfence of not more than an hour they returned to the bar. They were afked by the judge whether they had any bills or prefentments to make to the court. They faid they had none. The court called on the attorney of the diftrict to fay whether there was any bufinefs likely to be brought forward. He replied that there was none. Some of the grand jury then exprefled a wifh to be difcharged. Judge Chafe faid it was unufual for the court to difcharge the grand jury fo early in the feffion; it is not the practice in any circuit court in which I have fat. He turned round to me, and faid, Mr. Bedford, what is your ufual practice? I faid it depended upon circumftances, and on the bufinefs before the court; that when the court was fatisfied there was nothing to detain them they were difcharged. Mr. Chafe then turned to the jury, and obferved, "But gentlemen of the jury, I am informed that there is conducted in this ftate (but I am only *informed*) a feditious newfpaper, the editor of which is in the practice of libelling and abufing the government. His name is ———— but perhaps I may do injuftice to the man by mentioning his name. Have you, gentlemen of the jury, ever turned your attention to the fubject." It was anfwered, no. "But, refumed the judge, it is your duty to attend to things of this kind. I have given you in charge the fedition act, among other things. If there is any thing in what is fuggefted to you, it is your duty to

enquire into it." He added, " It is high time that this feditious printer fhould be corrected ; you know that the profpe-
rity and happinefs of the country depend upon it." He then
turned to the attorney of the diftrict, and faid Mr. attorney,
can you find a file of thofe papers ? He anfwered that he did
not know. A perfon in court offered to procure a file. The
attorney then faid as a file was found, he would look it over.
Can you, faid the judge, look it over, and examine it by to-
morrow at 10 o'clock. Mr. attorney faid he would. Mr.
Chafe then turned to the grand jury, and faid, " gentlemen,
you muft attend to-morrow at ten o'clock." Other bufinefs
was gone into, and the court adjourned about two o'clock.

On my way to judge Chafe's lodgings, I faid to him, my
friend, I believe you know not where you are ; the people of
this county are very much oppofed to the fedition law, and
will not be pleafed with what you faid. Judge Chafe clapped
his hand upon my fhoulders and replied, " My dear Bedford,
no matter where we are, or among whom we are, we muft
do our duty."

The next day we went into court about 10 o'clock. The
grand jury went to their chamber, and I believe Mr. Read returned with them into court. They were afked if they had
any thing to offer to the court ; and the attorney was called
on again to ftate whether he had found any thing in the file
of a feditious nature. He had a file of the papers before him,
and he faid he had found nothing that was a proper fubject
for the notice of the jury, unlefs a piece, relating to judge
Chafe himfelf. The judge anfwered, take no notice of that,
my fhoulders are broad and they are able to bear it ; but where
there is a violation of a pofitive law of the United States it is
neceffary to notice it.

Mr. *Harper*. Did judge Chafe fay nothing about a feditious temper in the town of Wilmington in Newcaftle county ?

A. I do not recollect that he did. The fubject has occupied my attention fince I faw Mr. Read's teftimony given
to the committee of enquiry of the Houfe of Reprefentatives ; and I have not been able to trace in my mind any recollection of the kind. What I faid to the judge fhews that
I did not hear fuch remarks. Another circumftance ftrength-
ens my conviction that no fuch remarks fell from him. There
was a publication in the Mirrcr on the 4th of July, giving an
account of the proceedings of the court ; in which many cir-

cumſtances that occurred appeared to me to be highly exaggerated; and yet in that publication no ſuch remarks are aſcribed to the judge.

Mr. *Harper.* Was there any thing authoritative or commanding in the language of judge Chaſe to the attorney of the diſtrict; or was what he ſaid in the nature of a requeſt?

A. It was a requeſt made in the uſual ſtyle of a requeſt.

Mr. *Harper.* Was the buſineſs conducted with apparent good humor?

A. It appeared ſo to me.

Mr. *Harper.* From what ſource did the printer obtain his ſtatement of the proceedings of the court?

A. The printer ſtated that he had it from a perſon in court.

Mr. *Randolph.* Was the title of the paper mentioned at the time?

A. I think not. I believe, I ſuggeſted the title, when enquiry was made as to the procuring a file.

Mr. *Rodney.* In what manner did the judge addreſs the grand jury?

A. In his uſual manner of ſpeaking; but without paſſion.

Mr. *Rodney.* Do you recollect whether on the 2d day there was not an unuſual concourſe of people in court?

A. I believe there was.

Mr. *Rodney.* Did not judge Chaſe aſk whether there were not two printers in town?

A. I believe he did aſk that queſtion.

Mr. *Rodney.* You do not recollect a ſuggeſtion by the diſtrict attorney that the paragraph you have alluded to did not come within the ſedition law?

A. I do not recollect it.

Mr. *Nicholſon.* Do you recollect the particular expreſſion of judge Chaſe when he aſked if there were not two printers?

A. He ſpoke very much in theſe terms—" Perhaps I am going too far—I may do the man injuſtice. Have you not two printers?"

Mr. *Nicholſon.* In the town or ſtate?

A. I do not recollect. I think it is more than probable that he mentioned the town.

Mr. *Nicholſon.* You are not certain whether judge Chaſe cited the title of the paper?

A. I am not certain.

Mr. *Nicholſon.* What induced you to conſider what he ſaid as applicable to the Mirror?

A. We had two papers printed in Wilmington, one of which was federal, and the other, the Mirror, democratic.

Mr. *Rodney.* Do you recollect whether it is the general practice in Delaware to difcharge the grand jury the fame day they are empannelled?

A. I believe it is the general practice.

Mr. *Randolph.* Do you recollect whether the judge, when fpeaking of the printer, faid, " and one of them, if report does not much belie him, is a feditious printer and muft be taken notice of. I confider it a part of my duty, and it fhall or muft be noticed. And it is your duty, Mr. attorney, to ex-amine minutely and unremittingly into affairs of this nature ; the times, fir, require that this feditious fpirit which pervades too many of our preffes, fhould be difcouraged and reprefled."

A. I have no recollection of fuch words.

Mr. *Harper.* Do you know who gave the information to judge Chafe about the printer—was it yourfelf ?

A. It was not—I had not the opportunity, as I came to town at a late hour.

NICHOLAS VANDYKE *fworn.*

Mr. *Harper.* Pleafe to ftate whether you were at the cir-cuit court for Delaware in the year 1800 ?

A. I attended the circuit court held in Newcaftle on the 27th and 28th June 1800. I was not prefent when the court opened ; but I think I entered the court houfe while judge Chafe was delivering a charge to the grand jury. After its delivery the grand jury retired ; they were abfent a fhort time ; and as well as I can recollect before and when they returned, I was either out of the court houfe, or engaged in converfation with fome perfons out of the bar. I think fo, as I have no recollection of the queftion put to the grand ju-ry, whether they had found any bills, and that put to the diftrict attorney. I entered the bar while there was a paufe, and filence prevailed. I recollect that the firft circumftance that attracted my attention was the obfervation of judge Chafe to the grand jury, that fince he had come among them, he had been credibly informed that there was a feditious print-er within the ftate, in the habit of libelling the government of the United States, and having received this information, he thought it his duty to call the attention of the grand jury to the fubject. He appeared to me to be proceeding to ftate the name of the printer; but he did not name him. He faid that might be doing injuftice to the man, or that it was improper in him. I cannot fay which was the term he ufed. I think he then afked the diftrict attorney if there were not two printers in the ftate. He anfwered, that there were. There was then fome converfation between the judge and the diftrict attorney. My impreffion was that it conveyed a requeft from judge Chafe to the diftrict attorney to enquire into the fubject on which he had previoufly fpoken to the jury. Mr. attorney faid that he had not feen the papers. The judge afked him whether he could not procure a file of them. I do not recollect that the name of the printer was mentioned then, or during the whole fittings of the court. Some perfon at the bar faid a file could be procured. Judge Chafe afked the attorney, if he could make the enquiry by to-morrow at 10 o'clock. About this time I heard fome obfervations made refpecting the difcharge of the grand jury on that day. Some of the gentlemen faid it was a bufy feafon, that they were farmers and were defirous of returning to their homes. Judge Chafe replied, that might be very true ; but that the bufinefs of the public was alfo important ; it muft be attended to ; and therefore he could not difcharge them. I do not pretend to fay I have purfued the language ufed. I have only attempted to give my impreffion of the facts that occurred.

Mr. *Harper.* Did you hear any fuch phrafe as this—that a feditious temper had manifefted itfelf in the ftate of Delaware, in Newcaftle county, and more efpecially in the town of Wilmington ?

A. I do not think I heard fuch expreffions.

Mr. *Harper.* What was the manner of judge Chafe in addreffing the diftrict attorney ?

A. His ufual manner; which is always warm and earneft.

Mr. *Harper.* Did he fay any thing that was authoritative or imperious to the diftrict attorney ?

A. It did not ftrike me fo.

Mr. *Harper.* But made a requeft in the ufual way ?

A. Yes, fir. On the fecond day a fhort time after I entered the court, fome perfon fpoke to the diftrict attorney, who foon after, as I fuppofed, went to the grand jury ; in a fhort time after he returned, and then the grand jury, with a file of papers. The judge enquired of the jury whether they had any thing to lay before the court. They faid they had not. The fame queftion was put to the diftrict attorney, who anfwered there was nothing, unlefs a certain piece againft judge Chafe. Judge Chafe faid that was not a proper fubject of enquiry; it was only matter that tended to libel the government of the United States, that was a proper fubject of enquiry for the grand jury.

Mr. Nicholfon. Is your recollection of what occurred very perfect?

A. I cannot fay that it is, after fo long a lapfe of time. I only ftate my prefent impreffions of what occurred.

ARCHIBALD HAMILTON *fworn.*

Mr. Harper. Pleafe to inform the court whether you were prefent at a circuit court for Delaware in 1800?

A. I recollect that I was prefent on the 27th of June. I arrived about ten o'clock, at which time judge Chafe was not there. Some time after, the court was formed, the grand jury was fworn, and judge Chafe delivered a charge. Having retired for about an hour, the grand jury returned to the bar. Judge Chafe afked them if they had any bills or prefentments to make. Their reply was that they had not. Judge Chafe then afked the attorney of the diftrict if he had no bufinefs to lay before them. He faid he had not. The jury requefted to be difcharged. Judge Chafe faid it was not ufual to difcharge them fo early, fome bufinefs might occur during the courfe of the day. He told them, he had been informed that there was a printer who was guilty of libelling the government of the United States—his name is——here he ftopped, and faid, " perhaps I may commit myfelf, and do injuftice to the man. Have you not two printers?" The attorney faid there were. Well, faid judge Chafe, cannot you find a file of the papers of the one I allude to? Mr. Read faid he did not take the papers, or that he had not a file. Some perfon then obferved that a file could be got at Mr. Crows. Judge Chafe afked the attorney if he could examine the papers by the next morning. Mr. Read faid, that under the directions of the court, he conceived it to be his duty, and he would do it.

On the fecond day the fame queftions, whether they had found any bills, were put to the grand jury. They anfwered that they had not. Mr. Chafe afked the attorney of the diftrict if he had found any thing in the papers that required the interpofition of the jury. He faid that he had found nothing which in his opinion came within the fedition law ; but there was a paragraph againft his honor. Judge Chafe faid that was not what he alluded to. He was abufed from one end of the continent to the other ; but his fhoulders were broad enough to bear it.

Mr. *Harper.* Did the judge fay any thing of a feditious temper in the ftate ?

A. I do not recollect any fuch expreffions.

Mr. *Harper.* Were you in the court the whole time ?

A. I was.

Mr. *Harper.* How were you fituated ?

A. I was directly under judge Chafe, and nothing could fall from him without my hearing it.

Mr. *Rodney.* Do you recollect whether he mentioned the name of the paper ?

A. I do not recollect that he did.

Mr. *Rodney.* What was the manner of the judge ?

A. I faw nothing unufual.

Mr. *Rodney.* Do you recollect whether his manner made any impreffion at the bar ?

A. On no body but the printer.

Mr. *Rodney.* Do you recollect that the diftrict attorney faid he conceived it his duty to enquire into matter of the kind alluded to ?

A. I do.

JOHN HALL *fworn.*

Mr. *Harper.* Were you prefent at the circuit court for Delaware held in June 1800 ?

A. I believe I was in court when they met, and when the grand jury were called, and returned into court. I have but a faint recollection of what paffed between the court and the jury after they returned ; I was at a confiderable diftance from the court.—I was not prefent the fecond day.

Mr. *Harper.* Do you recollect what occurred the firft day about a printer ?

A. I recollect that judge Chafe faid he was credibly in-formed there was a feditious paper publifhed in the ftate of Delaware—and he made enquiry of the jury whether any thing of that nature had come under their notice—They faid it had not.

Mr. *Harper.* What did judge Chafe then fay?

A. I cannot recollect particularly.

Mr. *Harper.* What did he fay afterwards?

A. There was fome converfation between judge Chafe and the diftrict attorney. The judge afked him whether he had feen any thing of the kind he had alluded to. He faid he had not. The judge afked him if he could procure a file of the papers.

Mr. *Harper.* Did judge Chafe fay any thing about a feditious temper in the ftate of Delaware, or New Caftle county, or in the town of Wilmington?

A. I do not recollect.

Mr. *Rodney.* Was Mr. Mc Mechon a member of the grand jury?

A. Yes, fir. He and judge Chafe went to court together.

GUNNING BEDFORD *called.*

Mr. *Rodney.* Did judge Chafe, in a converfation with you, fubfequent to the difcharge of the grand jury, complain that he could not get a perfon indicted in Delaware for fedition, though he could in Virginia?

Mr. *Bedford.* I have no diftinct recollection of that kind. I have fome indiftinct recollection that in a fmall circle of friends, though not to me perfonally, he faid fome fuch thing in a jocular way.

SAMUEL MOORE *affirmed.*

Mr. *Harper.* Were you in the circuit court held in Delaware in June 1800 when it met?

A. No, fir. I did not attend early enough on the firft day to hear the charge given to the grand jury. I think I did not attend before 12 o'clock. I attended as a juror. On the next day I attended early, and was in the court houfe when the court met. When the jury returned into court, enquiry was made whether they had any bills or prefentments to make. They anfwered no. The court then enquired of the attorney of the diftrict whether he had any bufinefs to lay before the grand jury. He faid he had not. While he was making this reply, he rofe, and laid hold of a file of newfpapers, which I took to be the Mirror of the Times, and while he was in the act of prefenting it, he obferved that he had not feen any thing that in his opinion required notice, unlefs it were a publication reflecting on judge Chafe, which did not appear to him to come under the fedition law. Judge Chafe anfwered, no, fir; they have abufed me from one end of the continent to the other; but it is the government, and not myfelf, that I wifh protected from calumny. Immediately after the grand jury were difcharged.

Mr. *Harper.* Have you ever feen the printed depofition of Mr. Read on this fubject? If you are acquainted with any particular circumftances relative to it pleafe to ftate them.

A. I no not know any particular circumftances refpecting it.

Mr. *Harper.* I mean to enquire whether there was any confultation?

A. If you mean a private converfation, it may be improper to ftate what may be confidered as confidential.

Mr. *Harper.* I will not then afk it.

Mr. *Nicholfon.* If thefe queftions are ftated with a view to impeach the teftimony of Mr. Read, I hope they will be put and anfwered.

Mr. *Harper.* I will ftate the object of the queftion. It is to difcredit the teftimony of Mr. Read by particular circumftances that occurred in a converfation between the witnefs and him. If the witnefs knows of no fuch circumftances I have been mifinformed.

Mr. *Rodney.* Confcious that nothing which can be ftated will in the leaft invalidate the teftimony of Mr. Read, it is my wifh, and that of the managers, to allow the fulleft liberty to the witnefs to ftate any thing he knows.

Mr. *Moore.* I will anfwer any queftions put, but unlefs directed I fhall not confider it correct to relate a confidential converfation.

Mr. *Harper.* I will wave all further enquiry, if the witnefs deem it indelicate.

Mr. *Moore* intimated that he did fo deem it.

Mr. *Randolph.* I will afk the witnefs if he ever had a converfation with Mr. Read on the fubject.

A. Frequently.

Mr. *Randolph.* I underftand you to fay that you do not know any thing that goes to invalidate Mr. Read's teftimony.

A. Yes fir.

Mr. *Randolph.* That is all we want.

Mr. *Hopkinfon* here adduced a charge delivered by chief juftice M'Kean in November 1797 in Philadelphia, printed in
Claypoole's paper in December 1797 (refpecting alleged libellous publications of William Cobbett.)

Mr. *Harper.* We will now adduce teftimony relative to
the 8th article. But before we call our witneffes, I will afk
a queftion or two of Mr. Montgomery.

Mr. MONTGOMERY *was called.*

Mr. *Harper.* Will you look at that paper. Is it the publication referred to in your teftimony as having been fent to the
prefs ?

Mr. *Montgomery.* Yes, fir.

Mr. *Harper.* Did you ever fend any other publication of
the fame kind to a newfpaper ?

A. No, fir.

Mr. *Harper.* I will offer this publication in evidence and
I will proceed to read it.

Mr. *Montgomery.* A fhort time after I returned home,
from my recollection at that time, I committed to paper
what I conceived to be the fubftance of the charge delivered
by judge Chafe, and made my comments upon it. The court
will obferve that it refers to other conduct of judge Chafe in
the ftate of Maryland.

Mr. Harper here read the paper above alluded to from the
Baltimore American of the 30th June, 1803, and added,
this is the temper of the witnefs, who has on a previous day
given his teftimony in this court.

Mr. *Harper.* I will now proceed to fhow that Mr. Montgomery, in his ftrong anxiety to get judge Chafe impeached,
has remembered things which nobody elfe remembers, and has
heard things which nobody elfe heard.

Mr. *Randolph.* I will afk of this court whether the witneffes we have called are not under their protection ?

The *Prefident.* If the counfel, in the teftimony they adduce, come up to what they ftate they can prove, they will
not be fubject to reproach; if they do not, they merit it.

Mr. *Randolph.* I have no objection to the counfel im-
pugning the veracity of one witnefs by the evidence of another,

and defcanting upon it; but I think they take an improper liberty when they undertake to fay before it is proved, that what is depofed by a witnefs never paffed.

The *Prefident.* I underftand the gentleman to fay that he will prove by another witnefs, that what has been depofed never did pafs.

Mr. *Harper.* Precifely fo, fir.

WILLIAM H. WINDER *fworn.*

Mr. *Harper.* I will afk you whether you was in the circuit court of the United States held at Baltimore, in May 1803 ? I will however previoufly obferve that it is not my intention to fay or to prove that the witnefs, when he depofed to certain facts, knew that they had not paffed. I mean only to impeach his correctnefs, and to infer that as he was angry, he gave to what he heard, the coloring of his own feelings.

Mr. *Winder.* I was prefent at that court when it was opened, and the jury empannelled, and I heard judge Chafe deliver his charge. After delivering the general and ufual charge to the grand jury, he faid he begged leave to detain them a few minutes while he made fome general reflections on the fituation of public affairs. He commenced by laying down fome abftract opinions, ftating that that government was the moft free and happy that was the beft adminiftered ; that a republic might be in flavery, and a monarchy free. He alfo drew fome diftinctions with regard to the doctrine of equal rights, and faid, that the idea of perfect equality of rights, more particularly fuch as had been broached in France, was fanciful and untrue, that the only doctrine contended for with propriety was, the equal protection of all claffes from oppreffion. He commented on the repeal of the judiciary fyftem of the United States, and remarked that it had a tendency to weaken the judiciary, and to render it dependent. He then adverted to the laws of Maryland refpecting the judiciary as tending to the fame effect. One was a law for the repeal of the county court fyftem. He alfo alluded to the depending law for the abolition of two of the courts of Maryland. He faid fomething of the toil and labor and patriotifm of thofe who had raifed the fair fabric (conftitution of Maryland) and faid that he faw with regret fome of their fons now employed in deftroying it. He alfo faid that the tendency of the general suffrage law was highly injurious, as under it a man was admitted to full political rights, who might he here to-day, and be gone to-morrow.

This is the amount of my recollection ; and I think I have stated the language of the judge in as strong terms as he himself used. Since I was summoned as a witness I have never seen the charge of the judge, or that published in the National Intelligencer, or by Mr. Montgomery. I concluded that it was most proper not to avail myself of those publications. My impressions, therefore, are altogether unassisted by them.

Mr. Harper. Did you attend carefully to the charge ?

Answer. I did. I am sure no part of it escaped me.

Mr. Harper. Did judge Chase appear to read it from a paper ?

A. I so took it. Occasionally he raised his eyes, but not longer than I should imagine a person would, who was familiarly acquainted with what he was reading.

Mr. Harper. Did you hear him use any of those expressions deposed by one of the witnesses—that the administration was feeble and inadequate to the discharge of its duties, and that their object was to preserve power unfairly acquired.—Did he use any such words ?

A. To my best belief he did not. I have a strong reason for considering my recollection on this point correct. Immediately after the charge was delivered I conversed with several gentlemen respecting it. It was complained of as harsh, and as containing reflections on those who had brought about the measures alluded to. I reflected on it, and the result on my mind was that it was couched in polite terms, and that the reflections it contained were entirely matters of inference.

Mr. Harper. Did the judge use any arguments against pending measures ?

A. Certainly.

Mr. Harper. Did he mention the present administration?

A. I believe not. If he had, it would have struck my mind very forcibly.

Mr. Harper. Did he use any such phrase as " degenerate sons ?"

A. I have a particular recollection of that, or some such expression. I considered it as a very happy allusion to events which occurred in the state legislature.

Mr. Harper. You confidered it as calculated to have a perfuafive influence ?

A. That was not my language. The fentiment I think was this. He regretted to fee fons taking part in deftroying the fair fabric their fathers had raifed. He fpoke feelingly on this point.

Mr. Harper. Had you any other converfation which tended to imprefs the fubftance of the charge on your memory ?

A. I do not recollect. I was very attentive to the charge. I obferved Mr. S. H. Smith to be prefent; and it was obferved at the time that we might expect to fee an accurate ftatement of the charge from him, as he could detail what he heard with great precifion. I recollect to have looked at the ftatement publifhed in the National Intelligencer at the time it appeared, and I thought it gave a faithful view of the fubftance of the charge—quite as ftrong as the charge itfelf.

Mr. Nicholfon. Did judge Chafe fay any thing of the motives of the members of the legiflature of Maryland ?

A. He did according to my impreffion.

Mr. Nicholfon. What were the motives he afcribed to them?

A. As I underftood him, the motive he afcribed to them, was to get rid of the judges, and not the fyftem.

Mr. Nicholfon. He did certainly then allude to the motives of the members of the affembly of Maryland ?

A. I think he did. If he did not, that was the impreffion produced on my mind by what he faid.

Mr. Nicholfon. Do you recollect whether judge Chafe did at the clofe of his charge recommend to the members of the grand jury to return home, and prevent certain laws from being paffed ?

A. I think that was the refult which he drew from what he had previoufly faid.

JAMES WINCHESTER *fworn.*

Mr. Harper. Pleafe, fir, to ftate to this court your recollection refpecting a charge delivered by judge Chafe in the circuit court of Maryland in May 1803 ?

Mr. Winchefter. As already ftated, that court fat in May 1803, in a room in Evans's tavern. The court and gentlemen of the bar fat round feveral dining tables. I fat on the left of judge Chafe ; and the jury were on his right. He addreffed a charge to them, the beginning of which was in the ufual ftyle of fuch addreffes. He then commenced what has been called the political part of the charge, with fome general obfervations on the nature of government. He afterwards adverted to two meafures of the legiflature of Maryland; the firft related to an alteration of the conftitution on the fubjed of fuffrage; the other contemplated an alteration in the judiciary. He commented on the injurious tendency of the principle of univerfal fuffrage and deprecated the evil effeds it was likely to have. Incidental to thefe remarks, he adverted to the repeal of the judiciary law of the United States. I fay incidental, for my impreffion was that his objed was to fhew the dangerous confequences that would refult to the people of Maryland from a repeal of their judiciary fyftem, and to fhew that as the ad of Congrefs had inflided a violent blow on the independence of the federal judiciary, it was more neceffary for the ftate of Maryland to preferve their judiciary perfectly independent. I was very attentive to the charge for feveral reafons. I regretted it as imprudent. I felt convinced that it would be complained of; and I am very confident from my recollection, and from the publications refpecting it, which I afterwards perufed, that all the political obfervations of the judge related to the ftate of Maryland.

Mr. *Harper*. Did the judge appear to deliver the charge from a written paper?

A. I have fat in the circuit court ever fince 1800—Judge Chafe has a kind of ftanding form in his charges on the general fubjed of crimes and offences. When there is much bufinefs expeded to be tranfacted he goes into a detailed view of the duties of a grand jury. When there is little bufinefs he contents himfelf with a charge of a different form. When he delivered this charge, he had in his hand a marble covered book.

Mr. *Harper*. (fhewing him a book.) Do you think this was the book.

Mr. *Winchefter*. I believe it was. There were occafional paufes during the delivery; he turned backwards and forwards; and read fedions from different parts of the book. At the conclufion of particular fentences he lengthened out the tones of his voice, and made a paufe, as if to arreft the attention of the jury. Though I cannot fay that there was not a word or expreffion introduced that was not written, yet my impreſſion is that he delivered the whole from the book before him.

Mr. *Harper.* Did you hear any expreſſions applied to the preſent adminiſtration, or was the adminiſtration mentioned at all?

A. My impreſſion is very ſtrong that neither the preſent adminiſtration was mentioned, or the views or deſigns of any member of it in any manner whatever. I am confident of this; becauſe if ſuch remarks had been uttered, they would have made a ſtrong impreſſion on my mind.

Mr. *Harper.* Did you ever hear the judge allude to ſuch topics in his charges?

A. I never heard judge Chaſe in any of his charges reflect on any adminiſtration. I have heard a great many charges of his, containing political matter, and they have been all rather calculated to ſupport the exiſting adminiſtration.

Mr. *Harper.* Have you heard any ſince 1800?

A. I recollect no political charge delivered by him ſince that time.

Mr. *Harper.* Was the general tenor of his charges ſince and before 1800 calculated to ſupport the laws?

A. I think there has been this difference. Thoſe delivered before 1800 called on the jury to ſupport the meaſures of the government as wiſe and upright; ſince that period he has made no alluſion to the meaſures of the adminiſtration.

Mr. *Harper.* But his general practice has been to recommend to them the obſervance of law and the ſupport of government?

A. He generally addreſſed the jury on the neceſſity of obeying the laws: that has been the tenor of his charges at all times.

Mr. *Key.* In a criminal caſe, when a queſtion of law ariſes, is not the opinion of the court always taken?

A. Except in a caſe which occurred between the preſent ſecretary of the navy and myſelf [The details of this caſe were not heard] I never knew an inſtance in which the direction of the court was not taken; and I know no inſtance in which counſel attempted to controvert the opinion of the court on a point of law.

Mr. *Key.* Have you ever known counſel addreſs a jury on a point of law after it had been decided by the court?

A. Never.

Mr. *Martin.* Would it not be deemed indecorous to do fo ?

A. I have always thought fo ?

Mr. *Nicholfon.* I will afk you whether judge Chafe recommended to the jury, on their return home, to ufe their exertions to prevent the adoption of a depending law ?

A. I do not know whether the recommendation came from the judge in language and terms. I rather think it flowed as an inference from what he had faid.

By a Senator. In any criminal or civil cafe, did you ever know the court give an opinion without being required by counfel ?

A. I recollect no inftance, except in a general charge to the grand jury, or in fumming up the teftimony at the end of the trial.

Mr. *Randolph.* I will afk whether the cafe you allude to is, after both parties have been heard, at the end of the trial ?

A. Certainly, fir.

Mr. *Martin.* I will afk you whether in any cafe, where the law is fettled, and counfel go into an argument on the point of law, the court do not frequently ftop them ?

A. It is difficult to give a correct anfwer to this queftion. It is certain that it often happens, that in arguments on points of law, the court check the counfel, and fay they are too clear to be controverted ; and, to prevent delay, beg the counfel to pafs over them.

TUESDAY, *February* 20, 1805.

The court was opened at 10 a. m.

Present, the Managers, accompanied by the Houfe of Reprefentatives ; and

Judge Chafe, attended by his counfel.

At the inftance of Mr. *Harper*, EDWARD TILGHMAN was called.

Mr. *Harper.* Do you recollect any inftance of an adjournment of the circuit courts of the United States ?

Mr. *Tilghman.* I recollect in the year 1801, that at a circuit court of the United States, where judges Tilghman, Griffith, and Baffet were on the bench, which was held at

Philadelphia, there was an adjournment on the 26th or 27th of October to fome day early in January enfuing. The court adjourned becaufe they were obliged to hold a court in Bedford, which was in the weftern diftrict of Pennfylvania. I recollect that in the court held in Philadelphia, they were not able to go through all the bufinefs before them, particularly in the cafe of Peter Blight's affignees. The court confulted with the bar on the adjournment, and the fentiment was unanimous that an adjournment could take place. After the court was held in Bedford, it was again held in Philadelphia, in the month of January ; the caufe I have mentioned was tried, and I believe feveral others.

Mr. *Harper.* What is the diftance of Bedford from Philadelphia ?

Mr. *Tilghman.* I believe between 100 and 150 miles. In the laft year in the month of May, while judge Wafhington was holding a court in Philadelphia, he learned that an attempt had been made to fet fire to his houfe ; in confequence of that circumftance and the fituation of his family he was obliged to leave town. He and judge Peters confulted on the courfe proper to be purfued in cafe the yellow fever fhould be in Philadelphia at the ufual time at which the court met, and it was agreed that judge Peters fhould in that cafe open the court and adjourn it over to January. This was agreed after confulting the bar, and I do not recollect that there was any difference of opinion among them. The court had commenced in April, and this determination was made fome time in May.

Mr. *Martin.* Did the judges after holding a court at Bedford return to their homes before the adjourned court was held in Philadelphia ?

Mr. *Tilghman.* According to my impreffion they certainly did, there was little or no bufinefs done at Bedford, where they either broke up the day on which they met, or on the day after.

Mr. *Randolph.* Have you ever known of a bill of exceptions in a criminal cafe in the courts of the United States ?

Mr. *Tilghman.* Never. I recollect in the cafe of the United States *vs.* Worrell, which was an attempt to corrupt Mr. Tench Coxe, the verdict was againft the defendant, and there was an arreft of judgment. There was a divifion of opinion whether it was an offence at common law, and there was a talk of a writ of error : it was faid at the bar a writ of error would not lie, and I think when it was mentioned to the court, they faid the fame thing under the idea that writs of error were confined to civil cafes.

THOMAS CHASE *fworn*.

Mr. *Harper.* Pleafe to look at that paper, (fhewing a paper.) Do you know the hand writing of it ?

Mr. *Chafe.* I do not.

Mr. *Harper.* Will you look at that book, do you know whofe hand writing it is ?

Mr. *Chafe.* I do.

Mr. *Harper.* Did you copy it ?

Mr. *Chafe.* I did.

Mr. *Harper.* This is exhibit No. 8, (charge of judge Chafe,) it contains the whole of the charge ; from what page did you copy it ?

Mr. *Chafe.* From page 13 to the words "fathers erected."

Mr. *Harper.* From what did you copy the book ?

Mr. *Chafe.* From a paper in my father's hand writing, except fome few words interlined by way of correction.

Mr. *Harper.* When did you copy it ?

Mr. *Chafe.* A few days before May term 1803.

Mr. *Martin.* Have you made any alterations in it fince ?

Mr. *Chafe.* No, fir.

Mr. *Harper.* We will offer this book in evidence.

PHILIP MOORE *fworn*.

Mr. *Harper.* Do you know that book ? (fhewing him the fame book above referred to)

Mr. *Moore.* Judge Chafe is in the practice of delivering his charges from a book. I faw him deliver his charge in May 1803, from a marble covered book, which I believe is the fame with that book.

Mr. *Harper.* Did he appear to read the whole time he was delivering that charge ?

Mr. *Moore.* He appeared to me to do fo ; he occafionally raifed his eyes from the paper before him, and fpoke with more than common emphafis, but he ftill appeared to fpeak from the book.

Mr. *Harper.* Did you hear any thing faid by him about the prefent adminiftration ?

Mr. *Moore.* I have never heard the judge in courts of juftice fpeak of the prefent adminiftration.

Mr. *Harper* Do you think in the charge he faid any thing about the adminiftration ?

Mr. *Moore.* I do not.

Mr. *Harper.* Had he made any fuch remarks, are there any peculiar reafons why they would have made a ftrong impreffion on your mind ?

Mr. *Moore.* I think they would have made a ftrong impreffion, as my impreffions were always in favor of the adminiftration, while judge Chafe's were againft them.

Mr. *Randolph.* Was there any recommendation to the jury, when they returned home to ufe their influence to prevent the paffage of certain laws ?

Mr. *Moore.* I do not know that there was, there may have been, but if there was, I have no recollection of it.

WALTER DORSEY *fworn.*

Mr. *Harper.* Pleafe to inform the court whether you were at a circuit court held at Baltimore in 1803 ?

Mr. *Dorfey.* I was.

Mr. *Harper.* Were you prefent when judge Chafe delivered a charge to the grand jury ?

Mr. *Dorfey.* I was.

Mr. *Harper.* Was you in fuch a fituation as to hear that charge ?

Mr. *Dorfcy.* I was.

Mr. *Harper.* Were you near Mr. Montgomery ?

Mr. *Dorfey.* I was ; I think there was only one perfon between us.

Mr. *Harper.* Did you attend to the charge ?

Mr. *Dorfey.* I attended to what is generally called the political part of it, becaufe it was novel, and contained fpeculations with refpect to government in general, and remarks on national and ftate laws.

Mr. *Harper.* Do you recollect any thing in it refpecting the adminiftration ?

Mr. *Dorfey.* I do not, I recollect a part of it relating to the ftate and national judiciary, and to univerfal fuffrage. I did not hefitate to ftate that it was an indifcreet thing; my attention was particularly drawn to it by feeing in the room the editor of a newfpaper, and from expecting that it would be the fubject of newfpaper animadverfion.

Mr. Harper. Do you think judge Chafe made any remarks relative to the prefent adminiftration?

Mr. Dorfey. I do not. I have no diftinct recollection of any fuch. I think if he had made fuch remarks, I fhould recollect them; there is another circumftance of which I am not pofitive, whether he did at the end of the charge, recommend to the jury to ufe their exertions to repeal certain laws of the ftate of Maryland, or whether I drew a conftruction in my own mind to that effect, from what he faid, I cannot fay, though it is impreffed on my mind that the former was the cafe.

Mr. Harper. Did he appear to read the charge?

Mr. Dorfey. He did, he appeared occafionally to throw his eyes off the paper.

Mr. Harper. Did he appear to throw his eyes off for a longer time than is ufual with a perfon who is reading his own compofition?

Mr. Dorfey. No, he did not.

Mr. Harper. You are of opinion that he read the whole from a book?

Mr. Dorfey. It appeared fo to me.

JOHN PURVIANCE *fworn.*

Mr. Harper. Pleafe to inform this honorable court whether you was prefent at a circuit court held at Baltimore in May 1803?

Mr. Purviance. I was.

Mr. Harper. State what happened on that occafion.

Mr. Purviance. I do not pretend to recollect every thing which occurred; but as I attended to what judge Chafe faid in his charge to the grand jury, I think I have a pretty diftinct recollection; as to the manner in which he delivered that addrefs, he appeared to me to read the whole from a written paper laying before him; I never expected that this enquiry would have been made of me, and after fuch a lapfe of time I can only fpeak of the impreffions now on my mind.

Mr. *Harper.* Do you recollect whether judge Chafe made any mention of the prefent federal adminiftration, and what was it?

Mr. *Purviance.* I have no recollection that he mentioned it, but as it was identified with the repeal of the law for eftablifhing the circuit courts of the United States, and fo far as the executive compofed a part of the legiflature he may have mentioned the adminiftration.

Mr. *Harper.* Was there any particular mention or allufion to the executive of the United States?

Mr. *Purviance.* No, fir, nothing of the kind; I have endeavored to retrace in my mind every thing which was faid, and I have not the fmalleft recollection that any remark was made upon the executive department of the United States.

Mr. *Harper.* Was there nothing faid about preferving power unfairly obtained?

Mr. *Purviance.* I think if fuch an expreffion had been ufed, it would have ftruck me forcibiy, for fhortly after the charge had been delivered, in a converfation among fome gentlemen on its contents, it was declared that the fentiments expreffed by judge Chafe were impeachable. I thought thefe kind of charges ought not to be delivered from the bench, but I did not obferve that any thing which had fallen was of a nature to warrant an impeachment.

Mr. *Harper.* Pleafe to inform this honorable court whether you are accuftomed to practice law in the courts where judge Chafe prefides?

Mr. *Purviance.* I am, fir.

Mr. *Harper.* Is it not his practice frequently to interrupt counfel?

Mr. *Purviance.* I think fo; but I always attributed it to his quicknefs of apprehenfion, which induced him rather to anticipate counfel than to liften to them; this I always afcribed to his fuperior fagacity.

Mr. *Harper.* Have you feen any difference in his interruptions between counfel with whom he was fuppofed to be on ill terms, and thofe with whom he was on good terms?

Mr. *Purviance.* I never obferved any difference in his conduct arifing from a confideration of perfons, but it always appeared to me to arife from the manner in which gentlemen treated the fubject.

Mr. *Harper.* Were there gentlemen at the bar, with whom judge Chafe was not on good terms?

Mr. *Purviance.* I think there were.

Mr. *Harper.* Did you ever know judge Chafe after having decided a point, hear counfel againft his own opinion, and upon hearing, induced to decide differently ?

Mr. *Purviance* ftated a cafe in which the judge had retracted his opinion upon argument in a cafe in which he had been employed, and added that notwithftanding the pride of opinion to which men were liable, he had obferved in judge Chafe an almoft unparalleled difpofition to hear his opinions contefted, and when miftaken to relinquifh them.

NICHOLAS BRICE *fworn.*

Mr. *Harper.* Pleafe to inform this honorable court whether you was at a circuit court held in Baltimore in May 1803, when a charge was delivered by judge Chafe to the grand jury.

Mr. *Brice.* I was there and attended to the charge very particularly.

Mr. *Harper.* Was that charge fpoken extempore or was it read from a book ?

Mr. *Brice.* I kept my eyes fteadily upon the judge, and I conceived that he read the whole from a paper, as is cuftomary with him in delivering a charge to the grand jury.

Mr. *Harper.* Have you a diftinct recollection of the latter part of the charge ?

Mr. *Brice.* I have not a recollection of the words, but I think I recollect their general nature and tendency.

Mr. *Harper.* Did he fay any thing refpecting the prefent adminiftration ?

Mr. *Brice.* Not in the flighteft manner, further than mentioning the repeal of the judiciary law of the United States, which he mentioned incidentally in the courfe of his obfervations on the alterations of the judiciary fyftem in the ftate of Maryland. One thing more I will add, with refpect to the advice which it is alleged he gave to the grand jury : fhortly after the charge was delivered in talking over this fubject with Mr. Stephen, I recollect that I rather thought it was an inference drawn from the charge, than any exprefs advice of the court on that point. Indeed I am pretty fure the words were not ufed.

Mr. *Martin.* Do I underftand you right ? You fay he had no allufion to the prefent adminiftration, but in connection with the repeal of the law of the United States as it was likely to affect the ftate of Maryland.

Mr. *Brice.* So far as I recollect he made ufe of no other expreffion, but mentioned the repeal of that law to fhew the evil tendency of fuch meafures as it regarded the judiciary of Maryland.

JAMES P. BOYD *fworn.*

Mr. *Harper.* Pleafe to inform this honorable court whether you were prefent at the circuit court held in Baltimore in May 1803, and what occurred at that time?

Mr. *Boyd.* I was there, but I do not know whether I was there at the opening of the court, but I was there when the charge was delivered to the grand jury. After judge Chafe had gone through that part of the charge which is an inftruction to the grand jury relative to the duties of their office, he proceeded to make fome further obfervations, to which I paid particular attention becaufe they were novel to me. I was under an impreffion at the time that judge Chafe was watched.

Mr. *Harper.* Did the judge read the charge from a book?

Mr. *Boyd.* To the beft of my recollection he did read it, but he caft his eyes off from time to time in the manner defcribed by Mr. Montgomery. I thought at the time the political part of the charge would bear hard upon him, becaufe I obferved Mr. Montgomery paying particular attention to the addrefs of the judge, which was an animadverfion upon the meafures Mr. Montgomery had been anxious to carry in the legiflature of Maryland. I do not however recollect the words which were ufed; thofe who paid it more attention are likely to be more correct.

Mr. *Harper.* Did that charge contain a fentiment like thofe you have heard, that the prefent adminiftration was weak or wicked, &c.?

Mr. *Boyd.* I have not a fcintilla of recollection of a word of the kind, no further than as an inference to be drawn from what was faid in relation to the repeal of the judiciary law. I have however a faint trace of the idea in my mind, not from my own recollection, but from having repeatedly heard it ftated that there was fuch a remark made in the charge.

Mr. *Harper.* Have you any reafon to believe that if fuch an expreffion had been ufed it would have ftruck you fo forcibly as to enable you now to recollect it, and what is that reafon ?

Mr. *Boyd.* The reafon is this, I thought a charge of that kind was both imprudent and impolitic ; and I have always thought political charges ought not to be delivered from the bench. If judge Chafe had then dropped a fentiment fo improper, reflecting on the prefent adminiftration of which he formed a part, I fhould have remarked it in a particular manner. And it is for this reafon I think he did not ufe it ; if he did, it has wholly efcaped my recollection.

WILLIAM M'MECHIN *fworn.*

Mr. *Harper.* Inform this honorable court whether you was prefent at the circuit court held at Baltimore in May 1803 ?

Mr. *M'Mechin.* I was prefent and heard the charge delivered by judge Chafe to the grand jury.

Mr. *Harper.* Was you in a fituation to hear the charge diftinctly, how near was you to the judge ?

Mr. *M'Mechin.* I was near the door of the room, about five yards diftant from the judge. I faw the judge delivering the charge, but whether he kept his eyes conftantly on the book I cannot fay, as I did not keep my eyes fteadily upon him ; but it appeared to me that he read from the book throughout.

Mr. *Harper.* Have you a recollection of the latter part of that charge ?

Mr. *M'Mechin.* I think I have.

Mr. *Harper.* Have you any recollection of his having faid any thing againft the prefent adminiftration ?

Mr. *M'Mechin.* I have no recollection of any thing of the kind, either that they were weak, or of their having unfairly acquired power ; fuch an idea was mentioned in no way unlefs it be inferred from the remark on the repeal of the law eftablifhing the fixteen circuit judges.

Mr. *Harper.* If fuch a fentiment had been uttered it would not have efcaped your notice ?

Mr. *M'Mechin.* I think it would not.

Mr. *Harper.* Had you any converfation about this charge, if you had, pleafe to inform when, with whom, and what was it ?

Mr. *M'Mechin.* About five minutes after the charge was delivered I left the court room : going down ftairs I met Mr. Montgomery and I afked him, or he afked me, what was thought of the charge ; after a few obfervations, he faid it was fuch an one as Mr. Chafe would be impeached for ; this drew my attention pointedly to the charge itfelf ; after this I heard of the publication in the American, but I did not fee it. I met afterwards with a publication in the Anti Democrat, which paper I took, purporting to be the charge of judge Chafe. I have converfed with gentlemen of both parties on the publication, and it appeared to them as it did appear to me, and as I ftill think it is, fubftantially the charge delivered by the judge.

Mr. *Harper.* Has that opinion refted on your mind ever fince you heard the charge and read the publication ?

Mr. *M'Mechin.* It has always fo refted on my mind, and I have never read any thing on the fubject fince ?

WILLIAM S. GOVANE *fworn.*

Mr. *Harper.* Was you at the circuit court of Baltimore in May 1803 ?

Mr. *Govane.* I was, and heard the charge delivered by judge Chafe. The room in which the court was held was a long one in a tavern, a range of tables formed the bar, and the feats around it were occupied by profeffional gentlemen. I went to the bottom of the table oppofite to judge Chafe and directed my attention towards him. Whilft he was delivering his charge he appeared to read it from a book, but generally ended the fentences by looking toward the grand jury ; except this circumftance he appeared to read the whole time.

Mr. *Harper.* Do you retain a diftinct recollection of the fubftance of what the judge faid ?

Mr. *Govane.* I think I do.

Mr. *Harper.* Do you remember any part containing animadverfions on the prefent adminiftration, fuch as that they were weak, feeble, or incompetent ?

Mr. *Govane.* I think no fuch words were ufed. If I could fwear to a fact negatively after fuch a lapfe of time, I could fwear that no fuch expreffions fell from the judge. He faid that a monarchy might be free and a republic a tyranny, and then proceeded to define what a free government was.

Mr. *Harper.* Then you have no recollection of any reflection made upon the prefent adminiftration ?

Mr. *Govane.* I have not the moft diftant idea that fuch an expreffion was ufed.

Mr. *Harper.* Would you have remembered them if they had been ufed ?

Mr. *Govane.* I think I fhould, as I had a converfation with a friend refpecting it foon after it was delivered ; and I paid particular attention to the charge, becaufe it came from judge Chafe, a man of great celebrity, and I wifhed to draw what information I could from fuch a refpectable fource ; every thing arrefted my attention, and it appeared that the attention of the whole company was fixed upon the judge.

JOHN CAMPBELL *fworn.*

Mr. *Harper.* Did you attend the circuit court held at Baltimore in 1803, and in what capacity ?

Mr. *Campbell.* I attended that court as a grand juror and was appointed foreman.

Mr. *Harper.* Do you recollect the charge that was then delivered by judge Chafe ?

Mr. *Campbell.* I recollect fome parts of it, but not the whole. I paid a particular attention to that part which defcribed my duties as a grand juror, and have fome recollection of the latter part. I kept my eyes conftantly upon the judge.

Mr. *Harper.* Did he read the charge, or fpeak it extempore?

Mr. *Campbell.* He appeared generally to read it, taking off his eyes from the book from time to time, but never for a longer time than what is ufual for men to exprefs the words they retain in their memory from their own compofition.

Mr. *Harper.* Have you a diftinct recollection of the latter part of the charge ?

Mr. *Campbell.* I cannot fay I have a diftinct recollection of any particular part of the charge, though I remember its general tendency.

Mr. *Harper.* Do you remember to have heard the prefent adminiftration cenfured as weak, feeble or incompetent, &c. ?

Mr. *Campbell.* I have not the flighteft recollection of any fuch expreffions, if they were ufed they have altogether efcaped my memory.

Mr. *Harper.* Was there any allusion to the present administration ?

Mr. *Campbell.* No, sir.

Mr. *Harper.* If such words were uttered, is there any circumstance which would have impressed them on your memory ?

Mr. *Campbell.* I should have thought them very improper,
and that would have fixed them in my mind, but I have no
trace of any such impression.

Mr. *Nicholson.* You gave a deposition before the committee
on this point ?

Mr. *Campbell.* I did, sir.

Mr. *Nicholson.* Did you say that the judge recommended
to the jury when they returned home, that they should use
their influence to prevent the passage of certain laws then
pending before the legislature of Maryland ?

Mr. *Campbell.* It does appear still to me that I heard some
such expression. I have thought of it repeatedly since, and I
continue to believe that the judge gave the jury that advice.

Mr. *Harper.* Was the exhortation made by the judge, or
is it an inference you draw in your own mind ?

Mr. *Campbell.* Some such expression fell from him, and
it is not an inference formed in my mind.

WILLIAM CRANCH *sworn.*

Mr. *Harper.* Were you present at the circuit court held
at Baltimore in 1803 ?

Mr. *Cranch.* I was. The court was held at Evans's tavern in Baltimore ; judge Chase was seated in an armed chair
at one end of a long table placed before him ; the grand jury
were on his right, some sitting on benches placed along the
wall and others standing. I stood myself about fifteen feet
from the judge, who was sitting during the whole time he was
delivering his charge : he generally held the book in his hand.

Mr. *Harper.* (shewing a book) Is that the book ?

Mr. *Cranch.* He appeared to be reading from such a book.

Mr. *Harper.* Did he read the whole, and did he read constantly ?

Mr. *Cranch.* He appeared to me to read the whole charge,
but I did not keep my eyes so constantly fixed upon him as
to declare positively that he did.

Mr. *Harper.* Were there variations in his manner of delivering the charge, as if he was at one time reading and at another fpeaking extempore ?

Mr. *Cranch.* He delivered fome parts with more emphafis than others. He often raifed his eyes from the book, but I did not obferve that he repeated more than one fentence without recurring to the book : he repeated no more than a man might repeat after running his eyes haftily over a paffage.

Mr. *Harper.* Did he raife his eyes for a longer time than a man might be fuppofed to do, who was reading a compofition of his own ?

Mr. *Cranch.* I do not think he did.

Mr. *Harper.* Do you recollect the latter part of the charge ?

Mr. *Cranch.* I recollect more of the latter part than of the beginning, becaufe I paid more attention to the latter part.

Mr. *Harper.* Do you recollect any fentiments expreffed relating to the weaknefs of the prefent adminiftration, and that they were not employed in promoting the public good, but in preferving ill gotten power ?

Mr. *Cranch.* No, fir, there was no fuch expreffion, as I recollect.

Mr. *Harper.* Was there any expreffion at all relative to the prefent adminiftration ?

Mr. *Cranch.* Not as an adminiftration ; nor any thing alluding to the adminiftration feparate from the government of the United States.

Mr. *Harper.* In what way was the government alluded to ?

Mr. *Cranch.* By alluding to the repeal of the act of Feb. 1801, for the eftablifhment of the circuit judges. I recollect no other meafure of the general government which was alluded to, or any allufion to the prefent executive.

Mr. *Harper.* I will now offer in evidence the book containing the charge of judge Chafe at Baltimore, which has been proved to be that from which he read his charge ; it will be unneceffary to read it, as it is left on file, and we wifh to fave the time of the court.

The written book was then returned to the clerk's table.

Mr. *Harper* faid he wifhed to afk a queftion of Mr. M'Mechin.

Mr. M'MECHIN was called, and Mr. Harper enquired if he had rightly underftood him, when he faid that a few minutes after he had left the court room he met Mr. Montgomery on the ftairs, and Mr. Montgomery ftated to him that judge Chafe would be impeached. Did Mr. Montgomery at that time fay for what he would be impeached, or that he would be impeached for reflecting upon the adminiftration ?

Mr. *M'Mechin.* He faid the judge would be impeached, but I do not recollect that he faid any thing about his being impeached for reflections upon the prefent adminiftration. I thought he felt hurt on the fubject of the alterations in the judiciary of Maryland, which had been much talked of, and for which he had been an advocate in the ftate legiflature.

Mr. *Harper.* In order to fhew that it is the cuftom of the courts in this country to deliver political charges to the grand juries (a practice which I am ready to admit is indifcreet) I wifh to be indulged in a narration of what has been the practice, and then this honorable court will be convinced that it did not originate with the prefent refpondent, but that he followed the track which had been a long time marked out. For this purpofe I will refer to feveral tranfactions which have taken place. Firft in the year 1776, on the 27th April, an addrefs was made to the grand jury in the ftate of South-Carolina, by William H. Drayton, (1ft vol. of Ramfay's hiftory of South-Carolina, page 103.) A further evidence that the cuftom obtained is derived from the addrefs of the executive council of Pennfylvania, wherein it is recommended that the judges of the fupreme court make mention in their charges of various fubjects of a political nature ; it is under date of October 8th, 1785. American Mufeum, vol. 1, page 228. I will alfo offer in evidence, a charge delivered by judge Iredell in Pennfylvania, previous to the trial of Fries in 1799. I will adduce that part only which may be denominated political.

I will alfo offer in evidence the general notoriety of the practice in this country for thirty years paft, to enforce from the bench political principles, and to defend political meafures ; a practice which we contend univerfally prevailed.

I will fubmit a paper yefterday referred to as evidence on the 7th article ; a charge delivered by chief juftice M'Kean on the 27th November, 1797. In this charge the learned judge, whofe eulogium has been fo boldly pronounced, difcuffes the doctrine of libels, and after a variety of pertinent obfervations, goes on as follows :

(Mr. Harper here read extracts from the above charge.)

Exhibit No. 7, contains extracts from the Mirror of the

Times, which are offered for the purpofe of verifying the ftatement of the refpondent ; the firft is contained in the paper of Wednefday February 5, 1800, and the fecond in that of February 8th.

Mr. *Randolph.* The exhibits are thofe which accompanied the refpondent's anfwer and pleas.

Mr. *Martin.* They are, and we here clofe our teftimony, adding only the letter of governor Claiborne, who has acted on the fame principle, and given to the world his political opinions on various fubjects.

Mr. *Randolph.* One of our witneffes has arrived in town, and we wifh that he fhould be called.

THOMAS HALL *was called and fworn.*

Mr. *Nicholfon.* Was you at Baltimore when the charge was delivered by judge Chafe, and do you recollect the language he made ufe of in addreffing the grand jury ?

Mr. *Hall.* I do not recollect the particular language ufed —I paid very little attention to what was there tranfacted.

Mr. *Nicholfon.* Do you recollect the fubjects generally, on which he fpoke ?

Mr. *Hall.* I have a general impreffion, but I cannot be particular.

Mr. *Nicholfon.* Did he mention the prefent adminiftration as weak and feeble ?

Mr. *Hall.* My impreffion is that he mentioned them, or I inferred it from what was faid.

Mr. *Nicholfon.* Did he mention them in fuch a way as to caft an odium upon them ?

Mr. *Hall.* I could not identify the language of judge Chafe, even if it were laid before me.

Mr. *Nicholfon.* Do you recollect his recommendation to the jury to ufe their exertions to prevent the paffage of particular laws ?

Mr. *Hall.* I think he ufed language in fubftance to that effect.

Mr. *Nicholfon.* In what way did he fpeak of the adminiftration ?

Mr. *Hall.* I do not recollect particularly the manner.

Mr. *Nicholfon.* Is it your general impreffion that he mentioned the adminiftration ?

Mr. *Hall.* I think he did, or elfe I inferred it from what he faid.

Mr. *Randolph.* Although you do not recollect the precife expreffions of the judge, you inferred from what he faid that his defign was to convey to the bye-ftanders the idea that the adminiftration was weak or wicked?

Mr. *Hall.* Yes, fir, thofe are my impreffions.

Mr. *Nicholfon.* Were you on the jury?

Mr. *Hall.* Yes, fir, I was on the petit jury.

Mr. *Rodney* here adduced a lift of the grand jury for the circuit court held in the year 1800 in the ftate of Delaware.

Mr. *Randolph* wifhed that Mr. George Hay might be called to explain part of his teftimony, that part which related to the converfation between the marfhal and himfelf, when the former was in purfuit of Callender.

GEORGE HAY *was accordingly called.*

Mr. *Randolph.* Did you endeavor to diffuade the marfhal from the execution of his duty in the arreft of Callender?

Mr. *Hay.* I certainly did not, and Mr. D. M. Randolph could not mean to convey to this honorable court that idea. I fhould have been prevented from doing this by two confiderations, one exclufively relating to myfelf, which I need not explain, the other, that I had a better opinion of Mr. Randolph than to fuppofe he would liften to any fuch fuggeftions. I did tell him that in my opinion he would not be able to get Callender, as I underftood that he had attempted to make his efcape, and that in the place in which he was, it would be impoffible for the marfhal to difcover him.

Mr. *Randolph.* Did you mention to him that he (Callender) would furrender at the next term?

Mr. *Hay.* I am not certain, but I believe I did.

Mr. *Randolph.* Were you at that time retained as counfel for Callender?

Mr. *Hay.* I was not retained as his counfel at that time, nor ever after; but I intended to appear in his defence for the fake of defending the caufe, not for the man.

Mr. *Randolph.* Were you averfe to proceed in the trial at that term for any particular reafon?

Mr. *Hay.* I did not wifh to appear before judge Chafe, from an impreffion that had been made on my mind in converfations with perfons who knew him. I conceived it would be an unpleafant bufinefs for me to carry into execution the intention I had formed to defend Callender. This impreffion arofe principally from the conduct the judge had manifefted towards Mr. Lewis and Mr. Dallas, on the trial of Fries, at Philadelphia. He had there, as I underftood, reftrained them from managing the defence in the way which they thought proper. I did not expect any greater indulgence or advantage than had been allowed on that occafion. I had therefore made up my mind to meet all the exigencies of the cafe with temper, but with firmnefs. The conduct of the judge on the trial of Mr. Thomas Cooper, had alfo its weight upon my mind. A great deal was faid about the judge's conduct on that trial, whether correct or not I do not fay; but it made me unwilling to appear as counfel before judge Chafe, though I was perfectly willing to undertake Callender's defence at the next term, before any other judge.

Mr. *Randolph.* What was the political complexion of the jury which tried Callender?

Mr. *Hay.* I am not perfonally acquainted with the gentlemen who compofed that jury. I believe fome of them did not live in the city of Richmond, but the impreffion on my mind was, and ftill is, that all the perfons on the jury were not only oppofed to Callender, but decidedly fo; and were diftinguifhed for the warmth of their political fentiments.

Mr. *Randolph.* Are you acquainted with colonel John Harvie; what is his political character?

Mr. *Hay.* I know colonel Harvie, but what is his political character I do not know. I lived at Peterfburg and he at Richmond. I only knew that it was faid that he did not vote with the republican party.

Mr. *Randolph.* Are you acquainted with Mr. William Radford; what are his politics?

Mr. *Hay.* He was ranked among thofe called moderate, but I am not well enough acquainted with him to decide upon his political character.

Mr. *Randolph.* Are you acquainted with Mr. Marks Vanderval, and what is his political character?

Mr. *Hay.* He is a very referved man, but has been uniformly regarded as a republican, though not a zealous one.

Mr. *Randolph.* In criminal actions, did you ever hear of a bill of exceptions being filed in Virginia?

Mr. *Hay.* Never, fir; there can be no fuch thing, it would anfwer no purpofe; becaufe from a criminal court there is no court which has appellate jurifdiction.

Mr. *Randolph.* But cafes are transferred from the diftrict courts to the general court.

Mr. *Hay.* There is a particular procefs for that purpofe; criminal cafes are not carried up after trial, for the decifion in that cafe is final; but if the diftrict court are unwilling to decide, it is then carried up to the fupreme court.

Mr. *Harper.* I underftood you to fay that it was your intention to argue the point. What point did you mean?

Mr. *Hay.* I meant to contend againft the conftitutionality of the fecond fection of the fedition law.

Mr. *Harper.* Did you not mean to argue it before the public, although you knew it would be unavailing if addreffed to the court? Did you mean by that argument to acquit the traverfer, or to produce a political effect out of doors.

Mr. *Hay.* I meant to addrefs my arguments to the court; if they fhould work the acquittal of the traverfer, or operate any wife in his favor, it was a thing to be defired; if they fhould affect alfo the public mind, that too was a defirable circumftance.

Mr. *Harper.* I afk you now whether you did not fay to the marfhal that Callender could not be defended, and that your object in requiring a continuance of the caufe, was to gain time, and bring the trial nearer that period in which it was probable he might get a pardon?

Mr. *Hay.* I have no recollection of having faid any thing of this kind, but if Mr. Randolph (the marfhal) fays that I expreffed myfelf to him in that manner, I fhall not contradict him.

Mr. *Harper.* I underftood him to fay fo in his teftimony.

Mr. *Hay.* I do not recollect it.

D. M. RANDOLPH was called in by Mr. Harper, and afked whether Mr. Hay had not faid to him that Callender could not be defended, and that his purpofe was to keep off the trial till the next court, in order to obtain a pardon.

Mr. *Randolph.* I do not recollect the words which were ufed, but I underftood that Callender could not then be defended, and that he would furrender himfelf at the next term. I think it proper to remark one thing further; there never was a pannel of the jury made out, or prefented to judge Chafe, or any other perfon, till the morning I made it out in court, before the commencement of Callender's trial, except in the cafe of the grand jury, when it is handed to the judge to appoint a foreman. In fetting down their names on the lift I arranged them according to my own idea of their refpectability.

Mr. *Nicholfon.* In your converfation with Mr. Hay, did he tell you that he wifhed to delay the caufe, in order to bring it nearer the time in which he might obtain Callender's pardon ?

Mr. *Randolph.* He did not ufe the words, but I thought he had it in his mind. I inferred it from the converfation.

Mr. *Randolph* wifhed to afk another queftion of Mr. HAY, who was thereupon called.

Mr. *Randolph.* Did you ever fay that Callender could not be defended ?

Mr. *Hay.* I cannot recollect what I may have faid on that point, but I recollect perfectly that I was impreffed with the idea, that he could not be defended, if the charge was either for writing or publifhing the Profpect Before Us, for thefe facts were too notorious to be called in queftion. But I did then think, and always fince have thought, that he might be defended on the ground of the unconftitutionality of the fedition law.

Mr. *Randolph.* Do you mean when you fay that he might be defended on the ground of the unconftitutionality of the fedition law, that you would not have defended him on any other ground, fuch as a flaw in the indictment, or a miftatement of the matter of the book in the indictment?

Mr. *Hay.* Moft certainly, fir, I meant to take advantage of any miftake or defect that might appear in the indictment, or in the evidence ; and that may be evinced by recurring to my objection againft the witneffes who were concerned with Callender in the publication, when I told one of them that he was not bound to give teftimony which would go to criminate himfelf.

P. N. NICHOLAS *called.*

Mr. *Key.* Do they ever arraign a perfon for a mifdemeanor in Virginia ?

Mr. *Nicholas.* I do not recollect that they do.

JOHN MONTGOMERY was called in, at the inftance of Mr. Nicholfon, who defired him to explain fome parts of his teftimony.

Mr. *Montgomery.* When I was before this honorable court the firft time, I ftated that I fhould not be able to ftate all the charge delivered by judge Chafe at Baltimore, or any particular part in the precife language which he ufed. From the examination of a great number of witneffes before this honorable court, I am induced to believe that I have been mifunderftood. When I firft ufed the word adminiftration, I ufed it not as the precife word he uttered, but what ftruck my mind as being his fenfe. The judge feemed to lay down a propofitiou that the adminiftration of government was fo and fo, and ftated that their acts were not guided by a view to promote the general welfare, but principally to keep themfelves in the poffeffion of unfairly acquired power. I thought the judge explained his pofition by his allufion to the repeal of the law creating the fixteen circuit judges, the general fuffrage law of Maryland, and the contemplated alteration of the judiciary law of that ftate ; I did not mean to ftate that he faid Mr. Jefferfon was weak or feeble, but that the adminiftration or the government was fo. This is the impreffion I then had, and now have with refpect to that part of the charge. But I did not then fay, nor do I now, that I ufe the precife words of the judge ; but I think I follow his fpirit and his meaning.

Mr. *Nicholfon.* At the concluding part of the charge did judge Chafe recommend it to the jury when they returned home to ufe their influence to prevent the paffage of the judiciary bill, or was that an inference from what he delivered ?

Mr. *Montgomery.* That part of the charge was in the exprefs words, and not an inference at all. I recollect that fhortly after I had a converfation with feveral gentlemen, who concurred with me in opinion that thefe expreffions were ufed; and I recollect that on the very day the charge was publifhed in the Anti Democrat, or the day after, I called thefe expreffions to the recollection of the fon of judge Chafe, and obferved that thefe parts were omitted in the printed ftatement.

Mr. *Harper.* I am defired by judge Chafe to make of this honorable court the requeft contained in the following letter, which I will read :

"" Mr. *Prefident*,

" The ftate of my health will not permit me to remain any longer at this bar. It is with great regret I depart before I hear the judgment of this honorable court. If permitted to retire, I fhall leave this honorable court with an unlimited confidence in its juftice ; and I beg leave to prefent my thanks to them for their patience and indulgence in the long and tedious examination of the witneffes. Whatever may be the ultimate decifion of this honorable court, I confole myfelf with the reflection that it will be the refult of mature deliberation on the legal teftimony in the cafe, and will emanate from thofe principles, which ought to govern the higheft tribunal of juftice in the United States."

The Prefident obferved that the rules of the Senate did not require the perfonal attendance of the refpondent ; whereupon judge Chafe bowed in a very refpectful manner, and withdrew.

Mr. HAY came again to the bar to explain the motives which induced him to undertake the defence of Callender.— He faid he was not without fome hope that his arguments againft the unconftitutionality of the fedition law, although they might not be conclufive with the court, would neverthelefs have fome weight with the jury, and might operate to produce the acquittal of Callender.

Mr. *Randolph*. On behalf of the managers, I have to requeft of the court, that further progrefs in the trial be poftponed until to-morrow, in order to give thofe gentlemen who follow, time to digeft, compare, and collate the great volume of teftimony which has been given. We fhall be ready to proceed to-morrow. There is alfo another reafon for this requeft ; we expect hourly fome important witneffes, and are in hopes that they will make their appearance in town before the next meeting of the court. If, however, this fhould not be the cafe, we fhall proceed without them. If they come, we prefume we fhall be permitted to take the benefit of their teftimony.

Prefident. I underftand that gentlemen have nothing further to offer.

Mr. *Randolph*. Not, fir, at this time.

M. *Harper.* I beg leave to ftate that we do not join in the motion for a delay, though we do not oppofe it.

Prefident. Is the courfe of the arguments on each fide un-derftood ?

Mr. *Nicholfon.* We underftand that the managers will open ; that reply will be made by the counfel for the refpondent ; and that the managers will then clofe.

Mr. *Key.* This is the ufual courfe, and we have no objection to it.

The court then rofe.

WEDNESDAY, *February* 20, 1805.

The court was opened at 10 o'clock.

Present, the Managers, accompanied by the House of Representatives in committee of the whole : and the counsel of Judge Chase.

Mr. *Nicholfon.* We expected a witnefs from Virginia ; but he has not arrived : a witnefs, however, from Maryland is prefent, whom we wifh to examine.

PHILIP STEWART *fworn.*

Mr. *Nicholfon.* Were you a member of the grand jury fummoned to attend the circuit court held at Baltimore, in May 1803 ?

Mr. *Stewart.* I was.

Mr. *Nicholfon.* Do you recollect any particular expreffions ufed by judge Chafe in his charge to the jury ?

Mr. *Stewart.* I have but an imperfect recollection. I have never feen the charge, nor have I heard it read fince it was delivered.

Mr. *Nicholfon.* Had you not fome reafon for attending to the charge, other than your duty as a grand juror ?

Mr. *Stewart.* There were fome things which ftruck my mind with fome force.

Mr. *Nicholfon.* Had you not been a member of the legiflature of Maryland ?

Mr. *Stewart.* I had.

Mr. *Nicholfon.* Did he not throw fome cenfure upon the members of that ftate legiflature ?

Mr. *Stewart.* I felt fomething of the kind, but I cannot tell his expreffions.

Mr. *Nicholfon.* Do you recollect his fpeaking of the fons of fome gentlemen who had affifted in framing the conftitution of Maryland, what were his expreffions ?

Mr. *Stewart.* If I were to hear the charge read I could perhaps point them out.

Mr. *Nicholfon.* I will ftate the queftion more precifely.— Did he ufe the words *degenerate fons,* and apply that epithet to the members of the legiflature ?

Mr. *Stewart.* To the beft of my recollection he did ; he fpoke of degenerate fons of fathers who had formed the conftitution of the ftate, which they were about to deftroy by the introduction of the general fuffrage bill.

Mr. *Nicholfon.* Did he recommend to the grand jury when they returned home, to ufe their influence to have fuch men elected as would vote againft the judiciary bill then pending before the legiflature ?

Mr. *Stewart.* I do not recollect.

Mr. *Harper.* I will afk you, fir, whether the word *degenerate* was inferred by you, or did you actually hear it.

Mr. *Stewart.* I believe I heard it.

Mr. *Martin.* Have you ever feen any publication of the charge ?

Mr. *Stewart.* I have not.

The *Prefident.* If no further witneffes are to be introduced, I would enquire whether gentlemen confider it neceffary to detain thofe who have been examined ?

Mr. *Nicholfon.* It is poffible that gentlemen may differ in their account of the teftimony ; but if there is no difpute on that point the witneffes I think may be difcharged.

Mr. *Martin.* There is a lift of the grand jury fummoned at the circuit court in Delaware ; I do not know for what it is filed ; until we are informed on that point we fhall be under the neceffity of detaining the witneffes from that ftate. Is it intended to fhew that there were men of different political fentiments on that jury ?

Mr. *Rodney.* We have nothing more to prove from that lift than what has already been ftated.

Mr. *Harper* faid the counfel for the refpondent would have no objection to difcharge all the witneffes ; but muft object to difcharging part of them.

The *Prefident*. If the gentlemen do not agree upon the difcharge of the witneffes, I will take the fenfe of the Senate upon the point.

Mr. *Harper*. The particular fituation of Mr. Tilghman's family requires his return to Philadelphia. I muft therefore requeft that his further attendance be difpenfed with.

The *Managers* confented, and Mr. T. was difcharged.

The queftion was then taken by the Prefident on the difcharge of all the witneffes, and loft ; there being 16 votes in the affirmative, and 17 in the negative.

Mr. *Rodney* requefted the difcharge of the witneffes from Delaware ; which being confented to by the refpondent's counfel, they were difcharged.

It may be proper here to notice that, from time to time, during the trial, witneffes were difcharged with confent of the parties.

The testimony having been closed on both sides,

Mr. EARLY rose, and addressed the Senate as follows :

MR. PRESIDENT,

THERE is no attitude, in which the government of this nation can be viewed, more completely demonstrative of the *efficacy* of its principles than that in which it is now placed. We are now occupied in an act well calculated to test the *practicability* of those principles, and to prove their fitness or unfitness for the condition of that country over which they are destined to rule. There is presented before this great depository of national justice, a highly important officer of the government, charged with acts violative of some of its leading and most essential principles. An officer who has been cloathed with the function of administering to a great and rising people the blessings of freedom in their most vital relations, is the object against whom charges of this serious nature are exhibited. He stands charged with violating the sacred charter of our liberties, and with setting at naught the most holy obligations of society. He stands charged with perverting the high judicial functions of his office for the purposes of individual oppression, and of staining the pure ermine of justice by political party spirit. These charges are founded upon transactions which have passed in review before an inquiring world, and which in the estimation of the representatives of the American government have cast a foul reproach on their national character. To this tribunal have they appealed for a vindication of that character. Hither do they appeal for the preservation of the dearest principles of their liberty, and for the sure support of their most sacred rights. It is here they must enter the complaints of the nation. It is here they must drag the *guilty* to punishment.

The first article, preferred by the house of representatives in support of their impeachment, charges a conduct upon the respondent, which strikes at one of the most vital principles of the government of this nation ; the right of " trial by an *impartial* jury." It ought never to be forgotten that the deprivation of this right was one of the injuries for which the people of this country put to the risk of a revolution all that was dear. Nor ought it to be forgotten that the security of this right forms one of the great *safeguards* of the federal constitution. " In all criminal trials " the accused shall enjoy the right to a speedy and " public trial by an *impartial* jury of the state and " district."

The relative rights of judges and juries have at some periods of judicial history been so little understood, and the limits of each so indistinctly marked, that the benefits of the institution of jury trial were left much at the mercy of *arbitrary and overbearing judges*. But it was reserved for the honor of modern times to dissipate this uncertainty so baneful to justice, and to fix down the establishment upon its only proper foundation ; that of the right to determine without control, both the law and the fact in *all criminal cases whatsoever*. This right has now been so long practiced upon in the United States, and may be considered as so well established, that it is scarcely to be expected we shall witness upon that point any difference of opinion. Still less is it to be expected that we shall witness such difference, when we are discussing principles which apply to cases capital. In such cases it is the glory of the laws of this country, that the offence of the accused should be left exclusively to the judgment of those least liable to be swayed by the weight of accusing influence. It is no part of my intention to deny the right of judges to expound the law in charging juries. But it may be safely affirmed that such right is the most delicate they possess, and the exercise of which should be guarded by the utmost caution and humanity.

The accused shall enjoy the right to a " trial by an *impartial* jury." We charge the respondent with deliberately violating this important provision of the constitution, in arresting from John Fries the privilege of having his case heard and determined by an impartial jury : For that the respondent took upon *himself* substantially to decide the case by prejudging the law applying thereto, at the same time accompanying the opinion thus formed and thus delivered, by certain observations and declarations calculated necessarily to create a prepossession against the case of Fries, in the minds of those who had been summoned to serve upon the jury, thereby making them the reverse of impartial.

These were the acts of a man who, from his own declarations, appears to have well understood upon what *points the defence would turn*. It was the act of a man, who it appears had been well informed of all that passed at the previous trial of Fries ; who knew that there was no dispute as to facts, and that the whole of the defence depended upon the discussion and determination of those very principles of law which he had thus prejudged, and upon the application of those authorites which he had thus excluded in the hearing and very presence of those who were to pass upon the life and death of the accused. No argument had been heard from counsel; no opportunity had been afforded to prove that the offence committed did not amount to the crime charged; no defending voice had been raised in behalf of the accused; but without being heard, and without having had any opportunity to be heard, his case was adjudged *against* him. I say, *adjudged against him without the chance of being heard.* For surely the case was adjudged against him, when the only point upon which it was defensible was determined against him, and that determination publicly announced from the bench. That this was done before the accused could possibly have had a chance of being heard is placed beyond contradiction by all the testimony. And that the judge knew the point, which he thus prejudged, to be the only ground upon which the defence rested, is perfectly clear. For from his own declarations at the time of announcing the opinion, it appears that he was well acquainted with all that had passed at the previous trial of Fries.

But, sir, we must look further into the progress of this transaction. It was not enough, that the poor trembling victim of judicial oppression should thus have his dearest privileges snatched from him by a prejudication of his case! It was not enough, that the impartiality of those who were to compose his jury, should be converted into a prepossession against him, by the imposing authority of solemn declarations from the bench! But the small remaining darling hope of life was to be smothered by a preclusion of his counsel from arguing the law to the jury. This fact, though sternly denied in the answer of the respondent, has nevertheless been established in a manner which

must irresistibly force conviction upon the mind.
Mr. Lewis affirms it positively. Mr. Dallas confirms
it in a manner peculiarly strong. Not being himself
present when the opinion was delivered to the bar, he
received from Mr. Lewis a statement of what had
passed, and in an address to the court afterwards repeated distinctly this statement, and particularly that part
which attributed to the judge a declaration that if the
counsel had any thing to say upon the law, they must
address themselves to the court and not to the jury.—
To this statement no reply was made by the court,
either correcting or denying it. Thus stands the evidence in the affirmative. Opposed to this we have
the negative testimony of Messrs. Rawle, Tilghman,
and Meredith, who have no recollection of any such
declaration. I address myself to those who well know
the difference between affirmative and negative testimony. I address myself to those who well know the
established rule in the law of evidence, that the testimony of one affirmative witness countervails that of
many negative ones; and I am sure that I address myself
to those who must feel the complete coincidence of
this rule with the dictates of common sense. Upon
this ground alone we might safely rest our proposi-
tion. But, sir, we will not rest it here. It appears
from the testimony of the witnesses on both sides, that
almost every observation from the counsel to the court
on the second day was predicated upon the idea that
something had been said on the preceding day re-
strictive of their privileges. These observations, although addressed to the court and carrying this feature prominent in their face, were neither contradicted nor corrected by the court. This was a strong
tacit admission of the correctness of the idea upon
which they were bottomed. But, sir, we have not
only this tacit admission, but we have in testimony,
this strong and impressive declaration from judge
Chase, that " the counsel might be heard in opposition

" to the opinion of the court, at the hazard of their cha-
" racters."

But, Mr. President, we have the positive admission of the respondent, in page 18 of his answer, that certain observations were made by him condemning the use of common law authorities upon the doctrine of treason, and also condemning authorities under the statute of treasons, but prior to the English revolution. (Here the passage was read.) By a recurrence to page 22 of the answer, it will be found that the respondent admits that these observations of his were made on the first day; yet, sir, nothing of all this is remembered by Messrs. Rawle, Tilghman, or Meredith. How light then, how extremely light must their bare want of recollection weigh against the positive affirmative testimony of Mr. Lewis, and Mr. Dallas.

Considering my position as uncontrovertibly established, I will proceed to observe, that the offence with which Fries stood charged was the highest possible offence which can be committed in a state of society. The punishment annexed to its commission was the highest possible punishment known to our laws. The accused was therefore entitled to every possible indulgence. In favor of life, not only every possible ground should be occupied by counsel to the jury, but every possible argument listened to and weighed with patience and forbearance : and it should never be forgotten, that judge Chase had such a conduct set as an example before him, in a previous trial of the same case. Yes, sir, a brother judge of his, who has since gone to the world of spirits, had set him an example conspicuous for the purity of its excellence, and which should have arrested his career in the commission of this cruel outrage upon all humanity. But judge Chase predetermines the law ; then prohibits counsel from proving to the jury that the law was not as laid down. This was in effect an extinguishment at once of the whole right of jury trial. All the privileges and all the benefits of that institution were swept at once from an American court of justice, and scarcely the external form preserved. The law was predetermined by the judge, and the accused was debarred from pleading it to the jury. Of what avail is it, sir, that the jury should be made judges of law and of fact, when the law is not permitted to be expounded to them? Of what avail is it that the accused should have a trial by jury, when he is prevented from stating and explaining to the jury the only grounds upon which his case is defensible? The right to hear and determine facts is *not more the right* of a jury, than the right to hear and determine the law. To deprive them then, of the privilege of hearing and determining the law, is as much a violation of their rights, as to deprive them of the privilege of hearing and determining facts. The right of the accused to be heard upon the facts to the jury, is not more his right, than the right of being heard upon the law to the jury. To deprive him then of the privilege of being heard upon the law to the jury, is as much a violation of his rights, as to deprive him of the privilege of being heard upon the facts to the jury.

But, sir, we are assailed by a train of reasoning on the part of the respondent, in exculpation of his conduct, which it may be proper to notice in part at this stage of the argument. He informs us in his answer, that the law of treason having been solemnly settled by prior adjudications, he was not at liberty to depart from the principles so settled, even had he thought them incorrect, and he enters into a lengthy discussion to shew the importance of uniform adherence to doctrines properly considered and solemnly established. It is no part of my intention to dispute either the correctness of the decisions previously made upon the constitutional doctrine of treason, or the propriety of an adherence to those decisions on the part of judge

Chase. For although I consider both extremely questionable, they yet appear to me to constitute no part of the present inquiry. This inquiry is whether the judge was authorized or can be excused for delivering an opinion upon the law before counsel were heard on the part of the accused, and for debarring counsel from the exercise of their constitutional privilege to address the jury on the law as well as the facts, thereby making the opinion thus prejudged and thus extrajudicially delivered completely decisive of the case. And give me leave to say, sir, that the reasoning, resorted to by the respondent to excuse this conduct on his part is, in my opinion, an aggravation of his offence. It is of importance truly that juries should be guarded against improper impressions from counsel, by having the law previously explained to them! And it is a favour to counsel to be informed that the ground they mean to occupy is not tenable, that they may look out for other resources! Would not this reasoning go to authorize a judge in all criminal prosecutions to settle the law before the case was heard? He has nothing else to do, sir, according to this doctrine, than to inform himself of the facts, as in Fries's case, and then before any trial is had settle the law; at the same time prohibiting counsel from arguing that to the jury. And if the reason that the law has been so solemnly settled that it cannot be departed from is to form an excuse, the more settled the law, the longer practiced upon, the stronger the reason. In every case of murder or theft then it is to confer a favour on the counsel to inform them what grounds are not tenable. It is of importance to instruct the jury what the law is upon the case, that they may be guarded against improper impressions, and then to render this object effectual prevent the counsel from arguing the law to the jury. In the case of Fries I hold it that the knowledge of the judge that the case depended solely upon legal principles is a circumstance highly aggravating his offence. He knew that there was no dispute as to facts, and that by thus prejudging the law, he fixed the destiny of the accused. But it was material to do this to guard the jury from improper impressions! My God! has it come to this? And is this the amount of our boasted constitutional right of jury trial, that they whose exclusive right it is to determine both the law and the fact, are to be guarded from improper impressions by the prejudged, extrajudicial opinion of him who possesses no right to determine either!

We are told by the respondent, that he not only never interdicted the counsel for Fries from arguing the law to the jury, but that he afterwards on the next day expressly offered to let them take as wide a range as they pleased. Mr. President, I must confess I have been disappointed. I had expected that much of the defence against the first article would have rested upon the transactions of that day. I had so expected, not because of any opinion of my own, that from them any substantial excuse could be extracted; but because public opinion had somewhat inclined to rest an excuse upon that foundation. For myself, it has been my misfortune to be unable to perceive in this part of the transaction any features other than such as afford additional proof of the unjust and oppressive intent with which the judge appears to have acted. Indeed, sir, the respondent must himself have considered the transactions of the second day, as dangerous topics. He has touched them lightly indeed. If his conduct had been so free from blame as is contended in the answer, why was an appearance of fairness to be cast over the scene by having the papers recalled upon which the opinion had been written, whilst the opinion itself remained? A short view of this part of the transaction may not be unimportant. It may afford us some strong proofs of the motives of the respondent. We are involuntarily lead to inquire why the papers were recalled? Was it because of the oppressive tendency with which they operated upon the case of the accused ? Was it because of any conviction on the part of the judge of the impropriety of the steps he had taken, or compunction for the cruel situation in which he had placed poor Fries? No, sir! The papers were recalled because of the firm and manly stand made by the counsel. It was because those counsel were men of characters too independent, and were governed by a sense of duty too high to submit to such a prostration of their rights. The determination to recall the papers was not taken until after it was seen that the counsel would abandon their cause rather than acquiesce in a conduct so oppressive and so injurious.

This recalling of the papers was a farce acted for the purpose of giving a specious appearance to the face of things; but the folly thereof could only be exceeded by the criminality of the first act. Was the crime the greater because the opinion was written? Was it the act of writing the opinion and throwing down the paper to the bar which constituted the evil to Fries? Or was it the formation of a prejudged and extrajudicial opinion completely decisive of the case, and the communication of that opinion in the very presence of those who were to try the accused? In my opinion it was the last. The evil was complete by the act of prejudication, and withdrawing the paper could have no possible effect. The case of the accused had been predetermined....had been extrajudicially predetermined....predetermined by the judge who had no right to determine it at all; and the counsel were left to the forlorn hope of convincing the judge that the opinion delivered by him was erroneous. "They might "be heard in opposition to the opinion of the court at "the hazard of their characters." This is his declaration on the second day.

If then I were asked, as were Fries's counsel, on the second day, by the other judge, and as I know many are now disposed to ask, whether, if an error had been committed, I would not suffer it to be corrected? I would answer that this was an act which from its nature admitted of no correction. It was a *crime* complete in its performance, and complete in all its baneful consequences. Repentance, even had there been any, could have afforded no relief; it came too late. As well might a man, after he had inflicted a mortal wound upon another, ask to be forgiven, because before the death of the wounded he was brought to relent, from an apprehension of the consequences. In my opinion, judge Chase had committed the sin not to be repented of.

As to the proffered permission to the counsel on the second day that they might proceed without the restrictions before imposed, it has been my misfortune to be unable to perceive either any proof of a disposition to relent on the part of the judge, or any privileges to the counsel which placed them or their client upon ground more advantageous than that on which they had before stood. On the contrary, I think I perceive in the whole of the judge's conduct taken together, on the second day, a deliberate design to impose upon the understanding of those present, by exhibiting the external form of fairness, whilst he continued to hold on upon the substance of injustice. For notwithstanding there appeared from his expressions at first a disposition to permit the counsel to argue the cause without any restraint, yet it ought to be kept in constant recollection, that when brought to explain himself, the general permission which had been thus apparently given, was subjected to restrictions of very serious import. The counsel were permitted to argue the law to the jury, but the manner in which they should do so, would be regulated by the court. The counsel were permitted to lay down the law, but should not read cases which were not law. That common law cases, and cases under the statute of treason, but prior to the revolution in England, were not law and should not be read. Look at the consequence! The counsel might argue the law to the jury, but were interdicted from the use of those authorities, which in their opinion bore most strongly upon the case, and upon which, it was within the knowledge of the judge, they had principally relied in the prior trial. They might lay down the law to the jury, but should not read cases which were not law. And who was to determine whether the cases offered by counsel were or were not law? The judge. And pray, sir, was not the right of the jury to determine the law, as effectually invaded by the judge's taking upon himself to determine each case as it was offered, as their right was invaded, by the judge's determining upon the whole together? I maintain, sir, that it is not the right of the judge in criminal, and especially in capital causes, to determine that any case is not law; for if he can determine that question as to a single authority, and upon that ground arrest it from the jury, he may do so as to all, and thus as effectually abolish the great privilege of trial by jury. I know it may be objected to this reasoning, that unless some restriction is imposed upon counsel, they may abuse their privileges by reading any thing however inapplicable to the jury. This, sir, is to suppose an extreme case, and it is never correct to reason from extreme cases. It is no proof against a privilege, that it is subject to be abused. And there is a security against extreme abuse in this privilege, from the regard which professional men necessarily feel for their professional reputation.

Here, Mr. President, we might close the argument upon the first article. But it is not possible; no, sir, not possible here to stop our reflections. When we review the ground which has been already travelled over; when in that review we behold an American citizen summoned to the bar of justice to undergo a trial in which his life is at stake; when we behold his judge, contrary to all precedent and in violation of every feeling of humanity, pre-occupying the only ground upon which the case of the accused was defensible, and closing upon him this only possible avenue to safety, truly I feel that my feeble powers of language are not competent to a description of the scene; it must be left to the strong expression of silence. For this transaction then in the name of the American people we denounce judge Chase. We denounce him for invading their most valuable privilege, *the trial by jury*. We denounce him for taking into his own unhallowed hands, the disposal of the life of an American citizen; and we invoke the justice of the nation to expiate by the proper punishment this most unholy sin.

The second, third, and fourth articles, exhibited by the house of representatives, charge the defendant with a course of conduct upon a particular trial which affords many grounds of accusation. In this case it is true no unfortunate individual was charged with an offence which demanded his life as an expiation; yet, sir, there were other rights involved equally sacred in the laws of a free country. The liberty and the property of the accused were the price of a conviction.

In casting our eyes over the ground upon which the different scenes of the transaction now about to be examined are spread, we are struck with a feature not usual in the history of human concerns. It would seem that even the restraint of appearances was no longer felt. We find the respondent setting out with a conduct, which seemed to prove that the fate of the accused was fixed. We find him pursuing a system of conduct throughout, which arrested from the accused some of his best established and most valuable privileges. We find him endeavoring to heap shame and odium on those who occupied the station of advocates, because they would not tamely yield to his unwarrantable invasion of long established rights.

Mr. President, notwithstanding the labored attempts
made by the defendant in his answer to exculpate himself from imputation in compelling Mr. Basset to serve
upon the jury in the trial of Callender ; yet, sir, I
must be permitted to say that those attempts appear
to me to be only the exertions of a mind conscious of
impropriety, and seeking to impose upon the understanding of others. The test adopted, by which to
try the impartiality of the jurors, in that case may possibly by some be held a correct one ; but the *manner*
of *applying* that test as then practised upon, is what
I believe can be accounted for upon no other supposition than that of a determination on the part of the
judge to procure the conviction of the accused.—
Upon what other principle can it be accounted for,
that the jurors should be asked " whether they had
formed and delivered an opinion upon the charges
laid in the indictment, when they knew not and were
not suffered to know what those charges were ? Why
else could it be laid down by the judge, that because
the individuals called to serve upon the jury, did not
know what charges were in the indictment (having
never seen it nor heard it read) that therefore they
could not have formed and delivered an opinion upon
the subject ? And why else did the judge, when this
monstrous logic was contradicted by the *fact* of one
of the jurors delivering in open court an opinion upon
the whole subject of those charges, without having
seen, or heard the indictment read ; why else did
the judge, in the teeth of this damning fact, order the
juror sworn ?

Every juror sworn might, like Mr. Basset, have
formed and delivered an opinion which concluded the
conviction of the accused, and yet because they did
not know that the subject matter of such opinion
constituted the charges in the indictment, having
neither seen it nor heard it read, the expression of
such opinion, created no disqualification.   Unworthy

evasion! An evasion which prevents the doctrine of disqualification in a juror from receiving any practical operation. An evasion which effectually puts at nought that principle of the constitution so often adverted to in a former part of the argument, that " the " accused shall enjoy the right of a trial by an impar- " tial jury." Upon this point I beg leave to read two authorities. [Mr. Early here cited 3 Bac. Abr. 176, and Co. L. 157 l.]

But we are told by the respondent in his answer, that the declaration made by Mr. Basset, did not disqualify him, because it contained no direct opinion as to the guilt of the *traverser*. This I understand to be the amount of all the labored reasoning and nice distinctions drawn by the respondent upon this point. There is, sir, a plain common sense rule to govern us upon this subject, which in my opinion is as safe in its application as it is reasonable in its principle. A juror must be *indifferent*. How must he be indifferent? What kind of indifference is this which is made necessary? The manner in which judge Chase has stated and explained this rule is certainly calculated to confuse and mislead. " The juror, says he, must " be indifferent between the government and the ac- " cused as to the subject matter."

Must the juror in reality be indifferent between the parties as to the subject matter of prosecution on- ly? Will not a prejudice against the accused, flowing from other causes, create a disqualification? I address myself to those who well know that partiality, arising from a variety of relations in society, as well as prejudice arising from a variety of causes, destroys that character of indifference necessary to render a juror competent, and that this partiality or prejudice need not relate to the subject matter of prosecution.

So also I apprehend that this character of *indifference* is as effectually destroyed by a prejudice as to the subject matter, without any prejudice as to the person. I mean the prejudice of a prejudication of the criminality of the subject matter. We meet with the rule every day, that it is good cause of challenge to a juror that he hath expressed an opinion upon the subject matter of prosecution. Wherefore then the manner of stating the rule, which we find adopted in the answer ? Most evidently to suit the respondent's case. What, sir, must a juror, to be so prejudiced as to be disqualified, have expressed an opinion not only that the subject matter of prosecution was criminal in law, but that the person prosecuted was the author of the crime ? Yes, sir, according to the doctrine of the answer, he must have prejudged both *law* and *fact*. In other words, although Mr. Basset had formed and delivered an opinion that such a book as " The Prospect Before Us," came within the sedition law, yet not having said that Callender was the author or publisher, he was still a competent juror. Suppose a man indicted for murder, in a case where there is no dispute as to the fact of killing (and here there was no dispute as to the fact of publishing) but the defence set up was that he was excusable. A juror has given his opinion, in reference to the act, that such a killing does amount to murder, but without saying that the person prosecuted was the murderer ; will any man say that this expression would not disqualify him ? I am bound to presume not. Sir, in the case of Callender, although Mr. Basset did not say that the person prosecuted was guilty, yet he did in effect say that whoever wrote or published the book was guilty. And give me leave to remark here that in prosecutions for libels, the question of law, as to their criminality, is generally the only question of dispute. The fact of publication is one about which there seldom occurs any difficulty, and has to be proven merely because not admitted. To have expressed an opinion then upon the question of law in such cases is substantially to have prejudged the

whole case. A juror under such circumstances cannot be called impartial. As well might it be alleged that judge Chase himself was impartial, as to the
case of Fries, after he had delivered the opinion which
we have before discussed.

We are told in the answer that the guilt of the traverser was not prejudged by Basset, for another reason ; that as the charges to make them criminal must
have been false, so Callender might have exculpated
himself by proving their truth. But, sir, the traverser was at liberty to rest his defence either upon a
justification or want of criminality in law, or upon
both. He was not bound to disclose which, nor could
the judge officially know which. Both and each of
these grounds were proper for the jury to determine
under the plea. The acquittal of the traverser then
did not depend exclusively upon the proof of the truth
of the charges.

Again we are told that the juror barely expressed
his opinion upon the book, as the contents thereof
had been represented to him. The same may be
said of almost every other case. Few, very few jurors
are spectators of a murder, or an act of treason. Any
opinion they may have formed and delivered of the
actual guilt of the person charged must be in nine
cases out of ten, from representation. Few, very few
of the jurors who were summoned in the case of Fries,
had been spectators of the acts which were alleged
to have been treasonable ; probably not one of them.
Yet we learn from the answer of judge Chase, that in
that very case several were repelled from serving, because of the opinions which they acknowledged they
had given. Such opinions must in nine cases out of
ten be bottomed upon representation. There are
numerous secret crimes, which from their very nature
preclude the possibility that an opinion concerning
them, however positive, and however decisive of the
conviction of the accused, should be founded upon

any previous knowledge of facts. And yet, sir, I presume no person will deny that in such cases, a juror may nevertheless so express an opinion as to disqualify himself from serving.

But, sir, the scene rises upon us. We have now to examine a part of the transaction for which, I had supposed, human invention might be tortured for a paliation in vain. I allude to the rejection of Mr. Taylor's testimony. The reason assigned for that rejection was, that the witness could not prove the truth of the whole of *any one charge.* Let us for a moment examine the consequences of this doctrine. According to the judge's own decisions then, as well as his doctrine now, each charge laid in the indictment must have constituted a separate offence. For it is explicitly declared both by Mr. Hay and Mr. Nicholas, that when an application was made to continue the case, because of the absence of some material witnesses, the application was rejected upon the ground, that it did not appear from the affidavit filed, that the witnesses so absent, could prove the truth of all the charges. That proof of the truth of a part only, would be of no avail, and that the whole must be proved to intitle the traverser to an acquittal. Each charge in the indictment then must have constituted a *separate offence :* for the charges cannot be made to help each other out. One charge, however, it seems might consist of different facts. This was the case with several in that indictment. It was particularly the case with the very charge, the truth of which Mr. Taylor was called to prove. " The President was a professed aristocrat. " He had proved faithful and serviceable to the British " interest." Here was a charge made up of two distinct facts ; so distinct in their nature, that the knowledge of their truth might not only rest with different persons, but was extremely likely not to rest with any *one* witness. Put the case of a man charged with any offence, murder, theft, or any other crime you please : There may be a string of facts upon the proof of which the defence may depend; some within the knowledge of one man; some within that of another. Was it ever heard of before, that because one witness could not prove the existence of all those facts, that therefore such witness should not be examined as to what he did know? Or if some of the facts depended upon written testimony, was it ever heard of before that therefore a witness should not be examined as to those resting in oral testimony? To these questions no man will answer in the affirmative. Why then was an unheard of and palpably absurd doctrine brought to bear in Callender's case? Was the defence of justification, under the sedition law of the United States, such an anomaly in its nature, that none of the established rules of jurisprudence would apply to it? Was it a thing so *entire* in its nature, that it could not consist of different parts? I have always been taught, and the respondent's answer confirms the principle, that a defence must apply to the whole of a charge. If then a charge consist of different parts, surely so must the defence. But according to judge Chase, be the parts ever so many, they shall not be proven, unless the proof can all be made by one witness, or unless it appear that the defendant has proof in reserve to establish all. I ask this honorable court how it can appear that the defendant has proof in reserve applying to all the parts of a charge? Suppose a witness called to substantiate *one part*, how is it to be known to the court whether there is or is not other testimony behind in the power of the party, by which the residue of the charge may be established? We are told by the respondent, that none of the questions propounded to colonel Taylor had any application to the charge, except the first, and this only to a part of the charge; and that this question was repelled because no proof was offered as to the residue. I answer, sir, that the judge had no right to know, nor were the counsel bound to disclose whether there was such testimony in reserve or not.

It is a new doctrine, sir, that the legal admissibility of testimony is to depend upon what the party can afterwards prove by other testimony. It is the right of the party to establish his defence as far as he can, and if he fail in establishing it completely, the evil is to himself alone. And permit me here to add, sir, that whether he succeed in establishing his defence or not, is a question for the jury to determine, and not the judge. The judge possesses no right to *determine* even after the testimony is finished, whether that testimony has or has not established the defence ; still less then can he before it is heard, determine that it will not make good the defence.

We are told in the respondent's answer that his rejection of colonel Taylor's testimony can be no proof of a determination on his part to oppress, as such an intention might have been gratified by the conviction of the traverser upon the other articles. This is true, very true, upon the principle that the judge and not the jury was to determine the question of law in criminal cases. If the criminality of the charges in point of law, was to be settled by the judge, his conclusion is certainly correct. But if, as I apprehend, the criminality of the charges was to be exclusively determined by the jury, then it was not entirely certain, that the judge might have been sure of his object, notwithstanding the tenth charge had been proved. For aught he knew, or ought to be presumed to have known, the jury might have been of the opinion that the other charges did not come within the sedition law, and might have therefore given a verdict of acquittal.

But, Mr. President, this apart, it is a novel proof of innocence to me at least, that a man should have the magnanimous boldness to disregard appearances. It is a novel proof of innocence that a man should possess a spirit daring enough to insult the common sense of mankind. Yes, sir, I yield to the respondent the full share of glory, which he is desirous of accumulating from this source.

The last of the three articles now under examination goes on to charge the defendant with various
acts of injustice, partiality and intemperance, highly
derogatory to his character as a judge, and equally
injurious to the reputation of the American bench.
Without fatiguing the patience of the honorable
court with an inquiry into the proofs and an investigation of the criminality of all the particulars
here enumerated, I beg leave to call their attention to
one part of the judge's conduct, which appears to me
to stand pre-eminent for its open defiance of all justice,
and its flagrant violation of the constitution of this
country. I allude to the refusal to continue the cause.
The reasons assigned for that refusal, were, we learn,
that it did not appear by the affidavit exhibited, and
upon which the motion for a continuance was founded,
that the witnesses, whose testimony was wanted, could
prove the truth of all the charges laid in the indictment. This conduct, Mr. President, strikes me as
being of the same family with the rejection of Mr.
Taylor's testimony. The charges in the indictment
are in number many. They embrace a numerous
collection of facts, some of them assimilated, others
extremely variant in their nature ; many of them in-
volving legal difficulties as to their criminality. Under the plea of not guilty, to the indictment, it was
competent to the traverser not only to prove the truth
of the charges in point of fact, but also to prove that
any of the charges were not criminal in point of law.
It was competent for the defendant to prove the truth
of a part of the charges, and to contend that the rest
were not seditious. Both these grounds of defence
were proper for the jury, and the jury possessed the
right to pass without control upon both. With what
propriety then could the judge pronounce from the
bench that to intitle the accused to a continuance, it
must appear that he could prove the truth of all the
charges ? What, sir, was the question of law as to

their criminality, a point which the judge here again arrogated to himself the exclusive right to determine, and that too before the traverser was heard? Indeed it would appear that in this case also, as in the case of Fries, the law was to be arrested from its proper organ, the jury, and to be exclusively passed upon by the judge himself. What other construction can be given to his determination that the truth of all the charges must be proven? There surely could be no necessity for this, unless they were all seditious within the act of congress. By determining then, that all must be proved true, the judge did determine that all were seditious. This, sir, it was the exclusive right of the jury to determine.

The constitution of this country has most wisely provided, that " the accused shall have compulsory " process for obtaining witnesses in his favor." Of what avail is this provision if time be not given for their attendance? Of what avail to grant the process, and, before the witnesses can by any physical possibility reach the place, force the accused to trial? This conduct, sir, is worse than mockery. It is an insult to the common sense of mankind. It is high treason against the majesty of the constitution of a free country. The constitution of the United States gives to the accused the right of process to compel the attendance of his witnesses. But judge Chase so administers, that the accused is indicted, arrested, tried, convicted and punished, all in the same term, whilst his witnesses are distant hundreds of miles.

After all this, Mr. President, surely we shall not be asked for proofs of corrupt intent. They are too thick upon every feature of the transactions which have been examined. The defendant is on all hands acknowledged to posses an acquaintance with the laws and constitution of his country, which yields not to that of any other man in this nation. He is on all hands acknowledged to possess talents which might do honor to any tribunal. With such knowledge and such talents, permit me to ask, if it was within the compass of possibility that he should mistake in points so familiar as those in which he is charged with criminal conduct? Although all things are possible, yet there are things the extreme improbability of which defies belief. Among those I rank the supposition of mistake on the part of judge Chase in the trial of James T. Callender. We might just as well be asked for proof of malice in a case where a man wilfully and without provocation kills another. In such a case as in the one now under consideration, the answer is that the criminal intent is apparent upon the face of the act. And there is a question, sir, which strikes me as applying itself with almost irresistible force to the present discussion: Can it be that such outrages should be committed upon the most ordinary principles of law and justice, and yet the conduct of the judge not be influenced by corrupt motives? Can it be that every thing should be done to favor the prosecution and stifle the defence, and yet justice be administered " faithfully and impartially and without respect to persons?" But if all this be insufficient, I pray this honorable court to recollect the declarations of the judge in relation to the case, as attested by several witnesses.

The fifth and sixth articles rest upon grounds so extremely simple, and so easily comprehended, that it appears totally unnecessary to fatigue the patience of the honorable court, by dwelling upon them.

The seventh article is as follows:

" That at a circuit court of the United States, for the district of Delaware, held at New-Castle, in the month of June, one thousand eight hundred, whereat the said Samuel Chase presided, the said Samuel Chase, disregarding the duties of his office, did descend from the dignity of a judge, and stoop to the level of an informer, by refusing to discharge the grand jury, although entreated by several of the said jury so to do; and after the said grand jury had regularly declared, through their foreman, that they had found no bills of indictment, nor had any presentments to make, by observing to the said grand jury, that he, the said Samuel Chase, understood, " that a highly seditious " temper had manifested itself in the state of Dela- " ware, among a certain class of people, particularly " in New-Castle county, and more especially in the " town of Wilmington, where lived a most seditious " printer, unrestrained by any principle of virtue, and " regardless of social order; that the name of this " printer was"....but checking himself, as if sensible of the indecorum which he was committing, added... " that it might be assuming too much to mention the " name of this person, but it becomes your duty, gen- " tlemen, to enquire diligently into this matter," or words to that effect; and that with intention to pro- cure the prosecution of the printer in question, the said Samuel Chase did, moreover, authoritatively en- join on the district attorney of the United States, the necessity of procuring a file of the papers to which he alluded, (and which were understood to be those pub- lished under the title of " Mirror of the Times and General Advertiser,") and, by a strict examination of them, to find some passage which might furnish the ground-work of a prosecution against the printer of the said paper : thereby degrading his high judicial functions, and tending to impair the public confidence in, and respect for, the tribunals of justice, so essen- tial to the general welfare."

The respondent stands here charged with a con- duct, than which, in my opinion, nothing could be more at war with his official duty—nothing more tar- nish his official character. The constitution and laws of this country certainly intended in erecting high judicial tribunals, that those who might be appointed to minister therein, should be impartial dispensers of justice between such as might resort thither for an adjustment of their differences. In public prosecutions, more especially was it intended that such dispensation should be made without respect to persons. In these, above all other cases, ought a judge to stand aloof from influence, free from predilection towards one, or prejudice against the other. Most peculiarly here is it his duty to stand firm at his post, resisting the overbearing influence of a powerful public, and protecting the rights of the accused in so unequal a contest. But judge Chase, disregarding these principles, always held sacred in a land of laws, converts himself into a hunter after accusations. He who, in the humane language of the laws, should be counsel for the accused, becomes himself an accuser. He, whose duty it is impartially to decide between the prosecutor and prosecuted, becomes himself the procurer of prosecutions.

I have always been taught that the character of an informer, in any station of life, was deservedly considered as the reverse of reputable. What then shall we say of him, who descends from the judgment seat of the nation, to inform against, and direct the prosecution of one, against whom he avows the strongest antipathy, and over whose trial he himself has to preside? Surely, sir, his thirst for punishment was great. Surely it was extreme indeed, when he could not wait for the tardy motion of the public prosecutors. If our judges are thus to turn informers; if they are thus to seek after objects for themselves to try, and themselves to punish; then indeed must this country, heretofore considered an asylum from oppression, become itself the nursery of oppression in its most odious form. And this government, heretofore the pride of humanity, will be held up as an object of scorn and derision to the nations of the earth.

The eighth article is in these words :

" And whereas mutual respect and confidence, between the government of the United States and those of the individual states, and between the people and those governments, respectively, are highly conducive to that public harmony, without which there can be no public happiness ; yet the said Samuel Chase, disregarding the duties and dignity of his judicial character, did, at a circuit court for the district of Maryland, held at Baltimore, in the month of May, one thousand eight hundred and three, pervert his official right and duty to address the grand jury then and there assembled, on the matters coming within the province of the said jury, for the purpose of delivering to the said grand jury an intemperate and inflammatory political harangue, with intent to excite the fears and resentment of the said grand jury, and of the good people of Maryland against their state government and constitution, a conduct highly censurable in any, but peculiarly indecent and unbecoming in a judge of the supreme court of the United States : and moreover, that the said Samuel Chase, then and there, under pretence of exercising his judicial right to address the said grand jury, as aforesaid, did, in a manner highly unwarrantable, endeavor to excite the odium of the said grand jury, and of the good people of Maryland against the government of the United States, by delivering opinions, which, even if the judicial authority were competent to their expression, on a suitable occasion, and in a proper manner, were at that time, and as delivered by him, highly indecent, extra-judicial, and tending to prostitute the high judicial character with which he was invested, to the low purpose of an electioneering partizan."

It is not my intention, Mr. President, to trouble the court with many observations upon this article ; not because of any opinion that it is unimportant. I believe it equally important with any in the catalogue. I believe it possesses a peculiar importance, in affording, from the testimony by which it is supported, proofs of the spirit by which judge Chase was usually governed in his official conduct.

There are features too in that part of the judge's official conduct charged in this article, which place him in a point of view awfully grand. We have heretofore been viewing him as bringing his talents to bear upon individuals. Here we see his genius rising, in the majesty of its strength, to far higher objects. Here we see him consigning over whole governments to the scourge of his own avenging wrath. Whithersoever he turned his eyes, whether to the state constitution and laws, or to the laws and constitution of the whole union, they were equally exposed to the whip and the rack.

Mr. President, there is no truth more forcible than that expressed in the language of this article, that " mutual respect and confidence between the govern- " ment of the United States and those of the indivi- " dual states, and between the people and those go- " vernments respectively, are highly conducive to that " public harmony, without which there can be no pub- " lic happiness." Indeed, sir, it may with truth be said, that this respect and confidence are *essential* to that harmony without which we can enjoy no public happiness. What words then can describe in its proper colors, the conduct of an officer of the highest judicial tribunal of the general government, who abuses the duty and perverts the privilege of his station to destroy the confidence and excite the odium of the people, against not only their state government, but that of the United States? He who was seated on the judgment seat of the nation to execute the laws of the union, converts that very judgment seat into a forum, from whence to pronounce a Philippic not only against the state government with which he there had no right to meddle, but against that very government under whose authority he was there sitting, and whose laws he was sworn there to execute. Not content with endeavoring to excite discontent and odium against the government of the state of Maryland, the congress of the United States must be held up as sacrilegious destroyers of the national constitution.

Mr. President, I have taken those views of this subject, which presented themselves most forcibly to my mind. I have finished all I intended to say upon the argument. There has, in my opinion, been established against the respondent a volume of guilt, every page of which calls for punishment at the hands of this nation. I leave the case and the respondent in your hands. I leave them where the constitution of this country has placed them. I leave them where I hope, and I believe, there will be found a different measure of justice from that which judge Chase has been accustomed to administer. I leave them where justice *will* be administered " faithfully and impartially, and " without respect to persons."

Mr. CAMPBELL then rose and spoke as follows :

Mr. PRESIDENT, and

GENTLEMEN of the SENATE,

It is with peculiar diffidence I rise, in compliance with the duty assigned me, to address this honorable court on this important occasion. Sensible of my own incompetency to do that justice to the investigation of this cause, which its importance, and the influence that the whole transaction is calculated to have on the jurisprudence of our country, would seem to require, I should have felt disposed to decline the undertaking ; but called upon by the representatives of the nation, to aid in supporting a prosecution which they have deemed it proper to institute for the public good, I conceive it my duty to yield up, in some degree, my own feeling to obey the voice of my country, and perform the duties imposed upon me thereby. Under this impression I shall endeavor to execute the trust reposed in me on this occasion, in such manner as the very short time left me from other public avocations, and the limited means of information on subjects of this nature, which the present situation of this place affords, will enable me. I feel, however, sir, considerable confidence in this undertaking, from the consideration, that there are other gentlemen associated with me on this occasion, who are fully competent to do complete justice to the subject. And a still higher degree of confidence arises from a perfect conviction, that the honorable members who compose this high tribunal, and who are to pronounce the final decision in this cause, are well qualified to investigate its merits ; and that their talents and experience are such as to preclude even the possibility of a defeat of justice taking place, in consequence of any deficiency that may exist in the exertions of counsel on either side.

The scene, presented to the nation by this trial, is more than usually interesting and important. One of the highest officers of the government, called upon by the voice of the people, through their representatives, before the highest tribunal known to our constitution ; that same tribunal that sanctioned his elevation ; to answer for the abuse of the power with which he had been entrusted. It is a melancholy truth, that derogates much from the dignity of human nature, but it is a truth that has been for ages established by experience, that high and important powers have a tendency to corrupt those on whom they are conferred. Few minds are possessed of sufficient integrity and independence, when elevated above the ordinary level of the great mass of their fellow citizens, to resist the impulse their high station gives them, to grasp at still greater powers, and prostitute those which they already possess.

Hence it has been the great exertion of all governments, who regard the rights and liberties of the people, and still must continue to be so, to watch over the conduct of the high and confidential officers of state, and guard against their abusing the powers reposed in them. For this purpose the mode of trial by impeachment was resorted to in very early times in that country from which we have derived most of our laws and usages. Near five hundred years ago, the representatives of the people in that nation felt themselves clothed with sufficient authority to check the abuses of power, in the highest officers under the crown, by calling upon them by impeachment to answer before the house of lords for their conduct, and punishing them for such acts as were unauthorised, illegal, or oppressive.

It was a wise and politic measure to have charges of this nature tried by the highest tribunal in the nation, that would not be *awed* by the great powers and elevated standing of the accused, nor influenced by the popular voice of the accusers, further than a strict regard to impartial justice would require. As I conceive, therefore, that pure and unstained impartiality ought to be the characteristic feature in the trial by impeachment, I shall for myself, and I conceive I may in the name of the representatives of the people, utterly disclaim any design or wish, that party considerations, or difference in political sentiments, should, in the remotest degree, enter into the investigation or affect the decision of this question. Yet in order to ascertain the motives that actuated the respondent, it may become necessary to notice the difference of political sentiments, so far as regarded the accused, and those who are stated to have been injured by his conduct, at the time those transactions took place, that gave origin to this prosecution.

In the view which I propose taking of this subject,
I shall in the first place notice the provisions in the
constitution relative to impeachment, and endeavor to
ascertain the precise object and extent of such provision so far as the same may relate to the present case.

The first provision in the constitution on this subject, (art. 1st, sec. 3.) declares, that the Senate shall
have the sole power to try all impeachments.

Here we discover the great wisdom of the framers
of the constitution. The highest and most enlightened tribunal in the nation is charged with the protection
of the rights and liberties of the citizens against oppression from the officers of government under the
sanction of law ; unawed by the power which the officer may possess, or the dignified station he may fill,
compleat justice may be expected at their hands. The
accused is called upon before the same tribunal, and
in many instances, before the same men, who sanctioned his official elevation, to answer for abusing the
powers with which he had been entrusted. Men who
are presumed to have had a favorable opinion of him
once, are to be his judges ; no inferior or co-ordinate
tribunal is to decide on his case, which might from motives of jealousy or interest be prejudiced against him
and wish his removal. No, sir, his judges, without
the shadow of temptation to influence their conduct,
are placed beyond the reach of suspicion.

The next provision in the constitution declares that
judgment in cases of impeachment shall not extend
further than to removal from office and disqualification to hold and enjoy any office of honor, trust, or
profit under the United States.

Here the constitution seems to make an evident distinction between such misdemeanors as would authorize a removal from office, and disqualification to
hold any office, and such as are criminal, in the
ordinary sense of the word, in courts of common law,
and punishable by indictment. So far as the offence

committed is injurious to society, only in consequence
of the power reposed in the officer being abused in
the exercise of his official functions, it is inquirable
into only by impeachment, and punishable only by removal from office, and disqualification to hold any office; but so far as the offence is criminal, independent of the office, it is to be tried by indictment,
and is made punishable according to the known rules
of law in courts of ordinary jurisdiction. As, if an
officer take a bribe to do an act not connected with
his office, for this he is indictable in a court of justice
only. Impeachment, therefore, according to the meaning of the constitution, may fairly be considered a
kind of inquest into the conduct of an officer, merely
as it regards his office; the manner in which he per-
forms the duties thereof; and the effects that his conduct therein may have on society. It is more in the
nature of a civil investigation, than of a criminal prosecution. And though impeachable offences are termed in the constitution high crimes and misdemeanors,
they must be such only so far as regards the official
conduct of the officer; and even treason and bribery
can only be inquired into by impeachment, so far as
the same may be considered as a violation of the duties of the officer, and of the oath the officer takes to
support the constitution and laws of the United States,
and of his oath of office; and not as to the criminality
of those offences independent of the office. This must
be inquired into and punished by indictment.

This position is strongly supported by the mode of
proceeding adopted by this honorable court in cases
of impeachment. You issue a summons to give notice to the accused of the proceeding against him; you
do not consider his personal appearance necessary;
you issue no compulsory process to enforce his personal attendance; and you pass sentence, or render
judgment on him in his absence. But in all criminal prosecutions, compulsory process must issue

at some stage of it to enforce the defendant's appearance; unless outlawry in England be considered an
exception, which, it is believed, is not resorted to in
this country, and his personal appearance is considered absolutely necessary; and in almost every case he
must be present when sentence is pronounced against
him. This construction of the constitutional provision appears to be absolutely necessary, to avoid the
absurd consequence that would arise from a different
construction; that of punishing a man twice for the
same offence, which could not have been intended by
the framers of the constitution. The nature of the
judgment which you are bound to render, and not to
exceed, appears also conclusive on this head. You
can only remove and disqualify an individual from holding any office of honor, trust, or profit. This cannot
be considered a criminal punishment; it is merely a
deprivation of rights; a declaration that the person is
not properly qualified to serve his country. Hence, I
conceive, that in order to support these articles of impeachment, we are not bound to make out such a case
as would be punishable by indictment in a court of law.
It is sufficient to shew that the accused has transgress-
ed the line of his official duty, in violation of the laws
of his country; and that this conduct can only be accounted for on the ground of impure and corrupt motives. We need not hunt down the accused as a criminal, who had committed crimes of the deepest die;
and this honorable court are not authorized to inflict
a punishment adequate to such crimes, if they had
been committed and could be established. With this
view of the meaning of the constitutional provision relative to impeachments, I shall proceed to examine
the articles now under consideration, and the evidence
given to support them. In the course of this examination, we apprehend, it will clearly appear, that the
whole conduct of the judge in the several transactions,
for which charges are alleged against him, *had its*

origin in a corrupt partiality and predetermination, unjustly to oppress, under the sanction of legal authority, those who became the objects of his resentment in consequence of differing from him in political sentiments; turning the judicial power, with which he was vested, into an engine of political oppression. So completely, it is conceived, has this motive pervaded the whole of his judicial transactions now in question, that there is not a single act charged in the articles of impeachment, that is not strongly marked with manifest oppression, springing from political intolerance, under the mask of administering justice. This is the corrupt origin from which have issued all the evils complained of; this has for ages been the scourge of society; and it is all important, that in our country, which is yet in its infancy, when this poisonous germ cannot have taken deep root, it should be crushed in its embryo, and not permitted to gather strength by the sanction of high and superior authority.

In order to observe some arrangement in the investigation of this subject, I propose to consider, first, under one general view, the conduct of the judge on the trial of Fries for treason, as stated in the charges contained in the first article; and,

Secondly, I will consider also under one general view, the conduct of the judge in the trial of Callender for a libel, as stated in the several charges contained in the second, third, and fourth articles of the impeachment. The fifth and sixth articles I will leave to be supported by those gentlemen associated with me in the management of this prosecution, who have been more conversant than myself with the laws of, and practice of the courts, in Virginia, upon which the support of these articles materially depend; and the remaining articles, to wit, the seventh and eighth, will be chiefly relied upon by me, to shew the spirit of oppression, partiality and political intolerance, that marked the whole judicial career of the judge, during the course of these transactions, thereby establishing more clearly the motives that actuated his conduct in the several acts charged as misdemeanors in the articles already noticed and relied upon.

In examining the first article, I shall rely upon the following positions:

First, that under the eighth article amendatory of the constitution of the United States, (referred to in this article of the impeachment) which secures to the defendant in all criminal prosecutions, the assistance of counsel, he is thereby entitled to the *right* of such counsel being heard in his defence by the court, before a decision be made and declared against him on the law arising in his case, and also, that such counsel should exercise their professional rights in making his defence, according to the known and established laws and usages of the nation, free from any arbitrary control or restriction whatever.

Secondly, that in the trial of Fries for treason, the judge did, by delivering an opinion in writing on the law arising in the case, before counsel were permitted to be heard in his defence, effectually deprive the defendant of any benefit from the assistance of counsel.

Thirdly, that he imposed on the counsel engaged for the defendant, arbitrary restrictions and control, in the exercise of their professional rights, unknown to, and unauthorized by the laws and usages of the nation, which compelled them to relinquish the defence of the prisoner.

Fourthly, I will then insist that this conduct was such a flagrant violation of his duty, as could only spring from corrupt motives, and a disposition to oppress those who became the objects of his resentment.

With regard to the first position, that counsel ought to be permitted to be heard for a defendant before a decision should be declared against him; and also that the counsel ought to be protected in the exercise of their professional rights, according to the usages and practice of courts, it appears to me substantially supported by the constitutional provision already noticed, securing to the defendant the assistance of counsel, and to be a necessary consequence of that provision; and essential, in order to give it effect. For in the first place, as to the law, of what use would the assistance of counsel be to the defendant, if a decision of the law arising in his case should be deliberately made up by the court, committed to writing to give it more solemnity and effect, and delivered, or made known, before such counsel were permitted to be heard in his defence? What hopes could the counsel entertain of being able to convince a court, that an opinion, thus deliberately formed, and solemnly made known, was incorrect and ought not to have been given? Surely if the right to the assistance of counsel, secured to a defendant, means any thing, it must mean that he should have an opportunity through his counsel, to make his case known to the court, to explain the law arising thereon, and shew, as far as it could be done, that according to the true construction of the law applying to his case, or under which he is charged, he is not subject to its penalties; before their opinion be declared on the subject, while the mind of the court is unbiassed, open to conviction, and capable of duly weighing the arguments that may be advanced on either side. But when an opinion is deliberately declared, or made known, against a defendant before he is permitted to be heard by counsel, his case is prejudged, the character of the court is committed in a very great degree to support such opinion, the arguments of counsel cannot be expected to be heard by such a court, with impartiality and fairness, that go to prove such opinion to be erroneous; and under such circumstances, the aid of counsel is a mere name without a benefit; a form without substance. But again. if such counsel were subject to the arbitrary control and restriction of a court, of every capricious and irritable judge; if they were not protected in the performance of their professional duties, so long as they acted within the laws of their country and the known usages and practice of courts, of what use would their assistance be to the accused, or what substantial aid could they afford him in making his defence? The counsel would have no rule to direct them in shaping their client's defence. When they had prepared to examine his cause in the manner heretofore usual in courts, and upon grounds, which they conceived most likely to establish his innocence and procure his acquittal, they might be stopped at the very threshold of the defence, surprised with a new and unheard of mode of proceeding; presented with a digested and formal opinion upon the very points they intended to contest; and informed that in the remarks they might be permitted to make to the court, to shew that such opinion was not correct, they must confine themselves in their endeavors to establish the doctrine they might advance, to the producing of authorities of a certain description; and must not extend their researches after decisions, on similar cases, beyond certain prescribed limits, as to time and the kind of decisions. Under such circumstances no counsel could render any substantial service to the accused; none would be found to submit to the tyranny of such a practice.

Further, it is conceived an universal rule of construction, that when a right is secured to any person, by a law, the means of acquiring the benefit of that right are thereby also secured to him. The constitution secures to the defendant in all criminal cases the assistance of counsel in his defence; the only means by which the benefits of that right can be obtained by such defendant, it is conceived, must be, by permitting counsel to be heard in his behalf, before his case is decided against him, and by protecting such counsel in the due performance of their professional duties. These rights are secured to counsel for the benefit of those for whom they are concerned, and whose interests they advocate; and not for their own advantage. And here it may be proper to observe, that though counsel may be considered in some respects as officers of the court, and in a certain degree subject to their control and direction; yet, it is certain, while they act within the line of their duty, and the known sphere of their action as counsel, their rights are as sacred as those of the court; and they are, in performing their professional duty, in a certain sense, as independent of the court, as the court are of them.

The *second* position proposed to be established and relied upon, to wit, that the judge did, in the trial of Fries for treason, by delivering an opinion in writing on the law arising in the case, before counsel was permitted to be heard in his defence, effectually deprive the defendant of any benefit from the assistance of counsel, is in part a deduction from the preceding position and supported by it. The fact of the judge's delivering an opinion in writing, in this case, against the defendant, previous to permitting counsel to be heard in his defence, is admitted by the judge in his answer, and is also established beyond a doubt by the evidence of Messrs. Lewis, Dallas, Tilghman, and indeed of all the witnesses on the subject. No difference exists in the evidence of the different witnesses with regard to the written opinion being delivered before the cause was heard. The statement briefly is, that after the court met, the jury were called and many of them answered and appeared; the prisoner was (Mr. Lewis believes) in court; the counsel assigned the prisoner, had not all got to the bar; when the judge handed down, or threw on the clerk's table, several papers, each containing the opinion of the court on the law that was to decide the defendant's fate: one of these copies, the judge said, was to be given to the counsel for the defendant; one to the attorney for the United States, and one to be delivered to the jury before they retired on the case. Some of the gentlemen about the bar began to copy these papers: Mr. Lewis, one of the counsel for the defendant, refused to receive or read it, declaring his hand should never be tainted by reading a prejudged opinion in any case, but especially in a capital one. The papers were subject to public inspection ; the jurymen then might, and probably did, read the opinion. Thus the formal opinion of the court on the law, being made known to the jury before the cause was heard, would bias their minds against the defendant, and render an impartial inquiry into his case next to impossible. The counsel had no hopes of changing an opinion thus deliberately and formally made up, and stamped with the solemnity of a written sentence ; the judge by deciding the law seemed to have decided the facts also, as he must have assumed them as proved, in order to found his opinion upon them ; and indeed the answer states that no doubts existed with regard to the facts, or evidence in the case on either side ; the jury would, therefore, consider such opinion as a decision of the whole case, and would be prepared, so far as they could be influenced by the judge, to pronounce the defendant guilty, before they heard the cause examined, or even a syllable of the evidence. In a case thus situated, how could the defendant be said to enjoy the benefit of the assistance of counsel ; when the whole case was decided before counsel was permitted to be heard; and no ground left for them to occupy. This mode of proceeding, adopted by the judge, was, therefore, a direct violation of the constitutional right secured to the defendant, of having the assistance of counsel in all criminal prosecutions ; for it cannot be pretended that to hear counsel after the cause was substantially decided, would be complying with the true intent and meaning of the constitution; for this would render the provision totally futile and useless, and would be calculated only to deceive unfortunate defendants, who might place reliance upon it. The judge, in delivering this opinion, introduced a mode of proceeding new and before unknown in our jurisprudence; and contrary to the known and established usages and practice of the courts in our country ; all the legal characters that have been examined as witnesses on both sides, and most of the witnesses to this article were legal characters, prove the fact, that no such practice ever did exist in this country ; not one solitary case can be adduced of a similar proceeding by a judge, either in this country, or in that from which we have taken most of our laws and usages. The writers on the laws of England afford no instance of this kind ; and it was left for judge Chase to introduce this extraordinary and before unheard of mode of administering justice.

But it is insisted on, by the judge in his answer, that the opinion was a correct one, as to the law of treason, supported by former decisions, and therefore, there would be no harm in making it known, at the time and in the manner he did ; that it could not mislead the jury, but would guard them against being imposed upon by the ingenuity of counsel. Though this reasoning may appear plausible at first view, it will be found, upon examination, to be falacious, tending to establish a dangerous doctrine, that would in principle go the whole length of justifying a judge, for dispensing with the intervention of a jury altogether in trials for crimes. If a judge may give a solemn opinion against a defendant in a criminal case, without permitting counsel to be heard in his behalf, when the party is entitled of right to the assistance of counsel, and then justify such conduct by shewing that the opinion itself was correct, and must have been delivered by him in some stage of the trial ; why may he not pass sentence of execution upon a criminal without the verdict or intervention of a jury ? And, when charged with this conduct as unconstitutional and illegal, justify himself by shewing that the sentence he passed was a correct one, that the facts in the case were notorious and admitted on all hands ; that the law was clear and had been established by former decisions that could not be shaken ; and that, therefore, the intervention of a jury could be of no service to the defendant, as they must find him guilty ; and that as he would have to declare the same sentence he had pronounced, after their verdict should have been rendered, it could do no harm to pronounce it without such verdict ; as it could not do an injury to pass a correct sentence at any time. This reasoning would be of the same kind with that advanced by the judge in the case before you, to justify him in delivering a written opinion, before the cause was heard, or the defendant permitted to make his defence by counsel ; for if in the one case it would be a violation of the constitutional right of a trial by jury, secured to defendants in criminal prosecutions ; so in the other case it would be equally a violation of the constitutional right secured to defendants of having the assistance of counsel in their defence. The reasoning therefore of the judge, if it proved any thing, would prove too much ; it would virtually destroy the most valuable provisions in our constitution for the protection of the rights and liberties of the citizen ; and authorise a judge or court at pleasure to dispense with constitutional restrictions, when they found it convenient so to do.

But in the present investigation, the correctness or incorrectness of the written opinion delivered by the judge, is not in question ; this opinion is not charged to be in itself incorrect or erroneous, but the offence charged is in the manner and time of delivering it ; the attempt therefore by the judge to justify his conduct, by insisting that the opinion delivered was correct and authorised by former decisions, is a mere evasion of the real charge alleged in the impeachment, and an exertion to prove what was not denied or put in question. It cannot, therefore, in fact aid the accused, or make his case better than it would be if such opinion had been evidently erroneous ; but it is not intended, in this place, to admit the correctness of the opinion delivered by the judge in writing, by not going into the discussion of it ; but this discussion of the opinion is omitted here, because its correctness or incorrectness is irrelevant to the present question, and, therefore, unnecessary to be discussed.

I will now proceed to consider the third position stated, to wit, that the judge did impose on the counsel engaged on behalf of Fries, arbitrary restrictions and controul, in the exercise of their professional rights, unknown to, and unauthorised by the laws and usages of the nation. In support of this part of the charge, there is the evidence of Mr. Lewis, who states that when the judge delivered the written opinion in the manner already noticed, he observed that on the former trials, there had been a great waste of time, by counsel making long speeches to the jury on the law as well as on the fact, and stated his disapprobation of their having been permitted to read certain statutes of the United States, relating to crimes less than treason, which he or the court declared they would not suffer to be read again, and that cases at common law, or under the statute law of England, previous to the English revolution, had nothing to do with the question, and that they would not suffer them to be read ; that they had made up their mind on the law. This is in substance the evidence of Mr. Lewis on this point ; and it is strongly supported by that of Mr. Dallas, who, though he was not present when this statement was made by the judge, yet corroborates the truth of it by the statement he made to the court afterwards on the same day, as made to him by Mr. Lewis, and by the circumstances that took place in consequence thereof. Mr. Dallas also states that the judge said, as he thinks on the next day, that in arguing upon the law the counsel must address the court alone and not the jury. The evidence of Messrs. Rawle and Tilghman, support most of these facts in substance, except as to the judge refusing to permit the statutes of the United States to be cited, and differ only as to the time at which the judge made these declarations ; these facts, therefore, are supported by evidence that cannot be shaken ; and were the evidence given by Mr. Lewis and Mr. Dallas, different from that given by Messrs. Tilghman, Rawle and others, more weight and credit ought to be given to the evidence of the former gentlemen than to that of the latter, though all may be men of equal integrity and veracity ; for there is a material distinction between the credit due to witnesses as men of integrity and veracity, and the weight or credit that ought to be given to their evidence as containing a correct and full statement of facts : two men may be of equal credibility in society, and equally tenacious of deposing the truth ; yet the evidence of the one, as to a particular transaction, may deserve much more weight and credit than that of the other, in consequence of his possessing better means of information, and being so circumstanced as to feel more interest in, and receive stronger impressions from the facts that may have taken place ; so in the the question before us, Mr. Lewis and Mr. Dallas felt the strongest interest in the transaction that took place ; their rights as counsel were invaded, and the impressions they received were strong, and not easily effaced. Mr. Lewis had the most correct means of information ; his attention was arrested by the paper containing the opinion being handed or offered to him ; the statement of the judge containing the restrictions already stated, immediately followed, to which he attended ; he could not, therefore, possibly be mistaken ; and the impression, so strongly made by so extraordinary a transaction, could not be erased from his memory. This was not the case with Messrs. Rawle and Tilghman; for though Mr. Rawle was concerned for the prosecution, he states he was much engaged with other business; the opinion delivered was also in favour of his side of the question, and of course the affair was not likely to excite so much the interest of those gentlemen, or make so deep an impression on their minds. The evidence, therefore, of Mr. Lewis and Mr. Dallas, may be considered as a correct statement of this transaction. These restrictions, therefore, imposed upon the counsel, of not citing such authorities as were usually permitted to be used, and not arguing the law to the jury, are unauthorised by the laws of our country, and contrary to the usages and practice of our courts of justice ; and in the case in question, amounted to a prohibition to argue the cause in any possible way that could be of the least service to the defendant. That these restrictions were unauthorised by the practice in our courts, is established by the evidence of every witness that has been examined to this point, who declared that no such restrictions had ever been imposed on counsel concerned in criminal cases, in any courts with which they had been acquainted, and particularly by the practice of the circuit court of the United States, in the same state, in the trial of the same cause before, and in other similar trials, when the utmost latitude was given the counsel in making their defence. This was, therefore, a direct and arbitrary innovation on the known and established modes of proceeding in courts of justice in criminal cases, and an unwarrantable attack on the privileges secured to defendants by the constitution and laws of the country. That judges are not authorised to substitute their own arbitrary will in place of law, and to dispense, at pleasure, with the established rules of proceeding in the tribunals of

justice, is proved by every principle of reason and of law.
To shew that this position has been expressly recognized by law writers, and legal decisions for ages, I
will refer the court to 2d Bac. Ab. (new edition) page
97, where it is declared that *judges are to determine
according to the known law and ancient customs of
the realm;* and to 4 Com. Dig. 418, where it is
stated that *judges ought to act conformably to law
and not according to discretion.* These authorities,
when we consider the country from which they come,
and the times in which they were written, strongly
mark the limits that ought to circumscribe the conduct of the judge. And shall the judges in our country assume greater latitude in their proceedings than
those of England, and depart at pleasure from what
are known to be the customs of the country? I should
presume not. But the judge states in his answer, that
decisions at common law, and before the revolution
in England, could throw no light on the doctrine of
treason here, but might mislead the jury; and therefore ought not to be admitted to be read, not being
law; and he wades into the dark ages of the history
of England, when the judges were corrupt and under
the influence of the crown. This reasoning of the
judge is evidently an evasion of the point in question. The object of the counsel for Fries, in wishing
to cite those authorities, both at common law and under the statute of Edward the Third, was not to shew
by them what the construction of the words of our
constitution with regard to treason ought to be; but
to shew first, the absurd and ridiculous lengths to
which those decisions had gone, in determining what
acts amounted to treason there, and then to prove that
since the English revolution, the judges in England
considered themselves bound by cases decided before
the revolution, and that as the decisions on treason in
England, since their revolution, were bottomed upon
those cases before the revolution, they ought not to

govern the courts in this country, in giving a construction to the words of our constitution, in order to determine what acts amounted to treason. This was evidently the object of the counsel, and it is proved to have been so stated by them, by the evidence of Mr. Lewis, Mr. Dallas, and Mr. Rawle. There was, therefore, no ground for the pretence the judge makes for refusing these authorities to be introduced.

It is admitted by the answer that the jury have the right to decide upon the law as well as upon the fact ; and if it were denied, it could be shewn by clear and undoubted authorities, of ancient and modern times. From what motives, therefore, and under what plausible pretence, could the judge refuse to permit the law to be argued before the jury ? How could they decide upon it properly, without hearing it discussed ? And with what color of reasoning can the judge say that the jury have the right to decide the law, and yet that they have not the right to hear it argued and explained by counsel ? Does not this shew the greatest absurdity, and prove that the accused must have had some object in view, that he did not chuse to avow, and that would not bear examination ? In this case there was no dispute about the facts ; the answer states, they were admitted on both sides. The judge makes up his opinion upon the law, commits it to writing, and makes it known as the opinion of the court, before the jury are impannelled in the case. For what purpose was counsel assigned to the defendant ? What remained for the counsel to examine or contest, when the facts were admitted and the law decided by the court ? Would not the assistance of counsel, under such circumstances, be to the defendant a mere phantom, a name without substance ? Was not the assignment of counsel, in this case, and with such views as the judge must have had, an useless ceremony, an empty compliance with form, a mere mock of justice ? The clear inference from the whole transaction must be, that the judge was determined the defendant should derive no benefit from the assistance of counsel, and only affected to permit them to argue the facts to the jury, because he knew they were not disputed, even by the defendant himself. It must, therefore, be a fair inference that the defendant was deprived of the assistance of counsel, by the unwarrantable, illegal, and unauthorized restrictions imposed upon them in the performance of their professional duties by the judge.

It remains, on this part of the subject, to shew that this conduct of the judge was such a flagrant violation of his duty, as could only spring from corrupt motives, and a disposition to oppress those who became the objects of his resentment. I lay it down as a settled rule of decision, that when a man violates a law, or commits a manifest breach of his duty, an evil intent, or corrupt motive must be presumed, to have actuated his conduct; as every man is presumed to know the law, and every officer or judge to understand his duty; and if the party will undertake to excuse himself, for misconduct, on the score of pure motives, and unintentional error, it is incumbent on him to make the same appear by satisfactory and incontestible evidence. In some instances, erroneous conduct may be explained, excused, or palliated, by the weakness or ignorance of the delinquent, and the circumstances that attend the case. But in this whole transaction, what marks of innocence, or pure motives are to be discovered? What excuse to be offered for the conduct of the accused? Ignorance of the law cannot be relied upon as forming a ground of excuse. The legal talents, long experience, and distinguished abilities of the judge, are too well known to admit of such a plea. It was no new and difficult case, wherein he might be easily mistaken. There were no former precedents to lead him astray. The proceeding was entirely new, and of his own inven-

tion; a total deviation from all former practice, and a
manifest innovation upon the established usages in our
courts of justice. The whole bar were agitated by
the proceeding; counsel of near thirty years practice
felt embarrassed and astonished at it. The common
sense of the whole audience appeared shocked at the
transaction, as being altogether new and extraordinary. The accused, in his answer, states, that he relied
upon the decisions of the circuit courts, wherein
judges Iredell and Paterson presided, with regard to
the law of treason, as forming a precedent from which
he would not even dare to depart. Why did he not
consider himself equally bound by the practice they
adopted in criminal cases? They gave the utmost latitude to counsel in making their defence to the jury,
both on the law and the fact, did not restrict them as
to the authorities they should cite, and delivered no
opinion until the cause was heard. Judge Chase reversed the whole of this mode of proceeding. What
good reason can be given for his adhering to their
opinion in the one instance, and totally departing from
their practice and example in the other? No excuse
can be formed for this conduct. This is the strongest
possible evidence of corrupt motives, of partiality, and
a determined design to overleap all former rules of
proceeding, to oppress the unfortunate defendant, that
was arraigned at his bar for trial. The whole course
of the judge's conduct in this transaction goes to
establish the same spirit of oppression. Counsel are
assigned the defendant, merely for the sake of form,
and, as it were, to mock him in his misfortunes.
The day of trial arrives. In the mean time the judge
makes up his opinion on the law arising in the case,
and, to add solemnity to the act, commits it to writing. There is no doubt, no dispute as to the facts.
The prisoner is brought to the bar. Not a voice is
permitted to plead his cause, until the solemn sentence of his legal conviction is made known; and

thereby the avenues of his defence, that might lead to his acquittal, for ever closed.

Here let us pause a moment, and behold the unfortunate, and, in the language of his able counsel, poor Fries, trembling before his condemning judge; stript of the aid of counsel, his only and forlorn hope ; the fatal fiat of his condemnation pronounced in the solemn language of a written opinion; and thus friendless, unprotected, and unheard, about to be consigned to the hand of the relentless executioner ! Let us view this spectacle, and then let me ask, if this can be considered an impartial administration of justice. I might here charge the accused with having knowingly and wilfully trampled on the laws of his country, and overleaped the bounds of legal justice, to oppress a friendless individual brought before him for trial. I might call upon this honorable court, to vindicate the character of insulted justice, and demonstrate to the American people, that when their rights and liberties are invaded, even though under the sacred sanction of judicial authority, this high tribunal will always be found ready and willing to avenge their wrongs and protect their interests.

But it is alleged by the judge, that the offensive written opinion, that had been made known, was withdrawn, and that next day full latitude was offered to the counsel to argue both the law and the facts to the jury. This was a fallacious offer; it came too late to be of service to the defendant, or excuse the judge. The act on his part was done; the offence was complete; and it was only the sternness of the counsel that made him retract. The impression had been made on the minds of the jury, that could not be erased....the flame had been kindled by the fire-brands he had scattered, which could not be extinguished by withdrawing the instruments that occasioned it. The experiment was as dangerous as it was novel, and can only be ascribed to the same spirit of oppression and political intolerance, that will be found to distinguish the whole conduct of the judge in his judicial career, during these transactions.

The respondent further insists, in his answer, that he cannot be impeached, except for some offence for which he may be indicted at law. This position cannot be supported by any fair construction of the provision in the constitution on this subject. It has already been attempted to be shewn in the view taken of this constitutional provision, that in order to support an impeachment, it is not necessary to shew that the offence charged, is an indictable one, but only that it is a breach and violation of official duty ; and I conceive that this is the only construction that can be adopted to give consistency to the constitution; to the mode of proceeding adopted under it in cases of impeachment; to reconcile with justice the nature of the judgment that must be rendered upon conviction, and to avoid the palpable absurdity that would follow a different construction, of punishing a man twice for the same offence. To the exposition already given of this provision in the constitution, I beg leave to refer the court as controverting the position here relied upon by the judge. But I would here further observe, in support of this doctrine, that according to the laws of England, a judge of a court of record is not accountable by indictment, for any thing done in open court, in his judicial capacity ; and that he may plead to an action brought against him, for any such act, that he did it, (that is, what he was charged with) as a judge of record; and it would be a good justification. In support of this doctrine the court are referred to 2 Bac. ab. (new ed.) page 97....2 Hawk. 123.... Jac. Law Dictionary, (new ed.) verbum Judges. It appears from the same authorities, that the judges in England, are accountable in parliament only, for opinions delivered by them in court ; and are not, for such opinions, to be questioned before any other tribunal. This is the great protection and security that judges of courts of record have, that they are accountable for their official conduct only to the legislature; and are punishable at law only for such acts as would be indictable offences, independent of their official character. This view of the subject renders the judges, so far as regards their judicial conduct, independent of all tribunals except the legislature; and is certainly better calculated to preserve the independence and dignity of the judges, than that contended for in the answer. I cannot, therefore, entertain a reasonable doubt, that the true intent and meaning of the constitution will support this doctrine; and that it will be sanctioned by the opinion of this honorable court.

Mr. Campbell here observed that he had closed the remarks he proposed making on the first part of the subject, and, finding himself indisposed, expressed a wish that the court would adjourn.

Whereupon, the court rose.

THURSDAY, *February* 21, 1805.

The court was opened at 10 a. m.

Present, the Managers, attended by the House of Representatives in committee of the whole: and The counsel of Judge Chase.

MR. CAMPBELL, *in continuation.*

I will now proceed, as well as my indisposition will permit, to examine in a brief manner the second part of the subject, containing the several charges founded on the trial of Callender, at Richmond, as stated in the second, third, and fourth articles of the impeachment. I will consider these several articles in the order in which the transactions on which they are founded took place in court. In order to ascertain the motives that actuated the judge, in this whole

transaction, it will only be necessary to view his conduct as proved, so far as the same relates to this subject, previous to the trial. The first account we have
of the intended prosecution, or I might say persecution, of Callender, is at Annapolis. Here the judge
received the famous book, called the Prospect Before
Us, upon which the prosecution was founded; and
here the determination was formed to convict and
punish Callender. The respondent said he would
take the book with him to Richmond; that the libellous parts had been marked by Mr. Martin, and that
before he returned he would teach the lawyers of Virginia to know the difference between the liberty and
licenciousness of the press; and, that if the commonwealth of Virginia was not totally depraved, if there
was a jury of honest men to be found in the state, he
would punish Callender before he returned from Richmond. This is the evidence of Mr. Mason, nearly in
his own words, and no person will pretend to doubt
its correctness. What language could be used, that
would more clearly shew the partiality and predetermination of the judge to punish Callender, and the
spirit of persecution by which he was actuated. Again,
on his way to Richmond, according to the evidence of
Mr. Triplett, the judge reviles the object of his intended vengeance; states his surprise and regret, that
he had not been hanged in Virginia; remarks that the
United States had shewn too much lenity to such renegadoes; and after arriving at Richmond, informs
the deponent, he was afraid they would not be able to
get the damn'd rascal that court. Thus evincing in
every stage of this business that intolerant spirit of
oppression and vengeance, that seems to have given
spring to all his actions. After the indictment is found
against Callender, the pannel of the petit jury is presented to the judge, he inquires if he had any of the
creatures called democrats, on that pannel, directs the
marshal to examine it, and if there were any such on it,

to strike them off. This is the evidence of Mr. Heath, whose character and standing in society are known to many of the members of this honorable court. And though his evidence is opposed by the negative declarations of Mr. Randolph, who affirms, that he did not present the pannel of the jury to the judge, or receive such directions; yet I conceive the court will give more weight to the affirmative declarations of Mr. Heath, with regard to these facts, than to the negative assertions of Mr. Randolph, who may have forgotten the transaction. This point rests upon the integrity and veracity of Mr. Heath. He could not receive the impression of these facts, unless the transaction had taken place; he could not reasonably be mistaken; the affair was new and extraordinary, and must have arrested his attention; and in this case there is no ground to make allowance for a treacherous memory; for it is not pretended that the witness, Mr. Heath, has forgot the facts, but that they never existed. If you do not, therefore, believe the statement he makes, it must follow that you admit the witness has wilfully and corruptly stated a falsehood; this I presume will not be admitted; but on the other hand, Mr. Randolph may have forgotten the transaction, in the bustle of business, and this will account for the difference in the evidence of the witnesses without impeaching the veracity of either; this mode of reconciling the evidence is agreeable to the rules of law. I take the facts, therefore, as stated by Mr. Heath, to be correct, and they afford an instance of judicial depravity hitherto unequalled and unknown in our country; a direct attempt to pack a jury of the same political sentiments with the judge, to try the defendant. This is a faint representation of the previous conduct of the judge, relative to this subject, before whom the defendant was about to be tried; or rather before whom he was to be called for certain conviction and punishment; for it ought not to be dignified with the name of a trial. With this view, therefore, of the temper and disposition of the judge, and of his previous conduct on this occasion, we will examine the first important step taken in the trial, in which the designs of the judge begin more clearly to unfold themselves, viz. his refusal to postpone or continue the trial until the next term, on an affidavit regularly filed, stating the absence of material witnesses and the places of their residence, being the second charge in the fourth article.

It is admitted by the respondent, in his answer, that an affidavit was filed, which he exhibits to the court, and a motion made thereupon by the counsel of Callender to continue his cause for trial until the next term ; and it is proved by the evidence of Mr. Hay and Mr. Nicholas, that as counsel for Callender, they insisted for a continuance of the case, on the grounds stated in the affidavit, and also on other grounds ; that they were not prepared to argue the law arising in the case, for want of time to examine the subject, and that the defendant was not, by the laws of Virginia, bound to come to trial that term. Here it may be proper to shew what are the grounds for a continuance known in law, and to inquire whether those stated in the affidavit come within the decisions heretofore made in courts of justice. On this subject I will refer the court to one authority only, but one equally respectable with any that can be produced on criminal law. Foster Cr. Law, page 2 and 3. Here Mr. Campbell read the case at length, and then observed, that this decision took place in a country where criminal law is executed with as much rigor as in any in the world where there is the shadow of liberty ; and yet the affidavit filed in this case, upon which a continuance was granted, only states the absence of material witnesses and the places of their abode ; the defendants were not required to state the facts that those witnesses would prove. In ordinary cases the courts do not require this, and in many cases it would be impossible for the defendant to know all that a witness could give in evidence ; nor is the defendant bound, except in extraordinary cases, to disclose the evidence that his witnesses, who are absent, can give, as it might endanger his defence and give an advantage to the prosecutor, if so disposed, to procure evidence, whether true or false, to controvert that of the defendant. The court in the case cited was held by a special commission from the crown, for the purpose of trying offenders for crimes of the deepest die, and such as are punished in that country with the utmost rigor ; yet the court continued the cases of those defendants for such a length of time, as was deemed sufficient to procure their witnesses according to the distances at which they resided. There were in this case no stated terms to which the court could adjourn and continue the causes ; they, therefore, fixed upon a reasonable time and adjourned over to such day, in order to enable the defendants to prepare for trial ; and it was observed by the court in that case as an additional ground for continuance, that the indictments had not been found until the court sat, and that, therefore, the defendants had not time to prepare for trial. This was the case with Callender ; he had no notice of this prosecution until after the indictment was found, and during the same term ; he, therefore, could not have had time to prepare for his trial. The affidavit he filed was stronger and much more full than that in the case cited ; it states the absence of a number of witnesses, whose evidence the deponent declares material to his defence. This would be sufficient to authorise a continuance upon a first application, and more ought not to have been required ; but the affidavit goes further, and states the substance, as far as the defendant knew, of the evidence the witnesses could give ; and also states the want of papers and

books, material to the defence, that could not be obtained without allowing a considerable time to procure
them. What more could be stated in an affidavit, for
a continuance on the gound of want of testimony, by
any defendant who wished to adhere to the truth?
Yet a continuance is refused ; and the judge states
in his answer as the principal cause of such refusal,
that the evidence of all the witnesses stated in the
affidavit to be wanting, would not prove the truth of
all the charges in the indictment, and would not,
therefore, make a complete justification if procured ;
and enters into an examination of the charges and
evidence to prove this position. This excuse of the
accused is founded on a train of the most fallacious
and sophistical reasoning that can be resorted to, and
is no more than a groundless apology, by which, if
possible, to evade the true question, and avoid the
odium that ought and must attach to such a transaction. It is not denied by the judge that the absent
witnesses would prove in part the charges in the indictment ; but he says it ought to appear, they could
prove the whole. By this rule, in order to obtain a
continuance, the party must shew to the court the
whole of the evidence necessary to support his case,
and the judge is to compare the evidence with the
charges, and must be satisfied that it is sufficient to
cover the whole of the case, or he will not grant a
continuance ; this doctrine is too absurd to require a
refutation ; it would destroy all the benefit that could
arise to parties from the right, so well established in
law, of continuing causes upon affidavit of absent material witnesses ; and subject the right to a fair and
impartial trial, to the mere arbitrary will of a judge,
who would thus assume the right to weigh the evidence wanted, and measure its materiality by his
prejudice against the party ; this would in fact, tend
in many instances to destroy the trial by jury, and
reduce it to a mere form without substance ; for the

party could not state on oath all that his witnesses could prove, once in a hundred times. But the answer states that the court proposed to postpone the trial for a month, and some of the witnesses go further than the accused himself and say for six weeks ; and this is relied upon as shewing the disposition of the judge to accommodate the defendant. This is a pretence to accommodate that could answer the defendant no valuable purpose. The absent witnesses resided at such great distances, that most of them could not be procured in that time, and this the judge well knew. He even states in his answer, that they lived at such great distances as left no reasonable ground to believe they could be procured at the succeeding term, being six months, and yet pretends that one month or six weeks would be sufficient. But here I must notice, that it is remarkable the counsel for the defendant never heard of this proposed postponement; and I must therefore conclude it was not seriously made ; but if it was it only proves that the judge was determined to try Callender himself, and would not, therefore, on any ground whatever, continue the cause to a succeeding term, at which he was not to be present. He had before determined to punish Callender, and could not trust his case to the management of any other judge. This is of a piece with the rest of his conduct on this occasion, and presents this honorable court and the world with an instance of the most flagrant abuse of common justice, under the sacred sanction of administering the law for the correction of offenders.

The next charge which I propose to examine is contained in the second article of the impeachment, and consists in the judge's over-ruling the objection of John Basset, one of the jury, who wished to be excused from serving on the trial of Callender, because he had made up his mind as to the book from which the words charged to be libellous in the indictment

had been drawn. The constitution secures to defendants charged with crimes, the right of a trial by an
impartial jury; any thing, therefore, that goes to shew
that a man has made up an opinion with regard to the
guilt or innocence of the accused, or with regard to
the matter in question, or decided it in his own mind,
proves him to be disqualified to serve as a juror, because it proves he is not impartial, has a bias upon his mind, and cannot be said to be indifferent.
The same doctrine is supported by the laws of
England. In order to shew this, I will refer the
court to 3 Bac. Ab. (new ed.) 756, and also Co. Litt.
158; where it is stated, if a juror has declared his
opinion, touching the matter in question, &c. or has
done any thing by which it appears that he cannot
be indifferent or impartial, &c. these are principal
causes of challenge; and therefore such juror would
be disqualified. Here it is manifest, that though
declaring an opinion is good cause of challenge to a
juror, if it is not necessary he should declare such
opinion in order to disqualify him; it is sufficient that
he has done something, whether making up an opinion, or doing any act whatever, by which it appears
he is not indifferent, is not perfectly impartial. The
objection, therefore, made to Basset as a juror, ought
to have been sustained, and he ought to have been excused from serving on the jury, upon two grounds.
First, because he had made up an opinion with regard to the matter of the charge against Callender.
This is proved by the evidence of Basset himself,
who says, he had seen in a newspaper, extracts stated
in the publication to have been taken from the Prospect before Us; and he stated to the court on the trial,
that he had made up his opinion, that those extracts
were seditious, and that the author of the book called
the Prospect before Us, or that from which these extracts were taken, was within the sedition act, and
therefore punishable under it. It was at the time no-

torious and well known that Callender was the author
of the Prospect before Us; it was equally notorious
and known, that the indictment against him was
founded on that book ; and Mr. Basset stated, he had
no reason to doubt that the extracts were taken from
that book as stated in the papers. Is it not, therefore,
clear, that forming an opinion with regard to the extracts, was forming an opinion with regard to the
matter charged as libellous in the indictment? No
reasonable doubt can exist on this point, and though
Mr. Basset did not hear the indictment read, as the
court refused to permit it to be read until the jury
were sworn, a measure under such circumstances as
extraordinary as it was new ; yet he knew the subject
matter it contained as well as if he had heard it. The
opinion, therefore, that he had made up his mind on this
subject, clearly proves he was not indifferent, was not
impartial; he had decided the guilt of Callender, in fact,
in his own mind, and could not be expected to shake
off the effect of such prejudication. He was, therefore, according to the constitution, and the law already
cited, disqualified from being a juror, having done
an act that shewed he was not indifferent, was not
impartial, and ought of course to have been excused from serving on the jury. He ought also to
have been rejected as a juror on a second ground ; because he had not only made up an opinion on the matter in question, but had declared that opinion in public. It is proved by the evidence of Mr. Basset himself, as well as by that of Mr. Hay and Mr. Nicholas,
and also by that of Mr. Robinson, that when he was
asked whether he had formed and delivered an opinion upon the charge in the indictment, he stated, that
although he had never heard the indictment read, yet
he had formed an opinion that the author of the Prospect before Us was within the sedition act. This, as
has been already insisted upon, was the same as forming an opinion upon the charges in the indictment,

as he knew the indictment was founded upon that book; and this opinion, which he had formed, he then declared in open court, in the hearing of all byestanders, and before he was sworn as a juror. This was, therefore, according to the rule laid down by the judge and the question he declared proper to be asked, a complete disqualification of Mr. Basset from serving as a juror on that trial. For he had formed and delivered an opinion on the matter in question. And what difference could it make, whether such opinion was delivered a minute or an hour before the juror was sworn on the trial, or a week, or a month before? Certainly the effect on his mind must be the same, and he must be equally unfit to serve as a juror in either case. On both of these grounds, therefore, Mr. Basset ought certainly to have been rejected from serving as a juror on the trial of Callender; and this is so glaring an innovation on the impartiality of trial by jury, (*the security* of our rights and great *bulwark* of our liberties,) that when taken in connection with the rest of the judge's conduct, it strongly evinces an overbearing disposition, that would not stop at the use of any means, however unjust and illegal, to obtain a desired object. He had told the marshal, if he had on his list of jurors any creatures called democrats, to strike them off. He, therefore, knew the political sentiments of those who were called as jurors, to be favorable to his wishes, as no doubt his direction was pursued. Mr. Basset had declared his opinion, that the author of the Prospect before Us was within the sedition law, who was notoriously known to be Callender. He therefore knew the sentiments of the juror; knew he must be disposed to convict the defendant, and for this reason he would not excuse him from serving on the trial, but would pervert the meaning of the law to make it subservient to his own views.

The next charge to be inquired into is that stated in the third article, in rejecting the evidence of colonel Taylor, a material witness in favor of the defendant, on the pretence that he could not prove the truth of the whole of one charge. In this instance the judge acted contrary to all former precedents in courts of justice, and without the shadow of law or reason to justify his conduct. Not a solitary case could be stated by any of the witnesses of a similar conduct in a judge. The rule here adopted, with regard to the admissibility of evidence, would deprive the jury of their undoubted right to decide on the credibility and weight of evidence, as well as on the extent to which it proved the matter in question; would transfer in substance this right to the court, and thereby shake to its very centre the fabric so justly admired and held so sacred, *of trial by jury.* It would make it necessary for the party to present to the court, all the evidence relied upon to make out his case. This evidence, the court or judge would first deliberately examine, compare it with the charges or case to be supported, and if it did not, in his opinion, prove the whole of one charge, or go the whole extent of the case to be established by it, he would reject it, and not permit the jury to hear it. This would strip the jury of the very prerogative that renders this kind of trial so much superior to all others, that of deciding on the weight and credit of evidence. There is a manifest distinction between the right which a judge has to decide upon the admissibility of evidence, on the ground of its being proper or improper according to the established rules of law, and the right here assumed of deciding upon the extent to which such evidence, that is admitted to relate to the matter in question, will go to support the case: the former is the exercise of a proper authority to prevent the admission of extraneous and improper matter, wholly irrelevant to the matter in question; the latter is an arbitrary assumption of power, to decide on the extent to which evidence admitted to be relevant, at least in some degree, would go to prove the matter in question; and is a direct innovation on the most sacred privilege of the jury. Nothing can be more absurd and dangerous, than the consequences that would flow from such a doctrine. The judge would first weigh the evidence himself, measure its extent, reject it at pleasure, and call this a trial by jury. But I must here be permitted to notice the reasoning resorted to by the judge in his answer, to excuse his conduct on this occasion, which is as dangerous and absurd, in its consequences, as it is subtle and evasive. It is stated by the judge, that the plea of justification must answer the whole charge, or it is bad on the demurrer; and that when the matter of defence may be given in evidence without being formally pleaded, the same rules prevail. This doctrine of the judge would require the party to shew, that the evidence he offered would cover the whole of his case, with the same exactness and formality that he would file a plea to avoid its being held bad on a demurrer: thus narrowing down the province of the jury, and subjecting the decision of all the facts as well as the law to the court. There is no rule of law to warrant such a proceeding, and it is manifestly contrary to all reasoning on the subject. The plea, in order to be good, must state matter sufficient to justify that part of the charge or suit to which it is put in; the demurrer admits all the facts stated in the plea that are well pleaded, but cannot admit facts that are not stated in it; therefore the plea must appear to contain sufficient matter of justification, or it will be held bad on demurrer; but no such rule was ever heard of before to apply to evidence offered to a jury. They alone are the proper and only tribunal to decide whether the evidence offered and given is sufficient to prove the whole matter in dispute or not; and if the jury be deprived of this right, there is nothing left them that deserves the name of a trial.

The judge insists, if he was mistaken, it was an error of judgment. This cannot be presumed. Ignorance of the law is no excuse in any man; but in a character of such high legal standing and known abilities as that of the accused, it is totally inadmissible and not to be presumed. How could any judge with upright intentions commit so many errors, or hit upon so many mistakes in the course of one trial, as are manifest in that of Callender. They must have been the result of design, and a predetermination to bear down all opposition, in order to convict and punish the defendant.

But it is stated that judge Griffin concurred with him in opinion, and this is insisted upon by the accused in different parts of his answer, as an excuse for the errors he committed, if, as he states, they were errors. This seems to be a kind of forlorn hope resorted to, when all other expedients fail. To this argument of the judge I would in this place answer once for all, that it can be no excuse for him, nor any justification of his offences, that another has been equally guilty with himself ; and it must strongly prove the weakness of his defence to rely upon this ground. Though judge Griffin has not yet been called to an account for his conduct on this occasion, that is no reason why he should not hereafter be made to answer for it. The nation has not said he was innocent, or that he will not be proceeded against for this conduct ; and there is no limitation of time that would screen him from the effects of charges of this kind, if they should be brought forward and supported against him hereafter. No ground of excuse therefore can arise from the circumstance of judge Griffin not having been called upon to answer for his conduct in this respect.

I will now proceed to notice very briefly the conduct of the judge in the subsequent part of this trial. Compelling the defendant's counsel to reduce to writing all questions to be asked the witness, was a direct innovation on the practice in our courts of justice, and tended to embarrass the management of and weaken the defence. It is proved by the testimony of all the witnesses, that no such practice ever prevailed in our courts of justice, for such a purpose as that avowed in this instance ; the only cases in which it is required to reduce to writing questions to be asked a witness, and the only cases in which it can be proper or consistent with reason and justice to do so, are those in which an objection is made to a question proposed to be asked, on the ground of its being improper and contrary to the rules of evidence ; and in order to ascertain the precise meaning and effect of the question, so as to decide on the objection made to it, it may be proper to require it to be reduced to writing, but it never was before done, so far as we can discover, for the purpose of ascertaining how far the witness could prove the matter in question, and whether he could prove the whole of one charge or not, and thereby decide whether the witness should or should not be examined. According to this rule the judge would first try the cause himself upon the evidence offered, by the questions thus reduced to writing, and if he did not consider such evidence fully sufficient to support the whole of the charge or case to which it was offered, he would reject it, and not permit the jury to hear a word of it, lest they might consider it stronger than he did, and give it sufficient weight to support the case to which it was offered. This mode of proceeding was left to be discovered and adopted by judge Chase. No other court or judge ever attempted in this manner to trifle with the rights of the jury, and establish a doctrine so tyrannical and oppressive ; but this is in perfect conformity with the whole of his conduct on this occasion; a preconcerted system of oppression, to bring the defendant, Callender, to certain conviction and punishment. For the same purpose the defendant's counsel were ridiculed, treated with indignity, and the whole audience entertained at their expense. They were frequently and abruptly interrupted in their arguments; charged with wilfully perverting the law, in order to impose upon and deceive the multitude; called boys by way of derision, and treated as mere mushrooms of the day, who ought to cringe submissively when they appear before a circuit court in which the honorable judge presided. He was facetious, witty, and sarcastic, as the occasion required; and it is pretended there can be no harm in this; it was all in jest and good humor! It is too serious a matter, Mr. President, for judges thus to jest and trifle with the rights and liberties of the citizen. Though this proceeding was levelled immediately at the counsel, it was the defendant who was the principal object of resentment, who was intended to be made an example of, and who felt the injury and became liable to the consequences of such illegal and unjust conduct of the judge.

Barely to notice the conduct of the respondent, at New Castle in Delaware, as charged in the seventh article, is sufficient to shew that he was there actuated by the same spirit of persecution and oppression that has, as already stated, marked the whole of his conduct during the course of these transactions. That he should descend from the elevated and dignified station in which he was placed as a judge, to hunt for crimes as a common informer against his fellow citizens; urge the jury to take notice of, and present certain persons sufficiently designated though not named; and press the attorney for the district to search for evidence among the files of newspapers to support a prosecution, was degrading to the sacred character of a judge, and was perverting the judicial authority to a mere engine of persecution to answer party purposes. Of the same complexion with this is the conduct of the respondent in delivering an inflammatory and disorganizing charge to the grand jury at Baltimore, as stated in the eighth article of the impeachment. This proceeding evinced a mind inflamed by party spirit and political intolerance : it was calculated to disturb the peace of the community, and alarm the people at the measures of government ; to force them by the terror of judicial denunciation to relinquish their own political sentiments and adopt those of the judge. This was the favorite object of this whole proceeding, and to obtain it no means were left untried. It was attempted to excite the fears of the public mind, to destroy the confidence of the people in the administration of their government. The judicial authority was prostituted to party purposes, and the fountains of justice were corrupted by this poisonous spirit of persecution, that seemed determined to bear down all opposition in order to succeed in a favorite object. Citizens of all descriptions felt alarmed at this new and unusual conduct. All the counsel at the bar, wherever the respondent went, though consisting of the ablest and most enlightened in the nation, were agitated into a general ferment, and the whole community seemed shocked at such outrages upon common sense ; for, to go to trial was to go to certain conviction. Is this, Mr. President, the character that ought to distinguish the judiciary of the United States ? No, sir. The streams of justice that flow from the American bench ought to be as pure as the sun beams that light up the morning. The accused should come before the court, with a well founded confidence that the law will be administered to him with justice, impartiality, and in mercy. When this is the case, he submits without a murmur to his fate, and hears the sentence of condemnation pronounced against him, with a mind that must approve the justice of the law and the impartiality of those who administer it.

The decision of this cause may form an important æra in the annals of our country. Future generations are interested in the event. It may determine a question all important to the American people; whether the laws of our country are to govern, or the arbitrary will of those who are entrusted with their administration. Mr. President, we, on this important occasion, behold the rights and liberties of the American people hover round this honorable tribunal, about to be established on a firm basis by the decision you will make, or sent afloat on the ocean of uncertainty, to be tossed to and fro by the capricious breath of usurped power and innovation.

END OF VOLUME FIRST.